Self and Story in Russian History

Sponsored by the Joint Committee on the Soviet Union and Its Successor States of the American Council of Learned Societies and the Social Science Research Council

(1983–1996)

Self and Story
in Russian History

Edited by

Laura Engelstein and
Stephanie Sandler

Cornell University Press

Ithaca and London

First published 2000 by Cornell University Press
First printing, Cornell Paperbacks, 2000

Printed in the United States of America

Library of Congress Cataloging-in-Publication Data

Self and story in Russian history / Laura Engelstein and Stephanie Sandler, editors.
    p. cm.
Includes index.
   ISBN 0-8014-3791-1 (alk. paper) — ISBN 0-8014-8668-8 (pbk. : alk. paper)
    1. Russia—Intellectual life—1801–1917. I. Engelstein, Laura. II. Sandler, Stephanie, 1953–   III. Title.
   DK189.2 .S45 2000
   947'.07—dc21

                         00-008839

Contents

CONTENTS

Preface

Self and Story in Russian History began as a conversation between the editors about our two disciplines, history and literature. We realized that some of the theoretical issues most interesting to us in our separate disciplines were seldom illuminated with help from the other, and we decided to create an occasion for this kind of conversation for colleagues working in different periods of Russian history and across several media of cultural expression. The Social Science Research Council, through the Joint ACLS-SSRC Committee on the Soviet Union and Its Successor States, agreed to fund a working conference at which papers, distributed in advance, would be discussed. Our chosen focus, self and story, was meant to elicit basic principles about the ideas of identity, self-creation, and narrative as they have evolved in the modern period in Russia.

The Introduction speaks at some length about the ideas that emerged in our conversations, but perhaps it is worth adding in this Preface some sense of why the confluence of self and story appealed to us as a topic for a small conference and for this collection of essays. We wanted a focus that could draw on recent theoretical innovations in the humanities, particularly one that would push historians and literary scholars to question the premises of their own disciplines and to see the usefulness and limits of another discipline. We suspected that some theoretical innovations, particularly those associated with psychoanalysis and deconstruction, would have had more impact on the study of Russian literature than on the study of Russian history, whereas others—for example, the theories of Michel Foucault—would have affected the study of history much more. We were interested to discover what time periods or forms of cultural expression might show affinities for certain theories, and we were hoping for some unexpected convergences and conflicts. A concentration on *story* seemed almost inevitable if one of our disciplines was history; by juxtaposing it to the idea of the self, the psychological aspects of history and narrative would be foregrounded, and, we hoped, some sense of the story Russia had told about itself would also be created in the process of our work together.

Our symposium was held in La Jolla, California, for twenty-five scholars, with lively and intense results. Debates about the premises behind papers were as probing as argument about conclusions or speculations. It seemed especially difficult to draw conclusions about the *present* state of ideas on self and story in Russia, where change is so rapid and instability so widespread that participants found it a challenge to agree on even such matters as what material might be most usefully studied, much less what approaches were the most fruitful. One result of that creative conflict was our decision not to include papers about contemporary Russia in this volume (a decision also propelled by the necessity of cutting down the size of our publication, which could not manageably include twenty-five essays).* It will be a wonderful result of our collaboration if others will now begin to work on *Self and Story in Russia Today,* and if, decades from now, the turbulent close of the twentieth century in Russia is seen as a moment of transition to a more stable and more comprehensible future.

We end by thanking all who participated in the 1996 symposium, the Social Science Research Council for its financial and organizational support, and particularly Susan Bronson, formerly of the Council, for her careful work and exceptional kindness as we prepared for the gathering and then moved toward the publication of these papers. Amherst College and Princeton University have enabled the publication of this volume through their research funding for faculty members. John Ackerman at Cornell University Press has also been an extraordinarily attentive and generous editor. Additional help in the editorial and publication process has come from Nicole Monnier and Jeanne Stolarski, both of whom we acknowledge with gratitude.

---

* Several of the essays not published in this volume have appeared in print elsewhere: Andrei Zorin, "Krym v istorii russkogo samosoznaniia," *Novoe literaturnoe obozrenie,* no. 31 (1998): 123–43; Yuri Slezkine, "N. Ia. Marr and the National Origins of Soviet Ethnogenetics," *Slavic Review* 55, no. 4 (Winter 1996): 826–62; Dale E. Peterson, "Civilizing the Race: Chaadaev and the Paradox of Eurocentric Nationalism," *Russian Review* 56 (1997): 550–63; and Helena Goscilo, "S(t)imulating Chic: The Aestheticization of Post-Soviet Russia," *Essays in the Art and Theory of Translation,* ed. Lenore A. Grenoble and John M. Kopper (Lewiston, N.Y.: The Edwin Mellen Press, 1997), 35–58; also as "Style and S(t)imulation: Popular Magazines, or the Aestheticization of Postsoviet Russia," in *Studies in Twentieth-Century Literature,* a special issue on Russian culture in the 1990s, ed. Helena Goscilo, 24, no. 1 (Winter 2000): 15–50.

The following abbreviations have been used for archival citations.

GARF   Gosudarstvennyi arkhiv rossiiskoi federatsii [State Archive of the Russian Federation]

GMIR   Gosudarstvennyi muzei istorii religii [State Museum of the History of Religion]

RGALI   Rossiiskii gosudarstvennyi arkhiv literatury i iskusstva [Russian State Archive of Literature and Art]

RGIA   Rossiiskii gosudarstvennyi istoricheskii arkhiv [Russian State Historical Archive]

OR-RGB   Otdel rukopisei, Rossiiskaia gosudarstvennaia biblioteka [Manuscript division, Russian State Library]

RO-BAN   Rukopisnyi otdel, Biblioteka Akademii nauk [Manuscript division, Academy of Sciences Library]

TsGIAM   Tsentral'nyi gosudarstvennyi istoricheskii arkhiv g. Moskvy [Moscow City Central State Historical Archive]

f.   fond [collection]

op.   opis' [inventory]

d.   delo, dela [file or files]

l.   list [sheet]

ll.   listy [sheets]

ob.   oborot [verso]

Self and Story in Russian History

Introduction

"Bolshevism," wrote Walter Benjamin in 1927, upon returning from a visit to Moscow, "has abolished private life."[1] In 1927 it was perhaps too early to announce the triumph of the collective over the individual, the social over the subjective. The New Economic Policy had been instituted in 1921 as a temporary reprieve for the vestiges of bourgeois culture, which Communism promised to eliminate but could not yet do without. By endorsing market relations and the accumulation of personal wealth, NEP had opened the door to self-indulgence, self-display, self-promotion, and self-gratification. It created a breathing space for the domestic pleasures of the private life imperiled by the regime's ideological commitments. Benjamin had correctly perceived, however, that the demands of political engagement, as well as the fragile basis of material existence, already threatened to make this inner world a thing of the past.

The Bolsheviks were willing to enlist the capitalist arts of selfishness in the service of economic and social reconstruction, but the society they were determined to build demanded a new kind of person. These refashioned men and women were conceived as self-sacrificing, self-denying, self-disciplined, and unselfish, but also as self-assured and heroic in their dedication to the common good. The New Woman would disregard her appearance and ignore the thrill of romance. The New Man would pour concrete with the fervor he might once have shown in winning a sweet-

---

[1] Walter Benjamin, "Moscow" (1927), in *Reflections: Essays, Aphorisms, Autobiographical Writings*, ed. Peter Demetz (New York: Harcourt Brace, 1978), 108; quoted in Svetlana Boym, *Common Places: Mythologies of Everyday Life in Russia* (Cambridge, Mass.: Harvard University Press, 1994), 73.

heart or making a fortune. In the 1920s such ideal types were embedded in narratives, both fictional and programmatic, that caricatured the past and predicted a shining future in which self and sensibility were radically transformed. No matter that people continued to fall in love, that tables were still set, even in communal kitchens, or that motherhood was always a civic virtue. The interiority and idiosyncrasy of the private person remained, in principle, unacceptable to the ideologically saturated regime.

Fast forward, now, to the end of Communism. Global capitalism asserts its dominance in the untapped markets of the post-Soviet world hungry for candy bars, kitchen cleansers, fashion magazines, cell phones, pornography, and personal computers. The greedy NEP-era egotist, destroyed by the onslaught of the first Five Year Plan, has returned as the "new Russian" (*novyi russkii*), still an object of ridicule but flexing his muscles in the corridors of power. What crueler irony—the New Man as Nouveau Riche! Free-market ideologues in the United States celebrate the vindication of private enterprise and the political virtues it is supposed to ensure: rule of law, individual rights, democracy. Even in the absence of political guarantees, Western businessmen join local entrepreneurs and former Soviet bureaucrats in making themselves rich.

Yet the happy world of the marketplace is not so happy, it turns out, certainly not for everyone whose lives it affects, and it is plagued by insecurities of its own. Marxists once critiqued the terms of bourgeois ideology, with its deceptive promise of liberty and justice for all, as a cover for economic class interests. Postmodern intellectuals focus on the power of ideology, reconceived broadly as a system of cultural forms and distinctions, to shape the way people think of themselves and their place in the world, ensuring the domination of some and the compliance of others. One of the most powerful weapons in this cultural arsenal is the figure of the independent personality, sure of his rights, convinced of his creative autonomy, ruthless in pursuit of material gain and sexual pleasure.

The story of the self-determining individual, the critics say, is a myth, the sense of personal sovereignty a psychological illusion. In fact, we are bound by the terms that define us, shaped by conventions that make us think we are free but actually enlist us in the job of self-regulation. We are not the masters even of our own cultural productions. In this iconoclastic vein, Roland Barthes announced the "death of the author" and Michel Foucault declared that same author to be a function of the text, powerless to control the meanings it may produce in the course of its existence. Feminists tell us the self is a marker that pretends to universality while excluding whole categories of actual persons from its attributes and rewards. Indeed, such exclusions are what the notion of self-governing individuality is designed to enforce: not everyone measures up. No self-respecting history of the Western self (or, as it is called, the "humanist subject") can nowadays do without a revisionist disclaimer pronouncing that subject more complicated than formerly thought: fragmented, gendered, self-deluded, illusory, "unstable."[2] And so are the identities these selves might claim.

Are we selfish or unselved? That is our Western conundrum. It is one that also affects post-Soviet Russians, who have not only engaged Western intellectual debates but who are experiencing the tensions inherent in modern capitalism firsthand. As always in its history, Russia participates in the world conversation but, as always, from its own point of view. The theme of the self—the articulation of individual difference, the literary and social evolution of personal and collective awareness, the relation of particularized identities to the formation of identity on a national scale—is not itself new to Russian consciousness. It is a theme that entered the Russian historical narrative at the start of the modern age. This volume offers a perspective on these two interspliced tales—the subjective and the collective—as recounted and interpreted by Russians, and as construed by historians and literary scholars looking in from outside the culture's bounds. Bringing their different sensibilities to bear on the common elements of time, text, and context, the present essayists explore a range of genres in which Russians have articulated the sense of self over the course of two hundred years, under the constraints of two political regimes and mobilizing a panoply of expressive resources.

As Sigmund Freud and Jacques Lacan have insisted, language is central to the articulation of subjectivity and self-awareness. People tell stories not only to communicate but also to discover who they are as distinctive beings, bound by relations of sameness and difference to the others whose cultural and emotional fields they share. The ideas of both Freud and Lacan were formally taboo in Soviet times, but their theories were known and subject to debate, if only in order to refute them. Though formalist criticism also ended up on the Party's ideological index, the principles of linguistic analysis derived from Saussurean and Jakobsonian structuralism provided a model for the semiotic approach developed by the Soviet-era Tartu school of literary analysis, which adopted as a major premise the centrality of language to the structure of meaning in both cultural and social terms. Ideas about language and identity, taken from both Russian and Western theorists, thus inform the essays of this book.

Over the course of Russian history, writers, thinkers, common people, and middling folk have found ways to explore their sense of where they fit in the scheme of things by fashioning particular dialects. They have spo-

---

[2] Marjorie Perloff, "Language Poetry and the Lyric Subject: Ron Silliman's Albany, Susan Howe's Buffalo," *Critical Inquiry* 25, no. 3 (Spring 1999): 405–8; Roy Porter, "Introduction," in *Rewriting the Self: Histories from the Renaissance to the Present*, ed. Roy Porter (London: Routledge, 1997).

ken in the name of communities, professions, and confessions, as creative individuals, sexual beings, and mortal creatures face-to-face with God and death. They have not only signaled to each other who they thought they were but have designed the inner architecture of the soul with instruments taken from the common store of cultural intelligibility. Their narratives have taken numerous forms. They come to us as records, explanations, and explorations, announcements, reflections, and enactments, operating at different levels of immediacy, abstraction, and self-awareness. Together they provide the material of Russian history itself, a story that identifies the personality of the nation.

In exploring the conventions governing narratives of self-expression and self-definition over so long a span, the essays, somewhat unconventionally, run in reverse chronological order, beginning in the twentieth century and ending in the eighteenth. Instead of charting a story either of progress or decline, from a historic point of origin to an outcome foreshadowed from the start, they follow some continuous threads but also focus on elements of paradox and disjuncture. The retrospective view underscores the extent to which current concerns shape our vision of what we leave behind: how an ever-unfolding present produces a continuously rewritten past. Lev Tolstoy tried valiantly to write a history of today, but, as Irina Paperno tells us, he was able to write only the history of yesterday. By moving progressively deeper into the past, the volume's essays call attention to the distance we travel to reach back in time and the particular location from which we approach our subject.

The subject of identity, both personal and collective, is on the agenda in the West, as well as in post-Soviet Russia. There the public is making the transition from a collectivist society with a clear national profile to a situation in which neither the dominant ethos nor the boundaries of political authority are clearly defined. Here we are reacting, perhaps, to an excess of certainty about who we are and what we represent. We are conscious of the ways in which established identities—whether national or local—may conceal or facilitate injustices. Where Russians are unable any longer to take very much for granted, we struggle to challenge a sometimes complacent world. The current intellectual climate encourages us to regard every expression of meaning and every assertion of identity as susceptible to reinterpretation. Yet our lives are governed by less rigorous demands. We see distinctions and recognize differences; and we also lump things together.[3] We call nations by their names, however many territories they have combined and languages conflated. We listen for the tonalities of diverse traditions. We revere the great writers, even as we deconstruct their texts, and we admire those who do the deconstructing. In the case of

---

[3] Perloff, "Language," 414; see also her quotation from Barthes, 407.

Russia, the great writers were often the first to tear themselves apart; the nation as a whole seemed the most self-doubting when it was vigorously in the process of constructing its self-image. What was modern Russia and who was to define it were complicated questions from the start. Peter the Great inaugurated the imperial era by breaking with the past. Importing European manners, institutions, and technology, he transformed the Romanov lands into a potent force among nations, a power to be reckoned with in modern terms. He was not the first Russian ruler to look to the West for cultural models, but he was the first to make disruption the signature of his rule.

Among Peter's boldest acts of cultural engineering was the refashioning of his subjects to conform to the latest Western type. He forced noblemen to shave their beards, abandon traditional attire, and usher their wives into public life. These changes, however cosmetic they may seem, carried an explosive symbolic charge. They imposed the rupture with tradition in personal terms on the self-consciousness of the elite. Peter did not, of course, invent the self as a framework for Russian lives, but the anguished question of national self-definition from that time on acquired a subjective dimension. The questions "who am I, and who are we?" were entwined in the minds of thinking persons, because the form the self now took clearly bore the mark of its European legacy. Rooted in the classical age, transformed by Christianity, the Renaissance, and the Enlightenment, the Western model of individuality was lodged in the self-defining, self-scrutinizing, self-activating person, quintessentially male, who was to emerge in the bourgeois era as master of the hearth and denizen of civil society.

Was selfhood, however, a necessary attribute of civilization? Was it something that every nation must acquire? In engaging the subject of the self as a feature of the Russian cultural landscape, one enters a discussion started by Russians themselves, indeed those very Russians most generously endowed with the necessary instruments of self-questioning: attention to upbringing, the cultivation of the mind, and a sense of civic location. By the nineteenth century the linked themes of person and patrimony had been elaborated into the intellectual styles of the Slavophiles and the Westernizers. The latter endorsed Peter's choice of the West as the model to be adopted; the former celebrated what they imagined to be specifically native traits. When Vissarion Belinsky complained in 1847 that in Russia "the personality is just beginning to break out of its shell," he eagerly anticipated its emergence. Not so the Slavophile Konstantin Aksakov, who praised the peasant commune as "an association of people who have renounced their personal egoism, their individuality, and express common accord." The commune, he wrote, "is a moral choir and just as each individual voice in the chorus is not lost but only subordinated to the overall harmony . . . so too in the commune the individual is not lost but merely renounces his exclusivity . . . and finds himself on a higher and purer level, in mutual harmony with other individuals motivated by similar self-abnegation."[4]

The participants in this dialogue all had their share of mixed feelings, however. For the exquisite arias of post-Enlightenment elite culture the Slavophiles had enormous regard. The cost of such achievements, however, was high and the advantages inaccessible to the common folk, whose traditional existence allegedly obeyed a different set of rules and exemplified more precious values. The Westernizers, too, were aware that the privileged upper crust in the great cities (especially the capital, St. Petersburg, built on a Western plan) and on wealthy estates, where French-speaking ladies presided over grand soirées and libraries were stocked with leather-bound volumes, was a world apart from the vast expanse of peasant huts and illiterate masses toiling from dawn to dusk, linked by fierce family ties and communal despotisms. The European model, furthermore, had lost its original luster. Russians who kept up with the latest in European thinking, knew the Enlightenment paradigm was under attack. The allegedly rational, free-standing self was taking a beating from collectivist, post-Romantic egalitarians, imagining new social contexts and the new selves they would breed. Influenced by early socialists such as Robert Owen and Charles Fourier, the Russian radicals and populists of the 1860s and 1870s agonized over the relation between the individual and the whole. The self that did the agonizing agonized about the very category of the self. Did intellectuals have the right to self-reflection? Were the instruments of culture that produced the individual subject a luxury that an agrarian country could ill afford?

The conviction that Russia has neglected the principle of individuality, for good or for ill—and all the more absolutely as one descends the social pyramid—has exercised a tenacious hold on both the native and foreign imaginations. Never very robust, even when commercial life flourished, the frail and largely elitist plant is sometimes thought to have withered away in the Soviet era. Yet the opening essays of this book question whether that regime in fact succeeded in replacing the principle of individuality with a collectivist ethos, as it boasted it had done and as its critics accused it of doing. Instead of documenting the alleged suppression of personal life along with individual rights, the authors ask how it was that a

---

[4] For an intellectual history of the term *self* as understood by nineteenth-century Russians, see *Constructing Russian Culture in the Age of Revolution: 1881–1940*, ed. Catriona Kelly and David Shepherd (Oxford: Oxford University Press, 1998), 13–25. Belinsky quoted in William Mills Todd III, "Storied Selves," Chapter 11; Aksakov quoted in Andrzej Walicki, *The Slavophile Controversy: History of a Conservative Utopia in Nineteenth-Century Russian Thought*, trans. Hilda Andrews-Rusiecka (Oxford: Clarendon Press, 1975), 257.

state aspiring to total control over private and public existence and notoriously hostile to individualized forms of expression nevertheless permitted—and in some sense even encouraged—attributes of selfhood to thrive. The self, though ideologically under siege, did not disappear. Rather, the cultivation of subjectivity was implicated in the very mechanics of the collectivist regime, on the level of everyday life as well as intellectual production.

The four thinkers that Caryl Emerson singles out offer an indigenous perspective on this subject. Navigating the ideological shoals of the Soviet academy, Bakhtin, Vygotsky, Lotman, and Ginzburg pursued the thematics of the self against all odds. Respecting the obligatory parameters of socially oriented discourse, their theories illuminated the unpredictable outcomes of the social process. All four, in Emerson's view, conceptualize the dynamics of the self in terms of creativity, seen as an interactive, not internal, dynamic. As she puts it, they considered "a self [to be] successful to the extent that it can transfigure what it encounters ready-made or given in the world." For Bakhtin, the matrix of self-definition was the dialogue—the fluid exchange among speaking subjects. Lydia Ginzburg put the accent on the subject's ability to participate in and appropriate elements of the social environment. She understood the creative process as occurring in response to what Emerson calls the pressure of "outside structures." Where Bakhtin chose Dostoevsky's idea-driven narratives as his model, Ginzburg preferred the socially and historically embedded plots and characters of Tolstoy. Compared with either Bakhtin or Ginzburg, Vygotsky and Lotman go farther in the direction of structural analysis, focusing on action and behavior rather than on narrative forms. Both are concerned with the social matrix, the coded forms that give meaning to individual lives and cultural landscapes.

Anna Akhmatova, the subject of Alexander Zholkovsky's essay, belonged to the same small world of highly creative figures who managed to carve an intellectual niche in the hard stone of Soviet cultural life. Like them she survived the worst years and found a voice that allowed her to be heard in some of the official registers (wartime patriotism, for example) but that more often clashed with the dominant tone. Akhmatova differed, however, from Emerson's critic-scholars in her refusal to hide. Bakhtin spent his professional life in the relative safety of a provincial backwater, to be discovered only in his waning days and achieve prominence after his death. Lotman found refuge in Estonia and took shelter in scientific structures of thought; Vygotsky exercised his courage in the laboratory; Ginzburg devoted herself to the study of how others articulated a personal style. Akhmatova, by contrast, turned her own personality into an instrument of expression, raising moral rectitude to the level of performance art.

A virtual icon of cultural resistance, Akhmatova organized her self-presentation around the drama of her own persecution. In a provocative and sober reading of this famous self-staging, Zholkovsky argues that although conceived in opposition to the repressive regime, the stories she told and the dramas she enacted exemplified its same discursive and representational principles. Cultivating her own charisma, she generated an extensive memoir literature among her friends and acquaintances, from which Zholkovsky copiously cites. Many of these texts establish their authors' own claims to recognition through the vicarious act of having known and written about her. This infinitely reflexive process shows how Akhmatova's performance and its reception served as vehicles of self-fashioning for the members of the countercultural elite. Yet despite the self-serving elements, or perhaps because of them, Zholkovsky accepts the eyewitness accounts as a reliable guide to what they describe. Not only do similar stories recur in different renditions, but the writers recount how Akhmatova herself dictated the tales she wished to see preserved. In some sense, her audience was her secretary and her archive, as well as her public. Other poets and writers have engaged in such practices of self-creation (most famously the Russian Symbolists), but Zholkovsky insists that Akhmatova's wish to control her legacy, like her sharp words of reprimand for those who mocked her or recorded deviant details, suggests a temperament different from the spirit of creative egotism that animated the aesthetic iconoclasts of pre-Soviet years. Her egotism, by contrast, had as much to do with control as with defiance, exerting, so Zholkovsky argues, the same monological grasp on meaning that characterized official Soviet culture in Stalin's time.

Both Emerson and Zholkovsky thus suggest that despite the collectivist ideology for which Soviet culture is known, cultivation of the self was in many ways congruent with the defining practices of that culture. Jochen Hellbeck goes even farther in seeing the production of a specifically Soviet self as central to the fulfillment of the regime's political aspirations. In contrast to Akhmatova, Hellbeck's protagonist, the writer Alexander Afinogenov, made his name as a Stalinist go-getter. An eager practitioner of Socialist Realism, he defined himself not against the political grain but by internalizing the regime's dominant values. Yet this undertaking involved an effort at self-delineation no less personal than the high-profile tactics Akhmatova employed in subversive ways. Hellbeck argues, in fact, that membership-in-good-standing in Soviet society did not entail the abandonment of individual sensibilities, but rather the mobilization of self-scrutiny in the interests of self-discipline. At the height of the purges, Afinogenov focused his writerly craft and psychological energy on self-reconstruction through the medium of a private diary. In his mind, there was no gap between devotion to the collective and cultivation of the self; indeed, one depended on the other. Accepting public criticism and attempting to conform to the Soviet ideal, Afinogenov used the language of religious conversion and spiritual purification. Despite some difficulties encountered in his professional life, he, like Akhmatova, survived the regime at its most ferocious.

The Soviet system applied a range of strategies for domination and control. Some were repressive in the ordinary sense, using fear and death to compel compliance. Others elicited cooperation in more devious ways. Inheriting both a religious and a secular tradition, the regime mobilized discourses of moral purity as well as modern techniques of social engineering. It could not, however, control the implications of these legacies. Akhmatova and Afinogenov utilized the religious idiom to very different effect; the literary semioticians drew on contemporary theory—linguistic, sociological, and psychological, some of it officially approved, some of it disparaged—to generate their own interpretive grids.

These narrators of the self from Soviet times all lived by the word; they were not average folk. Telling stories was how they defined themselves in both professional and personal terms. These exceptional cases are enough, however, to demonstrate that Soviet culture cannot be understood in direct opposition to a Western liberal model of civil society as the meeting place of autonomous souls. In the aftermath of the Cold War it is no longer surprising to observe that Soviet society was more complex than it may have seemed from the other side of the Iron Curtain. Kitchen curtains swung in the breeze, lives were lived and recorded, and consciences were cleansed as well as sullied. Stories were produced on command (as in Party-generated autobiographies and prison confessions) but also in private.

It is clear, moreover, that whatever the Soviet regime inherited from the past, it was nothing simple. Late imperial Russia was a society of intense discursive self-consciousness that came equipped with a morally oversensitive, highly literary intellectual elite, a growing urban public of catholic tastes enamored of material progress, and a political class dedicated to squaring the circle of conservative rule and economic advancement. Whether the empire was objectively "backward" (lagging on the developmental timeline to which other nations adhered) or overly attached to its self-conception as the repository of a timeless past is an issue that exceeds the competence of this volume. The essays that explore this cultural terrain demonstrate, however, that when Russians embraced the vocabulary of modern selfhood, they did so in their own way.

It was a vocabulary fraught with tensions suited to the hybrid character of the late imperial world. Even the First Person of the realm found himself caught in the snares of borrowed techniques and ambiguous meanings. Richard Wortman shows how Nicholas II tried to subordinate the vagaries of genre to his political needs. But the forms of representation resisted the imperial will, uncovering the contradictions in his own project. The sovereign was, of course, a figure whose person existed in a category of its own, embodying as it did the unitary character of absolute rule. Nicholas had only reluctantly established the State Duma in 1905 as a way to quell the revolutionary unrest of that year, but he resented the limitation on his absolute power. Even when insisting on the traditional nature of his mandate, however, Nicholas was obliged to speak in a modern tongue.

Films depicting the tsar in a domestic setting and journalistic accounts pretending to describe his private life highlighted the importance of his person and created a sense of intimacy that circumvented the institutions of political life, but the immediacy of the public's experience also undermined the tsar's pretensions to grandeur and the confidence he wished to convey. In mobilizing the "two selves" of Nicholas II, the intimate and the imperial, the tsar and his publicists wished to activate his connection to the populace at large and to underscore the exclusive focus of popular allegiance. Yet the use of modern techniques worked at cross purposes to deflate the monarch's dignity and cheapen his image as it proliferated on movie screens, postage stamps, scarves, and the pages of illustrated magazines. This representational confusion reflected the contradictions that impeded effective government on the eve of 1917, when the elected Duma delegates struggled with a ruler who wished they did not exist and had the power to ignore them. Even the sovereign, however, in his attempts to produce a convincing self with a carefully constructed purpose, discovered he was bound by the relational terms on which meaning depends. He could impede the participation of ordinary people in political affairs, but to govern he needed to influence the public mind, and this influence could not be controlled absolutely. In some ways the monarch was not sovereign after all.

The managers of the imperial persona wanted to use the resources of commercial culture to impose the values that same commercial culture had displaced on a public caught in the dynamics of change. But the conservative message embedded in the officially sponsored newsreels and memorabilia was contaminated by the form and context in which it appeared: the stuff of imperial self-advertisement was ephemeral; the monarch as object of public adoration shared the screen with the heroes and heroines of cheap melodramas. The world of popular entertainment was seductive and immediate, not authoritative and remote. It won the public's sympathy by engaging their emotions, desires, and dreams. It seemed, indeed, most personal when most formulaic.

At the opposite cultural pole from Nicholas and his demonstratively domestic wife, the New Woman of turn-of-the-century Europe and Russia went out to work and insisted on independence. Yet she, too, wanted her man. The dilemmas of self-representation and self-fulfillment that confronted this female icon of modern times were dramatically enacted on the silver screen. Intellectuals and officials had debated the question of women's place in public life since the mid-nineteenth century, but issues of gender-typing and postpatriarchal sexual conduct achieved a new vitality in the 1890s as cities grew and consumer culture expanded. The mass media created ready-to-wear types for the self-styled modern person to assume. Having purchased a ticket to fantasy, women in the darkened theaters were invited to imagine their femininity in different modes: the victim, the femme fatale, and, of course, the performer.

Louise McReynolds explains how Evgenii Bauer's melodramas offered scope to female stars while scripting the fantasy lives of female viewers. Instead of striving for mirror-like realism, actresses preferred the new style of exaggerated facial expression, creating characters broad enough to accommodate the projected desires and needs of those who watched them struggle with a range of motivations and ill-concealed fears. With his amplified emotionalism, Bauer exploited melodrama's potential for telling classic tales of women's downfall and betrayal. But the same films, as McReynolds points out, provided their female characters with disquieting victories that appealed to an audience of women seeking new role models for the new age.

Whereas the mass production of images of the tsar and stories about him did not enhance his exceptional status but had an unintended leveling effect, average Russian city dwellers used standard character types and standardized tales to produce stories of their own, which gave them a sense of distinction. This interactive dynamic is clearly evident in the case explored by Susan Larsen, who discusses the exceptional popularity of Lydia Charskaia and the outpouring of self-expression her stories provoked. Published in children's magazines, Charskaia's tales of young female friendship and adventure elicited countless letters from fascinated girl readers who identified with the fictional characters and their fates. The stories that Larsen examines include those of Charskaia's literary narratives, as well as those embedded in her readers' replies. Her novels provided the girls who read them with an opportunity to work through the complexities and contradictions of female identity. Larsen shows how the texts lent themselves to various kinds and levels of interpretation. Readers framed their responses in relation to the codes embodied in the fictional tales, but the response itself took the form of open-ended dialogue in which the girls commented on the meaning of what they read and imagined themselves in various roles. The act of writing connected them with the wide world and brought the world into their lives, influencing their choices and expectations.[5]

If narrative styles and prefabricated images were instrumental in enabling the Russian woman to design her modern self, so too did men find cultural guides to sexual self-definition. In the climate of relaxed censorship and heightened sexual awareness that followed 1905, the literary scene featured novels about prostitution and free love. The Western sexologists and Sigmund Freud were published in Russian translation. Even the topic of homosexuality came to public attention. The philosopher Vasilii Rozanov wrote about same-sex love as a natural (if less admirable) variation on human desire, while a few avant-garde cultural figures lived openly homosexual or bisexual lives and depicted homosexual characters in their fiction.[6]

The theme was nevertheless approached with caution. The Oscar Wilde case of the mid-1890s, a landmark in Western representations of the homosexual male, entered the Russian cultural lexicon through a series of mediations. In his reading of Russian reactions to the Wilde affair, Evgenii Bershtein shows how the scandalous figure was recontextualized by the contemporary Russian press and by Silver Age writers. Avoiding direct mention of Wilde's sexual behavior, Russians focused on his status as a creative personality and victim of persecution. Intellectuals saw him as a Nietzschean character, the center of his own dramatic self-representation, and a heroic devotee of aestheticism. Having emphasized the theme of suffering in Nietzsche's work, they depicted Wilde himself as a Christ-like martyr.

The Wilde figure thus construed provided either a model for male homosexual self-styling or a foil against which to define the same identity in different terms. It was embraced, for example, by Viacheslav Ivanov, who flirted with sexual variation in his own relationships and hailed the flamboyant Englishman as an amalgam of Christian and Dionysian motifs. Mikhail Kuzmin, by contrast, rejected the agonized martyr type in favor of

---

[5] For more on commercial literature, see Jeffrey Brooks, *When Russia Learned to Read: Literacy and Popular Literature, 1861–1917* (Princeton: Princeton University Press, 1985); Laura Engelstein, *The Keys to Happiness: Sex and the Search for Modernity in Fin-de-Siècle Russia* (Ithaca: Cornell University Press, 1992); Anastasya Verbitskaya, *Keys to Happiness: A Novel*, trans. and ed. Beth Holmgren and Helena Goscilo (Bloomington: Indiana University Press, 1999); Evdokia Nagrodskaia, *The Wrath of Dionysus: A Novel*, trans. and ed. Louise McReynolds (Bloomington: Indiana University Press, 1997); and Beth Holmgren, *Rewriting Capitalism: Literature and the Market in Late Tsarist Russia and the Kingdom of Poland* (Pittsburgh: University of Pittsburgh Press, 1998).

[6] On Rozanov, see Engelstein, *Keys*, chapter 8. On Freud, see Alexander Etkind, *Eros of the Impossible: The History of Psychoanalysis in Russia*, trans. Noah and Maria Rubins (Boulder, Colo.: Westview, 1997); Martin A. Miller, *Freud and the Bolsheviks: Psychoanalysis in Imperial Russia and the Soviet Union* (New Haven: Yale University Press, 1998); and, from the opposite perspective, James L. Rice, *Freud's Russia: National Identity in the Evolution of Psychoanalysis* (New Brunswick, N.J.: Transaction Publishers, 1993).

serene, classical images with which to represent male same-sex love. Yet even as he articulated an alternative to the russianized Wilde, Kuzmin addressed his critique to that model.[7]

The varied reception of the Wilde story, like the responses of Charskaia's readers, shows how interactive the process of cultural shaping could be. Sexual modernity was the joint production of image makers, storytellers, and their publics, whose members used the available cultural material in fashioning their private lives, just as the defining voices of Russian high culture adapted European discourses to their own ends. One of the most powerful discourses of the self in the modern period is the one developed by Sigmund Freud, who used narrative as a tool of therapy, diagnosis, and personal self-definition. Though known and appreciated in Russia, his was far from the dominant approach in these years. The Russian psychiatric profession, which took shape in the 1890s, eagerly embraced a range of Western theoretical models and curative techniques. As Cathy Popkin shows, however, narrative was a tool that Russian psychiatrists used sparingly and with paradoxical effect. In the case of patients who presented hysterical symptoms, somatic expression replaced narrative exposition; the sufferers were unable to explain, either to themselves or others, what was really wrong. Eliciting the story behind the symptoms was supposed to make them go away by revealing the psychological origins of distress. Instead of encouraging their patients, on the Freudian model, to achieve relief and self-knowledge by talking for themselves, Popkin observes, Russian practitioners often substituted their own words and abstract categories for the perspective their subjects might have offered. Popkin argues that, in the hands of professionals unsure of their scientific claims, the highly formulaic genre of the case study acted as a straitjacket to impede the free recital of personal woes and the creative process of self-repair. Only rarely do the patients' own stories emerge in the medical journals as evidence of illness and clues to a cure. The exceptions are all the more eloquent for involving people of little education who cannot explain themselves in writing and depend on being asked to speak for the opportunity to tell their stories and thus to emerge with a new consciousness of who they are or might be. In a careful reading of texts that do as much to obstruct as to illuminate, Popkin analyzes the transpositions effected by the case-study genre, while deciphering the voices they either silence or manage to transmit.

Psychiatrists influenced by Freud and Charcot saw themselves on a mission to relieve the silenced sufferers of their pain by reinterpreting their symptoms in the light of a seemingly objective scientific truth. Often, how-

---

[7] On Kuzmin, see John E. Malmstad and Nikolay Bogomolov, *Mikhail Kuzmin: A Life in Art* (Cambridge, Mass.: Harvard University Press, 1999).

ever, as Popkin suggests, the Russians were too insecure about their own professional authority to give their patients' narrative impulse full rein. A similar conflict confronted Russian political activists who adapted the analytic framework of Western political thought and modeled their behavior on Western political experience. They, too, believed that happiness depended on telling the right kind of story and assuming the identities these stories produced; they, too, imposed coherence on the messy stuff of unself-reflective existence. In their case, they aimed to instruct an assortment of factory laborers and part-time peasants in the mechanisms of the class struggle, equipping them for their role in the revolution envisioned in Western socialist thought.

Here, however, the similarities end. Psychiatrists sought to impose order on derangement, but radicals wanted to make rebels out of complacent men. The theater offered Social Democrats scripts on which to model the process of transformation. Drama provided roles and plots as templates for social action. Reginald E. Zelnik describes how Russian Social Democrats used Gerhart Hauptmann's 1892 play "The Weavers" to stimulate the activism of workers in a different context. Comparing the original German script with the Russian rendition, Zelnik shows the kinds of accommodations needed to make the foreign version comprehensible to local ears. Its basic elements did not, however, need translation. Its characters were not class-conscious proletarians but ordinary workers, of an old-fashioned sort, afflicted with all manner of human frailty. Indeed, Hauptmann's story was grounded in traditional terms of personal heroism, moral weakness, and tragic pathos that resonated with Russian workers' sensibilities and daily lives. Its very distance from the ideal made it an effective tool of political education. Using a ploy later codified in Soviet Socialist Realism, the sponsors of this pedagogical drama hoped the audience would identify with representations of an imperfect present (or past) in order to imagine a more perfect future in which their personal identities and collective circumstances would be transformed.

Transformation and instruction were also the goals of Lev Tolstoy, who turned the pedagogical apparatus upon himself, keeping a running moral account of his everyday existence. In the search for perfection, he too drew on foreign models, including Benjamin Franklin's diary and the thought of Immanuel Kant. By charting his daily life and all-too-worldly involvements, Tolstoy hoped to deprive that life of its appeal. The search for spiritual perfection connects his quest to that of Alexander Afinogenov, who used the self-scrutinizing diary to achieve the opposite aim of worldly acceptance. Tolstoy's story is the inverse of Afinogenov's in other respects: born to social preeminence, a figure of immense cultural authority, the great writer of fictions tried to craft a self that renounced privilege, fame, and even the joys of self-satisfaction.

In dealing with Tolstoy, a figure whose self-involvement is well known, Irina Paperno focuses not on the ironies of a life lived in self-contradiction but on the contradictions inherent in the generic demands of self-representation. How do the constraints of narrative limit the terms in which the self can be experienced and conveyed? As a diarist, Tolstoy is both practitioner of the genre and its anguished critic. Paperno catches him in this double act, showing how, and long *avant* the Foucauldian *lettre*, the dependence of the "reality effect" on its discursive matrix was already a subject of philosophical concern. Having tried to capture the flight of time and the evanescence of the present, to enact on the page the internal complexity of a person's self-awareness, Tolstoy finally despaired of his ability to plumb the essence of the fleeting moment. In the search for solace, he created handbooks of introspection, almanacs of assembled texts geared to faceless readers unburdened by the pressures of self-creation but hungry for guidance in their personal lives. Like Charskaia's tales and Bauer's melodramas, the formulaic scripts that Tolstoy collected appealed to the depersonalized public's interest in themselves. The almanacs of famous thoughts seem also to have offered some comfort to the famous author himself as he lay awaiting death and the final triumph of time over awareness.

The inadequacy of narrative forms to convey the subjective dimension of human existence did not seem to trouble this eager public, but it was a central preoccupation of Tolstoy's contemporary Fedor Dostoevsky, whom William Mills Todd III describes as having developed "a *negative* poetics for stories of the self." In *The Brothers Karamazov* Dostoevsky mimics the authoritative discourses that filled the journals in which the novel's installments first appeared. The stories told by lawyers in the courtroom and reported in popular accounts of trials are mirrored within the fictional text as a product of the author's art. The equally instrumental discourses of medicine and psychology are similarly invoked, only to demonstrate how seriously they fail to provide an adequate rendering of human nature. Dostoevsky uses the devices of fiction, itself a tissue of fabricated and purposeful tales, to explore the difficulty of being true to an existing reality, yet the inadequacy of such representations is itself a fact of life, which the novelist believed he was adequately reflecting. He thus produced a sense of the real, in full awareness of the complexity of the objects he attempted to evoke. By contrast, the lawyers he depicts do not doubt the effectiveness of their accounts and have little interest in the degree to which these accounts do justice to the objects they describe. The reality to which they aspire consists of the practical result of their inventions.

Dostoevsky was a professed conservative, hostile to the rational ethos of the modern secular world. His literary practice and the philosophical po-

sitions expressed in the very texture of his prose nevertheless spoke to issues of the moment and the future. As Todd explains, Dostoevsky articulated a very modern discomfort with modern certainties: his narratives are
exercises in unsettling the easy expectations about what constitutes character, self, coherence, and accurate representation. Psychological to the
core, Dostoevsky refused any single perspective or unitary view. In this
sense his work was at the forefront of Europe's own movement toward
self-questioning.

Although his narratives unmask the manipulations of stories that make
untroubled claims to truth, Dostoevsky was no skeptic. For him absolute
values existed, but not in the realm of logical syllogisms and worldly affairs. They belonged to the spiritual dimension, a domain inaccessible
through the efforts of exposition and justification his fictions expose—
the production of purposeful, seemingly coherent stories. The literary
theorist Mikhail Bakhtin inhabited a different world—one in which the
truths of scientific modernity dominated the discursive landscape. Yet it
was Bakhtin who used the example of Dostoevsky to argue for the virtues
of uncertainty, for the contingency of cultural expression, for the dynamic and illusory quality of the self. Bakhtin has become one of the
icons of modern interpretive theory, a specialist in ambiguity, complexity,
and subtlety surviving in a context that discouraged them all. Perhaps
there is something about the very insecurity of selfhood and its cultural
representations in the changing circumstances of the late imperial
regime that stimulated the development of modernism on Russian soil,
for Russians have been eminent practitioners of literary analysis and the
literature of fractured consciousness.

The hybrid and self-searching character of Russian modernity, in which
moral, spiritual, and rational elements intertwine, can already be de-
tected in its eighteenth-century roots. Catherine the Great's engagement
with the Enlightenment prompted her to endorse the rule of law, humane punishment, and public participation in civic life. As a patron of literature and the arts, she entered into dialogue with writers of the day,
permitted the establishment of private presses, and characterized the
Russian empire as a modern European state. As an absolute ruler, however, she was quick to penalize the expression of ideas with which she dis-
agreed and to use the power at her command to subdue any sign of popular insubordination. While promoting the development of a productive
intermediate class, she kept the peasants in bondage and the cultural elite
under threat of reprimand or incarceration.

Alexander Radishchev used the same enlightened ideas that Catherine
promoted from the throne to expose the contradictions of her reign. The
Journey from St. Petersburg to Moscow, which he published independently in
1790 and which landed him in Siberian exile, has been interpreted (most

emphatically, of course, by Soviet scholars) as an ideological tract denouncing serfdom and autocratic rule. Andrew Kahn argues, by contrast, that Radishchev did not intend to teach a political lesson but rather to create a morally exemplary writing self, as well as a morally implicated reader. In so doing, Radishchev articulated a concept of the individual as the bearer and shaper of the values that sustain a common world. Radishchev believed, Kahn writes, "that to be human is to be engaged in active relation to another individually or collectively." His tract, Kahn insists, was a work of fiction, whose purpose "is not to assert what knowledge and truth are, but rather to teach the reader that understanding comes from within." The narrator of the work does not deliver a sermon but "functions in the text as a moral spectator who sees the self in dialogical terms."

Radishchev, like Tolstoy, enjoyed the self-assurance of a well-born man. Both devoted their considerable cultural resources to the exploration of the moral questions that connected them to humanity at large. Yet reflection also played a role in the construction of humbler lives. For Ivan Tolchenov, the eighteenth-century provincial merchant considered by David L. Ransel, writing was not a means of professional self-definition. Tolchenov directed his practical activities, rather, toward attaining the social identity of a cultivated member of the upper crust. But as part of the project of self-transformation, he documented his efforts in the form of a daily account, supplemented by periodic summaries of longer perspective and more ruminative tone. The very act of recording marked him as belonging to the category of men whose interests transcended the mere pursuit of material existence, the province, supposedly, of the class into which he had been born. The story Tolchenov tells is imbued, however, with pathos and suspense; it reflects the increasing self-awareness that develops in tandem with the dwindling success of the enterprise itself. For the merchant both rises and falls, and the power of the narrative persona waxes as its author's economic and social fortunes wane. The cause of disaster is precisely his desire to make himself over in an aestheticized mode: his homes, his gardens, his leisure, and his diary are attributes of the kind of self to which he aspires. Self-reproach is part of this story. Craving status and recognition, he has indulged in luxury and wasted his means; he has ended lower, not higher, than he began. Like Tolstoy, Tolchenov repents his personal failings, but unlike the writer, who endlessly announced the desire to abandon his privileges for the purity of dispossession, the merchant regretted his fate.

The very fact, however, that a man of commercial origins thought of his life as a project in need of careful tending and worthy of being recorded in time—not just in the form of occasional jottings or the rendering of episodic events but in a continuous narration, reorganized retrospectively to make a well-told tale, in which the narrator achieves perspective on his own existence—testifies to the extent to which relatively ordinary lives, even in out-of-the-way places, had achieved a definition and value in their occupants' eyes. Such obscure personal documents should disabuse us of the assumption that the carapace of Russian high culture was transparently thin.

Indeed, even the most marginal of cultural communities at the far end of the social scale yields evidence of well-articulated selves telling tales that reveal a secure sense of social and psychological location. Such is the case of the true believers whom Laura Engelstein describes. Considerably humbler than the upwardly mobile Tolchenov, the members of this particular religious group were drawn from the prosperous peasantry and lowly town dwellers of the late eighteenth-century heartland. Following the call of a charismatic vagrant who styled himself as the reincarnation of Jesus Christ, these spiritual enthusiasts, known as the Skoptsy, submitted to the ritual of self-castration as a means of ensuring the salvation of their souls. Replenishing its ranks by recruitment, the community managed, despite continuous persecution under the tsarist regime, to survive for over 150 years until it was finally repressed in the late 1920s. In the course of this time, some members accumulated considerable wealth, but few acquired more than the rudiments of literacy and general culture. Under the pressure of the outside world, believers were nevertheless constantly compelled to render an account of their beliefs and practices. Some ultimately adopted the project of self-explanation as their spiritual mission.

Throughout their history, the Skoptsy used the telling of tales as a way of both defining and enacting their heretical creed—establishing the boundaries of their faith in relation to the Orthodox norm and confirming their adherence to a particular discursive style. Certain forms of storytelling protected them against the incursions of a hostile world. The choice of speech over silence, of writing over oral recital, had spiritual as well as practical consequences for individual believers and the community as a whole. Having concentrated for almost one hundred years on perfecting the arts of secrecy and evasion, at the turn of the twentieth century the few with access to the written and printed word began to reach out to the conventionally religious or even the secular world. These articulate brethren satisfied an impulse to self-expression which they shared with other self-taught writers from the common folk, such as the numerous blue-collar workers who, in the years around 1905, contributed to trade-union papers or sent their confessions to Maxim Gorky.[8]

[8] See, for example, Mark D. Steinberg, "Worker-Authors and the Cult of the Person," in *Cultures in Flux: Lower-Class Values, Practices, and Resistance in Late Imperial Russia*, ed. Stephen P. Frank and Mark D. Steinberg (Princeton: Princeton University Press, 1994), 168–184.

The view of self-renunciation as an attribute of poverty or traditional life may sooner reflect the egotism of the culturally well-endowed than the subjective experience of the less fortunate. As the parallel with Tolchenov suggests, Tolstoy's use of narrative as a corrective to self-indulgence may reflect the privileged outlook of just the kind of man he wished he could cease to be. And, as he realized himself, any narrative builds up the sedimentary rock out of which a person chisels a self-image. Despite the low level of literacy in the villages and factory districts in late imperial Russia, the culture of self-expression in fact reached well down the social scale. Exposed to readings from Scripture, the singing of spiritual verse, and the recounting of tales from the lives of saints, and accustomed to shaping distinctively local lore, the common folk employed whatever genres came their way. Those who learned to read or were read to absorbed the thrills of penny dreadfuls, the aphorisms of spiritual guidebooks, or the high-minded melodramas of socialist morality tales. The impulse to set oneself apart, whether in opposition to one's neighbors or in the company of kith and kin, clearly affected all kinds of people, no doubt even earlier than the mid-eighteenth century, when the stories in this volume begin. Yet it is rare to find a record of this quest. As more stories are discovered and heard, the chorus of voices gets richer, and each voice emerges in sharper relief.

CHAPTER ONE

Bakhtin, Lotman, Vygotsky, and Lydia Ginzburg on Types of Selves: A Tribute

CARYL EMERSON

A person can get sick and tired of everything except creativity. A person can weary of love, fame, wealth, homage, luxury, art, traveling, friends—absolutely everything. Under certain conditions, each of those will cease to seem purposeful. But not one's own creativity.

Lydia Ginzburg

In a happy paradox, the Soviet period—so rich in arbitrary evaluations and political oppression—knew a number of superior literary theorists who were wholly free from a hermeneutics of suspicion. Among them are the four very different thinkers considered in this essay. Mikhail Bakhtin, Lev Vygotsky, Yuri Lotman, and Lydia Ginzburg contributed to a distinctly trusting Russian "psychology of literary creativity." Each considered at length how the self might work optimally inside a fiction, outside in life, and in that borderland between self and other called "authoring"; for each, a self is successful to the extent that it can transfigure what it encounters ready-made or given in the world, and (however troubled, needy, resistant, or self-sufficient that material might seem) enhance rather than diminish its energy and potential. This self, whether nurtured in a literary text or exercised in the outside world, certainly knows weakness and vice. But it is not presumed to be inherently neurotic, self-pitying, or pathological. Such grim orientations of the spirit are not taken as sign of any special strength or depth, nor equated with the courage to accept reality and look it in the eye. Reality—the givens of our world—must be shaped, not merely accepted. The transformation of negative or tragic material is not so much heroic or exceptional as it is a routine obligation.

Jotting from 1944. Lidiia Ginzburg, *Pretvorenie opyta* [The Transformation of Experience] (Riga / Leningrad: "Avots" / Assotsiatsiia 'Novaia literatura,' 1991), 86.

These four thinkers postulate that the self is naturally healthy—by which they appear to mean it is perpetually capable of learning and by definition is robust enough to withstand hostile or destructive responses to its outreaching instincts. Moral worth, the loving embrace of community, a striving toward self-affirmation and wholeness are understood to be *normal*.

The extraordinary work Vygotsky accomplished with blind, deaf-mute, and learning-disabled children in the 1920s is one inspirational result of this presumption of spiritual health.[1] Bakhtin, in the same decade, displayed a kindred optimism in his study of Dostoevsky—which has been credited with presenting a rosier, more benevolent, more constructive image of the human spirit than that conflicted novelist could ever have endorsed himself. Lotman, in his luminous treatments of Russia's greatest poet, returned again and again to Pushkin's almost fanatical tenacity and physical courage, in art and in life; as the scholar wrote of the poet to Boris Egorov in 1986, "Life is that hard, granite material which wants to remain a formless chunk, resisting the sculptor, threatening to kill him after collapsing on top of him. Pushkin is the sculptor, triumphing over the material and subjecting it to himself. . . . A striving not to give in to circumstance was one of Pushkin's most consistent impulses."[2] And Ginzburg, arguably the most melancholic of the four, jotted down in her

---

[1] In 1925–26 Vygotsky organized a laboratory for the psychology of abnormal childhood (which was to become the Experimental Defectological Institute in 1929) under the People's Commissariat for Public Education. His studies in this field, collected under the title "Osnovy defektologii" in L. S. Vygotskii, *Sobranie sochinenii v 6–i tomakh*, vol. 5 (Moscow: Pedagogika, 1973), were pathbreaking in their time. Human handicap is real, Vygotsky argues, but its psychological effects are socially imposed. Whatever its equipment at birth, a body will always posit itself to itself as whole (at no time does a child who has been blind from birth feel "plunged into darkness"); a bodily defect is felt as such only *culturally*. Isolating and emphasizing that defect ignores the "tons of health" innate in each organism. For a lucid discussion of this work in English, see Mikhail Yaroshevsky's biography *Lev Vygotsky* (Moscow: Progress Publishers, 1989), especially "The Abnormal Child in the World of Culture," 96–132.

[2] Lotman to B. F. Egorov, 20–21 October 1986, in Iu. M. Lotman, *Pis'ma 1940–1993*, ed. B. F. Egorov (Moscow: Shkola 'Iazyki russkoi kul'tury,' " 1997), 346. This eloquent letter continues: "Just consider: it's as if his whole life 'worked out': exiles, persecutions, no money at all, prohibitions . . . and how does one have to present this to students? 'Pushkin was exiled to the south. This turned out to be extremely timely, in that the romanticism that had spontaneously ripened in him received the necessary shaping.' Pushkin is exiled to Mikhailovskoe (he is in despair, all his plans and contacts are severed. Viazemskii writes with absolute seriousness that the Russian countryside in winter is the same as a prison and that Pushkin will take to drink). And we say (and correctly): 'The stay in Mikhailovskoe was a fortunate circumstance for shaping Pushkin's sense of history and of the [Russian] people, here he discovered folklore.' " Or the poet's final days: "Here he is, lying with his intestines torn apart and a shattered pelvis. The pain, apparently, is not to be believed; but in response to Dal''s words: 'Don't be ashamed of your pain, if you groan it will be easier,' he answers startlingly: 'It's ridiculous that this nonsense has overpowered me, I don't want . . . ' And that was when he could hardly speak from pain. [Doctor] Arend said that he had attended at thirty duels and had never seen anything like it."

private notebook for 1943 (in an entry entitled "Affirmation and Denial") the observation that Russian literature, for all its celebrated nihilism, had never been given to wholesale repudiation. "It is untrue," she declared, "that great thought in the humanities is always pessimistic."[3]

The mental gesture here is characteristic. Over her long life, Ginzburg developed a remarkably frank and humble set of principles to help the mind (and especially the mind of the scholar-intellectual) survive with its chronic reflexivity intact. "Happy people never evoke envy in me, even if they are very happy, nor irritation, even if they are very satisfied," she wrote wryly in 1928. "The ability to be happy is a concrete psychological skill, just like intelligence, courage, or kindness. For me it is more important to talk for an hour with a happy person than with an intelligent one. I've grown accustomed to intelligent people; I know from experience that one smart person cannot tell another smart person much that is new and interesting (especially if they share the same field). But a happy person, even if he is—however unlikely this might seem—a philologist, is always a revelation, a concretely material solution to one of life's basic tasks."[4] That same year, 1928, Ginzburg jotted down in her notebook: "A very important day in my life (it happened in Moscow) was the day I realized that spiritual pain cannot serve as the basis for ceasing to work, and in general for violating a regular mode of life. . . . The important thing: personal anguish is no reason to shun the task at hand—this was a happy discovery."[5] None of the four was inclined to indulge the self in what it might consider its legitimate sense of hurt. And none was convinced that acceptable levels of happiness need come at a terrible price (dishonesty, evasion, withdrawal)—nor, as Freud had intimated, that we pay for civilization with our individual discontent.

For all their underlying benevolence, however, their thought is not cast in the utopian, maximalist mode that fueled so much official Soviet theorizing during those years. Little in it is based on the logic of material production or class identity, and none of it is predicated on the sudden arrival of some better promised time. All four were adapters rather than rebels; to the uncommon nonsense of their highly politicized time and place, they tended to respond with commonsense methodologies and a pragmatic sobriety. Perhaps for this reason, all authored literary criticism of high caliber and strong philosophical bent—although each sees human personality as equipped in a different way to confront its problems.

[3] "Utverzhdenie i otritsanie" [1943] from "Zapisi 40-kh godov," in Ginzburg, *Pretvorenie opyta*, 96–102, especially 97, 99.

[4] Lidiia Ginzburg, "Iz starykh zapisei" [1928], in the anthology *O starom i novom* (Leningrad: Sovetskii pisatel', 1982), 387.

[5] "<1928>" in Lidiia Ginzburg, "Zapisi 20–30-kh godov [iz neopublikovannogo]," *Novyi mir*, no. 6 (June 1992): 144–86, especially 166.

Bakhtin's dialogic self (open, negotiating, distinct from every other self and irreplaceable in time and space) is constructed to work largely with words. Lotman's semiotic self (code-using, game-playing) works with behavioral signs. Vygotsky's developmental self (linear, physiologically defined) has at its disposal maturational stages and an arsenal of "tools." Ginzburg's "societally conditioned" (*obuslovlennyi*) self, with its delicate, permeable boundary between life's traces and literary texts, combines in varying proportion all three.

Each thinker, too, has a favorite literary genre and creative author through which the chosen model of the self is set off to its best advantage. For Bakhtin, the author of choice is Dostoevsky and his polyphonic novel of ideas. For Vygotsky, it is Shakespeare and the genres of classical and Renaissance drama (Vygotsky's master's thesis, later incorporated into his 1925 treatise *The Psychology of Art*, was devoted to *Hamlet*). Ginzburg's center of inspiration is dual, Lev Tolstoy and Petr Viazemsky, both exceptionally long-lived writers of great breadth and versatility for whom the quasi-autobiographical, quasi-fictional "human document" (letter, diary, notebook) was a fundamental mode of expression. To speak of "favorite genres and authors" for Yuri Lotman is quite impossible, for this polymath enriched all he touched and he touched upon so much; but for images of the narrated or narrating self, most useful is probably Lotman of his middle period, when he was given to investigating Romantic-era conventions and behavioral codes, culminating in his commentaries and literary biographies of Pushkin and Karamzin.

These scholars knew of and respected one another's work. But they were not disciples or mentors for each other in any strict sense. In fact, they were sooner wary of one another than indiscriminately enthusiastic; their models of the self emerged independently, out of their own methodologies and most basic convictions about what constituted legitimate data on the psyche and its optimal means of nourishment. For my purpose here, these four thinkers can be grouped around two poles; in each case, similarities that initially link each pair will open out into more interesting differences. In what follows, I will try to defend this peculiar procedure of a grouping that leads to a differentiation—and then invite further speculative juxtapositions (that is, the creation of dialogues where there were none) by passing the thought of all four through one highly productive concept: Vygotsky's notion of "interruption."

Bakhtin and Ginzburg: The Self as Utterance

The first group we might call, affectionately and informally, the *logos*-philes: Mikhail Bakhtin and Lydia Ginzburg. Although their work engages many aspects of human behavior, their mature and recurring focus is philology in the root sense. For them, in the beginning—and at the end—was the Word. To emphasize this point is not to ignore the manifest fact that language is a pivotal concern for all four thinkers. But in Bakhtin and Ginzburg we encounter a special reverence: verbal consciousness and its manipulation is demonstrably the *dominant*, that place where the identity of the self coalesces first, validating the resultant world with the most resonant authority. Thus the word-centeredness of these two scholars means more than the routine acknowledgment that all writers must sooner or later go through words to make their point; their personal notebooks—a crucial part of their legacy—reveal an orientation toward the uttered or recorded word *as toward a primary reality*. "Language and the word are almost everything in human life," Bakhtin jotted down late in life. "But one must not think that this all-embracing and multifaceted reality can be the subject of only one science, linguistics."[6] Ginzburg admitted to something of the same bias. "Anything that is not expressed in words (either spoken aloud or said to oneself) has no reality for me; or, more accurately, I lack the organs of perception for it," she confessed. "All the joys and sorrows of life reach us through clots of words."[7]

Although Ginzburg was no special fan of Bakhtin's work (she appreciated his mental energy but was unconvinced by his methods),[8] the two scholars hold certain enthusiasms in common. They share a faith in the growing polysemy and flexibility of the word as the surest guarantee of human survival. Both are well known as theorists of Russian Realism— whose teleological unfolding toward the genius of Dostoevsky (for Bakhtin) and Tolstoy (for Ginzburg) gives the work of both a faintly Hegelian cast. For each, realistic prose is above all a carrier of real-life ethics; and for the fictional or quasi-fictional selves that populate such prose, a realistic outlook is compatible with an increase in human freedom, that is, an increase in the absolute amount of non-predeterminedness in the world.[9] Consciousness testing the constraints of a "genre

---

[6] "The Problem of the Text in Linguistics, Philology, and the Human Sciences: An Experiment in Philosophical Analysis" [1959–61], in M. M. Bakhtin, *Speech Genres and Other Late Essays*, trans. Vern W. McGee (Austin: University of Texas Press, 1986), 118.

[7] See Sarah Pratt, "Introduction" to "Lydia Ginzburg's Contribution to Literary Criticism," in *Canadian-American Slavic Studies* 19, no. 2 (Summer 1985), 123 (reference is to "Iz starykh zapisei" in Ginzburg, *O starom i novom*, 396–97, misprinted in *CASS* as p. 385).

[8] Bakhtin made no known reference in print to the work of Ginzburg, but she did on occasion comment on Bakhtin—usually with reservations. See her "Razgovor o literaturovedenii" [1978], in Ginzburg, *O starom i novom*, 43–58.

[9] See, for example, Bakhtin's definition of the novelistic hero as one whose fate and situation is always inadequate to him, in "Epic and Hero," in *The Dialogic Imagination: Four Essays by M. M. Bakhtin*, ed. Michael Holquist (Austin: University of Texas Press, 1981), 37; also Ginzburg's elaboration of nineteenth-century realism as "a poetics of the non-predeter-

boundary" fascinated them both. If Ginzburg was occupied throughout her life with the dynamics of the "human document"—letter, diary, confession, autobiography, memoir, notebook (one person's verbal trace or recorded version of a life event)—then Bakhtin focused on those "life and speech genres" maximally close to the speaker's present, genres that were in principle open-ended, valuing them as the essential building blocks of the novel. Perhaps it is no accident that the work habits and, as it were, ego ideal of both these scholars—as glimpsed through their own personal notebooks and the memoirs of others—reveal curiously similar self-images. Both appear relatively isolated, only sporadically identified with official institutions and their subsidized networks, unacquainted with childrearing and its complex preverbal dependencies, given to communion in the middle of the night with a beloved text, each one a "person seated at a writing desk" (*chelovek za pis'mennym stolom*): in sum, anchorites for culture, devoted to the written word as culture's most reliable mediator.

However, in their meditations on the self (professional as well as literary), Bakhtin and Ginzburg diverge in crucial ways. Bakhtin's model of author-hero relations grew out of an interest in ethics and the philosophy of consciousness, that is, the responsibilities of a singular, answerable "I" cast into a given culture. To the end of his life he prided himself on being—in the root sense of the word—an eccentric, a radical innovator, and a loner. Evidence suggests that Bakhtin was of a kindly, aristocratic, intellectually stubborn, phlegmatic nature; he was tolerant of others' opinions because, by and large, he was unthreatened by them and rarely altered his own point of view in response to them. Preferring to be seen as a philosopher and "thinker" (*myslitel'*) rather than as a literary specialist (*literaturoved*), he resisted identification with any ideological "tendency," officially decreed standard, or school, and he disdained public rank.[10] The dialogues that really mattered to life were already deeply and gloriously contained within the literary and philosophical texts that were his primary nutrient. He might well have divined that the art of the ages is not here to prepare us for *this* life, which inevitably passes amid its own miserable hopes and fears, in "small time"; far more likely, our selves exist in this life to prepare us—albeit always inadequately—for the rich inventory of ideas and experiences that will continue to interact and coexist in art. In this Bakhtinian concept of "great time" there is, to be sure, more than a hint of values precious to a Formalist poetics. But Bakhtin's philosophy was in-

---

mined" in chapter 2, "Logika realizma," of Lidiia Ginzburg, *O literaturnom geroe* (Leningrad: Sovetskii pisatel', 1979), 57–88, especially 62–63.

[10] For more on this interpretation of Bakhtin's persona, see Caryl Emerson, *The First Hundred Years of Mikhail Bakhtin* (Princeton: Princeton University Press, 1997), chapters 1 and 2.

finitely more ambitious. One memoirist recalls how Bakhtin, in an off-hand way, remarked that yes, of course, the formal study of literature (*literaturovedenie*) was, "after all, a parasitical profession."[11]

Ginzburg had none of this Olympian striving after first principles. Raised among Russian Formalists who knew the value of precise definitions, structures, and codes, not only was she devoted to the strictly academic, somewhat distancing aspects of philology; she also never confused that professional practice with the fate or "feel" of life. (In a famous remark, she declared that "bacteriologists do not need to love bacteria and botanists do not even need to love plants"; they must, however, "love the *science* of bacteria and plants,"—not just the scholarly results but the very process of study, "the subject itself.")[12] What is more, as a close student of Tolstoy and his hypersensitivity toward societal pressure, Ginzburg keenly appreciated hierarchies and the crippling effect on the private self of public failure and professional shame. For all the chasteness and fastidiousness of her private notes, about such topics Ginzburg is not proud. Consider, for example, the portraits of the self as loser—excruciating in their simplicity—that we find in her notebooks from the 1940s, such entries as "The Failure" (*Neudachnik*) or "A Place in the Hierarchy." Writing "for the drawer" or "for the ages" is less likely to be heroic than simply unnatural, Ginzburg observes. A hidden creative striving, one that is destined only for oneself, is distorted, unverifiable, unhealthy, wounded; "it is a sad creativity, not fixed in place through confrontations with the present, not tensed up in expectation of glory or failure and a constant, lofty sense of urgency."[13]

In her moving, quasi-autobiographical account of life during the Leningrad Blockade, Ginzburg expands on this insight—and thereby enters obliquely into dialogue with those two attractive aristocrats and polemical nonjoiners, Bakhtin and Tolstoy. She remarks on the enormous satisfactions that her protagonist "En" experienced getting ready to go out to his bureaucratic job: at last "he was not only starving and eating, now he was working too."[14] The very triviality of the work was its consolation. Every day, after the lonely terror of hauling water and chopping firewood, here, on official terrain, "a series of professional gestures began: joking with one's comrades, arranging something with a secretary, sending a manuscript off to a typist, dropping in on the boss's office, commu-

[11] G. B. Ponomareva, "Vyskazannoe i nevyskazannoe ... (vospominaniia o M. M. Bakhtine)," in *Dialog. Karnaval. Khronotop*, no. 3 (1995): 59–77, especially 66. Interview with Ponomareva, November 1994.

[12] "Razgovor o literaturovedenii," 43.

[13] "Neudachnik" [1944] and "Mesto v ierarkhii" [1943] appear in Ginzburg, *Pretvorenie opyta*, 83–95 and 112–120. Sentence quoted from "Neudachnik," 85.

[14] From chapter 2, "Uchrezhdenie," in "Zapiski blokadnogo cheloveka, chast' vtoraia," in *Pretvorenie opyta*, 6. Subsequent quotation on p. 8.

nicating something on the office phone to another department that had messed something up": all of it makework, dimly perceived as dispensable during a time of "starvings and bombardments" but life-sustaining precisely because a self that could afford to be engaged in superfluous activities was a self that had energy to spare, that could begin to relax and *belong*. "After the oppressive cave-dwelling quality of his domestic activities," Ginzburg writes, "these official bureaucratic gestures eased the tension— through an experiencing of form, of conventionality." Such conventions and comforting hierarchies are often the product of centralizing, "official" forces in a culture, constraints that for Tolstoy were altogether morally disgraceful and for Bakhtin were theoretically tolerable only when routinely challenged by jesters or destabilized by misfits from below. For Ginzburg, however, striving to ascend along their axis or satisfy their ritual requirements is a normal, healthy appetite of the self. The locus for this activity is no carnival square or defiant, heroic theater but a city under siege, Petersburg from the perspective, say, of Akaky Akakievich, the poor clerk in Gogol's "Overcoat." For reasons one can not reconstruct theoretically, Ginzburg suggests, most people will go to great lengths to fit in.

In this connection one might contrast the reluctance with which Bakhtin commented on his own life with Ginzburg's two lucidly cool essays, written in her final decade, that attempt to explain to a younger, appalled generation what motivated her contemporaries to support, and then to acccommodate, the Revolution.[15] How could she, as a fifteen-year-old schoolgirl, have worn a red ribbon on the streets of Odessa in 1917? More seriously, how could she have spent the summer of 1938 with colleagues in the Pskov region, boating and picnicking, when Leningrad lay under the shadow of the Terror? As Ginzburg writes in the second of these essays, among the basic regulatory laws of human social behavior are "accommodation to circumstances," "justification of a necessity (including an evil) if resistance is impossible," and "the indifference of a person to whatever does not directly touch him."[16] All three mechanisms, in differing proportion for each survivor, operated throughout the Stalinist period—although "with interruptions and obstacles to decency." As regards her own self, Ginzburg admitted to a weakly developed sense of justification because of her "inborn tendency to analyze," but noted that "the mechanism of indifference worked without a hitch" (226).

Is an analysis of the embarrassed or compromised self made more palatable when formal mechanisms (rather than the raw, unmediated

---

[15] L. Ia. Ginzburg, "Eshche raz o starom i novom (Pokolenie na povorote)," in *Tynianovskii sbornik: Vtorye Tynianovskie chteniia* (Riga: Zinatne, 1986): 132–41; and its sequel in " 'I zaodno s pravoporiadkom . . . ,' " in *Tynianovskii sbornik: Tret'i Tynianovskie chteniia* (Riga: Zinatne, 1988): 218–30.

[16] " 'I zaodno s pravoporiadkom,' " 218–19. Further page reference given in text.

moves of conscience) govern it? Alexander Zholkovsky has addressed just this issue of Ginzburg's distinctively "formal-intimate" way with emotions and words.[17] Closely analyzing one of her prose passages—one that deals, significantly, with the inexpressibility of its subject matter in prose—he points out that Ginzburg was wont to raise the most "lyrical-poetic" themes with the most formulaic abstractness. The effect is one of "dryness and pseudoscienticity" (*sukhost' i naukoobrazie*), but this effect, he argues, was a deliberate act of defamiliarization, an invasion of scholarly rhetoric into the poetic realm. The discomforting freshness we feel on reading her is the result of that dissonance, and its impact is stronger than the more predictably packaged satisfaction to be had from the same "message" transmitted through a poem.

Such meditations on the self, especially if culpable and in search of adequate genres of self-expression, were not foreign to Bakhtin. His passion for reconstructing maximally generous contexts for every utterance and his astonishing tolerance have appeared to some as all too accommodating. ("Even a word that is known to be false is not absolutely false," Bakhtin wrote near the end of his life; it "always presupposes an instance that will understand and justify it, even if in the form: 'anyone *in my position* would have lied too.' ")[18] When called upon to explain his life by disciples eager to canonize him, Bakhtin avoided confronting morally awkward or compromising situations and displayed no interest in devising for these difficult situations anything like an ethical typology. His oral memoirs, seventeen hours of taped interviews recorded in 1973, come to an end with the late 1920s—and emphasize the lives and reactions of others, not his own.[19] If Ginzburg, equipped with Formalist devices, analyzed the cumulating effects of outer life on the private self (and on her own self) for fifty years, the nonformalist Bakhtin changed his paradigms only with exceptional slowness, and documented the direct effects of the world on his own self hardly at all.[20]

---

[17] Aleksandr Zholkovskii, "Mezhdu zhanrami (L. Ia. Ginzburg)," in Zholkovskii, *Inventsii* (Moscow: Gendal'f, 1995): 154–57. A version exists in English, with some shift of emphasis: Alexander Zholkovsky, "Between Genres," *Canadian-American Slavic Studies* 28, nos. 2–3 (Summer–Fall 1994): 157–60. References here are to Russian text.

[18] "The Problem of the Text in Linguistics, Philology, and the Human Sciences: An Experiment in Philosophical Analysis," in Bakhtin, *Speech Genres*, 127.

[19] See *Besedy V. D. Duvakina s M. M. Bakhtinym*, ed. S. G. Bocharov et al. (Moscow: Progress, 1996). The interviews were originally serialized, with some editorial cuts, in the journal *Chelovek*, 1993–95.

[20] Near the end of his life, Bakhtin did make some revealing comments when pressed by his close friends. To Sergei Bocharov in 1974 he remarked that during the early Soviet period there was "almost complete moral disintegration" and "scorn for moral foundations reigned supreme"; when asked by Bocharov whether this cynicism also affected him, Bakhtin replied: "Mmm, yes, in part I felt that way too, after all, we had betrayed everything—our homeland, our culture." "And how could one avoid betraying?" Bocharov asked. "By perishing," Bakhtin answered. In Bocharov's memory of this conversation, Bakhtin "said all this with a bright face

To sum up: while researching "human documents," Ginzburg—in this as in so much else, Tynianov's disciple—never forgot the integrative role of literary devices, social and literary convention, the anxieties and *pressures* of history. In her attentiveness to outside structures she closely resembles her junior colleague, Yuri Lotman. And as her many returns to the site of creative melancholy and public anguish attest (her loving attention to the earnest, terminally awkward Vissarion Belinsky being a case in point), she intuitively senses a limit to what words can do to relieve this pressure in any immediate sense. In fact, words often serve to exacerbate that tension.[21] In contrast, Bakhtin is without social ambition and without chagrin. He prefers to live—and never ceases to assure his favorite literary personalities that they too live—in a category he calls "great time." In that visionary chronotope, all words, however inept or excruciating their local reverberations, will find a context that is appropriate to them and thus will be heard. As a theoretician, Bakhtin is at his best in just such an all-forgiving space. There he can downplay devices as well as constraints. He can celebrate those selves that hear many options within what had seemed like only one; his ideal selves are those that defy convention or that register relatively little pressure from external systems (or at least none that cannot be cast off): the fool, the rogue, the breakaway novelistic hero. Not surprisingly, Ginzburg is superb on mediation and the technical problem of narrators. Bakhtin, for whom everything really interesting about the authoring process is flexible, modifiable, two-way, is brilliantly insightful on the general problem of authorial "access" but is relatively indifferent, I would argue, to the precise structuring of narrative voice that accounts for the text we actually read. He is loath to award to any single narrating self that potentially stifling envelope of control over other human material. Bakhtin loves Dostoevsky, Goethe, and menippean satire because, in his interpretation, those novelists and that genre favor heroes who live by open-ended ideas. Ginzburg loves personal letters and quasi-autobiographical genres because, in her understanding, people live by embarrassment.

Thus we circle round to our opening comparison. Both these gifted *logos*-philes acknowledge language as our most efficient socializing agent and repository of personality. But Ginzburg, with her discrimination and humility when it comes to hierarchies and institutions, has a better overall

---

and rather cheerfully." See S. G. Bocharov, "Ob odnom razgovore i vokrug nego," *Novoe literaturnoe obozrenie*, no. 2 (1993): 70–89, quotation on 83. An abridged translation appears as Sergey Bocharov, "Conversations with Bakhtin," trans. Stephen Blackwell and Vadim Liapunov, *PMLA* 109, no. 5 (October 1994): 1009–1024, cited passage on 1020.

[21] See especially Part Two, "Belinskii and the Emergence of Realism," of "The 'Human Document' and the Construction of Personality," in *On Psychological Prose*, trans. and ed. Judson Rosengrant (Princeton: Princeton University Press, 1991), 58–101.

sense than does Bakhtin of the pragmatic, often mortifying social conversations filling "general life," the *obshchaia zhizn'* that shapes each individual. This feeling for the "pressure of the general" is most clearly sensed in her appreciation of the prosy, deeply embedded Tolstoyan self: morbidly alert, self-critical, able to be badly hurt even by what it detests, that self remains a "mobile, changeable, yet *identifiable* structure."[22] Bakhtin, for whom words serve primarily to generate fresh options, rarely allows dialogue to conclude, amalgamate, or "generalize" anything. Social life, too, is a take-it-or-leave-it affair. Bakhtin prefers to work with a singular "I" and a singular "other": each is presumed to be a mutual, ongoing helpmate to the other, and their openess to continual renegotiation matters more than whatever wounds (or even joys) might be inflicted.

Finally, Bakhtin and Ginzburg must be said to differ in their mature concepts of aesthetic form as it relates to depiction of personality in the Realist tradition. For Ginzburg, the literary hero is ultimately a *structure*: "the unity of the literary hero," she writes, "is not a sum but a system, with dominants that organize it."[23] Since social history is also a system, these two structures condition one another constantly—and only a painstaking analysis of reciprocal pressures can yield anything approaching the truth of their interaction. As we know, this hypothesis, at base Tolstoyan, about the exceptional difficulty of telling a true story or writing a true history, was never resolved by Tolstoy himself. (Uncompromising and revising furiously until the end, Tolstoy eventually came to welcome memory loss as a type of liberation; for a lucid discussion of this conflict as reflected in the diaries, see Irina Paperno's essay in this volume.) Ginzburg, more humble and self-limiting than Tolstoy in all respects, tackles this difficult task by selecting human documents that manifestly interact with history in analyzable ways. Belinsky's letters to Bakunin or Herzen's life and writings—unlike an account of the Battle of Borodino or even "The History of Yesterday," Tolstoy's earliest surviving literary effort—can be seen to have aesthetic form, motivation, genesis, an ideational skeleton.

In his approach to selves as well as to plots, Bakhtin cannot be said to do structures. He really only does middles. He pays little attention to genesis; he assures us that no end is ever final because words, once spoken, enter a dialogue from which they can never be fully retrieved or repossessed (and thus never killed). He is, in fact, wholly indifferent to a fear of death—one reason, perhaps, why the Tolstoyan universe (permeated by this fear and by elaborate preparations for this event) struck him so often as crabby and flat. The Bakhtinian self, in its mature redaction, is tough,

---

[22] For the initial quotation, see Ginzburg, *On Psychological Prose*, 249, and in general the phenomenon of *obuslovlennost'* (rendered by Rosengrant not quite successfully as "causal conditionality"; the term means more the "conditioned and conditionable nature" of the self).

[23] Ginzburg, *O literaturnom geroe*, 90.

inspiring, buoyant. It is experienced but not burdened. And surely this is so partly because such a self is not in fact perceived as a structure with a burden to bear; it is sooner a site of exchange. Or, better, a site of interchange, for there are few goods that any party can be said to bring to the encounter "ready-made." Value and form accrue in the gesture of addressing an other, in desiring to address another, and in desiring to be addressed (the precise good in hand is less important). This state of mutual receptivity, a plenitude without accumulation, the young Bakhtin called "aesthetic love." One might compare such a Bakhtinian self with Ginzburg's more somber concentration on "conditionedness" (*obuslovlennost'*) and convention (*uslovnost'*), qualities of a self that lives more cautiously, more by accretion, and is therefore more vulnerable: a "conditioned, conditioning, and conventional structure" that literally fears for its life. It is along this fault line that hardcore dialogism—with its insistence on the continual "outsideness" and verbal negotiability of each person or utterance vis-à-vis every other—must part company with the socially modifiable dialogic interaction that Ginzburg considers foundational to human definition, and that she so admires in Tolstoy's art.

It is not only along the fault line of the social that Bakhtin and Ginzburg differ, however; the internal landscapes of their prototypical selves differ as well. The Bakhtinian self acknowledges no equivalent of a Freudian "Id" with its inner (but presumably universal) drives. It also appears to know no firm or punitive "Superego." It can be stabilized only in categories that originate in a concrete consciousness external to it. And thus, in order to optimize its choices in the world, the viable personality will strive to expose itself to a multiplicity of inputs, perspectives, and discourses from outside—that is, it will strive toward a maximally "novelized" state. How would Ginzburg respond to this paradigm? She would applaud its absorptive qualities, its capacity to generate new potentials, its facility to learn from others' utterances. But I believe it would strike her as unrealistically open-ended, as too indifferent to the self's tendency to absorb (and to crave, be sensitive to, be hurt by) *whole structures*, not just words and "options," presented to us by the outside world. For this reason is she drawn to the vulnerable and confessional sides of Tolstoy. The Tolstoyan self is open, certainly—immeasurably more so than the Classical or Romantic personality-masks that fulfill predictable binary "functions" in literary plots associated with those earlier eras. But this self is open to hurt almost more than to love, because shameful events adhere in it with ruthless tenacity. The transitoriness of content in Bakhtin's model, the continual mutual self-abnegation required as each "I" places itself in hostage to every other "I" and thus its dependence on a steady supply of interested, benign, and articulate others before the basic ingredients for selfhood can accumulate, would fail to persuade Ginzburg. To a greater extent than Bakhtin, she believes in sustained introspection, in an "I" that always risks being thrown back on a solitary speaker. This "I" *must* cohere more than provisionally, because the "outside" as the source of all diversity and value is not necessarily enriching or benign. Conventional and societal pressures are disorienting, tempting, dangerous, real; they require accommodation, justification, hard choices. Ginzburg is wedded to the Tolstoyan model of the self, I think, not only because it is a "complex, multidimensional structure"—a case could be made that Dostoevsky's heroes, in Bakhtin's polyphonic treatment of them, are also that—but because the Tolstoyan personality necessarily "performs a variety of functions and fulfills a variety of tasks."[24]

Precisely this multiplicity of contradictory pressures and tasks, so characteristic of the Tolstoyan plot, separates the Ginzburg-Tolstoyan type of hero from the prototypical Bakhtin-Dostoevsky one. When Bakhtin, at the end of the 1920s, developed his model of the polyphonic self, he solved the problem of the self's diffuseness and transitoriness in a radical way: by positing "idea-persons" as the fulcrum of Dostoevsky's novels. Idea-persons do not need a multiplicity of tasks. In fact, they do not need an outer plot at all (taking his cue, perhaps, from the fact that Dostoevsky attends little to ordinary, everyday stable life, Bakhtin controversially insists that plot events mattered little to the novelist); all they need is a place to talk out their ideas. In his 1961 notes for revising the Dostoevsky book, Bakhtin credited Dostoevsky with the discovery of the "self-developing idea"[25]—but one might ask, is such "self-development" in fact compatible with real dialogue among human beings? Compared with Pierre Bezukhov or Konstantin Levin (genuinely confused, evolving personalities, with many stubborn habits but with few stubborn convictions), does the obsessed Raskol'nikov or Ivan Karamazov learn a thing from any other person? Or, for that matter, does the saintly sinner, Sonya Marmeladova? In the "plotless" polyphonic novel, my self has my idea, your self has yours, and—although characters do crave each other's presence as witnesses and confessors—we can get by feeding these ideas to each other until each has ripened and the novel is over. Perhaps this lonely, essentially autonomous dynamic was part of what Ginzburg sensed, and disliked, in Bakhtin's critical readings. An honest monologue, presented by its author as such—the one, say, that structures Ginzburg's beloved Proust—can be investigated without apology on its own terms. But Bakhtin's polyphonically designed selves too often pretend to a need for dialogue where in fact there is none.

---

[24] Ginzburg, *On Psychological Prose*, 252.
[25] "Toward a Reworking of the Dostoevsky Book," in Mikhail Bakhtin, *Problems of Dostoevsky's Poetics*, ed. and trans. Caryl Emerson (Minneapolis: University of Minnesota Press, 1984), 284.

Our first pairing might be summarized in the following way. By temperament a modified structuralist, deeply influenced by her reading of William James, Ginzburg proffers a model of the self that is inescapably conditioned, *obuslovlennyi*, pressured from the outside in. It is palpably acted upon by human conversation, hunger, fear, official hierarchy, and every other physiological and social constraint that impinges on it in a given space. In her model, as implicitly in Tolstoy's, ideas pass through us; they are used as needed to help human beings realize their chosen tasks. Tasks, in return, tell us who we are. It is perhaps significant that we cannot imagine Ginzburg, so superbly work-oriented, ever praising carnival—that release from imposed obligation, conventionality, and shame.

Bakhtin, inspired by philosophies of religion and drawn to laughter as a personal antidote to terror, is far more susceptible than is Ginzburg to states of pure potential. Thus he is routinely credited with caring more about time than space, evidenced by his preference for the present tense (or very near future) over the past, his passion for loopholes, his always only penultimate words, his tendency to ask not "who am I?" but "how much time do I have to become something else?" In the Dostoevsky book, Bakhtin comes as close as he ever will come to a synchronic (almost a structuralist) view of the world, in which words and ideas stand in for bodies. "Interaction and coexistence," the god-terms of that study, do not take into consideration the origins, biological maturation, cumulative learning experience, or inevitable death of individual organisms.[26] For an integration of irreversible time and physiological development into the personality—and for some serious (in the sense of noncarnival) attention to the outer behavior, not only the verbal identity, of this personality—we must turn to our second cluster: Lev Vygotsky and Yuri Lotman.

Vygotsky and Lotman: The Self as Staged

The linking of these two names will strike some as counterintuitive. In the West, it is Ginzburg who has been anthologized alongside Lotman as

[26] In the later carnival self, of course, time is experienced entirely as cyclical or "folkloric," detached from the irreversible biography of any individual consciousness. It is in his (lost, now largely reconstituted) study of Goethe and the *Bildungsroman* that Bakhtin gives us the middle ground: close readings of a genuinely "developmental" chronotope that can approximate the emphasis Ginzburg gives to "life conditions." In Bakhtin's thought, the interaction of cyclical with linear, and of structured with unstructured, is complex. Suffice to say it here that because Bakhtin is unsympathetic to mechanical systems does not mean he is partial to chaos or believes that human beings prosper amid mess. He was, as Michael Holquist has lucidly argued, an *organicist*, a proponent of living or "body" systems. For the distinction between living and nonliving systems as Bakhtin (and as contemporary biologists) define it, see the excellent essay by Michael Holquist, "Dialogism and Aesthetics," *Late Soviet Culture from Perestroika to Novostroika*, ed. Thomas Lahusen with Gene Kuperman (Durham: Duke University Press, 1993), 155–76, especially 172–74.

fellow traveler in the semiotics of culture.[27] And much more highly publicized than Lev Vygotsky as protostructuralist has been the parallel between Vygotsky's language-learning maps and Bakhtin's hypotheses about outer dialogue internalizing into "innerly persuasive words," and from there into patterns of thought.[28] I will argue here, however, for a kinship between Vygotsky and Lotman—and for their common distance from Bakhtin— along another axis. Reflexology (where Vygotsky began) and semiotics (the field Lotman so powerfully shaped) both depend upon the sign. Each thinker greatly expanded the relevance of signs to the study of personality, in life and in art. Their curiosity in this realm might be contrasted to Bakhtin's, who, throughout his long life, chose never to deepen or make more sophisticated his understanding of the sign (znak), willing to leave it the rather crude, mechanical, binary Saussurean instrument that was criticized by his circle in the 1920s. He was equally dismissive of bundles of signs, or codes. The code has no "cognitive, creative significance," he wrote in one of his final notebooks; it is a "deliberately established, killed context."[29] To be sure, we should not make too much of this startling remark, a casual private jotting whose implications were nowhere worked out. But we should also not ignore the fact that as a statement it is, of course, not true: codes can be cognitively and creatively significant to an enormous degree.

Here we arrive at the truly instructive comparison between Bakhtin and the Lotman-Vygotsky group as typologists of the self. Bakhtin never seriously entertained the ways in which personality—and especially the poetic (not the prosaic) personality living in a highly "convention-driven" era— might actually be weakened and made more desperate by endlessly renegotiable dialogue; and conversely, how such a personality might become *more* creative, more capable of initiative and of honorable activity, when confronted with the challenge of manipulating many vigorous codes. For this reason, one might argue, Vygotsky had so much of interest to say about *Hamlet* and Lotman became such a fine Pushkinist—whereas Bakhtin dismissed stage drama as a form of monologue and (although certainly not without wisdom on the Russian Romantic period) he tended to "read backwards" from his beloved Dostoevskian novel into earlier pe-

---

[27] See, for example, *The Semiotics of Russian Cultural History: Essays by Yurii M. Lotman, Lidiia Ia. Ginzburg, Boris A. Uspenskii,* ed. Alexander D. Nakhimovsky and Alice Stone Nakhimovsky (Ithaca, N.Y.: Cornell University Press, 1985).

[28] A role was played in this linkage by my own early essay, "The Outer Word and Inner Speech: Bakhtin, Vygotsky, and the Internalization of Language," originally appearing in *Critical Inquiry* 10, no. 2 (December 1983): 245–64. For a later treatment, see James V. Wertsch, *Voices of the Mind: A Sociocultural Approach to Mediated Action* (Cambridge, Mass.: Harvard University Press, 1991), chapter 3, "Beyond Vygotsky: Bakhtin's Contribution," 46–66.

[29] The full text reads: "A context is potentially unfinalized; a code must be finalized. A code is only a technical means of transmitting information, it does not have cognitive, creative significance. A code is a deliberately established, killed context." "From Notes Made in 1970–71," in Bakhtin, *Speech Genres,* 147.

riods of Russian literature, often governed by manifestly different dominants. As David Bethea argues eloquently in an essay on Lotman's use of codes in relation to literary biography,[30] a semiotician at work on a Romantic biography would have to value equally the given codes of the era (codes still worthy of respect, not mocked or "novelized") and the subject's own personal response to those codes. The biographical subject does not necessarily resent or resist this struggle between social codes and the more fluid, spontaneous self. "Lotman is suggesting that the [semiotically creative] type of personality (here Pushkin, later Karamzin) has a special orientation toward the text of its life," Bethea writes. "It finds a way *to use* the codes and behavioral norms for its own benefit, as an artist works with his medium . . . [Here Bethea cites Lotman's preface to the Polish edition of his biography *Aleksandr Sergeevich Pushkin*] 'a sculptor cannot complain of the fact that the granite presented to him is too hard, because the resistance of the material enters into the energy-supplying moment of creation.' " One could, of course, go further with this metaphor. Without the code there would be no medium, just as without the granite there would be, for the sculptor, no art.

In Lotman's understanding, then, a successful biography is a balancing act. It must coordinate "texts generated by the personality according to the laws of a grammar arising *ad hoc*" (inevitably softer and more idiosyncratic) with the hardness, the non-negotiability of "socio-semiotic norms," whose violation could result in real scandal (real duels, real death).[31] The players can resist, or they can enjoy the game. But crucial for the scholar to remember is that the defining lines between these two types of text are themselves historically conditioned. In a 1985 essay devoted to the special challenge of writing popular biography,[32] Lotman inquires how the conscientious biographer should react to the persistent rumor that D'Anthès, infamous for having killed Pushkin in a duel, arrived at that encounter protected by a chainmail vest. For all the ingenious research on the topic, proof cannot be had one way or the other.[33] But it is most unlikely, Lotman concludes, that D'Anthès, a run-of-the-mill courtier, would have

---

[30] David M. Bethea, "Iurii Lotman in the 1980s: The Code and Its Relation to Literary Biography," in Arnold McMillin, ed., *Reconstructing the Canon: Russian Writing in the 1980s* (London: Harwood Academic Publishers, 2000), 9–32. Bethea opens his essay with a juxtaposition of Lotman and Bakhtin as two models for the biographical self. The metaphor of the poet and the "granite of life" was a favorite of Lotman's.

[31] See Iurii Lotman, "*Aleksandr Sergeevich Pushkin. Biografiia pisatelia*. Predislovie k pol'skomu izdaniiu [1990]," in E. V. Permiakov, ed., *Lotmanovskii sbornik* (Moscow: Its-Garant, 1994), 85–88. Comment on granite and the sculptor, cited by Bethea above, is on 86.

[32] Iurii Lotman, "Biografiia—zhivoe litso," in *Novyi mir*, no. 2 (1985): 228–36. All quotations on p. 235.

[33] This "breastplate scandal" has a long history. For a brief summary in English of scholarly attention to the "homicide, not duel" hypothesis, see the colorful and engrossing reconstruction of Pushkin's final year by Serena Vitale, *Pushkin's Button*, trans. from the Italian by Ann Goldstein and Jon Rothschild (New York: Farrar, Straus, and Giroux, 1999), 244–46.

had the originality and risk-taking instincts to deceive in this way. The slightest wound would have led to a discovery of the vest; D'Anthès would have been exiled from his regiment, from polite society, from respectable women, from the company of the emperor. For his era and class, "terror at violating conventional rules of honor was infinitely stronger than terror at losing one's life." So while the chainmail vest is by now unverifiable, the basic emotions—fear, shame, terror, pride—leave a reliably conventional trace; for "like all human actions," Lotman observes, "corruption, crimes, and temptations are also historical." In reconstructing the story of a past self, biographers must resist the urge to universalize or essentialize even the deepest human responses.

From this it follows that Lotman and his school, to a far greater degree than the Bakhtinians, would see powerful disadvantages in any model of selfhood that prevented personality from coalescing into recognizable, transcribable forms, into conventional units that can be rendered visible for biography. Lotman turned often to this theoretical problem as it was made concrete in various historical periods, asking: what gives a person the "right to a biography," or the right to become a biographer?[34] How does the concept of a biographical self enter cultural memory? Whereas the "unique self" appears to delight and satisfy Bakhtin, striking him as relatively unproblematic, Lotman, with his larger systemic vision, is more reluctant to bestow that quality and considers it a fraught area for the responsible cultural historian. Selves become social types. In eras with weakly developed forms for registering the uniqueness of a self, individuals who do not govern their behavior by approved, recognized codes or choices might be perceived simply as having an "undeveloped sense of personality." Or the entire culture might be classified by later historians as one governed by an "impersonal collective" in which "personality as a principle had not yet emerged" (365). To complicate the picture still more, a multiplicity of acceptable forms for transcribing biography need not increase their truth value. As soon as biography gets a biographer (as soon as a Saint's Life identifies its storyteller), and when that author receives in turn the "right to a biography" of his own (369), the likelihood of undecodable, confounding interplay between real-life event and mythologized self-construction greatly increases.

Here again we see the extraordinary appropriateness of a semiotician such as Lotman for Romantic-era biography—and especially as chronicler and interpreter of Pushkin's life. For all his precocity, Pushkin still belonged (in Monika Greenleaf's strong statement of this position) to the "pre-psychological age of Russian literature"; thus he "found it 'impossible

[34] See as exemplary his "Literaturnaia biografiia v istoriko-kul'turnom kontekste (k tipologicheskomu sootnosheniiu teksta i lichnosti avtora)," in Iu. M. Lotman, *Izbrannye stat'i v trekh tomakh* (Tallinn: Aleksandra, 1992), 1: 365–76. Further page numbers in text.

to write about himself' and recoiled from exposing the smallest detail of his inner life as if from an abyss."[35] Public life, for him, was governed not by gestures of spontaneous honesty but by a code of honor. Unlike the later novelists Turgenev, Dostoevsky, and Tolstoy—among whom Bakhtin felt so at home, and for whom confession, exposé and autobiographical intimacies became primary literary matter—Pushkin, even in his friendly letters and casual jottings, practiced a more impersonal access to the psyche. He respected mediated, stylized behavior. For a semiotic reading of the self is *not* a Bakhtinian dialogue where both sides can always be loosened up by talk. It more resembles a formal game, conducted within fixed parameters and agreed-upon codes, a competitive sport between players who know the rules and are pleased to pit themselves against them.

It has been my hypothesis, then, that the "dialogue of ideas" inherent in Bakhtin's Dostoevskian model of the self (run largely by "idea-persons" and verbal utterances), and the fluidity (*tekuchest'*) of Ginzburg's Tolstoyan model (run by a mixture of conversations and conditions, but with deep pleasure always to be had from correct placement of the words), together situate those theoreticians of prose at some distance from Vygotsky and Lotman. That second pair of thinkers concentrates not only on the *word* but also, and perhaps predominantly, on the *scene*, on gesture and embodied action, and on the specifically irreversible— and at times unutterable—decisions that the self makes in collaboration with others.[36] For Vygotsky as pedagogue, the site for this activity was the "learning scenario" and specifically the "zone of proximal development,"[37] the most precious and efficient environment for a child. For Lotman it became the "behavioral complex," which he studied in specific periods ("The Decembrist in Everyday Life," "The Poetics of Everyday Behavior in Russian Culture of the Eighteenth Century") and applied

---

[35] Monika Greenleaf, *Pushkin and Romantic Fashion: Fragment, Elegy, Orient, Irony* (Stanford: Stanford University Press, 1994), 344.

[36] Of great interest, but beyond the scope of this essay and complicating its thesis, are the obvious affinities between Vygotsky / Lotman's bias toward behavior and Lev Tolstoy's commitment to the essentially wordless scene as perfect communication situation (epitomized by Kitty and Levin's "declaration" of love over the chalkboard). Whereas it is true that Tolstoy did not wholly trust the action of words (and did not trust "ideas" at all, at least as honest prompts to behavior), close analysis would show, I believe, that the goal of even the stumbling scenes is to release, at last, the right verbal cues to the correct "moral feeling"— which ends up revealed as Tolstoy's own. Such was Viktor Vinogradov's thesis in his 1930s work on Tolstoy's stratified inner monologues, conclusions not incompatible with many of Ginzburg's observations.

[37] For Vygotsky's exposition of this zone, see chapter 6, "The Development of Scientific Concepts in Childhood: The Design of a Working Hypothesis," in Lev Vygotsky, *Thought and Language*, trans., rev., and ed. by Alex Kozulin (Cambridge, Mass.: MIT Press, 1986), 147–209, especially 187–89. The title of this important book remains mistranslated, even in its revision: *Myshlenie i rech'* specifically implies the processes of "thinking and speaking," not their product or schematic residue (thought, language).

with great craft in his creative biographies of Karamzin and Pushkin.[38] If Bakhtin and Ginzburg, for all their differences, were drawn to the formal (and fictional) structure of long novels, maximally open to personal idiosyncracy, then Vygotsky and Lotman were both ultimately drawn to drama, to plotted spectacle, and—if the task required a prose narrative— to the challenge of teasing out, from the non-negotiable processes of real lived biography, an inspired pattern.

As common ground for my second cluster it is significant, I think, that both Vygotsky and Lotman (the former early in his career, the latter at the end) were curious about research on the binary neurological functions of the human brain. With varying degrees of figurativeness, each applied this information to his readings of literary works. Each experimented with "cognitive maps" that identified at what point a simple sign (*znak*), functioning as a reflex, evolved into a more complicated code that could govern personalized behavior and produce contextual meaning (*smysl*).[39] At the end of this essay, our three humanists will be passed through one fundamental concept developed by Vygotsky in his work on the integrative functions of the central nervous system: the notion of "interrupting a reflex." Here the "behavioral-dramatic" pair of thinkers, with their interest in space, plots, and signs, and the *logos*-philes in their capacity as theorists of the open-ended novel and the private notebook, set one another off to mutual advantage.

Vygotsky, a committed and flexible Marxist, distrusted both introspection and idealism as methods for gaining access to the psyche.[40] But he did not endorse, at the other pole, the natural-science or "objective" view of behavior regulation that held sway in the early 1920s, Pavlov's school of "reflexology." The task of developmental psychology, Vygotsky believed, lay somewhere in between: to determine those points at which biological

---

[38] "Dekabrist v povsednevnoi zhizni (bytovoe povedenie kak istoriko-psikhologicheskaia kategoriia)" [1975] and "Poetika bytovogo povedeniia v russkoi kul'ture XVIII veka" [1977], in Iu. M. Lotman, *Izbrannye stat'i v trekh tomakh*, 1: 248–68 and 296–336. Translations of both essays exist in Ju. M. Lotman and B. A. Uspenskij, *The Semiotics of Russian Culture*, ed. Ann Shukman (Ann Arbor: Michigan Slavic Contributions no. 11, 1984): 71–123 and 231–56. Lotman's two studies in the biographical genre are *Aleksandr Sergeevich Pushkin: Biografiia pisatelia* (Leningrad: Prosveshchenie, 1981), and, in the "Writers about Writers" series, *Sotvorenie Karamzina* (Moscow: Kniga, 1987).

[39] For an essay that compares Lotman's and Vygotsky's contributions to semiotics (and to two types of "inner speech," the first "poetic" [rhythmic, irreplaceable, individualized] and the second "philosophical" [spatial, paraphrasable, content-oriented]), see V. S. Bibler, "Iu. M. Lotman i budushchee filologii," in *Lotmanovskii sbornik*, 278–85. Bibler, a philosopher of consciousness, is also well known as a Bakhtin scholar (*Mikhail Mikhailovich Bakhtin ili poetika kul'tury*, 1991).

[40] For this survey I am indebted to Yaroshevsky, *Lev Vygotsky*, "From Reflexology to Psychology," 67–95; and a documentary account of Vygotsky in the 1920s: A. A. Leont'ev, *L. S. Vygotskii* (Moscow: Prosveshchenie, 1990), chapters 1–2.

maturation (both physical and mental) intersects with organized external stimuli. At these crossover nodes, self-confidence is high and learning is always profoundly efficient. Thus Vygotsky had no patience with the standardized intelligence test or the conventional examination environment in public schools (he considered both little better than Pavlovian stimulus-response scenarios, further debased by anxiety and fear). Reflexology was magnificent science in its own sphere—but it was not for humans. The development of a human self could be assimilated neither to plants (as in Kinder*garten*), nor to household pets.[41] Human nurturing requires a kindling of emotions and a triggering of ability through specifically *"cultural* irritants," and these, Vygotsky averred, involve not so much physiological sensations as they do the complex, sophisticated, socially conditioned stimuli of language and art.

Early in his career, Bakhtin had devised a tripartite model of the self. This self knows an "I-for-myself" that is fluid, hypothetical, lacking verbal expression, and then a more presentable "I-for-the-other" and "the-other-for-me" constructed out of images and evaluations originating in the external world.[42] Vygotsky too devised a triadic model for personality formation. As a practicing physiologist and developmental psychologist, however, he could not be content with static metaphors, nor could he presume a simultaneity of all working parts throughout the life of the organism. Always alert (as Bakhtin often was not) to the body's maturational imperatives, Vygotsky's three-stage model of a person's emergence into culture began with what was "in oneself" (*v sebe*), then moved to what was "for others" (*dlia drugikh*); finally, in an interiorization model that is reminiscent of Bakhtin, to what was "for oneself" (*dlia sebia*).[43] At all stages of this sequence, language is key.

Areas of compatibility between Vygotsky and our other, more literary thinkers now begin to emerge. Again we see evidence that a "hermeneutics of suspicion"—to return to Paul Ricoeur's useful distinction invoked at the beginning of this essay—is simply not persuasive to these four Russian thinkers, who doggedly, luminously remain devoted to a

---

[41] Picking up on Pavlov's analogy that conditioned reflexes function like the hooking-up activity of a *telefonistka* (a telephone operator, the reliable and obedient intermediary at a switchboard), Vygotsky remarked: "Pavlov's idea basically comes down to this: what people thought the telephone operator was doing (the soul) was in fact being done by the apparatus itself (the body, the brain). Ergo, the telephone operator was not a soul." L. S. Vygotskii, "[Konkretnaia psikhologiia cheloveka]," in *Vestnik Moskovskogo universiteta*, ser. 14, no. 1 (1986): 52–65, especially 58.

[42] The model is developed throughout the early philosophical essay "Author and Hero in Aesthetic Activity," in *Art and Answerability: Early Philosphical Essays by M. M. Bakhtin*, trans. and notes by Vadim Liapunov (Austin: University of Texas Press, 1990): 4–256, but especially 36–42.

[43] Vygotskii, "[Konkretnaia psikhologiia cheloveka]," 53.

"hermeneutics of recovery of meaning." For all of them, however, meaning is never recuperated in a static way; it is designed to grow (as does the meaning of words) with each further exchange or with the passing of time. Each tends to discount innate or programmed scenarios for the psyche, especially those that dictate inevitable repression or shame. All four thinkers take as real, not illusory, the possibility of shaping environments and attitudes creatively through an assimilation of language—for again, in their view, mastery of the word ameliorates and connects, it does not naturally alienate. Words are not, of course, all-powerful. But since human beings are such richly endowed and outreaching creatures, they are more likely to be distracted (that is, more likely simply to forget) than they are to "repress"; and since the mind is structured to internalize others' experiences before it learns to express itself, we may assume a continuity between "inner" (mental) and outer (socially dialogic) modes of communicating and remembering. No censors need to be tricked, no illicit energies need to be discharged. Above all, we are social creatures who can be seen and heard; and that which can be seen and heard can always be positively addressed.

For Vygotsky, however, the benevolent "outsideness" of a stimulus is only half the solution to optimizing human intelligence. The stimulus must occur at the right moment in an organism's development (read a novel out loud to an eighteen-month-old infant and she will not understand it; fail to read that novel to her in her eleventh year and a precious resource is lost, she'll never be as receptive again). The stimulus also has to be somehow aslant of the norm, in excess of it. In the spirit of early Formalism, Vygotsky insisted that the conscious self always develops *outside* of system, estranged momentarily from it; human beings learn creatively only when their automated reflexes are blocked or "interrupted" and they are thus obliged to pause. Since a reflex can give back only what has been programmed, in the "expected order of things" we would experience no unexpected growth and no leap of consciousness. It follows that in living creatures engaged in higher-order activities, the "reflex arc" is maximally interrupted: "inefficient" in terms of one's current economy, incomplete, it is chronically, continually being delayed by one or another "speech irritant." Vygotsky argues that any interruption of physiological or mental routine by some outside thing, person, or word endows our inner reactions with flexibility and new depth. Physiologically, human thought could be understood as an *interrupted reflex.*

Hesitation, then, is the mark of humanness. The temporal gap between a stimulus and a reaction to it ranks high among the factors separating us from Pavlov's dogs. One begins to see why Vygotsky was so preoccupied throughout his life with Shakespeare's *Hamlet*; indeed, the "physiological" reading of that play which Vygotsky provides in *The Psychology of Art*, taken together with his "maturational" reading of *Eugene Onegin,* are the literary highlights of that youthful monograph.[44] Paying tribute to the canonized German tradition of *Hamlet* criticism with its refrain of a weak and vacillating hero, Vygotsky's critique is largely taken up with what he calls "the enigma of Hamlet's failure to act." Vygotsky dismisses the obvious reasons for Hamlet's hesitation to kill Claudius: why trust a ghost (especially one who by all indications comes not from Purgatory but from Hell); Hamlet's concern that he is mad; a normal fear of death on the part of the hero; his resentment that he was born to set things right; the playwright's practical consideration that an unhesitating act of retribution by the heir to the throne would have ended the play in the first act. But he refuses to endorse the traditional Russian view of Hamlet as limp and ineffectual, a "superfluous man" *avant la lettre.* He concentrates instead on the magnificent, courageous, consciousness-expanding series of "interruptions" in the hero's reflexes, which give rise to the great monologues, to the oddly unmotivated turns of plot, and to the casual wholesale slaughter at the end. Every goal toward which this multiplaned, contradictory tragedy moves is eventually undermined (195); both external and internal spectators are deceived in their attempt to create an "arc" of expectation for the plot. In this most universally human of plays we are left hanging between "words, words, words" and "the rest is silence." Profoundly out of sympathy with Aristotle, this most interrupted drama is the most creative and human one.

The Interrupted Self as the Space of Consciousness

Let us now turn to our other three thinkers and stitch them in. On its own, the notion of "interruption" is fearfully broad; to be profitably used by any given thinker upon any text, one would have to ask, at the very least, "what interrupts what?" Where does the author first seek primary unity: in the figure or in the ground, with the personality or with the field? We might begin with Bakhtin in his high polyphonic phase. "Interruption" is what separates the dialogic from the monologic self. As we have seen, Bakhtin's convictions everywhere speak out against mechanical system, against a steady or integrated state of anything, against any definitive centralization of authorial control. Everywhere he champions the overwhelming power of the utterance (often unexpectedly, even to its speaker) to rearrange reality on its own. Both Vygotsky and Bakhtin

[44] Lev Semenovich Vygotsky, *The Psychology of Art,* trans. Scripta Technica, Inc. (Cambridge, Mass.: The MIT Press, 1971): 166–96 (chapter 8, "The Tragedy of Hamlet, Prince of Denmark"); reading of Pushkin's *Eugene Onegin* on 222–28. Further page numbers in text.

put the literary text in the place reserved for the "interruptant" or "irritant" in classical reflexology. But these two thinkers diverge as regards the literary genre most effective as a site for this learning. In a 1993 essay entitled "Life Experience and the Drama of Development of Personality (Vygotsky's Final Word)," Mikhail Yaroshevsky takes on Vygotsky's abiding fascination with drama in contrast to Bakhtin's passion for the novel.[45] For Vygotsky, he notes, the unit of analysis is always *experience*. And experience must be a three-dimensional, fully staged, thickly embodied affair, in which (as in the well-made play) one's maturational level, emerging sense of individual personality, and ability to act—not just talk—alongside others combine with an environmental stimulus to produce confrontational social behavior that ends in genuine learning, in a type of closure. Bakhtin, in contrast, did not believe that confrontation (or even Dostoevsky-style catastrophe) finalized anything.[46] As Yaroshevsky notes, for Bakhtin "the center of analysis, both in matters of art and of personality, is a person's consciousness, not a person in all the fullness of bodily and spiritual being. . . . However, consciousness—no matter how one might interpret it as a living and dialogic thing—is not the only 'measuring stick' for human personality" (88). What Yaroshevsky senses here is that under polyphonic conditions, an event (*sobytie*) need not be an embodied experience with a one-way result. It can simply be a "co-being" (*so-bytie*), two or more consciousnesses interrupting or interacting verbally with one another on an ideational plane, potentially without end. Development is not an issue, nor is death.

At the other end of this spectrum there is Yuri Lotman during much of his distinguished career. If Bakhtin's primary focus was always on the *figure*, on the differentiated and rebellious unit that resists resolution, then Lotman proved himself to be an excellent student of grounds. His early work was inspired by information theory and impersonal functions. In contrast to Bakhtin, who evinced little interest in spatially distributed norms as the regulator or standard for a given self,[47] Lotman in his struc-

---

[45] M. G. Iaroshevskii, "Perezhivanie i drama razvitiia lichnosti (Poslednee slovo L. S. Vygotskogo)," *Voprosy filosofii*, no. 3 (1993): 82–91. Important to note here is the Russian word *perezhivanie* [experience as process, life experience] as distinct from *opyt* [which, like the French *expérience*, can cover an experience, an experiment, and a trial or essay]. This article exists in English as M. G. Iaroshevskii, "Experience and the Drama of the Development of Personality (L. S. Vygotsky's Last Word)," *Russian Studies in Philosophy* 36, no. 1 (Summer 1997): 70–83.

[46] Consider these passages from "Notes to a Reworking of the Dostoevsky Book" in *Problems of Dostoevsky's Poetics*: "The problem of catastrophe. Catastrophe is not finalization. It is the culmination, in collision and struggle, of points of view. . . . Catastrophe does not give these points of view resolution, but on the contrary reveals their incapability of resolution under earthly conditions. . . . By its very essence it is denied even elements of catharsis" (298).

[47] For a discussion, see I. L. Popova, "Ob esteticheskoi norme u M. Bakhtina," in K. G. Isupov, ed., *M. M. Bakhtin i filosofskaia kul'tura XX veka* (St. Petersburg: Obrazovanie, 1991), 1:48–54. Popova argues that as Bakhtin understood the term, a norm received its obligatory

turalist phase viewed the matter geographically: "an *event* in a text is the shifting of a persona across the borders of a semantic field."[48] These events are arranged in a hierarchy of visibility, depending upon their "meaningful departure from the norm" (234). In certain genres and situations, Lotman asserts, neither death nor love register as events, regardless of their significance for the selves involved (235). Personalities are above all agents—and an agent is simply "one who crosses the border of the plot field (the semantic field); the border for the agent is a barrier" (240). Even in his later, more organic, and least binary phase, Lotman retained his affection for rivalry, not cooperation, across a boundary.[49]

Because of their highly marked structuralist and polyphonic starting points (the former favoring system, the latter disdaining it), Lotman and Bakhtin are read, and properly, as strong critics. Each has generated a "school" and presents a profile that one can embrace or reject; indeed, postcommunist criticism in the mid-1990s enjoyed pitting one approach against the other.[50] But we should note that both scholars, in the second half of their careers, introduced self-correctives that significantly soften the opposition. Bakhtin tightened his structures up: he drew back from the eternally "interruptible" polyphonic model of the self as well as from the vacuous carnival self, turning his attention to "speech genres" and other social constraints on individual utterance. And Lotman, in his remarkable final volume *Culture and Explosion* (Kul'tura i vzryv), discusses topics that would seem to lie squarely in the center of Bakhtin's world: the limitations of a Jakobsonian model of "code and message," the benefits to be had from multilanguaged environments and permanent untranslatability, the inadequacy of all systematized content, the virtues of interruptibility, and—drawing on and polemicizing with Pushkin—the nature of poetic inspiration.[51] Very much in the spirit of Vygotsky's "interrupted re-

---

force from "the authority of its source, the authenticity and precision of its transmission" (49), and that such nondialogic criteria were unacceptable to him.

[48] Jurij Lotman, *The Structure of the Artistic Text* [1971], trans. Ronald Vroon (Ann Arbor: Michigan Slavic Contributions no. 7, 1977), chapter 8, "The Composition of the Verbal Work of Art," 233. Further page references in text.

[49] See, for example, chapter 9, "The notion of boundary," in Yuri M. Lotman, *Universe of the Mind: A Semiotic Theory of Culture*, trans. Ann Shukman (London: I. B. Tauris, 1990), 131–42.

[50] See, for example, the Moscow-based thick journal *Novoe literaturnoe obozrenie* (henceforth *NLO*), which openly espouses a pro-Lotman position against the Bakhtinians, themselves served by half a dozen established journals. For a sampling of the polemics, see A. M. Ranchin, "Iskushenie Bakhtinym," *NLO*, no. 3 (1993): 320–25; Iurii Murashov, "Vosstanie golosa protiv pis'ma: O dialogizme Bakhtina," *NLO*, no. 16 (1995): 24–31; A. T. Ivanov, "Bakhtin, Bakhtinistika, Bakhtinologiia," *NLO*, no. 16 (1995): 333–37; and Mikhail Gasparov's riposte against careless dialogism in the humanities, "Kritika kak samotsel'," *NLO*, no. 6 (1993–94): 6–9.

[51] Iu. M. Lotman, *Kul'tura i vzryv* (Moscow: Gnozis, 1992). Consider this sampling of chapter titles, in light of Vygotsky's procedures discussed above: "A System with One Language" [not a positive or possible thing], "Gradual Progress," "The Interrupted and the Uninterrupted," "Semantic Intersection as an Explosion of Meaning." Further page references in text.

flex," Lotman defines life itself as a sort of punctuated equilibrium, where certain types of progress cannot be gradual or gridded in advance; for this reason, he surmises, *sluchai*, or chance, often contains the highest degree of informationality (27–29). The task of art is to create a fundamentally new level of reality, one distinguished by a sharp increase in freedom in exactly those areas where the self in life is not free (232–34). The aesthetic "makes possible not only the forbidden, but also the impossible." For that reason alone, Lotman intimates, art has a moral dimension. In real, unscripted life, one can always blame an immoral act on necessity, but one cannot thus rationalize a despicable artistic creation. All great art is "a thought experiment permitting us to verify the elusiveness of the various structures in the world" (235).

Lydia Ginzburg remains somewhat apart from these shiftings and reconceptualizations. One possible explanation might be found in her writerly serenity. Part structuralist, part personalist, her thought never partakes of extremes; in her work on the literary and real-life self, she does not represent entities as "invading" or "interrupting" each other wholly unexpectedly. A figure is not assimilated to a ground simply to benefit systematic analysis, nor is a ground ignored on behalf of freedom for the figures that live on it. Multiple variables constantly condition one another. In this methodology, Ginzburg was highly consistent. Her work on the lyric manages to be both technical and socially contextualized at once (a rare accomplishment for prosodists); her investigation of the literary hero begins with the modest task of "recognizing a unity" and sets as its goal an exposition of the process whereby "stable forms assimilate new social material uninterruptedly flowing into it."[52] It is hard to get a scandal out of Ginzburg. For this reason, perhaps, her close readings of individual literary texts remain among the most thoughtful and least paraphrasable of our four philosophical critics.

Do the four thinkers discussed here represent a "Russian school"? On the far side of Soviet communism and its failed attempt to transform the human psyche, it is perhaps time to reexamine that label as well. These Russians are scholars of world scope. Under the most trying conditions and confronted with sobering practical lessons at every turn, they produced theories of the self that are at base antifoundationalist and contingent while giving nihilism an exceptionally wide berth. Their voices should be part of the debates over moral and evaluative discourse that now provoke such stimulating controversy among philosophers and literary experts (Charles Taylor, Martha Nussbaum, Richard Rorty) in the academies of the West.[53] But Russian contingency is not ours. There are

---

[52] Ginzburg, *O literaturnom geroe*, 4.

[53] For a lucid survey of the state of this debate by the early 1990s, see David Parker, *Ethics, Theory and the Novel* (Cambridge: Cambridge University Press, 1994), especially chapters 1–3.

more palpable traces of the ideal in it. For if it is a cliché of American culture that our ideal is not that which is perfect but that which works (in general, our values remain pragmatic ones), then underneath our pragmatic "working models" is very often a presumption of personal alienation, of lonely autonomy and lack of trust. To erect a network of logical and legal defenses against mutual suspicion and subversion of meaning feels natural and right. Precisely here do these four Russian thinkers differ from current Western critical fashion. Each is unembarrassed to rely, in a theoretically rigorous way, on more old-fashioned positions: a trust in words, a reverence for the transformative powers of art, and self-discipline in the presence of love.

CHAPTER TWO

The Obverse of Stalinism: Akhmatova's
Self-Serving Charisma of Selflessness

ALEXANDER ZHOLKOVSKY

In every revolution, the main issue is power.

V. I. Lenin

"Poetry is power," Osip Mandelstam once said to Akhmatova in
Voronezh, and she bowed her head on its slender neck.
Banished, sick, penniless, and hounded, they still would not
give up their power.

Nadezhda Mandelstam

A Storied Self

The life and works of the poet Anna Andreevna Akhmatova
(1889–1966) offer a sustained example of self-presentation that is
grounded in historical circumstances in ways one would not have easily
suspected. What follows is an attempt to reread the Akhmatova myth as a
set of stories told of oneself and received, repeated, and institutionalized
by the surrounding culture. The case of Akhmatova is especially challenging because of the poet's well-known stoic opposition to the reigning political climate of the time: her essential affinity with the totalitarian discourse of her oppressors can only be discerned through a fresh parsing of
the text of her literary and personal life, usually construed in hagio-
graphic tones.[1]

The epigraphs are respectively from: a common Lenin poster, and Nadezhda
Mandelstam, *Hope Against Hope. A Memoir* (New York: Atheneum, 1970), 170.

[1] For "hagio-biographies" of Akhmatova, see Amanda Haight, *Anna Akhmatova: A Poetic
Pilgrimage* (New York: Oxford University Press, 1976), and Roberta Reeder, *Anna Akhmatova:
Poet and Prophet* (New York: St. Martin's Press, 1994); see also my review of the latter:

Fortunately, the task is facilitated by the unabashed conspicuousness of Akhmatova's self-image making. Forestalling the needs of biographers, Akhmatova used to give her visitors "guided museum tours of herself"[2] and play to them what she called "gramophone records" (*plastinki*)—vignettes from her life.[3] She often spoke as if "for the record"[4] and "was not above ghosting her own biography."[5]

> She came to believe . . . that all her indiscretions would be divulged by her biographers. She lived . . . aware of her biography. . . . "It is all in our hands," she would say, and: "As a literary critic I know. . . ." One part of her longed for a canonized portrait without the follies and foibles inevitable in any life, especially that of a poet.[6]
>
> [P]eople . . . said . . . that she "corrected her biography" . . . [She] declared herself . . . to be the chronologically first Akhmatova specialist to whose *objective* opinion all later specialists would have to give particular weight.[7]

Here is how she went about providing "objective" data.

> She persuaded Vera Alekseevna Znamenskaia to write her memoirs, but . . . did not find in them what she had expected. . . . A[nna] A[ndreevna] would get angry and even quarrel with Vera Alekseevna, but then she recalled wisely that the very initial period of her relationship with [the poet Nikolai] Gumilev [Akhmatova's former husband, executed by the Soviets in 1921 on dubious charges] should be remembered by Valia [Sreznevskaia]. . . . Valeriia Sergeevna went ahead and wrote, but [Akhmatova] did not like her notes . . . although much of it was written according to her own words. Some of it they corrected together, and Valeriia Sergeevna once again copied it out in her own hand, at [Akhmatova's] insistence. This copybook written by Valeriia Sergeevna was rejected by Anna Andreevna.[8]

With similar bias Akhmatova shaped her versions of her historic role. According to Sir Isaiah Berlin, she believed that, "we—that is, she and I—

Alexander Zholkovsky, "Anna Akhmatova: Scripts, Not Scriptures," *Slavic and East European Journal* 40, no. 1 (1996): 135–141.

[2] I. Metter, "Sedoi venets dostalsia ei nedarom," in *Ob Anne Akhmatovoi: Stikhi, esse, vospominaniia, pis'ma*, ed. M. Kralin (Leningrad: Lenizdat, 1990; henceforth *OAA*), 387.

[3] Nika Glen, "Vokrug starykh zapisei," in *Vospominaniia ob Anne Akhmatovoi*, ed. V. Vilenkin and V. Chernykh (Moscow: Sovetskii pisatel', 1991; henceforth *VAA*), 634.

[4] Anatoly Nayman, *Remembering Anna Akhmatova* (New York: Henry Holt, 1991), 163.

[5] Catriona Kelly, "Anna Akhmatova (1889–1966)," in her *A History of Russian Women's Writing. 1820–1992* (Oxford: Clarendon Press, 1994), 219.

[6] Nadezhda Mandelstam, "Akhmatova," in *Anna Akhmatova and Her Circle*, ed. Konstantin Polivanov (Fayetteville: The University of Arkansas Press, 1994; henceforth *AAHC*), 121.

[7] Nayman, *Remembering Anna Akhmatova*, 81.

[8] I. N. Punina, "Ob Anne Akhmatovoi i Valerii Sreznevskoi," in *VAA*, 27.

inadvertently, by the mere fact of our meeting, had started the cold war and thereby changed the history of mankind. She meant this quite literally; and . . . saw herself and me as world-historical personages chosen by destiny to begin a cosmic conflict. . . . I could not protest . . . since she would have felt this as an insult to her tragic image of herself as Cassandra—indeed, to the historico-metaphysical vision which informed so much of her poetry. I remained silent."[9] Berlin identifies the fundamental connection between Akhmatova's personal fears as a subject of Stalin's regime and her charismatic self-image. The paranoia, more or less legitimate under the circumstances, develops into a mania grandiosa, which, in turn, energizes her personal myth, in an instructive instance of the paradoxical opposition / symbiosis between dissident poet and totalitarian leader—of the sort perceptively analyzed by Gregory Freidin with respect to Osip Mandelstam.[10] Akhmatova's brooking no contradiction from Berlin, therefore, evidences not so much her unreasonableness as her adherence to the laws of charismatic mythmaking.

Indeed, as a disciple of the Silver Age masters of "self-creation" (*zhiznetvorchestvo*)[11] and as a witness to the production of Stalin's "cult of personality," Akhmatova had a keen understanding of these laws. "When Brodsky was tried and sent into exile . . . she said: 'What a biography they are making for our Ginger. As if he had gone out and hired someone to do it.' And to my question about the poetic fate of Mandelstam, whether it was not overshadowed by his fate as a citizen . . . she replied: 'It's ideal.' "[12]

On occasion, the "hiring" metaphor would be reified. In the 1920s, Akhmatova engaged the services of a younger friend, P. N. Luknitskii, to work on the biography of Gumilev. In his diary, he noted her instructing him as follows: " 'You mustn't forget that this biography you are compiling is perhaps a most severe indictment. . . . You must gain an understanding of every detail, plow through all this debris . . . create the *true* image of Nikolai Stepanovich. . . . You may overly narrow that image and make mistakes.' . . . She realized that creating such a biography was also a work of art . . . an act of creation like any other."[13]

[9] Isaiah Berlin, "Anna Akhmatova: A Memoir," in *The Complete Poems of Anna Akhmatova*, ed. Roberta Reeder, trans. Judith Hemschemeyer, 2 vols. (Somerville, Mass.: Zephyr Press, 1990), 2:38.

[10] Gregory Freidin, *A Coat of Many Colors: Osip Mandelstam and His Mythologies of Self-Presentation* (Berkeley: University of California Press, 1987), 1–33; for a recent variation on the traditional view, see Clare Cavanagh, "The Death of the Book à la russe: The Acmeists under Stalin," *Slavic Review* 55, no. 1 (1996): 125–35.

[11] On the concept of *zhiznetvorchestvo* see *Creating Life: The Aesthetic Utopia of Russian Modernism*, ed. Irina Paperno and Joan Grossman (Stanford: Stanford University Press, 1994).

[12] Nayman, *Remembering Anna Akhmatova*, 6.

[13] P. N. Luknitskii, *Vstrechi s Annoi Akhmatovoi* (Paris: YMCA-Press, 1991), 1: 232–33.

Akhmatova considered plain wrong and punishable all biographical statements about Gumilev, herself, and Mandelstam that were not authorized by her. "She passionately hates—and fears—authors of *biographies romancées*. [She says:] 'I'd like to set up an international tribunal and give severe sentences to the likes of J. Carré, Maurois, Tynianov.' "[14] She also insisted on securing proper portrayals of herself in the sphere of visual arts.

> Once she read in someone's memoirs . . . published abroad that she was not pretty. . . . From that day on she began to collect photographs . . . where she looked pretty and pasted them in an album . . . heaps of pictures.[15]
>
> [L. V.] Gornung asked Anna Andreevna to take her photograph *lege artis*. Anna Andreevna gladly gave her consent. She loved being "immortalized."[16]

Indeed, today Akhmatova is among the photographically best-documented literary celebrities.

A sculptor recalls the discussion he had with her during a session: "[Akhmatova:] 'And what is the point of sculpting such a fat nape [*kholka*]? Can it really be so huge? . . . I hope that the model fully deserves that the artist not set in relief all such details.' Now there was nothing I could object to in this. Indeed: the model was so important and noble, sophisticated to the utmost degree in her views of art. . . . I decided to eliminate the fat excrescence in the area of the seventh neck vertebra, popularly known as *kholka*."[17]

Even highly esteemed artists, such as A. G. Tyshler (1898–1980), were not spared Akhmatova's peremptory "editing" of her image, as reported by a younger poet: "[I asked]: 'Lydia Iakovlevna, what's the matter with this drawing?' On the wall of L. Ia. Ginzburg's apartment there is a framed profile of Anna Andreevna by Tyshler, in which the Roman hump of her nose has been erased and corrected in a soft and unsure line with a different pencil. . . . 'Anna Andreevna corrected it. They were together in evacuation in Tashkent, and Tyshler drew her there. . . . She maintained that he did not do the nose right—and corrected it.' "[18]

As for storytelling proper, it lies at the core not only of Akhmatova's self-fashioning strategies but also of her innovative contribution to Russian lyric poetry. In this, she drew on the traditions of the nineteenth-

---

[14] Sophie Ostrovskaya, *Memoirs of Anna Akhmatova's Years 1944–1950* (Liverpool: Lincoln Davies, 1988) 37.

[15] Nadezhda Mandelstam, "Akhmatova," in *AAHC*, 128.

[16] S. V. Shervinskii, "Anna Akhmatova v rakurse byta," in *VAA*, 292.

[17] Vasilii Astapov, "Seansy v Komarove," in *OAA*, 407.

[18] N. V. Koroleva, "Anna Akhmatova i leningradskaia poeziia 1960-kh godov," in *"Svoiu mezh vas eshche ostaviv ten' . . .": Akhmatovskie chteniia* 3, ed. N. V. Koroleva and S. A. Kovalenko (Moscow: Nasledie, 1992), 123.

century novel, compressing its narrative *topoi* into the background of her laconic poems.[19] To do so, she coopted the Nekrasovian prosaization of lyric poetry—with the important modification of narcissistically arranging the narrative element around her persona. Narcissistic manipulation is also evident in the mode of her entrance, in the 1930s, into the field of literary scholarship. "Akhmatova's research article on Pushkin's tale in verse *The Golden Cockerel*[20] was written with the assistance of [the scholar] N. I. Khardzhiev. 'I was ill,' Anna Andreevna liked to recall, 'and Nikolai Ivanovich sat facing me and asked: 'What do you want to say?' and he wrote it down for me himself.' "[21] The manipulative streak conspicuous in this episode—whether fact or one of her fictions—is not an isolated occurrence. Akhmatova was keen on power play, noticing it in others and practicing it herself. Of the Symbolist poet Viacheslav Ivanov she remarked, acidly: "He was a desperate self-advertiser . . . a highly experienced fisher of men, a virtuoso! He, a forty-four-year-old man, would get grey-haired ladies to escort him around. . . . He knew how to establish himself everywhere."[22]

In fact, similar self-promotion was one of Akhmatova's own fortes—be it within her circle of admirer-helpers[23] or vis-à-vis the Soviet literary and political establishment all the way up to Stalin himself. Her version of the 1946 Zhdanov campaign against her, Mikhail Zoshchenko, the journals *Zvezda* and *Leningrad*, and the liberal Western-leaning intelligentsia in general characteristically reduces the dramatic plot to only two star performances—hers and Stalin's:

> She also believed that Stalin became jealous of the applause she got: in April 1946, Akhmatova recited her poetry in the Hall of Columns in Moscow and the public stood up to applaud. Standing ovations were due, in Stalin's opinion, only to himself, and here was the crowd applauding some poetess.[24]
>
> Rumor had it that Stalin was furious because of the passionate reception given to Akhmatova by the audience. According to one version, after

---

[19] This was first noted by Osip Mandelstam, in his early 1922 review, "Letter about Russian Poetry" (see his *Complete Critical Works and Letters*, ed. Jane Gary Harris [Ann Arbor: Ardis, 1979], 158), and Boris Eikhenbaum, in his 1923 monograph "Anna Akhmatova" (see his *O poezii* [Leningrad: Sovetskii pisatel', 1969], 140).

[20] "Posledniaia skazka Pushkina" (first published in 1933); see Anna Akhmatova, *Sochineniia*, 3 vols. (Munich: Inter-Language Literary Associates, 1968), 2: 197–222.

[21] E. G. Gershtein, "The Thirties," in *AAHC*, 140.

[22] Lidiia Chukovskaia, *Zapiski ob Anne Akhmatovoi*, vol. 1 (Moscow: Kniga, 1989), vol. 2 (Paris: YMCA-Press, 1980), 2: 451–52; henceforth referred to by volume and page only.

[23] About this, see Beth Holmgren, *Women's Works in Stalin's Time: On Lidiia Chukovskaia and Nadezhda Mandelstam* (Bloomington: Indiana University Press, 1993); Zholkovsky, "Scripts"; and Aleksandr Zholkovskii, "Strakh, tiazhest', mramor (Iz materialov k zhiznetvorcheskoi biografii Akhmatovoi)," *Wiener Slawistischer Almanakh* 36 (1996): 119–54.

[24] Chukovskaia, *Zapiski*, 2, x.

some such event Stalin inquired: "Who organized the standing ovation [*vstavanie*]?"[25]

The latter question, usually perceived as Stalin's willful projection of his own insidious ways onto an innocent poet, is not all that absurd: a unanimous standing ovation does take organizing, albeit not necessarily of the crude sort Stalin specialized in. His irate acknowledgment of Akhmatova's charismatic techniques was a sui generis tribute to her mastery. As for his contribution to the "making of her biography," it was perhaps even more "ideal" than what he, according to her, had done for Mandelstam (and what other Soviet leaders later did for Brodsky): she was subjected to harsh, but by the same token spotlighting, persecution, yet spared literary or literal liquidation.

To turn from storytelling to playacting: Nadezhda Mandelstam recalls how Akhmatova once told her on very short notice before appearing in public that they should instantly turn themselves into beauties.[26] A similar statement is recorded by Lydia Chukovskaia: "Seeing me off, Anna Andreevna said by the door, 'Tomorrow I . . . have to look good.'—'Can you?'—'All my life I could look as I wished: from beautiful to ugly' "[27] Akhmatova's theatrical abilities rivaled her narrative prowess, although her actual dramatic and fictional prose writing was practically nonexistent. Where narrative and drama did work for Akhmatova was in her short lyrics and in her *zhiznetvorchestvo*. Both achievements were in tune with the twentieth-century democratization of culture and advent of mass-media manipulation of the wider public. Despite all her differences from the avant–garde, Akhmatova's "emplotting" of her poetry and life was akin to their strategy (nowadays prevalent) of valuing gesture and self-promotion over texture.[28] That is probably why her lyrics travel across national and linguistic borders better than those of her rival contemporaries Pasternak and Mandelstam: proportionately, less is lost in translation, not because there is less poetry, but because there is more posture.

Commenting on the contradictions among memoirists' versions of the Akhmatova image, the Dutch scholar Kees Verheul proposed distinctions among her various scripts: "1. The stories about the persona . . . that . . . enhance the artistic image created by Akhmatova. . . . 2. The stories about

[25] Glen, "Vokrug starykh zapisei," in *VAA*, 631.

[26] Nadezhda Mandelstam, "Akhmatova," in *AAHC*, 128.

[27] Chukovskaia, *Zapiski*, 2: 31–32.

[28] In the provocative formulation by a postmodern poet, "Vo vsekh derevniakh, ugolkakh by nichtozhnykh / Ia biusty vezde by postavil ego / A vot by stikhi ia ego unichtozhil— / Ved' oblik oni prinizhaiut ego" ("In all the villages, [all] nondescript necks of the wood, I would install [Pushkin's] busts. But as for his verses, I would annihilate them—for they do diminish his image"), Dmitrii Aleksandrovich Prigov, *Sovetskie teksty* (St. Petersburg: Izd-vo Ivana Limbakha, 1997), 226.

the actress . . . who created her own persona and sometimes treated this activity with . . . irony. 3. Finally, the stories about Akhmatova the person . . . who engaged and quite often did not engage in the above, with irony or without."[29] The last point raises the intriguing question of the enigmatic core "person" hiding within the constructed roles, personae, and performers. A related issue is that of the audience, whose reception of Akhmatova's stories and acts was crucial to her art of self-presentation. Despite the "regal" image Akhmatova strove to produce, she, unlike Pushkin's archetypal poet-tsar, who is supposed to "live alone,"[30] could not stand loneliness.[31] Rather, like the proverbial king on the stage, she needed a retinue to make her appear royal.

Akhmatova was very deliberate in deploying her skills of impressing immediate and distant admirers. Unlike the Futurists and quite like the Acmeist and the consummate "lady" she was, Akhmatova relied not so much on direct, provocative, or laid-bare indoctrination but rather on covert suggestion, leaving her receptive audiences with a sense of (co-)authorship.

> She had a special way of adjusting opinions held about her in the desired direction. . . . "I have a way of unobtrusively floating my own thoughts to people. And in a little while they sincerely believe that the ideas are their own."[32]
>
> I observed how Akhmatova created her own legend—as if surrounding herself with a strong magnetic field. A strong concoction of premonitions, coincidences, private omens, fatal accidents, secret dates, non-meetings, and three-hundred-year-old trifles was always boiling in her magic pot. . . . The pot was hidden from the reader.[33]

The effectiveness of these strategies resulted from that blend of submission and domination that was so characteristic of Akhmatova's lyrical as well as life-textual persona and is highly relevant to our "Stalinist" theme.

Akhmatova and Mayakovsky: A Story with a Prehistory

One telltale instance of Akhmatova's techniques of self-presentation features her relationship with Mayakovsky. The problem "Akhmatova *vs.*

---

[29] Kees Verheul, "Neskol'ko posleakhmatovskikh vospominanii," in *"Svoiu mezh vas eshche ostaviv ten' . . . ,"* 49.

[30] See Pushkin's 1831 sonnet "Poetu" ("To the Poet"), with its programmatic statement: "You are tsar: live alone" ("Ty tsar': zhivi odin"), in A. S. Pushkin, *Polnoe sobranie sochinenii,* 10 vols. (Leningrad: Nauka, 1977), 3: 165.

[31] For more detail see Zholkovskii, "Strakh."

[32] Nayman, *Remembering Anna Akhmatova,* 81–82.

[33] Ign. Ivanovskii, "Anna Akhmatova," in *OAA,* 615.

Mayakovsky" was posed by the critic Kornei Chukovskii as early as 1920,[34] and, despite later modifications by other scholars,[35] has been read since in terms of stark opposition. But the actual picture was more complex. The two poets paid respectful attention to each other's work, if only in order "to know the enemy."[36] Akhmatova liked reminiscing about their 1915 chance encounter on Morskaia Street, of which both poets had had a mystical premonition.[37] Mayakovsky was alarmed by rumors of Akhmatova's suicide after the execution of Gumilev; she, in turn, reacted with compassion, if somewhat condescendingly, to Mayakovsky's suicide.[38] And in 1940, on the tenth anniversary of Mayakovsky's death, Akhmatova wrote a poem that was a panegyric to his prerevolutionary image and thus a covert polemic with his official Soviet icon.[39]

In 1956, Lydia Chukovskaia noted in her diaries that, "The editors of the *Literary Legacy* [Literaturnoe nasledstvo] asked Anna Andreevna to write her recollections of Mayakovsky. " 'I refused,' she said. . . . 'Actually, I never really knew him—only from afar. . . . And why should I run after his chariot? I have my own. Besides, he always badmouthed me in public, and it doesn't become me to praise him.' "[40] But then, the 1940 poem was also written "from afar"; more likely, the problem lay in their general competition and in a never-forgotten specific offense.

The invitation was renewed a year later:

[34] Chukovskii's article (see "Akhmatova and Mayakovsky," in *Major Soviet Writers: Essays in Criticism*, ed. Edward J. Brown [New York: Oxford University Press, 1973], 33–53) was published in 1921, after a series of his 1920 lectures in Moscow and Petrograd, on "Two Russias (Akhmatova and Mayakovsky)," where Akhmatova was made to represent the old, sophisticated, churchgoing Russia and Mayakovsky, the new, nihilist, Soviet one; she stood for intimacy and silence, Mayakovsky for public speechmaking and shouting, etc.

[35] According to S. A. Kovalenko ("Akhmatova i Maiakovskii," in *Tsarstvennoe slovo: Akhmatovskie chteniia 1*, ed. N. A. Koroleva and S. A. Kovalenko [Moscow: Nasledie, 1992], 168) and V. Vilenkin (*V sto pervom zerkale* [Moscow: Sovetskii pisatel', 1990], 41), both were major poets, troubadours of "unhappy love"; and, according to Kovalenko (ibid., 173), both were victims of the Soviet regime in general and censorship in particular.

[36] See I. S. Eventov, "Ot Fontanki do Sitsilii," in *OAA*, 360–379; Kovalenko, "Akhmatovai Maiakovskii,"167; and V. Katanian, *Maiakovskii: Khronika zhizni i deiatel'nosti* (Moscow: Khudozhestvennaia literatura, 1985), 520, where Mayakovsky is quoted saying, after reciting an Akhmatova poem in his powerful voice, that while "expressing refined and fragile emotions, the poem itself is not fragile at all; Akhmatova's verses are monolithic and can withstand the pressure of any voice without cracking." Akhmatova, in turn, is known to have "mentally 'tried on' Mayakovsky's fate" (Kovalenko, "Akhmatova i Maiakovskii," 163).

[37] Katanian, *Maiakovskii*, 100; Kovalenko, "Akhmatova i Maiakovskii," 166.

[38] Kovalenko, "Akhmatova i Maiakovskii," 166; N. Reformatskaia, "S Akhmatovoi v muzee Maiakovskogo," in *VAA*, 542.

[39] On this poem, "Mayakovsky in the year 1913" ("Maiakovskii v 1913 godu"), and other aspects of the interrelationship between the two poets, see also L. F. Katsis, "Zametki o stikhotvorenii Anny Akhmatovoi 'Maiakovskii v 1913 godu,' " *Russian Literature* 30, no. 3 (1991): 317–36.

[40] Chukovskaia, *Zapiski*, 2: 140 (entry for March 12, 1956).

She showed me [the editor of *The Literary Legacy* Il'ia] Zil'bershtein's letter . . . asking her to write . . . her recollections of Mayakovsky. She seems willing to me, but alas [he] made a grave tactical error. He enclosed . . . a fragment from the memoirs of [Mayakovsky's beloved] L. Iu. Brik, who relates
how Mayakovsky always liked Akhmatova's poems and often quoted them.
That would be fine, but, unfortunately, Brik goes on to tell how he deliberately, for fun, would mangle them. A poet can hardly hear with equanimity
her poems being crippled. It seems to me that these manglings caused Anna
Andreevna physical pain. In any case, she is not going to write.[41]

Zil'bershtein's mistake was, indeed, only "tactical," since Akhmatova
did have prior knowledge of Lily Brik's memoirs. The relevant passages
had been brought to her attention in 1940 by I. S. Eventov in the course
of his attempts to persuade her to participate in a memorial concert,
where she eventually did read her poem "Mayakovsky in 1913."[42] The interview began with his declaration of interest in studying Mayakovsky's
work. " 'Studying,' Anna Andreevna repeated with evident coolness. . . .
'Then you probably know that Mayakovsky once publicly, from the stage,
made fun of me, reciting my 'The Grey-Eyed King' ('Seroglazyi korol','
1911) to the tune of the vulgar song 'A Cocky Merchant Rode to the Fair'
('Ekhal na iarmarku ukhar'-kupets').' "[43]

Eventov did know about this, as he did about the notorious "purge of
contemporary poetry" at the Polytechnical Museum in January 1922.
There, Mayakovsky had declared that in light of the tasks of revolutionary
poetry, "many remain overboard," including Akhmatova with her "chamber lyrics."[44] Eventov succeeded in getting Akhmatova to change her mind
by showing her his own excerpts from Lily Brik's memoirs, which proved
that in the years 1915–1916, "Mayakovsky, who was in love . . . most often
recited Akhmatova . . . and sometimes even sang, to some completely incongruous tune, his favorite lyrical lines. He liked her poems and made
fun not of them but of his own 'sentiments,' which he was unable to hold
in check."[45] Eventov was also able to "humbly report" (*dolozhil*) to
Akhmatova that "in Brik's manuscript, the incident with 'The Grey-Eyed
King' was . . . clarified: 'Mayakovsky often recited others' poems in the
street, as he walked. . . . We sang these poems in unison and we marched
to them . . . selecting tunes to fit the original poem rhythmically but
sound incongruous because of a clash in meaning."[46] In the same way,

---

[41] Chukovskaia, *Zapiski*, 2: 192 (entry for February 13, 1957).

[42] Also, Lily Brik's memoirs soon appeared in *Znamia* [The Banner], no. 3, 1940.

[43] Eventov, "Ot Fontanki," 361. In August 1922, Mayakovsky had publicly nicknamed her
"Akhmatkina" (Katanian, 232).

[44] Eventov, "Ot Fontanki," 361.

[45] Eventov, "Ot Fontanki," 362.

[46] Eventov, "Ot Fontanki," 362–63.

Mayakovsky and Brik would also perform verses by David Burliuk, Sasha Chernyi, Mikhail Kuzmin, and other poets, not just "The Grey-Eyed King."[47] Moreover, the mongrelization of that poem was meant in part as a theoretical experiment: "A. Fevral'skii, who attended the Moscow recital where Mayakovsky publicly sang these lines to the tune of 'The Cocky Merchant,' later told [Eventov] what exactly preceded that episode: the speaker was demonstrating to the audience how unexpectedly a poetic text can be turned around when it is used as a bare rhythmical scheme without attention to its meaning."[48]

Parody, of course, was not a Futurist monopoly, geared only toward throwing the classics from the steamship of modernity. At the time, parody came to be understood by literary theorists as the prime mover of literary evolution in general. Contemporaneous with Kornei Chukovskii's article was Yuri Tynianov's pioneering formulation of a "theory of parody"[49] focused on Dostoevsky's spoofing of Gogol in the comic guise of Foma Opiskin—a treatment not much different from that which Mayakovsky dealt Akhmatova. The subversion of authoritarian literary systems (in particular, that of Gogol) through a parodic invasion by "other voices" (in particular, those of Dostoevsky's characters) was also to become central to the Bakhtinian school of thought.[50] In this context, Akhmatova's defensive reaction to Mayakovsky sounds rather monological (corroborating Bakhtin's view of poetry as opposed to the novel).

No less evident, on the other hand, are Akhmatova's efforts to overcome such one-sidedness. Relenting a little, she tells Eventov of her encounters and affinities with Mayakovsky. "I realized that in our first conversation, Anna Andreevna was not above playing games [*nemnozhko khitrila*]. . . . She knew perfectly well how much Mayakovsky treasured her name and poetry."[51] The same attraction / rejection was to be noted by Chukovskaia some fifteen years later. But this time around rejection won out—perhaps because of Akhmatova's growing concern for her own

[47] The list of poets futuristically mongrelized by Mayakovsky should also include Pushkin, as evidenced by the famous paraphrase in "The Jubilee Poem" ("Iubileinoe," 1924) from *Eugene Onegin*: "Kak eto / u vas / govarivala Ol'ga?.. // Da ne Ol'ga! / iz pis'ma / Onegina k Tat'iane. // —Deskat', / muzh u vas / durak / i staryi merin, // ia liubliu vas, / bud'te obiazatel'no moia, // ia seichas zhe / utrom dolzhen byt' uveren, // chto s vami dnem uvizhus' ia" ("How did your Olga used to say? Oh, no, not Olga—from Onegin's letter to Tatiana. Like, your husband is a fool and an old gelding, I love you, you absolutely must be mine. Right away in the morning, I should be certain to see you later in the day"), Vladimir Maiakovskii, *Polnoe sobranie sochinenii*, 13 vols. (Moscow: Khudozhestvennaia literatura, 1957), 6: 50.

[48] Eventov, "Ot Fontanki," 363.

[49] See Iu. Tynianov's 1921 article, "Dostoevskii i Gogol' (K teorii parodii)," in his *Poetika. Istoriia literatury. Kino* (Moscow: Nauka, 1977), 198–226.

[50] See, especially, S. G. Bocharov, "Perekhod ot Gogolia k Dostoevskomu," in his *O khudozhestvennykh mirakh* (Moscow: Sovetskaia Rossiia, 1985), 161–209.

[51] Eventov, "Ot Fontanki," 365.

"chariot,"[52] aggravated by her systematic official victimization, which culminated in 1946 but had been accumulating ever since Chukovskii's 1921 article.[53]

Akhmatova had refined formidable skills of psychological self-defense, of which the games she played with Eventov were but an innocent example: "Akhmatova, stung by most of the critical judgments, which *volens nolens* distorted her artistic image, made a point of regally ignoring Mayakovsky's rude attacks, considering them . . . extraliterary phenomena."[54] If such was her "real-life" reaction, an even higher level of sublimation was achieved in her art. "In her poetry she was more fair and positively balanced than . . . in her oral pronouncements. Poetry was where she was able to rise above the . . . 'all too human.' . . . In her 'commemorative' poems about Mayakovsky, whom she . . . perceived in a very complex way, and also about Pasternak and Tsvetaeva, she spoke of them casting aside all psychological and other overtones . . . in a voice of sublime affirmation and acknowledgement."[55]

Similar sublimation mechanisms informed an unexpected sequel to the story of the mongrelized "Grey-Eyed King." The actor Aleksei Batalov, who as a young man had observed Akhmatova during her postwar stays with his mother Nina Ol'shevskaia and her second husband Viktor Ardov on the "legendary Ordynka" Street in Moscow, remembers that, "Anna Andreevna let herself treat her most famous poems with irony. And this did not contradict a bit her . . . regality. . . . The most merciless public mockery of [her] poems took the form of a show. The guests whom she entertained in such a way . . . would freeze . . . as if in a bad dream. I can testify that Anna Andreevna herself . . . directed . . . this entire domestic entertainment. Of course, the story has a prehistory."[56]

According to Batalov, the prehistory was as follows. The Ardovs had befriended the returned émigré *chansonnier* Aleksandr Vertinskii and once arranged a surprise performance in his honor, which included Batalov's parody of him—to his sheer pleasure.

> Gradually I adjusted so well to his gestures and intonations that I could easily replace the text. . . . An especially incongruous and funny effect was

---

[52] Also, by the end of the 1950s the association with Mayakovsky may no longer have had any political use for Akhmatova.

[53] "To the end of her life—and hardly in fairness—Akhmatova held that precisely this article was the source of almost all her further misfortunes" (Vilenkin, *V sto pervom zerkale*, 45); see also Kovalenko, "Akmatova i Maiakovskii," 171, and M. Budyko, "Rasskazy Akhmatovoi," in *OAA*, 465.

[54] Kovalenko, "Akmatova i Maiakovskii," 174.

[55] D. Maksimov, "Ob Anne Akhmatovoi, kakoi pomniu," in *VAA*, 124.

[56] Aleksei Batalov, "Riadom s Akhmatovoi," in *VAA*, 563–64.

achieved when I sang the poems of Mayakovsky in the style of [Vertinskii's] salon *romans*. Anna Andreevna time and again made me repeat these parodies. . . . Once, in the presence of many guests . . . she said: "Alesha, do you . . . remember what Aleksandr Nikolaevich [Vertinskii] sings to my verses?" . . . I tried to beg off the dangerous act. "No matter," she smiled, ". . . you may use some others, the way you take from Mayakovsky." . . .

[E]ven adapting Mayakovsky would not sound as unnatural and unmasking as in the case of Akhmatova, because . . . Akhmatova's pointedly feminine confessions and emotions, when combined with the gestures and the strictly masculine position of Vertinskii, would border on clowning. . . . To help me . . . Anna Andreevna started prompting a choice of her poems. Now I felt completely confused—they were lines from her best . . . lyrics. . . . In such moments Akhmatova's eyes, despite her regally calm posture, would light up with a slyly mischievous stubbornness and she seemed ready to accept any rules of the game. Prompting, like an experienced conspirator, every word, she finally made me sing the first lines, and the song gradually acquired its funny form. . . .

Akhmatova publicly organized and staged this parodic act, with which she would often "treat" new guests. Many of them, I believe, still have not forgiven me for what I did to Akhmatova's lyrics . . . unaware of the origins of this parody [and] that sly wisdom and inner freedom with which Akhmatova dealt with any works of art, including her own.[57]

Similar scenes, with Akhmatova's friend the actress Faina Ranevskaia in place of Batalov, are described by Nataliia Il'ina:

> To an oriental tune of her own invention, rolling her eyes and twisting her arms, Ranevskaia sang: "You don't love me, don't want to look my way. . . ." God Almighty! . . . In the author's presence these lines are spoofed, mocked! Yet we were shaking with laughter—both the song's author and I. . . . Akhmatova, wiping her eyes . . . would beseech: "Faina! Now, 'The Seamstress.' . . . Akhmatova laughed herself to tears. I also wept. But not only out of laughter. Out of amazement and admiration. Ranevskaia called Akhmatova "rabbi." . . . I started calling her jokingly "ma'am." . . . This mixture of reverence and familiarity . . . gave our relationship a new tinge. I would ask: . . . "Don't you think, ma'am, that you are simply a genius?" . . . "Don't flatter me, I don't like it, as the merchant in Ostrovsky used to say."[58]

The secret dynamics of these self-therapeutic psychodramas becomes clear once their deeper origins are uncovered. The way Akhmatova played the Mayakovsky–Vertinskii card, artfully directing others to rehearse and enact it but not divulging to them its *real* "prehistory"—the

[57] Batalov, "Riadom," 565–66.
[58] Nataliia Il'ina, "Anna Akhmatova, kakoi ia ee videla," in *VAA*, 575.

1920s' traumas—is very informative. It demonstrates her manipulative expertise at remaining the only one who knows what the show is all about and who pulls the strings from behind the scenes. The heart of the matter concerns the apparently marginal presence of the principal villain: Mayakovsky. By performing his texts Vertinskii-style in the presence of Vertinskii himself and with his explicit approval, Batalov unwittingly achieves two effects crucial to Akhmatova's game. Batalov both avenges her—pours balm over her still-festering wound, and suggests to her a felicitous directorial find—the staging of a parody of herself in her presence and thus definitively laying to rest the problem of her vulnerability to humor.

That the parodic acts of Batalov and Ranevskaia stage-managed by Akhmatova were power moves on her part—*tours de force* in the full sense of the word—was not completely lost on the participants. Batalov goes on to say that, "In such . . . barbaric entertainments . . . I always glimpse a certain manifestation of a hidden force, of the clarity of the author's view of the world and her place in it. . . . Anna Andreevna never fenced in her territory, never exempted either herself or her poetry from the surrounding life."[59] The observation about "barbarism" is corroborated by Il'ina's reference to a "mixture of reverence and familiarity," as well as the stylistics of her own discourse, with its "ma'am" and "genius." This is echoed by the renowned scholar V. V. Ivanov: "Akhmatova was rumored to like the way [Isidor] Shtok treated her, calling her 'old woman' to her face and telling her only funny stories. . . . I heard about parties that Akhmatova attended where the guests in their verbal incontinence went pretty far down the road of Bakhtinian carnival."[60]

Akhmatova had not always possessed such a readiness to serve as the butt of ridicule—consider the long time it took her to cope with Mayakovsky's antics. A similar observation, this time "in the perspective of everyday life" (*v rakurse byta*), was made by her friend the literary scholar and translator S. V. Shervinskii: "One day [in 1936] . . . walking on a steep riverbank, she stumbled; for a moment, a shadow of fear crossed her face, but I realized that Akhmatova was frightened by the prospect not of falling but of looking ridiculous. That was a possibility she could not allow."[61] Akhmatova's constant preoccupation with the impression produced by her poetry and person is well attested by memoirists. Could her attitude towards laughter at her expense have undergone such an effective change by the time of the postwar carnivals? To be sure, Akhmatova

---

[59] Batalov, "Riadom," 566.

[60] V. V. Ivanov (who has written professionally on Bakhtin and on carnival), "Besedy s Annoi Akhmatovoi," in *VAA*, 479.

[61] S. V. Shervinskii, "Anna Akhmatova v rakurse byta," 282.

now did have the humor aimed at herself, but she designed the Ordynka happenings in such a way that the deflation of her sublime image would only enhance its "regality": "This majestic woman, who knew how to petrify those in her presence, had a perfect pitch for humor, and the principal attribute of such a pitch is . . . the ability . . . to see oneself in a comic light."[62] This, however, was by no means an unexpected, independent laughter coming from the outside and threatening to actually subvert her greatness the way Mayakovsky's mockery once had. On the contrary, the mockery was scripted and directed by Akhmatova herself. Having painstakingly reproduced all the aspects of the traumatic situation—singing to an incongruous tune, disrespectful familiarity, inversion of gender roles, collective laughter—she made a point of changing only one, but decisive, aspect of it: she assumed complete control of the event.

One is reminded of Chukovskaia's account of another occasion: "Anna Andreevna sat grandly in the middle of the couch and majestically presided over the wisecracks."[63] What better way to take the sting out of the debasing spoofs of her poetry than by "presiding over" their replays? A more sinister parallel can be drawn with the truly regal carnival direction in the color sequence of Sergei Eisenstein's *Ivan the Terrible* (which segues into the murder of the would-be pretender to the throne, Prince Vladimir Staritskii)—and with its real-life prototype: Stalin's grotesquely "humorous" treatment of the victims of his carnivalized purges.[64]

Such usurpations of carnival do demonstrate the strength of their organizers, not in the sense of openness to the liberating play of laughter but rather in the sense of its power-oriented manipulation within the bounds of a secured territory. This refutes Batalov's claim about Akhmatova's lack of territoriality.[65] As for humor, under such duress, it inevitably undergoes a mutation. If successful, it acquires self-complacent and even barbaric overtones; if not, it turns subversively against the would-be potentate. Indeed, in her later years Akhmatova could be blinded by her semiofficial fame.

> When reading, one was expected to . . . exclaim in reaction. . . . The newspaper item was supposed to elicit either approbation or indignation. I occa-

---

[62] Il'ina, "Anna Akhmatova," 573; for more detail on Akhmatova's intimidating presence, see Zholkovskii, "Strakh."

[63] Chukovskaia, *Zapiski*, 2: 15.

[64] See Alexander Zholkovsky, "Eisenstein's Poetics: Dialogical or Totalitarian?" in *Laboratory of Dreams: The Russian Avant-Garde and Cultural Experiment*, ed. John E. Bowlt and Olga Matich (Stanford: Stanford University Press, 1992), 249–51.

[65] On Akhmatova's treatment of the issue of "boundaries" in a 1915 poem, see Alexander Zholkovsky, "To Cross or Not to Cross: Akhmatova's 'Sacred Boundary,' " in *Approaches to Poetry: Some Aspects of Textuality, Intertextuality and Intermediality*, ed. Janos Petofi and Terry Olivi (Berlin: Walter de Gruyter, 1994), 248–64.

sionally messed up. I would exude approval, but indignation was expected because . . . of something Anna Andreevna did not like. . . . So, here I am, en-
thusing, and from her face and angrily narrowing eyes I can see that I'm out
of sync. I try to realign myself as I go, hoping . . . for a hint as to what exactly
I should be indignant about. . . . And she, who could see ten feet below the
ground, she, the wisest, the omniscient . . . she stopped sensing falsehood![66]

One is tempted to conclude, charitably, that fame and power had finally
succeeded in corrupting the aged martyr-poet. But then, a similar narcissistic lack of detachment was evident to Kornei Chukovskii almost half a
century earlier.[67]

Akhmatova's attempts to exorcise parody by presiding over it herself
may have had a literary source in her avowed all-purpose mentor and
model: Aleksandr Pushkin. In his "little tragedy" *Mozart and Salieri*
(Motsart i Sal'eri, 1830), there is an episode in which Mozart brings a
blind street fiddler, overheard by him massacring his music, in order to
share this campy pleasure with Salieri. Pushkin's Mozart is true to his historical prototype, who had included in *Don Giovanni* a fragment from *The
Marriage of Figaro* travestied by the primitive performance of invited musi-
cians.[68] However, Pushkin's (somewhat less historical) Salieri fails to find
this funny: he does not "feel like laughing, when a despicable clown /
Dishonors with his parody [an] Alighieri."[69]

Akhmatova knew her Pushkin well, including the *Little Tragedies*
(Malen'kie tragedii, 1830),[70] and this episode could well have been on her

---

[66] Il'ina, "Anna Akhmatova," 592.

[67] On March 26, 1922, he wrote in his diary about visiting her:

> With the gesture of a hostess entertaining an important guest she gave me . . . a mag-
> azine . . . "They really berate me! . . . This Gollerbakh . . . look what he writes about
> me. . . . It turns out that Akhmatova's maiden name is Gorenko!! How dare he?" . . .
> One could sense that here was the core passion of her life. . . . "What a fool! . . . As a
> schoolgirl I bought doughnuts in their bakery—it doesn't follow from this that he can
> call me . . . Gorenko."
> To test my impression, I told her . . . that in my Studio there was a split . . . : some are
> for, others against [her]. "And, you know, among the opponents there are sensitive
> and clever people. . . ." This excited Akhmatova so much that she felt she had to affect
> indifference, started looking into the mirror, arranged her bangs, and said in a worldly
> manner: "Very interesting, very! Bring me . . . this paper."
> I felt a terrible pity for this hard-living woman. She has somehow completely con-
> centrated on herself, on her fame—and barely lives through anything else." (Kornei
> Chukovskii, *Dnevnik 1901–1929* [Moscow: Sovetskii pisatel', 1991], 201–2)

[68] On Pushkin's use of Mozartian self-quoting, see Boris Gasparov, "Ty, Motsart, nedostoin
sam sebia," in *Vremennik pushkinskoi komissii. 1974* (Leningrad: Nauka, 1977), 115–23; on
Mozart's own similar games, see Boris Kats, "Iz Motsarta nam chto-nibud'," in *Vremennik
pushkinskoi komissii. 1979* (Leningrad: Nauka, 1982), 120–24.

[69] I.e., Dante (who, incidentally, was another of Akhmatova's idols); see Pushkin, *Polnoe sobranie*, 5: 308.

[70] See, for instance, her 1947 article, "*Kamennyi gost'* Pushkina," in her *Sochineniia*, 2:
257–74; for an astute analysis of Akhmatova's reading of her own constructed self and life-

mind as she staged the Ordynka parodies of herself. Fancying herself a Mozart, she did manage to shed at least some "Salierisms." For instance, Chukovskaia's typically "Salierian" assumption about the artist's physical suffering when exposed to a mongrelization of his / her work hardly captures the essence of Akhmatova's reaction, which was rooted not so much in the aesthetic sphere but rather in that of power politics. Similarly, it was probably Il'ina's initiative to play Salieri to Akhmatova's Mozart with her "you-are-a-genius" adulation,[71] although Akhmatova's coy encouragement is not irrelevant.

And yet, distance herself as she would from Salieri, Akhmatova could not boast the blithely unconcerned self-sufficiency of Pushkin's Mozart. Her "obedient vassals" Batalov and Ranevskaia do not qualify for the role of a street fiddler messing up the maestro's work in a random pub. Akhmatova's control of the performance is reminiscent if not of Salieri then of another quasi-Salierian Pushkin character: Silvio, who insists in "The Shot" ("Vystrel," 1830) on exercising vengeful power over his "Mozartian" rival (Count B***) even as he attains his personal best in letting him go.[72]

In summing up the differences between the aesthetic credos of Pushkin's Mozart and Salieri, a Pushkin scholar writes that, "The tragedy shows clearly what Salieri does *not* have: boldness and freedom, the unpredictability . . . of a genius, his unboundedness by the artificial barriers of the 'low' and the 'high,' the 'proper' and the 'improper,' that divine play . . . that lets him find material for his art everywhere. To Salieri, this creative freedom and unboundedness look like frivolity and lack of discrimination . . . humiliating ease and irrationality."[73] This sounds strikingly similar to Akhmatova's jealous view of Pasternak's brand of creativity, as reported by her younger friend and secretary, the poet and critic Anatoly Nayman:[74]

---

text into Pushkin's *Stone Guest*, see Stephanie Sandler, "The Stone Ghost: Akhmatova, Pushkin, and Don Juan," in *Stanford Slavic Studies*, vol. 4, no. 2 (*Literature, Culture, and Society in the Modern Age: In Honor of Joseph Frank*, part 2) (Stanford: Stanford University Press, 1992), 3–49. Akhmatova's special interest in Pushkin's Salieri is evidenced by one of her "Northern Elegies," variously numbered Third and Fifth: "Menia, kak reku . . ." ("Me, like a river . . ."). Stylistically and metrically this autobiographical self-portrait in blank iambic pentameter is patterned on Salieri's opening soliloquy, with which it also shares the more specific motifs of "an existential and creative turn" and "creative envy"; see Anna Akhmatova, *Sochineniia* (Paris: YMCA-Press, 1983), 3: 79–80, and Pushkin, *Polnoe sobranie* (Leningrad, 1978), 5: 306–7.

[71] See his lines: "Ty, Mozart, bog, i sam togo ne znaesh'; / Ia znaiu, ia" ("You, Mozart, are a god, and you don't know it yourself. I know, I [do]"), Pushkin, *Polnoe sobranie*, 5: 310.

[72] Silvio was also very important for Dostoevsky (see Paul Debreczeny, *The Other Pushkin: A Study of Alexander Pushkin's Prose Fiction* [Stanford: Stanford University Press, 1983], 114–19), who, in turn, was "number one" writer for Akhmatova (about which presently).

[73] B. Gasparov, "Ty, Motsart," 122.

[74] To be sure, there is always the chance that Nayman had read Boris Gasparov.

[H]er . . . principles . . . set boundaries to the freedom and unpredictability of [her] writing, and thus to [her] genius. "An everlasting childhood is his prize,"[75] she had written of this aspect of Pasternak's gifts, with admiration but also condescension, and not without a hint of sarcasm, as if to say, "Enough is enough." His poems bubbled over the edge of an Acmeistically structured universe . . . ; his lapses of taste . . . which she did not forgive him for. . . . In short, he "put himself above art," as Chukovskaia records her saying. . . . I [once] said to her that, dispensing with flattery, Akhmatova was not a genius but some kind of *anti-genius*. She listened to this without pleasure.[76]

Uncannily, Akhmatova's remark about "putting oneself above art" echoes Salieri's insistence on the uselessness for "art" of Mozart's cherub-like soaring to ever-new artistic heights.[77]

The Stalin Metaphor

We have seen Akhmatova pressing her consummate self-presentation skills—narrative, directorial, histrionic—in the service of her carefully constructed persona: ostensibly weak, fragile, and victimized but actually strong, manipulative, and powerful. Even as she gets plaudits for self-deprecation and openness to ridicule, she is, in fact, busy secretly performing an aggressive-defensive exorcism of that same laughter. Are these, however, sufficient grounds for interpreting her strategies in a "Stalinist" key? Why not try reading Akhmatova as an old-world autocratic *barynia*, a vainglorious *femme fatale*, a limelight-crazy bohemian star, or in some other way that would plausibly naturalize the observed tendencies without bringing up the ultimate charge?

Akhmatova can probably be read as any and all of the above lesser despots, but it seems more productive to construe her personality and strategies of survival as part and parcel of the culture of her totalitarian times. Warring parties tend to develop mutual affinities. In the so-called "Stockholm syndrome," hostages adopt the value system of their captors. The *Zeitgeist* principle presupposes a certain cultural unity of the mutually opposing groups. Thus, Ovid, despite being banished by Augustus from Rome and dying in exile, ended up being a great representative of the Augustan epoch. Or, to consider a case closer to home:

[75] See Akhmatova's 1936 poem "Boris Pasternak" (*Sochineniia*, [1967], 1: 234–35), with the line: "He has been awarded some sort of eternal childhood" ("On nagrazhden kakim-to vechnym detstvom").

[76] Nayman, 212–13.

[77] See Salieri's lines: "What's the use if Mozart lives on and achieves new heights? Will he thus elevate art?" ("Chto pol'zy, esli Motsart budet zhiv / I novoi vysoty eshche dostignet? / Podymet li on tem iskusstvo?"), Pushkin, *Polnoe sobranie,* 5: 310.

Bakhtinian polyphonism is usually perceived as a protest against the monologism . . . of Stalinist ideology. . . . But Bakhtin insists precisely on the totality of the carnival, whose point is the dissolution of the autonomy of the human body and existence. . . . Bakhtin is highly antipathetic to liberal and democratic values. . . . His portrayals of carnival are born of the experience of the Revolution and the atmosphere of Stalinist terror. . . . Yet his purpose was by no means their critique . . . but rather their theoretical justification as an eternal ritual act. . . . To be sure, Bakhtin was not a Stalinist. But he was still less of an anti-Stalinist. . . . A major theme of Russian culture at that time was the aesthetic justification of the epoch. . . . The totalitarian style of the 1930s' mentality is also . . . represented by those, who, while not sharing the Apollonian illusions of worldly power, were nonetheless ready for the Dionysian sacrifice.[78]

Akhmatova herself would hardly have settled for the role of a *barynia*, superstar, *femme fatale*, or some other similarly modest figure. "Anna of all Russia"[79] set her sights higher. She perceived and narrated herself as an actor on a world-size stage, locked in a direct and mortal combat with Stalin the supreme villain, and this fateful match-up kept her charismatic batteries charged. Accordingly, she made sweeping, prescriptive pronouncements as someone invested with ultimate ideological and cultural authority. She preferred, "clearcut formulation[s]: The best city in the world [is] Paris, the best country in the world, Italy";[80] "Dostoevsky is most important to me [*samyi glavnyi*]. In general, he is the most important."[81] Akhmatova's predilection for "the most, the best, the number one" values, which went back to her early years, when it was found unacceptable by Blok,[82] was to resonate later in paradoxical unison with the Stalinist appointment of ideologically correct icons, one per cultural slot, mirroring the strict hierarchical nomenclature of Stalin's command system in every sphere. In actual life, the establishment of such a simplified chain of authority was facilitated by the physical elimination of the competition through purges and the moral cleansing of those beyond historical or ge-

---

[78] Boris Grois, "Mezhdu Stalinym i Dionisom," *Sintaksis*, no. 25 (1989), 94–97; see also Boris Groys, "Nietzsche's Influence on the Non-official Culture of the 1930s," in *Nietzsche and Soviet Culture: Ally and Adversary*, ed. Bernice Rosenthal (New York: Cambridge University Press, 1994), 367–89.

[79] This appellation, going back to the ninth of Marina Tsvetaeva's "Verses to Akhmatova" ("Stikhi k Akhmatovoi," 1916), has been used as the title of a recent hagio-biography: Igor' Losievskii, *Anna vseia Rusi: Zhizneopisanie Anny Akhmatovoi* (Kharkov: Oko, 1996).

[80] Mikhail Ardov, "Legendarnaia Ordynka," in *Chistye prudy. Al'manakh*, no. 4 (Moscow: Moskovskii rabochii, 1990), 675.

[81] Nataliia Roskina, "Good-by Again," in *AAHC*, 187.

[82] "I will never accept [*nikogda ne pereidu cherez*] your '*vovse* ne znala,' u '*samogo* moria,' '*samyi* nezhnyi' . . . postoiannye '*sovsem*' " (Aleksander Blok, in *VAA*, 43). Incidentally, this obsession with superlatives belies the allegedly "low-key" image of Akhmatova, opposed by Chukovskii to the "loud-mouthed" Mayakovsky.

ographical reach through defamation. Ironically—and tragically, the same processes led to the elevation of Akhmatova, an unpurged survivor who came to accumulate, inherit, and stand for the literary legacy of an entire era.[83]

Akhmatova's amalgam of fear, defensiveness, and domineering is a characteristic instance of siege mentality—so typical of Stalin, his regime, and the entire "socialist camp." Akhmatova the "iron lady"[84] manifested in a grand way the defensive strategies developed by the average *homo Sovieticus* under the regime's enormous pressure. Hence the sympathetic chord struck among her contemporaries by her eminently closed personality: her cult of silence and other means of suppressing information (viz., her refusal to take down her poems, reluctance to write letters, and destruction of existing correspondence, in particular, that with her ex-fiancé V. G. Garshin)[85] and her replacement of her "real" person with the invented, narrated, and staged selves devised to hide her "iron" core beneath outward fragility.[86]

The constructed quality of Akhmatova's personality and the dynamics of her "power through weakness" were shrewdly discerned by her friend and mentor, the poet N. V. Nedobrovo, who wrote in his 1915 review of her book of poetry *Rosary* (Chetki):

> [A] very strong book of power-full [*vlastnyi*] verses . . . a desire to imprint oneself on the beloved, somewhat coercive [or even rapist: *nasil'nicheskii*] . . . an unrequited love . . . which by its ability all of a sudden to disappear instantly induces the suspicion of inventedness. . . . Akhmatova's very voice . . . displays a lyrical soul that is harsh rather than too soft, cruel rather than tearful, and obviously domineering rather than oppressed. . . . An unsuspecting observer . . . has no idea that were these very same pathetic holy fools . . . to return to the world, they would walk with their iron feet over his living worldly man's body; then he would discover the cruel power . . . of the capricious ones . . . who had shed tears over trifles.[87]

---

[83] K. Chukovskii, *Dnevnik*, 219; Nayman, 211–12.

[84] In response to an awed junior contemporary's compliment, "You all seem as though you are made of iron," she quipped: "Those not made of iron perished long ago" (Budyko, 499).

[85] See Zholkovsky, "Scripts."

[86] A memoirist remembered her saying about an old *babushka*'s impression of her: "Poor old thing! She pities me so! . . . She thinks that I am a weakling. She has no idea that I am a tank!" (V. G. Admoni, "Znakomstvo i druzhba," in *VAA*, 342). In connection with "strength through weakness," worth note are the manifold parallels with the ostensibly "modest" and "disembodied" appearances assumed by Soviet leaders, as discussed in Aleksander M. Etkind's "Psychological Culture," in *Russian Culture at the Crossroads: Paradoxes of Postcommunist Consciousness*, ed. Dmitri N. Shalin (Boulder, Colo.: Westview Press, 1996), 112–13.

[87] See N. V. Nedobrovo, "Anna Akhmatova," in Akhmatova, *Sochineniia*, 3: 474, 487–89.

Akhmatova's "intimidating cruelty" sensed by Nedobrovo did materialize later, in the way she struck awe in the hearts of her friends, admirers, and the wider public and would not hesitate to cut off—making them virtually "unpersons," Orwellian-style—her acquaintances, including Chukovskaia.

The imperious, indeed, "imperial," image that she liked to project and that others chose to validate by playing along, and the bureaucratic Soviet clichés that she was wont to use quasi-ironically linked her to the surrounding power-ridden cultural atmosphere. The "Russian-imperial" overtones of her image, far from contradicting her "Stalinist" affinities, actually reinforced them. Her programmatic conservatism—emphasis on memory, love of marble monuments, her own statuesque figure and personality, her dogmatic reliance on classical quotations,[88] her prescriptive cultural rankings (of books, artists, cities, pastimes),[89] the growing traditionalism of her versification[90]—all these turned out to be profoundly in tune with the neo-imperial Stalinist "Culture Two" (in the sense of Vladimir Papernyi's seminal book).[91]

Lydia Chukovskaia, in trying to puzzle out the arbitrary humiliation and excommunication to which she, Akhmatova's devoted younger friend, helper, and chronicler of many years, was subjected by Akhmatova in Tashkent in 1942 (the split lasted through 1952), sketched the following scenario: "As far as I understand it now, Anna Andreevna did not want to break up with me definitively; she wanted to provoke my question: 'Why are you angry with me?' Then she would have explained to me my guilt, I would have apologized, she would have magnanimously forgiven me. . . . But my conscience did not bother me, I could find no cause for guilt."[92]

[88] See Kelly, "Anna Akhmatova," 209, 220.

[89] For an extensive list of such dogmatic formulations by Akhmatova, see Zholkovskii, "Strakh," 135–36.

[90] See Mikhail Gasparov, "The Evolution of Akhmatova's Verse," in *Anna Akhmatova 1889–1989: Papers from the Akhmatova Centennial Conference, June 1989*, ed. Sonia Ketchian (Oakland, Calif.: Berkeley Slavic Specialties, 1993), 68–74.

[91] See Vladimir Papernyi, *Kul'tura Dva* (Ann Arbor: Ardis, 1985).

[92] Chukovskaia, *Zapiski*, 2: xvi. Additional light has been shed on the matter by a recent communication from Mikhail Meilakh, who has known both parties. In a letter to me (in the fall of 1996, undated, ending with a stipulation that, in quoting it, I should mention his reservations regarding some of my "interpretations of Akhmatova's behaviorism"), he reports what he had heard from Chukovskaia:

> In Tashkent . . . the ladies in waiting . . . the "Akhmatissas," started, in Akhmatova's presence, a game: each one had to state what she loved Akhmatova for. . . . Akhmatova listened benevolently to the ladies' pretentious compliments; when the turn of Chukovskaia, who could not stand the game, came, she simply said: "For the poetry," to a mocking response from the ladies; Akhmatova did not defend her, to say the least. Lydia Korneevna got up, left, and never visited Akhmatova in [the next] ten years. . . . Both then and later she blamed Akhmatova and always insisted on this. . . . [But] in her diaries [i. e., in Chukovskaia, *Zapiski*, vol. 2] she passed in silence over the reasons for the quarrel, which makes her attitude even more sympathetic [to us].

Chukovskaia's insightful conjecture may be due to the subliminal familiarity of this psychological script. The sadistic silent treatment by which the would-be infallible senior partner forces the junior one not only to submit to her will but masochistically to "understand" her own guilt and the senior's righteousness underlies a well-known plot by Akhmatova's "number one" writer: Dostoevsky's "The Gentle Spirit" ("Krotkaia," 1877). This is hardly a coincidence. According to an American scholar, in her poem "Prehistory," "Akhmatova is portraying herself as Dostoevskii's literary heir. The paternal legacy is . . . a gift associated with cruelty. . . . Cruelty . . . has been associated with Dostoevskii's art since . . . N. K. Mikhailovskii's . . . Zhestokii talant . . . (1882). It was also a quality ascribed to Akhmatova's lyric talents by N. V. Nedobrovo."[93]

To expand the analogy, one could complement "cruelty" with "miracle, mystery, and authority," which constituted the tools of power prized by *The Brothers Karamazov*'s Grand Inquisitor and were also among Akhmatova's favorite poetic motifs and self-fashioning strategies. Indeed, the husband character in "The Gentle Spirit" is a close relation of Dostoevsky's "Grand-Inquisitorial" types—and of their progeny in the subsequent dystopian literature and real-life totalitarian dystopias with their insistence on rituals of recanting, self-criticism, and reeducation. In the

---

Chukovskaia's silence has now been in part broken in the Appendix to vol. 1 of the latest edition of her diaries: Lidiia Chukovskaia, *Zapiski ob Anne Akhmatovoi*, 3 vols. (Moscow: Soglasie, 1997), 1: 341–521, which includes also a commentary and additional quotations from Chukovskaia's notebooks by one of the volume's editors, her daughter Elena ("Liusha") Chukovskaia (516–21). These long-concealed and heavily self-censored notes (dating back to 1942 as well as later years) paint a picture of the diarist's bitter rivalry with Akhmatova's new "court," headed by the renowned actress (and probably Akhmatova's lover at the time) Faina Ranevskaia, whom Chukovskaia portrays as a corrupt and debauched ("sovershenno rastlennaia," 505) plotter and drunkard, while harshly accusing Akhmatova herself of connivance, mercilessness, and betrayal.

This entire story calls for further study, especially given the repeated repression of details and motives by the diarist, who is desperately at a loss whether to report, forgive, or forget and excise the damning evidence about her suddenly fallible and fallen idol:

"It would have been easier for me to be wrong than to see her—unkind, unfair, mistaken, not understanding" (1943; 516; cf. already in the earlier version: "I viscerally [*krovno*] wanted for me, not her, to turn out to be guilty, for an implicit trust in her absolute nobility was my best possession [*dostoianie*]," Chukovskaia, *Zapiski*, 2: xvii). "I continue reading my Tashkent diary. So far I do not see . . . how or whether I should touch upon the quarrel and the bad, unattractive [*nekrasivye*] features of AA's life" (1998; 517). "I'm not up to delving into the Tashkent horrors—the most awful period of my life since 1937 [!]—the disloyalties, betrayals, thieving . . . the unseemly, un-noble behavior of AA" (1982; 518). "There is a lot there [in the diaries] that is unnecessary [*lishnego*], which ought to be destroyed" (1993; 510). "I was reading my Tashkent diaries. AA looks so [bad] there that I'm cutting [*vyrezyvaiu*] a lot. . . . It can't be left as is" (1993; 520). Comments Elena Chukovskaia: "This is the last entry in L. K.'s diaries regarding the Tashkent notebooks. She managed to destroy certain words, lines, pages, but did not have the time to prepare her notes for publication. She clearly did not want to write about that time" (1996; 520).

[93] See Susan Amert, *In a Shattered Mirror: The Later Poetry of Anna Akhmatova* (Stanford: Stanford University Press, 1992), 90.

story, the husband's treatment of his wife results from his passing on to her the victimization to which he himself had been subjected earlier in life. Similarly, Akhmatova's "purging" of Chukovskaia (and some others) can be read as replicating her own persecution at the hands of Stalin and his henchmen.[94]

To be sure, the legitimacy of the "Stalinist" metaphor is among the many questions raised by my unorthodox interpretation of Akhmatova's life-text. But a metaphor is not an equation, and Stalin remains the ultimate paragon of totalitarian power and thus a useful point of reference. While it is obvious that Akhmatova (whose practical power was negligible and ethical-political stance well-nigh irreproachable) cannot be compared with Stalin in terms of actual mass victimization, the metaphor does hold on its proper, figurative level. In fact, in the domain of literary and personal reputations, where Akhmatova did wield considerable moral authority, she is known to have resorted to ostracism and character assassination.

Another meta-interpretational issue concerns the comparative validity of the various testimonies used in piecing together Akhmatova's totalitarian image. Some of the sources could be questioned as suspected or even proven secret police informers, others as envious literary or personal rivals, still others as disaffected former friends / helpers, squirming victims of her imperious treatment, traders in second- and third-hand gossip, and so on and so forth. It stands to reason, however, that such a discriminating approach should follow, not precede, the sketching of a broad integral picture based on the striking mutual agreement among the otherwise highly diverse witnesses. Their unanimity is evidence if not of the accuracy of the emerging individual portrait, then certainly of its collective acceptance and desirability. The stories that are told and retold about Akhmatova clearly conform to a commonly cherished model of "awesome authority."[95] In this, they are not so different from those told about Stalin by generations of Soviet people, including intellectuals and dissidents, in the mixed spirit of fear and fascination.[96]

Akhmatova's strategies of resistance and survival through an obverse replication of the regnant power structure were not exceptional. One analog is Alexander Solzhenitsyn, the once- and ever-hardened *zek* (Gulag prisoner) in whom Akhmatova clearly saw a kindred soul: his indomitable

[94] For Stalin, too, Dostoevsky was a "number one," except that he showed his appreciation by effectively silencing the author of *Devils* out of official literary history. In Stalin's twilight (and my dawning) years, Dostoevsky was not even taught in Soviet high schools; Akhmatova was—as the culprit of the 1946 attacks.

[95] "Awesome," rather than "Terrible," might be a more accurate English rendering of the epithet *Groznyi* in the sobriquet of Tsar Ivan IV.

[96] For a reasoned collection of such jokes, see Iurii Borev, *Staliniada* (Moscow: Sovetskii pisatel', 1990).

opposition to the regime was sustained by his hidden, at least for a time, authoritarian core. Other strategic options available to and explored by Akhmatova's great contemporaries included such scenarios as: enthusiasm / disappointment / suicide (Mayakovsky), enthusiasm / collaboration / Aesopian critique / silence (Eisenstein), defiance / submission / suicide (Tsvetaeva), defiance / exile / collaboration / purging (Mandelstam).[97]

A tellingly different existential course is instanced by the constructed literary and personal self of Akhmatova's fellow survivor and poetic rival Boris Pasternak. Reifying his master trope "my sister—life,"[98] Pasternak fashioned a program of "fraternization" with women, friends, adversaries, and political realities, which, however, could be practiced only up to a point, beyond which it proved to be but a utopian metaphor and had to be discarded in favor of another similar program-metaphor.[99] This strategy can be seen to underlie Pasternak's entire tortuous journey from a rather unreserved acceptance of the Revolution (especially, that of February 1917) to an ambiguous, partly Aesopian collaboration in the 1920s to a period of ecstatic, if somewhat self-imposed pro-Stalinism in the early '30s and eventually to a more or less open rupture with the Soviet system and a clinging to (Russian Orthodox) Christianity in the '50s.

The affinities among these various life plans show how essentially limited were the available scenarios, overdetermined by both the objective realities of Stalinism and the subjective attitudes inherited from the culture of the Silver Age and from the nineteenth-century "populist" tradition. Against this background, Akhmatova stands out as an ultimate paradox of resistance–cum–replication. The indisputable force of her poetry and persona lays a strong claim on a lasting place in the Russian literary canon—as perhaps the most durable specimen of the siege culture of her time.

---

[97] See Freidin, *A Coat*, and M. L. Gasparov, *O. Mandel'shtam: Grazhdanskaia lirika 1937 goda* (Moscow: RGGU, 1996).

[98] For more detail, see A. K. Zholkovskii, "O zaglavnom trope knigi 'Sestra moia—zhizn'," " in *Stanford Slavic Studies*, vol. 21 (*Poetry and Revolution: Boris Pasternak's "My Sister Life,"* ed. Lazar Fleishman) (Stanford: Stanford University Press, 1999), 26–65; for a comparative analysis of the "survivalist" component in the self-fashioning strategies of Anna Akhmatova, Boris Pasternak, and Mikhail Zoshchenko, see A. K. Zholkovskii, "K pereosmysleniiu kanona: sovetskie klassiki-nonkonformisty v postsovetskoi perspektive," *Novoe literaturnoe obozrenie*, no. 29 (1998): 55–68.

[99] See B. M. Gasparov, " 'Gradus ad Parnassum' (Samosovershenstvovanie kak kategoriia tvorcheskogo mira Pasternaka)," in *"Byt' znamenitym nekrasivo . . .": Pasternakovskie chteniia*, no. 1, ed. I. Iu. Podgaetskaia et al. (Moscow: Nasledie, 1992), 110–35.

CHAPTER THREE

Writing the Self in the Time of Terror: Alexander Afinogenov's Diary of 1937

JOCHEN HELLBECK

At an extraordinary meeting of the Moscow playwrights' association convened on April 27, 1937, two of its most prominent members, Vladimir Kirshon and Alexander Afinogenov, were accused of having engaged in a Trotskyist conspiracy against the Soviet system. Kirshon's and Afinogenov's refutations of these charges were not accepted by their fellow writers, and both were expelled from the Party a few weeks later. Kirshon was arrested, and he died in 1938. Afinogenov remained free for the time being; shunned by most of his former colleagues, he retired to his dacha in the writers' colony of Peredelkino, where he lived in near-total seclusion. While remaining uncertain of his fate and observing the waves of arrests that engulfed the residents of Peredelkino, Afinogenov kept a voluminous diary. In fascinating detail, the diary shows how the playwright grappled with the reason he had become a target of the terror campaign and what motivated the purge policies as a whole.

On the basis of Afinogenov's diary, this essay seeks to introduce an understanding of the Stalinist purges that departs from the prevailing views of the Terror as either an expression of naked state power applied against Soviet society or an arbitrary process, defying rational explanation.[1] The

Many of my ideas on the Stalinist terror have crystallized in conversations with Igal Halfin and Peter Holquist, and I gratefully acknowledge their support. I also thank the participants of the Maryland Workshop on New Approaches to Russian History for their comments and suggestions. Support for the writing of this article was provided by the Michigan Society of Fellows.

[1] The former view, which goes back to the old totalitarian paradigm, is maintained by Robert Conquest, *The Great Terror: Stalin's Purge of the Thirties* (New York: Macmillan, 1973), and Robert Tucker, *Stalin in Power: The Revolution from Above, 1928–1941* (New York: W. W.

issue that most preoccupied Afinogenov throughout the purge period was himself. The Party's vigilance campaign confronted him with the question of who he was and whether he could change. Was he a Bolshevik at heart, or had he been corrupted in his soul? If so, was the corruption fatal, or could it be reversed? Remarkably, these questions had preoccupied the playwright long before his expulsion from the Party, as can be gleaned from his pre-1937 diary. In this light the Stalinist purges appear as the culmination of a revolutionary agenda of purification, involving both the social realm and individual selves, pursued jointly—if not always harmoniously—by the Soviet state and members of society.[2] The self in this context was evaluated in terms of the quality of the soul. Self-purification for Afinogenov meant conforming to the strict standards of Communist morality in thoughts and deeds.

The essay addresses the role of the diary in actualizing Afinogenov's program of self-transformation, treating the diary less as a mirror of Afinogenov's experience of the Terror than as a tool that he applied to himself to remake himself.[3] The focus is not so much on how he wrote *about* himself as it is on his attempt to *write his self*, to actualize himself in the very act of writing.

In examining Afinogenov's diary of 1937, the essay touches on the barely explored issue of subjectivity in an illiberal modern state. As the diary amply illustrates, Afinogenov relentlessly sought to mold himself, such that his self-definition assumed the properties of a project—an unfinished piece of work on the self. In many ways the shape of this project was determined by the agenda of the Stalinist regime, which supplied the conceptual vocabulary of purification and corruption with which Afinogenov articulated his sense of self. Yet the diary as a medium of self-actualization acted as a corollary of the regime's attempts to mold the populace into

---

Norton, 1990). "Revisionist" historians have identified personal, institutional, and ideological tensions underlying the purges, but they are at a loss to explain the overarching dynamic of the terror phenomenon (*Stalinist Terror: New Perspectives*, ed. J. Arch Getty and Roberta Manning [Cambridge: Cambridge University Press, 1993]). For an overview of the historiography, see Johannes Baur, " 'Großer Terror' und 'Säuberungen' im Stalinismus. Eine Forschungsübersicht," *Zeitschrift für Geschichtswissenschaft*, no. 4 (1997): 331–48.

[2] Here I have been inspired by recent investigations conducted in the area of cultural studies which draw attention to larger narratives of social transformation and purification underlying the Soviet project: Katerina Clark, *Petersburg: Crucible of Cultural Revolution* (Cambridge, Mass.: Harvard University Press, 1995); Eric Naiman, *Sex in Public: The Incarnation of Early Soviet Ideology* (Princeton: Princeton University Press, 1997); Boris Groys, *The Total Art of Stalinism: Aesthetics, Dictatorship, and Beyond* (Princeton: Princeton University Press, 1992).

[3] This approach is informed by Michel Foucault's concept of "technologies of the self." See *Technologies of the Self: A Seminar with Michel Foucault*, ed. Luther Martin et al. (Amherst: University of Massachusetts Press, 1988); also Michel Foucault, "The Subject and Power," in Hubert L. Dreyfus and Paul Rabinow, *Michel Foucault: Beyond Structuralism and Hermeneutics* (Chicago: University of Chicago Press, 1983).

prototypes of the New Man and Woman. By means of his journal, Afinogenov actively embraced the Soviet revolutionary call for radical self-transformation, converting it into a relationship of interiority. The figure of the New Man, his case suggests, came to life not simply as an effect of Soviet official ideology but through individual acts of creative self-inscription into the political order. Moreover, the Stalinist purges appear as more than a purely repressive policy. The inquisitorial practices pursued by the state also had a productive effect, in the sense that they highlighted the significance of the self in the Bolshevik system and induced individuals to engage in specifically Soviet modes of self-constitution. The present essay thus explores a powerful personal, indeed spiritual, dimension of the Soviet project, which has been scarcely recognized to date.[4]

It may be wondered how personal and "authentic" a diary produced by a professional writer can be, all the more so in the Stalinist context, when the diary might fall into the hands of the security police. The essay addresses this question by reflecting on the origins and purposes of the diary, by observing shifts in narrative techniques over a long time period, and by juxtaposing Afinogenov's diaristic self to his self-presentation in public.

Born in 1904, Afinogenov rapidly established himself as one of the foremost Soviet playwrights. By the early 1930s he was regularly corresponding with Stalin, whom he regarded as his supreme literary mentor, and to whom he would submit drafts of his plays for criticism. One of Afinogenov's plays, devoted to the life of a Red Army commander, was read before its official premiere in the apartment of the People's Commissar for Defense, Kliment Voroshilov. Yet his work did not remain uncontested. In 1933 Afinogenov experienced his greatest failure to date with the play *Lozh'* (The Lie). Both Stalin and Gorky harshly condemned the script for distorting the Communist Party. As Gorky observed, all Party members were rendered shallow and in shades of grey, in contrast to the lively portrayal of the corrupt characters.[5] Even though Gorky was not a Party member, he could recognize a Bolshevik's personality. "A Bolshevik is interesting not for his faults," he lectured Afinogenov, "but for his virtues. His faults are rooted in the past which he is tirelessly destroying. His virtues, however, are rooted in the present, in the work of building

---

[4] Notable exceptions include Stephen Kotkin, *Magnetic Mountain: Stalinism as a Civilization* (Berkeley: University of California Press, 1995), and Igal Halfin, "From Darkness to Light: Student Communist Autobiography during NEP," *Jahrbücher für Geschichte Osteuropas* 45, no. 2 (1997): 210–236. Subjectivities and mechanisms of subjectivization under Stalinism are explored in greater detail in Jochen Hellbeck, "Laboratories of the Soviet Self: Diaries from the Stalin Era," Ph.D. diss., Columbia University, 1998. This essay is a very condensed adaptation of chapter 7 of the dissertation.

[5] One of the Bolshevik characters bore the evocative name Comrade Graypants [*Seroshtanov*].

the future. . . . We have to train ourselves to appraise the past and the present from the vantage point of our future goals."[6]

In the eyes of his critics, Afinogenov had failed to meet the demands of Socialist Realism, which was emerging at the time as the binding aesthetic for Soviet art. In depicting phenomena of contemporary life, Socialist Realist art was to be informed by a vision of the preordained Communist future. By contrast, Afinogenov's play dwelled solely on present deficiencies and their roots in the past,[7] suggesting that the playwright doubted the Bolsheviks' capacity to will the new socialist world into existence. Indeed, the reproach that in spite of his Party membership, Afinogenov did not fully grasp what constituted a real Bolshevik and that his plays therefore showed Soviet reality only "from the outside" and through a "distorted mirror," was repeated in official reviews of Afinogenov's work over the next few years.[8]

In the course of 1936 the playwright faced an increasing barrage of official criticism. He received a first reprimand in March in connection with the campaign against formalism. Later in the year his most recent piece, *Hail, Spain!* (Saliut, Ispaniia!), premiered in Moscow. The initial response was favorable. *Pravda* wrote approvingly that the performance elicited standing ovations, and emphasized in particular the play's powerful emotional effect on a delegation of visiting Spanish soldiers from the war.[9] Only a few days later, however, after Stalin and other Bolshevik leaders had seen a performance, *Hail, Ispaniia!* as well as all of Afinogenov's other plays currently on stage were suddenly withdrawn from the repertoire of Soviet theaters.[10] Afinogenov's diary strikingly reveals how the playwright attributed the misfortunes in his professional life to personal shortcomings, while admonishing himself with ever-greater urgency to change, to better himself both as a writer and as a human being, so as to earn back Stalin's trust:

12/28/1936 Went through old notes and letters. . . . Can't I possibly derive from all this a lesson for the future? Is it possible that these admonitions will

---

[6] *Gor'kii i sovetskie pisateli: Neizdannaia perepiska* (Moscow: Sovetskii pisatel', 1963), 34. A copy of the manuscript of *Lozh'*, covered with Stalin's scolding remarks, is desposited in RGALI, f. 2172, op. 2, ed. khr. 2. For Stalin's criticism, see Aleksandr Karaganov, *Zhizn' dramaturga: Tvorcheskii put' Aleksandra Afinogenova* (Moscow: Sovetskii pisatel', 1964), 297; Nikolai Afanas'ev, "Ia i On: Aleksandr Afinogenov," in *Paradoks o drame: Perechityvaia p'esy 1920–1930-kh godov* (Moscow: Nauka, 1993).

[7] Regine Robin, *Socialist Realism: An Impossible Aesthetic* (Stanford: Stanford University Press, 1992), 61.

[8] See, for instance, B. Polianskii, "Krivoe zerkalo (O p'esakh Afinogenova)," *Sovetskoe iskusstvo*, December 11, 1936: 8.

[9] *Pravda*, November 28, 1936: 8 ("Ispanskie delegaty na spektakle 'Saliut, Ispaniia' ").

[10] See Afinogenov's diary entries of November 29 and December 2, 1936. The damning article in *Sovetskoe iskusstvo* (see note 9) appeared shortly after Stalin's viewing of the play.

remain empty words and that my life will go on as before? No, no, no! How many times have I already said "no". . . . I must break, break away from every-thing—and from myself in the first place.[11]

1/29/1937... Now I have to work in such a way as to be again worthy of [Stalin's kindness].

Afinogenov had kept a diary since 1926. Except for a period of roughly two years, from 1936 to 1938, this diary has survived only in fragments—scraps of mostly undated typewritten sheets without a clear sense of cohesion or sequence. The original text had been torn to pieces by none other than Afinogenov himself: in preparing his plays, he repeatedly went through his diary with scissors, cutting out numerous passages and arranging them thematically.[12] The diary thus functioned as a sketchbook for the author's literary work. For the most part, diary entries abound in observations of Afinogenov's daily environment: conversations at home and with colleagues, street scenes, thoughts on nature, human psychology, and reflections on political life. Beyond this, however, the diary manifested a striking self-reflexive quality. With the help of the diary Afinogenov turned his gaze inward, critically assessing the nature of his self. For the most part he chided himself for not living up to the ideal norm of a Soviet writer and human being. This harsh self-criticism was accompanied by calls for self-renewal. On New Year's Day of 1935, looking back on his development over the past year, he wrote: "Confusion, depression, . . . and the search for myself, in constant uncertainty. . . . And only now has it suddenly become clear that I can't go on living like this."[13] Almost exactly one year later, in late December 1935, he noted: "Nothing real has been done, the year was spent at the expense of what had been done in the previous year. . . . Isn't this parasitism?"[14] Afinogenov attributed the cause of his problem to the corruption of his soul. The success of his early plays had brought him fame and induced him to indulge in the

---

[11] A. N. Afinogenov, *Izbrannoe v dvukh tomakh*, vol. 2: *Pis'ma, dnevniki* (Moscow: Iskusstvo, 1977), 399.

[12] Afinogenov's diary notes of the period before 1937 have been preserved in two parts: the first, consisting of the rump diary of each year, and the second, in the form of several folders containing clippings from the diary, which are arranged in thematic fashion. These themes include: "mode of life" (*byt*), "things," "celebrating the New Year," "children," "thoughts and feelings," "theater," "music," etc. (RGALI, f. 2172, op. 1, ed. 124). Large parts of Afinogenov's diary were published during the Soviet era: Afinogenov, *Pis'ma, dnevniki*. His diary of 1937 and 1938, however, was locked away in the *spetskhran* and became available to researchers only recently (RGALI, f. 2172, op. 3, ed. 4–6). Some of this material has now also been published: A. Afinogenov, "Dnevnik 1937 goda," *Sovremennaia dramaturgiia*, no. 1 (1993): 239–53, no. 2: 223–41, no. 3: 217–30. Unless otherwise noted, citations from Afinogenov's diary of 1937 and early 1938 are drawn from the archival manuscript.

[13] Afinogenov, *Pis'ma, dnevniki*, 273.

[14] Ibid., 336.

pleasures of life. As a result, he had become lazy and complacent and stopped struggling. In this connection, he regarded setbacks in his career—such as the failure of *The Lie*—as welcome opportunities to remake himself.[15] Keeping the diary on a regular basis made possible a continuous process of baring and cleansing the self, which Afinogenov likened to the results of prayer: "The significance of a prayer is the cleansing before the beginning of the day. The cleansing of the soul. This is not that stupid, of course not in the form of a memorized prayer, but like this: by reflecting on the day to come as well as on the past day . . . —gymnastics of the soul."[16]

While Afinogenov entered the year 1937 considering himself a personal failure and resolving to break with his former life, he also regarded the same period as a critical juncture for the Soviet system as a whole. In November 1936 the Eighth Congress of Soviets had ratified the new Soviet Constitution, which was officially praised as the most democratic in the world. Among other civic entitlements, the Constitution foresaw a secret ballot in elections to all the state's representative bodies, including the newly established Supreme Soviet. The first election to the Supreme Soviet was scheduled to take place in late 1937. Official propaganda portrayed the Constitution as the legal foundation underpinning the ever-purer socialist society. At the same time, the Party leadership increased its calls for cleansing the Soviet social body of remaining impurities—of Trotskyist enemies as well as corrupt, degenerate Communists. For Afinogenov, the official campaign of purification and Bolshevik self-criticism signified an "enormous turn" (3/28/1937), and he declared: "The Constitution is not just a scrap of paper! This is what many don't understand, oh so many!" (3/17/1937). Commenting on the first wave of arrests of suspected enemies of the people, he noted:

> *4/5/1937* Oh, what a gigantic turn: History itself is breathing on us, and we are given the joy of witnessing these turns, when Stalin chops off all and everything, all the unfit and weakened, the degenerate and empty. . . . Life has now taken a turn toward the new and the real. Only like this, and in no other way, can we march toward real communism. Whoever says otherwise, lies!

Afinogenov's diary reveals how deeply he was involved from the start in the campaign of purification launched by the Stalinist state, which was to

---

[15] Ibid., 237 (undated entry of 1934).
[16] Ibid., 338 (undated entry of 1935). On another occasion Afinogenov deplored his ongoing lack of "concentrated calm and ability to control [himself]." To work on his composure, he called upon himself to regularly record on paper all the "interesting" and "essential" aspects of life: "This needs to be done on a daily basis, for about ten to fifteen minutes per day . . . , like an exercise, like playing scales, like saying one's tables, until it becomes a habit, just like brushing one's teeth at night" (ibid., 244; undated entry of 1934). For other religious themes, see ibid., 226 (undated entry of 1934).

culminate in the Great Terror of 1937–38. The purge campaign unfolding in the country at large illustrated for him the necessity to embark on a similar program of self-purification. Already in early 1937—before he became a target of the terror campaign—Afinogenov understood the purge as a last chance for him to redeem himself and demonstrate to everybody that he was a Bolshevik at heart.

At about the same time, Afinogenov's diary changed noticeably in character as the introspective gaze became ever more prominent and in the end eclipsed the other function of the diary as a writer's sketchbook of outside events and observations. The focal point of Afinogenov's diary in 1937 was himself.[17] Thus, to the extent to which the Stalinist regime increased its demands for the unmasking of Trotskyist enemies and called upon citizens to lay bare their inner stance toward the socialist system in public, Afinogenov by means of his diary proceeded to scrutinize and cleanse his soul. This close interaction between the purge policies of the Soviet state and such mechanisms of inner purification would characterize his diary throughout the period of the Stalinist terror.

While shifting in focus and style, diary entries of this period grew longer and more frequent. Hardly a day passed on which the playwright would not write at least one typewritten page, and often his diary entries of a given day spanned three or more pages. If members of Soviet society are thought to have ceased writing their diaries as the regime stepped up its repressive policies, in Afinogenov's case the Terror induced a veritable explosion of autobiographical writing. The Stalinist purges emerge in this light not as an expression of absolute estrangement between state and society but as an intense synergetic link between individuals and the state, in which the respective agendas of social purification and individual work on the self culminated and fused. The phenomenon of terror, Afinogenov's diary suggests, was far more than a policy threatening the integrity of the self from without; it had a profoundly self-constitutive quality, which was expressed in torrents of confessional writing designed to cleanse and rework the self.[18]

Against this background, we can more fully understand the fateful meeting of the Moscow playwrights of April 27, 1937. The principal reason why it was convened was the fact that the literary critic and erstwhile secretary of the Russian Association of Proletarian Writers (RAPP),

[17] This is not to imply that the diary stopped having a literary purpose. The place and function of Afinogenov's diary in his literary work are discussed below.

[18] A huge volume of confessional literature produced under the supervision, and often on the direct order, of Stalin's security police remains in the archives of the KGB, inaccessible to most researchers. The introspective and self-transformative purpose of the Stalinist confession is highlighted in two recent publications from the KGB archives: Vitaly Shentalinsky, *Arrested Voices: Resurrecting the Disappeared Writers of the Soviet Regime* (New York: Free Press, 1996); " 'Prosti menia, Koba . . . ' Neizvestnoe pis'mo N. Bukharina," *Istochnik*, no. o [*sic*] (1993): 23–25; see also Hellbeck, "Laboratories of the Soviet Self," introduction and chapter 3.

Leopol'd Averbakh, had been exposed as a Trotskyist enemy a few days earlier.[19] Before RAPP was dissolved in 1932, Afinogenov had been a leading activist in the organization, and thus Averbakh's arrest cast a dark shadow of suspicion on him as well. The opening speech, by Vsevolod Vishnevskii, was wholly devoted to Averbakh and the need to excise from the playwrights' association all members of Averbakh's camp. The gist of Vishnevskii's accusations was directed against Vladimir Kirshon, who was present at the meeting. But clearly Afinogenov was another target of the gathering, being third in the assigned speaking order, following Vishnevskii and Kirshon.[20]

Kirshon vigorously refuted Vishnevskii's accusation, insisting on his absolute purity as a Communist. Like Kirshon, Afinogenov began by refuting the specific charges made against him, namely that he had been involved in a conspiracy with Averbakh to undermine the Soviet system. But he then used the public forum to expose his own inner corruption, and by cleansing himself reverse the process of degeneration. He admitted to a series of errors and mistakes, "much more serious" than those with which he was charged and impossible to summarize in the fifteen minutes that he was allowed to speak. After a week of sleepless nights he had been able to realize clearly what kind of person he was. Through his contacts with Averbakh and other "literary chiefs" (*literaturnye vozhdi*), he had "unnoticeably absorbed, drop by drop, the very poison of unprincipledness and cultivated in his relationship with others an ignorant and boorish attitude of conceit and bureaucratism which this literary premier [Averbakh] had fully exemplified." These qualities had "corrupted" (*gubili*) Afinogenov, too. Under Averbakh's influence he had turned away from the Party and produced pieces which were "absolutely not what the country wanted and demanded of me. I did not understand how it happened that I forgot how to listen to the country and forgot how to write." Afinogenov summarized his confession with the words: "As a person, as a writer and Party member, I began to degenerate."

---

[19] The Averbakh affair was prominently featured in Soviet newspapers on April 23, 1937, the fifth anniversary of the dissolution of RAPP, which had led to the unification of Soviet literature. Averbakh had been arrested earlier in the month: he was the brother-in-law of former NKVD chief Genrikh Iagoda, who in turn had been indicted as an enemy of the people in early April 1937 (*The Modern Encyclopedia of Russian and Soviet Literature*, vol. 2, ed. Harry B. Weber [Gulf Breeze: Academic International Press, 1978], 1–2).

[20] The stenographic protocol of the Moscow meeting is preserved in RGALI, f. 631, op. 2, ed. 220–24. The meeting adjourned in the late evening of April 27, reconvened the following day, and lasted until May 3 due to the great number of speakers. The enormous volume of accusatory and confessional speech produced during the meeting provides further testimony to the self-actualizing effects of the Stalinist purges. For an elaboration of this argument see Jochen Hellbeck, "Speaking Out: Languages of Affirmation and Dissent in Stalinist Russia," *Kritika* 1, no. 1 (2000): 71–96.

Afinogenov affirmed, however, that his current situation constituted a turning point in his life. The charges made against him had given him a final opportunity to "understand and appreciate" his past life "as a life that clearly destroyed me, gradually at first, but then increasingly faster." He declared that he had "realized, conclusively and absolutely, the essence of the poisonous disease called the 'Averbakh leprosy'—a disease that required surgical intervention." In concluding, Afinogenov implored his colleagues to acknowledge that he had broken with his past once and for all and taken the first step on the difficult road of self-renewal.

His plea was ignored by the assembly of playwrights. Several fellow writers conceded that Afinogenov's confession had been sincere, unlike Kirshon's defense, which amounted in their eyes to a "crafty lawyer's speech" that would scarcely save him. Yet in its very sincerity, Afinogenov's speech demonstrated to them just how alien he was to the spirit of the Party. As one speaker, a certain Chicherov, remarked, it was this lack of understanding of "the real role of the Party" that constituted "one of the gravest sins of his dramaturgic work of recent years." In the course of the four-day meeting, more than thirty writers spoke out against the "henchmen of the Trotskyite Averbakh," Kirshon and Afinogenov. The association passed a motion to discuss their removal from the board of the Writers' Union.[21] Both Afinogenov and Kirshon were expelled from the Party in May 1937.[22]

Returning to Afinogenov's diary, it is striking to note how closely his personal record replicated the self-accusation in which he had engaged two days earlier. Using the medium of his private diary, Afinogenov produced another full-fledged confession, expanding on his public narrative. Just as in his speech, Afinogenov confessed his sins in the service of self-purification:

4 / 29 / 1937 Days of great cleansing! The more evil and terrible the words addressed to me become, the more my spirits rise. These words aren't terrible at all, and the people are not a bit evil; they are saying the truth, seen from

[21] *Komsomol'skaia Pravda*, April 29, 1937: 4; April 30, 1937: 4.

[22] *Literaturnaia gazeta*, May 15, 1937: 1; see also Afinogenov's diary entry of May 20, 1937. Kirshon was arrested shortly afterward, and he died in 1938, while probably still in prison (Wolfgang Kasack, *Lexikon der russischen Literatur des 20. Jahrhunderts*, 2d, rev. ed. [Munich: Verlag Otto Sagner in Kommission, 1992]: 536–37). It is quite possible that Afinogenov escaped arrest because of his complete confession, in which he bared his soul to the Party, while Kirshon's initial refutation of the accusations against him may have hardened the suspicion that he was concealing his anti-Soviet essence, and thus contributed to his subsequent arrest. On the very last day of the meeting of the Moscow playwrights, Kirshon submitted to a degree of self-criticism, admitting that the last few days had forced him to reevaluate his former life. Yet at the same time he had the audacity to "seriously reproach" his fellow comrades for the harshness of their sudden accusations against him. The stenographic protocol recorded "noise in the room" (RGALI, f. 631, op. 2, ed. 224, l. 51).

their viewpoint. And I have pronounced a much more cruel verdict on myself, and therefore the people's verdicts have already stopped worrying me.

Afinogenov interpreted the purge campaign as a long-awaited opportunity for him to change and be saved. In this connection he relished each public accusation leveled against him by his writer colleagues, for the more severely he was criticized, the more he would be able to recognize and denounce his sins and the purer he could become.

Afinogenov then detailed the work he had already performed toward his self-renewal. The diary passage makes clear how central a role the public confession to the meeting of playwrights played in this project of reworking. It was the act in which he had renounced, indeed killed, his former self, a necessary precondition for the type of "rebirth" Afinogenov sought. Harking back to his speech at the meeting of playwrights, where he had spoken of the need for a "surgical intervention" to remove the Averbakhian remnants from within him, Afinogenov now reported in his diary that he had successfully carried out an operation on himself:

> I put myself under the knife; I took out not only the stomach but the heart as well. I killed the self inside me—and then a miracle happened: Having already given up all hope and preparing myself for my physical death, I suddenly understood and saw the beginning of something new, a new "self," far removed from previous agitation and fuss, a "self" that appeared out of the mist of all the best that had ever been in me and had faded, vanished, evaporated since then. And now it turns out that it has not faded or evaporated; it has not died completely but laid the beginning of a new—if still very weak and small—beginning, in which the new master of my body speaks together with me.

In describing how he shed his former self and invited a new master into his body, Afinogenov employed a narrative of radical conversion akin to the Christian notion of rebirth. Rebirth in Christian theology is the act by which the Christian believer reaches the stage of salvation, leaving behind his old sinful nature and attaining a new life in God's spirit.[23] In the Soviet context, rebirth was frequently used as a trope to describe the inner transformation an individual undergoes by joining the Communist Party. By joining the Party, the initiate reached a new plane of insight and understanding; he was "born anew," "saw," "knew," and "spoke of" new things,

---

[23] "Rebirth," in *New Catholic Encyclopedia* (New York: McGraw-Hill, 1967), 12: 123–25. Rebirth in Christian theology is, however, only one variant of an age-old trope of rite of passage, in which "in order to be created anew, the old . . . must first be annihilated." The initiates "receive protracted instruction from their teachers, witness secret ceremonies, [and usually] undergo a series of ordeals" (M. Eliade, cited in Katerina Clark, *The Soviet Novel: History as Ritual* [Chicago: University of Chicago Press, 1981], 178).

for in that moment he left the world of profane reality and entered a realm of higher knowledge and vision.[24]

The notion of rebirth was essential to Afinogenov's subjectivity in the context of the purges, for it allowed him to accommodate his past sins while at the same time giving him the assurance that he would eventually be saved. Since rebirth presupposes the existence of a prior, sinful self, Afinogenov could identify this self as the "degenerate playwright Afinogenov," as he had been labeled by his public accusers but as he also saw himself. By the same token, however, he was able to renounce this self through the act of confession. By undergoing a symbolic death prior to being reborn, he could claim that he had emerged as a new, pure being who had nothing in common with the old Afinogenov. In his diary he remarked that the attacks against him in the Soviet newspapers were being directed against a "dead body which by a misunderstanding is called by my name" (4/29/1937).

Even after having successfully shed his former self and been reborn as a new person, Afinogenov faced a major problem: how credible was his claim to self-renewal in the face of the unceasing stream of attacks and denunciations against him? This problem was made even more serious by his critics' rejection of the very premise on which Afinogenov had based his self-renewal, namely, that he was a degenerate Party member, an erring Bolshevik who had temporarily slid from full consciousness but was now firmly back on track. As will be remembered, at the meeting of playwrights Chicherov had declared that Afinogenov was in reality not a Bolshevik but an individual alien to the spirit of the Party. In the same vein, *Literaturnaia gazeta* remarked on the occasion of Afinogenov's expulsion from the Party: "All of Afinogenov's activities . . . show that the only reason he can't be called a degenerate [Party member] is that he has always been a person who was fundamentally alien to the Party."[25] As if in response to these annihilating voices, Afinogenov stated programmatically in his diary: "This new self is a person whose word the people will hear at some point, and they will understand that this word is the word of a Bolshevik, no matter what!" (5/2/1937) Given Afinogenov's exclusion from the collective, the diary remained practically the only available medium in which the new person of the Bolshevik he was determined to become could raise and train his voice.

It would be misleading, however, to reduce Afinogenov's diary of 1937 to a narrative of self-fashioning in a Bolshevik vein. Rather, the diary speaks to us in several voices. It portrays an individual excluded from the collective, desperately trying to make sense of his personal existence in re-

[24] Clark, *Soviet Novel,* 174; Halfin, "From Darkness to Light."
[25] *Literaturnaia gazeta,* May 20, 1937: 1.

lation to the overall political process engulfing him. In rapid succession, expectations are paired with doubts, hope with despair. Only days after his confession and self-renewal, Afinogenov spoke of himself very differently in his diary, maintaining that he was innocent and suspecting that his denunciation was part of a "devilish" fascist conspiracy seeking to "annihilate talented Soviet artists" (4/30/1937, 5/2/1937).

Yet for all the instability of self-definition that these entries suggest, it is intriguing to see how Afinogenov's notion of himself was affected by the official decision to expel him from the Communist Party on May 20, 1937. In his entry of that day, he described the meeting of the Party section of the Writers' Union during which Party Secretary Aleksandr Fadeev, "with a stony face called me a vulgar and philistine person, a degenerate bourgeois, and a good-for-nothing artist." All members of the section then openly balloted to exclude him from the Party. When the meeting turned to a different point on the agenda, Afinogenov got up and left the room "in deadly silence." As soon as he was outside, he regained his "calm, bordering on happiness," because he knew that he was "not guilty of anything." Later in the day, Afinogenov noted in his diary, a writer colleague, Il'ia Sel'vinskii, visited him at home to "comfort him and cheer him up":

> We spoke about the entire life of a person, which can't be lived without making mistakes. And then when you have to account for a mistake, all of a sudden everybody forgets about all the good things that this person could have done in his life and which he probably did do. Like Gretchen, who lived her entire life in a chaste and pure, sinless and good way. But she had only to commit the one sin with Faust for all her previous piety and goodness to go from the threshold of heaven straight to hell. (5/20/1937)

In likening himself to Gretchen, Afinogenov admitted to a sin so grave that it offset all the good deeds he had performed in the past and could send him to damnation. This passage suggests how much Afinogenov's expulsion from the Party, which stood for the public exposure of his sinful self, compelled him to accept his depravity even in an unofficial setting such as the private conversation he had with Sel'vinskii. Moreover, Afinogenov felt obliged to record this conversation in his diary, thereby qualifying and, to an extent, invalidating the proclamation of innocence he had just made. As Afinogenov further noted, he spent the days and weeks following his expulsion from the Party researching the concepts of fall from grace (*grekhopadenie*), sacrifice, and redemption. In works by Cervantes, Bruno Frank, and Dostoevsky, he hoped to find models of spiritual guidance:

Now, in solitude, he felt at last the urge to understand which he had not had at all previously. To understand the philosophical foundations of life. He wanted to read not for the sake of some kind of "education," but because he needed an immediate answer to the questions of how to go on living with people, how to relate to them, and how to conduct himself. (5/25/1937; see also entry of 6/2/1937)[26]

Afinogenov understood his expulsion from the Party during the Great Terror as a manifestation of his fall from grace. Both in his conversation with Sel'vinskii and by means of his diary, he fashioned himself as a faithful Bolshevik who had strayed from the path of virtue and truth. By the same token, he used the public campaign against him to stage a process of personal conversion and self-renewal. This extensive effort in self-fashioning strikingly demonstrates how much an individual living through the Stalinist Terror actively enrolled in the ongoing purge campaign, even though he had been branded as an enemy and thus been turned into a victim of the Terror. As Afinogenov saw it, the purge compelled each individual to question whether he or she was sufficiently pure and worthy to be accepted into the newly founded socialist community and thus to withstand the Party's scrutinizing gaze. This was the essential question the playwright was grappling with in his diary throughout the purge campaign. Afinogenov thus regarded the Stalinist purges less as a policy of annihilation threatening the integrity of his self than as an incentive to rework himself, with the prospect of restoring and perfecting the self.

In his attempt to emerge from the purge as a new person, Afinogenov resolved to make drastic changes in his life. Shedding his former corrupted self entailed first and foremost an end to the oblivious and pleasure-seeking lifestyle in which he had indulged in the past. But it also meant leaving behind circles of former friends and colleagues, exposure to whom had corrupted him. Afinogenov once observed in his diary that most of his former acquaintances had turned out to be "enemies": they had been "either arrested or picked to pieces" (7/26/1937). But with mass arrests taking place around him and his suspicion that many more

---

[26] From the very inception of his diary in 1926, Afinogenov mostly used the third person (*on*) when referring to himself. This strategy may suggest how much the diaristic self already inhabited the domain of Afinogenov's literary work. The autobiographical "he" of the diary occupied the same level as the individual characters of his plays, who were also sketched out on the pages of the diary, thereby creating a degree of interchangeability between them. In the context of the Stalinist purges, however, Afinogenov often shifted to the first person. His use of the pronoun "I" can be read as an indication of the emotional immediacy with which Afinogenov experienced the purge campaign. The choice of pronoun can thus be correlated to the intensity of the imperative of self-scrutiny and self-change weighing on Afinogenov. Throughout 1937 he hardly ever used the third person when confiding his existential anxieties.

acquaintances were soon to be arrested as enemies of the people, Afinogenov went even further in his search for self-purification. In his eyes, the entire city of Moscow, where arrests were most frequent, came to represent a site of pollution. The playwright resolved to avoid exposure to this dangerous source of contamination and to pursue instead an isolated existence in his dacha in Peredelkino: "On the whole, every trip to Moscow is a nervous shock. You mustn't go there anymore, you must live alone by yourself, you must rest and be glad that you are alive and can lie in the sun without thinking about anything except your small and simple life, which alone you understand (6/8/1937)."

Afinogenov implicitly juxtaposed the pure, "small, and simple life, which alone you understand" to a morally depraved treacherous world filled with hidden enemies intent on betraying his trust. This implicit contrast becomes apparent in the following entry in which the playwright dreamed of leaving behind his impure social environment and seeking refuge in a remote place on earth:

> 7/26/1937 ... become a hermit, settle either alone or with my wife and the baby—and not depend on anybody, nor be connected to anybody. I'm afraid of people now, although I have this occasional urge to sit with them and talk, but I'm afraid. This was such a life lesson, when the people whom you trusted most of all turned out to be traitors and enemies. Now, except myself, I don't trust anybody. I can't vouch for anybody and I want to go far away and live in such a way that I don't have contact with anybody.

In the context of the mass purges taking place around him and the revelation of more and more ugly, depraved individuals, the logic driving Afinogenov's program of self-purification led him to celebrate a solitary existence in nature, outside his social environment. In his quest for complete purity he thus came to extol values wholly at odds with the Bolshevik notion of man as a collective being with a civilizing mission: "*5/18/1937* He loved his loneliness so much that in the mornings, when getting up light and refreshed, he implored his fate that this loneliness would last as long as possible." Living Robinson Crusoe-like in his patch of self-imposed exile, and in the midst of continuous waves of arrests, which were also taking their toll among fellow residents in the writers' colony, Afinogenov discovered a new notion of a "life for himself":[27]

---

[27] Afinogenov in fact likened himself to Robinson Crusoe a number of times during this period (e.g., diary entry of 5/1/1937). This reference is extremely suggestive. The story of Robinson Crusoe has long been recognized as a "laicized transposition" of the puritan autobiography (G.A. Starr, *Defoe and Spiritual Autobiography* [Princeton: Princeton University Press, 1965]). During his prolonged stay on the island, Crusoe reaches a point of conversion through intense study of the Bible. He recognizes that his exile expresses God's punishment for his sinful behavior in not heeding his father's wish that he not go to sea (Kaspar von

7/19/1937 They played cards; he had a streak of luck. Then they drank tea and ate sweet pirogi with cherry filling. Then he went home, it was a warm summer night. Strolling under the stars, he whistled and tenderly thanked life that it was now so clear and peaceful for him. He suddenly understood that he had always wanted such a peaceful life, be it even at the price of such a terrible catastrophe. It didn't matter. Now he was not needed by anybody and what made him happy was that he could live for himself.

Afinogenov conceptualized his new ideal of self-determination by opposing it to an alienated existence, which he identified with his identity as a Party member. It was only a small step from embracing the new ideal of a solitary life to condemning the former life spent in the service of the Party:

> *7/7/1937* Strange things are happening to me. Since the age of fourteen I haven't belonged to myself. First the Komsomol, then the Party. I always carried the consciousness of some sort of sacrifice on my shoulders. I was a soldier and honestly served in the ranks; I did everything that the Party ordered me to do and had never any bad thoughts about it. . . . But now they suddenly began to suspect something and removed me ignominiously from the ranks. As if they had mutilated my eye and said: Now we don't need you, go where you want. And at first, ah, what terrible days of isolation and solitude these were. . . . Oh well, I had to leave the ranks. I took my bag and left. And then, as I was leaving town and following my nose, I discovered for the first time since my distant childhood the happiness of a free step. You are not needed by anybody; yes, nobody needs you; go where you want and work for the benefit of the people and the country, but by yourself and inconspicuously, for you are not needed. How wonderful it is that nobody is pursuing you with calls to meetings, or with orders to write an article or to give a speech and say something boring. . . . Oh, how wonderful—to go and work where you deem it necessary.

Afinogenov no longer viewed his expulsion from the Party in terms of an absolute loss or a fall from grace. On the contrary, he described his former life as an act of self-sacrifice. Now that he was no longer a soldier in the ranks, executing Party orders, he discovered a new sense of freedom and purpose: an insignficant but peaceful and stable existence. In describing his expulsion from the Party, Afinogenov used a revealing metaphor. He likened this event to a mutilation of his eye. This explains why Afinogenov insisted repeatedly that he was no longer of any use to anyone: his forcible removal from the Party entailed the loss of his eyesight, a loss of the superior vision that he had previously possessed as a

---

Greyerz, *Vorsehungsglaube und Kosmologie: Studien zu englischen Selbstzeugnissen des 17. Jahrhunderts* [Göttingen and Zurich: Vandenhoeck & Ruprecht, 1990]: 182).

Communist and a writer. This vision had bestowed on him particular social responsibilities as an engineer of human souls, and it was precisely
the loss of this burden of responsibility that Afinogenov had in mind
when hailing his new existence as someone "who was not needed by anybody."

Just as urgently as Afinogenov embraced the ideal of an individual existence, however, he began to repudiate it within only a few weeks. His diary
entries of July and August 1937 are filled with passages hailing his arrival
at a new stage of consciousness. The first of these, written only three days
after the playwright's dream of becoming a hermit, starts with the following words: "7/29/1937 The entry may be entitled 'Return to Life'....
This is a day on which I suddenly felt that life is bustling around me....
Again the lines of the newspapers are enlivening me as they have done before." Indeed, Afinogenov continued, his own "small fate" was

> excluded from the general stream of life. But does this small fate really mat-
> ter? And the consciousness that what matters is not my case and my lament-
> ing about my unfair expulsion, this consciousness brings me back to life.
> Only to a different life.... This feeling of being close to life fills you with hap-
> piness, you listen again to the words of the "Latest News," you read about the
> record harvest, about the flight of the Chkalov team and the reception for
> them in the Kremlin, and all this makes you happy and excited. And again
> you awake from the lethargic sleep. The knockout is over, and the person be-
> gins to live.

Afinogenov now referred to the dreams he had entertained earlier
about an autonomous life as moments of "lethargic sleep," as a "knockout" phase, implying that he had lacked any consciousness when recording those thoughts. By contrast, the "return to life" subsumed his reinte-
gration into the Soviet system and his renewed participation in the heroic
life of the collective and in the course of history itself. As long as his personal existence evolved away from the collective body of the Soviet
people, it remained small and insignificant. Only in aligning himself with
the Soviet system could he realize himself as a person.

Afinogenov described a similar turning point a few days later, referring
to it as an "awakening." As he now disclosed, he had spent the past nights
waiting to be arrested. But now he knew that his fears were unfounded.
Why should he be arrested? "Over there, at the Lubianka, there are intelligent people. In spite of their busy schedules and all the stressful work,
they see down to the roots of everything . . . , and no wave will force them
to arrest someone innocent" (8/4/1937). In the entry of the following
day, Afinogenov once more celebrated his "fundamental and unusual
break," namely, his newfound certainty that he was not slated for arrest.
He felt embarrassed that only a few days before he had confided his fears

to the diary. To underscore how different he now felt, he even questioned the authorship of those despairing thoughts: "Where did these thoughts spring from? Who wrote them?" (8/9/1937).

Afinogenov seemed to be implying that there were two different persons living inside him, who assessed the political situation in opposite terms and therefore also pursued contrasting means of self-realization. One lived in permanent fear of arrest and dreamed of a solitary existence which would shelter him from the corrupt social environment. The other, by contrast, disclaimed the likelihood of arrest and, indeed, the impurity of the social order, calling for the individual's integration into the Soviet system. It would be tempting to view these diverging notions of individual autonomy and social self-integration as expressions of Afinogenov's private and public selves, with Afinogenov privately yearning for personal independence and freedom, while maintaining in public an image of himself that would conform to official Soviet norms. The fact that these contrasting identities were played out in Afinogenov's private diary would seem to suggest how much the writer's official self-image interfered with his own self-definition and how difficult it was for him to retain a private sense of himself distinct from the social identity prescribed by the Soviet regime.[28]

Yet this interpretation, which emphasizes the disparity between private and official self-definitions and proceeds from a belief in the primacy of the private domain, obscures the links between Afinogenov's diverging assessments of himself. If we stop treating individual entries of a given day in isolation from each other, and view them instead as elements of a larger narrative structure, Afinogenov's diary emerges as a form of spiritual writing, organized in such a way as to enact the experience of conversion. Afinogenov described this conversion variously as a return to life, a new birth, or the attainment of a higher consciousness and purity. The diary thus served as a means of furthering his personal salvation.

Conversion was the founding experience for a Communist. Communists could make no credible claim to Party membership without proving that they had experienced a conversion in their lives. For all their variations, Communist autobiographies from the early Soviet period, which

---

[28] Russians who have lived through the Stalinist regime frequently refer to this phenomenon of two irreconcilable spheres as a split consciousness or a "dual soul" (*dvoedushie*). See L. A. Gordon and E. V. Klopov, *Chto eto bylo? Razmyshleniia o predposylkakh i itogakh togo, chto sluchilos' s nami v 30–40-e gody* (Moscow: Izdatel'stvo politicheskoi literatury, 1989), 221–42; Bernd Bonwetsch, "Der Stalinismus in der Sowjetunion der dreißiger Jahre. Zur Deformation einer Gesellschaft," *Jahrbuch für historische Kommunismusforschung* 1 (1993): 11–36 (here: 34–36). In a variation on this theme, Stephen Kotkin writes that members of Stalinist society simultaneously inhabited two different realities: the profane world of the everyday, in which dissatisfaction with living conditions seems to have been widespread, and a higher, sacred reality of official Bolshevik dogma, which allowed individuals to rationalize away their criticisms of the regime, and which presented the socialist system as the best of all possible worlds. Kotkin, *Magnetic Mountain*, 225–30.

had to be written as part of the application process for Party membership, described a conversion experience dividing the lives of candidates into two phases: an early phase marked by material backwardness, passivity, and a lack of consciousness, and a mature, active, and conscious phase induced by the candidate's exposure to the teachings of the Communist Party.[29] It was on the strength of a Communist's insight into the historical role of the Party and his ensuing conversion that he acquired his vanguard status as a leader of progressive mankind.

Afinogenov well realized, however, that conversion could not be reduced to the experience of a single act of rebirth, such as he had described it in his entry of April 29, 1937, following his self-critical speech at the meeting of Moscow playwrights. As would also be the case with a Christian believer, his conversion was rather a lifelong process, to be reenacted and reaffirmed time and again. The initial act of seeing the light and turning in one's tracks, whatever its dramatic quality, constituted only a prelude to an extended spiritual life. As a scholar of Christian conversion has written, after the "initial startled awakening," the convert has to remain "steadily alert to signs of saving grace and backsliding, always questioning the genuineness of the former and fearing false security. . . . Assurance, like joy, grief, or fatigue, generates its own other set of dangers such as pride, despair, or complacency. Each achievement can thus spark another cycle of guilt and self-testing."[30]

In the period following his exclusion from the Party, Afinogenov through his diary writings consistently tried to turn in his tracks and reach a purer form of consciousness which he sometimes referred to as a "second stage" (*vtoraia stepen'*) of comprehension. For example, he once wrote how angered he was by the behavior of a number of colleagues—among them his former friend, the writer Vsevolod Ivanov—who had not only voted to expel him from the Writers' Union but were now even spreading the news about his supposed arrest. "How can one live among such double-dealers, cowards, and fainthearted types!" Afinogenov exclaimed (9/10/1937). Looking back on this incident from the vantage point of the following day, however, Afinogenov took a different stance: "*9/11/1937* Yesterday I didn't succeed at all in reaching the second stage. . . . Today it worked, and I'm happy about it." Now, Afinogenov wrote, he understood the all too human motivations of Ivanov's behavior; no longer indignant, he reacted with understanding and compassion. By the same token, the diary also recorded instances when Afinogenov was unable to sustain a conversion and reverted to his old self. On October 2, 1937, he noted his enthusiasm for a recent speech in which Stalin had declared that enemies were frequently those who showed excessive zeal. In

---

[29] Halfin, "From Darkness to Light."

[30] Kathleen M. Swaim, *Pilgrim's Progress, Puritan Progress. Discourses and Context* (Urbana: University of Illinois Press, 1993), 139.

striking contrast, the diary entry of the following day resounded with despair: "*10/3/1937* What a leaden depression! . . . Now that I've retreated from my confidence and fallen back into my ordinary state, I'm suddenly afraid that I won't be able to hold out, that I might lose my mind." A few weeks later, Afinogenov again wrote that he kept returning to his customary doubts and fears, reprimanding himself: "Why did you become weak?" (10/25/1937).

This dialectical pattern of certainty and self-assurance giving way to doubts which in turn are dispelled in the name of a higher consciousness can be observed not only in the sequence of diary entries but even within single entries. A large number of Afinogenov's diary entries from the period of his exclusion from the Party are filled at the outset with doubts, despair, and complaints about the writer's inability to comprehend his position. Typically these entries end on a confident and optimistic note, with Afinogenov hailing his rediscovered sense of belonging and purpose.[31] The function of the diary was to dispel existing doubts and dissonance to achieve a higher form of consciousness and unity. Afinogenov himself likened the emergence of a new "insight" (*prozrenie*) to an "almost mystical miracle through which I was reborn" (9/24/1937).

In fact, an underlying conversion motif serves as the foundation for the entire structure of Afinogenov's diary from the onset of the purge campaign. It is the narrative of a gradual coming to light, a progression that at the outset is at best tortuous and marked by frequent backslidings, but increasingly becomes steady and determined. Back in May 1937, on the day of his exclusion from the Communist Party, Afinogenov confided to his diary how little he could make sense of that act. No longer an active participant in the unfolding of history, he felt brutally pushed about by a force external to him and therefore was uncertain over his fate (entry of 5/20/1937). In retrospect, though, from the vantage point of the late summer of 1937, Afinogenov referred to the weeks and months following his loss of Party membership as a long knockout phase. This had been a time filled with doubts, fears, and escapist dreams of leaving this world. As much as he condemned this phase, it served an important purpose: as the realm of the unconscious, it functioned as an indispensable backdrop against which Afinogenov could experience the unfolding of his Communist consciousness. The narrative of conversion and rebirth simply could not function without a previous degeneration and death. It was as such, as a period of backsliding and weakness of mind, that Afinogenov integrated his doubts and his incipient criticism of Communist Party policies into the overall conversion narrative of his diary.

---

[31] For the period of May to October 1937 alone, this pattern can be identified in the following entries: 5/1, 5/10, 5/13, 5/18, 5/23, 7/7, 7/28, 8/4, 8/8, 8/9, 9/4, 9/5, 9/9, 9/25, 10/4, 10/6, 10/7, 10/14, 10/19, 10/25, 10/26/1937.

In the fall of 1937, Afinogenov repeatedly voiced the expectation that he would soon be readmitted to the Soviet collective. In his eyes, the celebration of the twentieth anniversary of the Revolution on November 7 and the elections to the Supreme Soviet in early December represented the threshold of the new socialist society. He expected the Stalinist purges to culminate and reach their logical end at the close of 1937, when the new political order would have come into being, staffed by a new generation of pure Soviet citizens and freed from all the impurities of the past. He, too, could belong to this new order, thanks to the efforts he had made to purify his self. Yet, to be reintegrated into Soviet society, it was equally important for Afinogenov to engage in socially useful work and demonstrate his devotion to the collective:

> *9/12/1937* Everything else will come by itself, but first you have to perform honest work for the country and its best people. These people, right now they are marching across Red Square. The radio is transmitting their laughter, their shouts of hurrah, and their merry songs. Right now you are not among them; that hurts terribly. But earn the right to join them again! . . . This right can only be earned through work . . . , not through any letters, protests, complaints. None of this will do; there have been too many complaints and letters.

Only work—and here he had in mind literary work—was going to save him, Afinogenov suggested, not petitions nor proclamations of innocence. This remark is very revealing of Afinogenov's understanding of the nature of writing in the Soviet realm. To be legitimate and socially useful labor, writing had to leave the descriptive mode and become transformative. This was not the case with the petitions and protests he had composed in the wake of his expulsion from the Party, for they had harped on the injustices or errors committed in his case and thus merely invoked a present, static sense of himself. The only acceptable way to write about the self was by means of a narrative of self-transformation and self-renewal.

The specific project through which Afinogenov hoped to redeem himself as a Soviet writer was a novel—the first novel of his career. In the diary, this idea of writing a novel can be traced back to 1935, but it was not until late 1937 that he began to take on the project in earnest. Entitled *Three Years* (Tri goda), the novel was to span the period from December 1934 to the end of 1937. It was to trace the development of its protagonist, Viktor, through the stages of personal degeneration, crisis, and subsequent recovery.[32] By means of the novel, Afinogenov sought to convey how the Soviet population had experienced the Stalinist purge campaign:

---

[32] See diary entries of 12/18/1937 and 12/22/1937. The novel was never completed. The first nine chapters appeared in *Teatr*, no. 3 (1958). The hero's degeneration and rebirth

12/18/1937 A novel about the summer of 1937 in Moscow, about what happened to all of us, how it became possible to liquidate a whole stratum of enemies without disturbing the country, and how the people experienced this.[33] The novel will be written in such a fashion that Stalin will say: "good." This is a very bold promise to myself, but only in this way will it be possible to raise the thing to the level of those great works required by the people and the present time.

In a diary entry, Afinogenov sketched out a central scene of the projected work. A character, possibly the main protagonist, returns to Moscow after serving his term of exile. He meets an old friend who has already written him off. "Emerging as if from the next world," he

rushes to say everything: how he was returning as a totally different person; that he himself had changed as much as this wonderful city. These "Moscow meetings" are numerous. . . . A man returns to Moscow who had left the city on purpose: he had once been unjustly insulted and he didn't have the energy to fight for his rights, so he left, offended. But then he returned, already as another person, reconciled, and he sees those who had turned away from him before. (10/11/1937)

The central purpose of the projected novel was thus to convey how the purge policies of the Stalinist state had induced an individual to work on, and in the process renew, his self. Obviously, one of the goals for Afinogenov in writing this autobiographically inspired novel was to underscore the self-transformative work he had performed. The novel was to serve as a token of his successful self-renewal as an individual and as a claim for readmission to the circle of Communist writers. Throughout his career, Afinogenov was an intensely political writer, devoting his plays to problems attending the various stages of building socialism. Now his plan to write a novel about the issues of personal degeneration and renewal in the context of the purges shows how much he recognized the self as the most pressing issue of his time.

Against the background of the novel project, Afinogenov's diary appears in a new light. Notwithstanding its highly personal character, the diary retained a distinct literary purpose throughout the purge period. While attempting to resolve personal uncertainties and fears, Afinogenov emplotted them in such a way as to make them fit the structure of his

---

parallels the evolution of Soviet system at large: the hero's cycle occurs between late 1934 and late 1937, exactly when the purge program was formulated and carried out.

[33] The purges were carried out invisibly, Afinogenov argued, so that the removal of bad, diseased elements would not negatively affect the labor process of the otherwise healthy social body. Afinogenov thus stressed the secrecy of the purges as a virtue. By contrast, most Western historians regard it as a sign of the Bolshevik regime's embarrassment and culpability.

novel. Yet the diary differed from the projected novel in one important way. (To be sure, a comparison between the two works has to remain somewhat speculative, since the novel never materialized, except for a few initial chapters as well as outlines and scattered scenes recorded in the diary.) Both the diary and the novel narrated the same themes of personal degeneration, work on the self, and self-renewal. In this respect, the diary served Afinogenov as an ongoing autobiographical construction site. It was a laboratory of the self, revealing the inner workings of the soul, including its darker aspects: doubts, weaknesses, sins. Most importantly, the diary narrative was open-ended; it referred to an unfinished, ever-expanding self-project. The novel, by contrast, even though it also addressed impurities of the soul, would have presented a finished, harmonious picture of the human psyche. The novel narrative spanned a full—and, from the beginning, preordained—cycle of degeneration and regeneration, logically culminating in the hero's salvation. This distinction suggests that Afinogenov never intended to publish his diary *as is*. Rather, it was to serve as a literary quarry from which to carve the material needed for his novelistic self-presentation. From this standpoint, it made sense for him habitually to cut his diary into pieces, integrating the segments he deemed most worthwhile into his published works.

Afinogenov was acutely aware of how crucial a role the diary played in his quest to regain himself, not just as a writer but also as a Soviet citizen and Communist. In the fall of 1937, while reviewing the events of the preceding spring and summer, he wrote that his diary had "saved" him:

> The notes have saved me. Every night I sat down and wrote out what I had carried in me during that night, all the oppressive thoughts in my mind. And as soon as these thoughts spilled onto paper, I felt relieved. My mind and my heart were relieved of the pressure; it was as if another person had assumed the burden of my somber thoughts and given me time to rest. He did not just entertain these thoughts, he also preserved them, so that I would not return to them and could forget them without much ado, which also happened. This is why it is sometimes so strange to read about the past. Surprised, you ask yourself: did this really happen? Did I really think this? And the paper answers: yes, precisely like this. . . . But the fact that you are already so removed from this indicates how far you have traveled since. We, the white pages, mark this road with the regular landmarks of every single day that you have lived. (10/7/1937)

Freeing him from the burden of his "black thoughts," the diary figured as a garbage dump of sorts, onto which the playwright could unload all the trash accumulating in his soul, all that was illegitimate in the Communist world and that he regarded as expressions of his impurity. Yet, by the same token, and somewhat paradoxically, Afinogenov stressed the virtue of looking back at his qualms and despair as a way to memorize them.

This was necessary to prevent his ever returning to such a state of mind and to experience the distance he had traveled since leaving his old, impure self behind. The diary thus provided him with perspective on his self-renewal. The sequence of daily entries constituted, in his own words, milestones on the path from darkness to light, along which he was traveling. One of Afinogenov's principal goals in keeping his diary throughout the period of Terror was thus the production of a visible record of self-development.

Self-constitution in the Bolshevik vein was for Afinogenov an unending process of self-renewal, a constant work on the self, which he accomplished through writing. To stop on this road would mean to retreat into one's present, and hence imperfect, self. And stasis was tantamount to degeneration: "*11/16/1937* Right now, today . . . I got up with the desire to somehow move on: not to stop *thinking* and *accumulating* what I've already begun to accumulate, always *looking back* and *examining myself, not allowing myself to become my former self,* if even only a tiny bit" (emphasis in original).

Conversely, purity could be experienced only in the act of purification, in the very struggle against the lingering impurities within. As an instrument of purification, writing was supposed to eradicate impurities and at the same time, excavate a pure essence within, which Afinogenov understood as the Communist essence in his soul. Tellingly, he discovered this pure essence, "the best" that was in him, on November 7, 1937, the day when the Revolution summoned a new generation of young leaders into existence, which was also the day of Afinogenov's own rejuvenation:

> *11/7/1937* Today, in accordance with my behest, I looked through the notes of the last two years. Carefully, every single day. My impression: a massive amount of time spent in vain, and of an inability to use the circumstances for work; a lot of futile meetings, of grudges at every occasion, of vain expectations for something better, and it appeared to me that this "something better" would inevitably come from someone else but that I myself should just sit there, fold my arms and wait for this person. Only now do I understand that the best is within me. And this summer, these feverish thoughts of mine, my notes—they are the best that is in me. . . . But with respect to the diary entries for 1935 and 1936 . . . , I have to leaf through them and remind myself how fortunate that no road leads back to this empty wasted life, that ahead of me lie arduous work and new tasks that are so different from my entire easy past. The harder the life in front of me becomes, the more fruitful it will be.

Afinogenov welcomed the obstacles that marked the distance he had already traveled and the road still ahead of him. The more challenges, doubts, and weaknesses he encountered, the more effort he expended to overcome them and the purer he would emerge as a result. This mode of self-constitution and self-perfection, defined as an unending process of work and self-transcendence, was most glaringly present in Afinogenov's diary of the Terror, and this was the chief reason why he considered this period as the most precious in his entire life.

Convinced that by now he had reached the level of inner purity expected of a Communist, Afinogenov petitioned for his rehabilitation in December 1937. The playwright concluded the fateful year 1937, which had nearly destroyed him, with exclamations of gratitude for the opportunity that he had been afforded to regain himself as a person and be reborn. Writing that 1937 was the "year of [his] birth," Afinogenov undoubtedly also had in mind many other Party members and writer colleagues for whom this year had brought destruction and death (12/30/1937).

On January 18, 1938, the Central Committee issued a resolution admitting that many Communists had been unjustly expelled from the Party in preceding months. They had been the victims of enemies in the Party and state administration who concealed their true faces behind the appearance of overzealous vigilance. In the weeks following the Central Committee resolution, thousands of Party members were reinstated nationwide, Afinogenov among them. Yet the purge went on, shifting its target to overzealous opportunists (*perestrakhovshchiki*) who had furthered their careers by denouncing "honest" Communists.[34]

In the wake of his reinstatement to the Party and while working on his novel, Afinogenov turned to his diary again, with the intention of cutting out segments and transferring them to the outline of his novel. As may be recalled, he had practiced this habit ever since keeping the diary. Yet with respect to his diary notes of the Terror period, he made an exception:

> *2/9/1938* Yesterday, while working on the novel, I took scissors to the "reserve fund"—the diary of 1937. I felt sorry about destroying the pages. So much is connected to them. But I did not get to the fateful dates and notes. I mustn't touch them; after all, I remember my New Year's resolution to read these notes more often!

In his eyes, the diary of 1937 stood out as a monument: it was material evidence of the process of his renewal and of his new identity as a true Bolshevik. In this respect the diary of this period was no less important than Afinogenov's Party membership booklet which he kept looking at with unceasing wonder during the days following his reinstatement.[35] Afinogenov had to preserve the diary notes of the most critical period in his life in order to know that he was truly one of the new Soviet men. It is

---

[34] Robert Thurston, *Life and Terror in Stalin's Russia, 1934–1941* (New Haven: Yale University Press, 1996), 108.

[35] RGALI, f. 2172, op. 3, ed. 6 (diary entries of 2/7/1938, 2/8/1938, 2/10/1938).

only for this reason that his diary notes of the Terror period have survived intact to the present day.

In late 1938 Afinogenov sent a draft of his most recent play, *Moscow, Kremlin*, to Stalin for his evaluation. Around New Year of 1939 he received a brief note from Stalin, addressed to "Comrade Afinogenov," in which the leader apologized for being too busy to read the manuscript. In his diary, Afinogenov noted exuberantly:

> There it is, the beginning of the New Year! A personal note from *Stalin* himself! I couldn't believe this, and read and reread it. For the first time in so many years, *His* hand is writing to me again, and suddenly [I felt] a new surge of inspiration, of gratitude to *Him*, a new desire to work and write—to write! . . . Tears flowed down my face. . . . I wept out of gratitude for what I had found, for the fact that I, too, have now been given the opportunity to . . . become a true engineer of the soul. (Emphasis in original)[36]

In the following years Afinogenov wrote several plays which were staged in theaters throughout the Soviet Union to critical acclaim. Within days of the German invasion of June 1941, Afinogenov produced a play devoted to the war against fascism (*On the Eve* [Nakanune]). Yet the novel in which he wanted to distill his personal experience of the Stalinist purges remained incomplete. Afinogenov died in Moscow in October 1941, on the eve of a mission to England and the United States to give a series of lectures on the heroic struggle of the Soviet people against their fascist invaders. He was killed by a bomb during a German air raid.[37]

[36] Cited in Afanas'ev, "Ia i On," 348.
[37] Karaganov, *Zhizn' dramaturga*, 515.

CHAPTER FOUR

Publicizing the Imperial Image in 1913

RICHARD WORTMAN

New Modes of Representation

From the reign of Peter the Great, Russian monarchs sought to vest
themselves in European personas that reflected current Western ideals of
rulership and culture. At the same time, they presented themselves as em-
bodiments of the Petrine ethos of state service, subordinating the gratifications of private life to the superordinate goals of the imperial state.
Nicholas II ascended the throne in 1894 unburdened by the imperative
to transcend or deny his self. His model was contemporary royalty, particularly the English royal family and aristocracy, who had adopted many of
the individualistic tastes of nineteenth-century middle class society.
Marriage and the family, personal religious piety, healthful sport and
recreation, all were of paramount concern to him, competing with and often outweighing official obligations. His authority, Nicholas was convinced, demanded no self-transformation on a heroic mythical pattern.
He saw himself as a human being ordained by God and history to rule
Russia autocratically. Following the precepts of the national myth introduced during the reign of Alexander III, he believed that the Russian
people, specifically the peasants, were devoted to him personally, a conviction that he held tenaciously in spite of the widespread insurrections
among the peasants in the first years of the twentieth century.

This article is based on Chapter 14 of my book *Scenarios of Power: Myth and Ceremony in
Russian History*, Volume 2: *From Alexander II to the Abdication of Nicholas II* (Princeton:
Princeton University Press, 2000).

A disjuncture between the transcendent image of the autocratic emperor and Nicholas's own self-representation was evident from the beginning of Nicholas's reign. But it became particularly acute after the ebbing of the Revolution of 1905 and the establishment of representative institutions in Russia. He then began to demonstrate his bond with the masses of the peasants. This bond was not a sentiment of gratitude for a generous monarch bestowing benefactions on the people, as it had been characterized for Alexander II; nor was it the union of tsar and people through the Orthodox Church as proclaimed during the reign of Alexander III. It was represented as a spiritual bond between simple religious people—between the tsar who ruled and the peasants who wanted to be ruled without restrictions on the power of their "little-father" (*batiushka*) tsar.

Following the example of his European counterparts, Nicholas used great historical celebrations and mass publicity to appeal to popular feeling. While Nicholas disliked the public functions of the court, he appreciated the adulation of crowds of people and publicity of his warm domestic life. At the historical celebrations—the bicentenary of the battle of Poltava in June 1909, the jubilee of Borodino in August 1912, and the tercentenary of the Romanov dynasty in February and May 1913—he presented himself as heir to the traditions of Peter the Great, Alexander I, and the first Romanov tsars. He stood and chatted with groups of peasants as if they were kindred spirits, evoking a bond between tsar and people that presumably showed him to be a truer representative of their feelings than their elected deputies.

Nicholas's publicity campaign reached its height during the tercentenary of 1913. Pictures of the tsar and the imperial family appeared on new postage stamps, commemorative coins, and kitsch, the souvenirs of celebrations. Films showed a mass public scenes of the imperial family at ceremonies and episodes from Russia's past. Articles in the press and a widely circulated official account of Nicholas's life acquainted a growing reading public with his habits, tastes, and ostensibly democratic predilections.

The new genres of representation assured that the tsar's image would be conspicuous during the celebrations of 1913. But at the same time, their coarse forms and context could associate the lofty figure of the tsar with the everyday and commonplace. Mass-produced coins lacked the finish and class of the old limited editions. Stamps were cheap slips of paper that ended up in the trash. Actors could give inept or vulgar portrayals of the tsar on the stage. Newsreels were screened in sequence with trite romances and crime stories. Descriptions of the tsar's personal life gave him an aspect of the ordinary that was devastating to the worshipful admiration the tsar still hoped to command.

The new genres coexisted with the traditional elevation of the tsar as all-powerful autocratic monarch working, with superhuman effort, for the power and expansion of the empire. They introduced a dichotomy into imperial imagery, creating symbolic confusion in the midst of the political crises of 1913 and 1914. But this problem eluded Nicholas, who saw publicity as a confirmation of his broad popularity and the strength of his alliance with the masses of the Russian people against the educated classes and the institutions they dominated.

The commemorative rubles issued on the occasion of the Romanov tercentenary made clear both the possibilities and the perils of the new forms of publicity. For Nicholas's coronation in 1896, the government had circulated 190,845 commemorative rubles, nearly three times the number of 66,844 for Alexander III's coronation in 1883. For the tercentenary celebration, as many as 1.5 million commemorative rubles were issued. The increased numbers brought the commemorative ruble to a broader public beyond the court, the administration, and the armed forces.[1]

But the rise in production was accompanied by a noticeable decline in quality. The busts of Nicholas, bareheaded, dressed in the uniform of the Imperial Rifles, and Michael wearing the Monomakh cap decorated the obverse of the coin (Fig. 1). A breakdown of a die after the minting of the first 50,000 resulted in a flattening of the image of Michael, giving him a ghostly look. The jeweler F. P. Birnbaum wrote, "the layout of portraits is unsuccessful in both the decorative and sculptural respect," and a polemic in Novoe vremia focused on whom to blame for the failure. The numismatist S. I. Chizhov criticized the "market" appearance of the ruble, which was not, in his eyes, "a work of art." He pointed out that "the artist should not have placed a Greek design that has no relationship to the Romanov house on both sides of the ruble."[2] The tercentenary medal, which also bore images of Michael and Nicholas, prompted further dissatisfaction. A. I. Spiridovich, the chief of palace security, wrote that it was "as ugly as possible, and one asked, stupefied, how our mint could strike such a medal on the occasion of so memorable a jubilee."[3]

[1] Robert G. Papp, "The Road to Chervonets: The Representation of National Identity in Russian Money, 1896–1924," Unpublished paper for American Numismatic Society Summer Seminar, 1996, 10, 16–17, 19.

[2] Papp, "The Road to Chervonets," 17; F. P. Birnbaum, "Iubileinyi rubl', medal'ernoe iskusstvo i Monetnyi Dvor," in T. F. Faberzhe, A. S. Gorynia, and V. V. Skurlov, Faberzhe i Peterburgskie iuveliry (St. Petersburg: Zhurnal Neva, 1997), 357–60. The article was originally printed in Iuvelir' in 1913; S. Chizhov, "Iubileinye rubli 1912 i 1913 godov," Numismaticheskii sbornik (Moscow, 1915), 101–2.

[3] General Alexandre Spiridovitch, Les dernières années de la cour de Tsarskoe-Selo (Paris: Payot, 1929), 2: 357, 401.

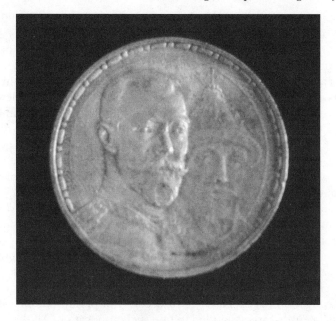

Figure 1. Tercentenary Ruble, 1913.

The issue of postage stamps carrying the portraits of Romanov tsars on January 1, 1913 represented a more fundamental break with imperial traditions. In Europe, the faces of monarchs began to be printed on postage stamps in the middle of the nineteenth century. The decision to introduce the practice in Russia was certainly made with the consent of Nicholas, who was an ardent philatelist. Of the tsars, Nicholas's portrait was represented most frequently—on the seven-kopek, the ten-kopek, and the five-ruble stamps. The seven- and ten-kopek stamps, intended for single-weight letters sent in Russia and abroad, gave his portrait the broadest dissemination. Peter the Great was shown on the one- and four-kopek stamps, Alexander II on the two-kopek, and Alexander III on the three-kopek. Of the pre-Petrine tsars, Alexei Mikhailovich appeared on the twenty-five-kopek and Michael Fedorovich on the seventy-kopek.[4]

Stamps had to be canceled, and devout Orthodox and supporters of the monarchy condemned what they regarded as a desecration of the sa-

---

[4] Michael Ercolini, "An Introduction to the Stamps of the 1913 Romanov Issue," *The Journal of the Rossica Society of Russian Philately*, no. 122 (April 1994): 11–14; *Niva*, January 5, 1913, 20. A. F. Giers refers to Nicholas and stamp collecting. A. F. Girs, "Vospominaniia byvshego ofitsera L.-Gv. Preobrazhenskogo Polka i Minskogo Gubernatora A.F. Girsa o svoikh vstrechakh s Gosudarem Imperatorom Nikolaem II" (Bakhmeteff Archive of Russian and East European Literature and History, Columbia University), 11.

cred image of tsar. Bishop Nikon, writing in the official organ of the Holy Synod, deplored the number of kopeks printed beside the tsars' faces as demeaning of the pious tsars worshiped by the people. Worse, he wrote, "these portraits of the tsars must be soiled with a postmark, as if to profane us all the more." Nikon asked himself if he was still living in Russia, "or has the kike come and conquered our tsardom?" The newspaper *Zemshchina*, an organ of the extreme right-wing Union of Russian People, pointed out that the law specified sentences of penal servitude for those who defiled the imperial image. Many postmasters refused to desecrate the face of the tsar with postmarks and left stamps uncanceled. The government suspended the series in February 1913 but resumed printing it later that year.[5]

The mass production of souvenirs with portraits of members of the imperial family troubled the censors in the Ministry of the Court, but apparently not the emperor or empress. The ministry received applications to produce a variety of household items carrying the portraits of members of the imperial family, among them trays, candy boxes, metal cases, china, and calendars. "The placing of the portraits of imperial personages on objects having a utilitarian character is usually not permitted," an official of the court censorship responded to one such application. All the requests, however, were approved, sometimes with restrictions, as in the case of a request to market scarves with the portrait of the tsar. The censor authorized this "as long as these are of a size not suitable for use as handkerchiefs."[6]

The effort to popularize the image of the tsar in 1913 even led to the lifting of the ban of the presentation of Romanov rulers on the stage, which had been in effect since 1837. Enforcement had been irregular, but the rule had been consistently applied to grand opera.[7] For example, at the end of all performances of Mikhail Glinka's *Life for the Tsar*, a procession led the newly elected Michael Romanov into Moscow, but the curtain always fell before he appeared. The gala performance at the

---

[5] Bishop Nikon, "Vera Khristova ne terpit dvoedushiia," *Tserkovnye vedomosti*, February 9, 1913: 283–84.

[6] "Ob izdaniiakh kasaiushchikhsia 300–letiia Doma Romanovykh," RGIA, f. 472, op. 49, d. 1083, ll. 70, 134, and passim. The growth of the market, however, exceeded the capacity of the office of court censors, and some items, like a cheap jubilee medal produced by a private firm, had not even been submitted for approval. Ingeborg Kaufmann, "Das dreihundertjährige Thronjubiläum des Hauses Romanov: Russland 1913," Masters thesis, Humboldt University, Berlin, 1996, 68–69.

[7] In the early twentieth century, the censorship permitted three different performances showing Peter the Great, one of them a comic opera, and one play about Catherine the Great. However, proposals to portray Michael Romanov, Fedor Romanov, and Alexander I in plays marking the anniversary of 1812 were refused. "Po povodu izgotovlennoi Lefortovskim Otdeleniem damskogo popechitel'stva o bednykh v Moskve kinematograficheskoi lenty s izobrazheniem sobytii za vremia 300–letiia tsarstvovaniia Doma Romanovykh," RGIA, f. 472, op. 49, d. 1252, l. 27.

Mariinskii Theater in St. Petersburg in February 1913, however, concluded for the first time with Michael's entry into Moscow. He marched in a procession of the principal historical figures of the early seventeenth century. Michael, played by Leonid Sobinov, rode in a gilded carriage led by companies of musketeers. With two boyars at his side, he received bread and salt from groups of boyars and a golden goblet from the oldest, Andrei Trubetskoi.[8]

Permission was also extended to the Malyi Theater in St. Petersburg, which presented Tsar Michael in a play of E. M Bezpiatov, "Oh, Quiet Light" (Svete tikhii), about the period of the election. The performance took place only after the censors' objections had been overridden by authorization from the throne.[9] The Ministry of the Court also permitted both the Moscow Malyi Theater and the Aleksandrinskii Theater to present three excerpts from Nicholas Chaev's drama "The Election of Michael Romanov," including the scene of the meeting of the Great Embassy with Martha and Michael in the Ipat'evskii Monastery. When the cast sang "God Save the Tsar!" at the close of the performance, the actor Davydov, who played Michael, amazed the audience by raising his voice above all the others. Shouting the final hoorah he extended his arms forward and threw his hat into the air, to loud hoorahs from the crowd.[10]

The medium of film was most congenial to Nicholas, for it enabled him to establish direct visual contact with a mass audience without jeopardizing either his privacy or security. It also made his ceremonies and celebrations known to large numbers of his subjects, many of whom were illiterate or could not hope to witness them firsthand.[11] From 1911–14 the censors approved more than one hundred requests to screen newsreels of the tsar submitted by such firms as Pathé, Khanzhonkov, Drankov, and Gaumont. These films gave the public glimpses of Nicholas at various ceremonial occasions, including the Borodino festivities, the tercentenary processions in Petersburg and Moscow, the Blessing of the Waters, military reviews, parades of the play regiments (*poteshnye*), the launching of ships, and receptions of foreign dignitaries. Moviegoers also could see the

---

[8] The procession at the conclusion of *Life for the Tsar* reproduced the picture in the 1672 album, reprinted in 1856: *Kniga ob izbranii na tsarstvo Velikogo Gosudaria, Tsaria, i Velikogo Kniazia Mikhaila Fedorovicha* (Moscow: Sinodal'naia tipografiia, 1856). See also *Russkoe slovo*, January 18, 1913: 4; February 23: 3; *Birzhevye vedomosti*, February 22, 1913: 5.

[9] *Russkoe slovo*, January 18, 1913: 4.

[10] *Moskovskie vedomosti*, February 23, 1913: 3; March 3, 1913: 2–3.

[11] Court censors freely gave permission to film imperial ceremonies with the tsar, even though the ban on *showing* films of the imperial family remained in force until 1910. Yuri Tsivian, *Early Cinema in Russia and Its Cultural Reception* (London: Routledge, 1994), 126. On censorship and the film, see Yuri Tsivian, "Censure Bans on Religious Subjects in Russian Films," in Roland Cosandey, André Gaudreault, Tom Gunning, eds., *Une invention du diable? Cinéma des premiers temps et religion* (Sainte-Foy: Les presses de l'université Laval, 1992), 76–77.

emperor and his family attending ceremonies in the Crimea. A newsreel of his birthday celebration in 1911 showed Nicholas crossing himself continuously during the religious services. Others presented scenes of the empress at the "Day of the White Flower" for the Red Cross in Yalta and the family's visit to the estate of Prince Lev Golitsyn, where the tsar examined the prince's vineyards and caves.[12]

The censors tried to ensure that the screening of these films took place with the appropriate dignity and not in sequence with figures of lovers and bandits. They, in effect, understood the reception of early film programs, discussed by the film historian Yuri Tsivian—that the combination of short film subjects on a single program raised the possibility of associating one with the other. The censors prescribed that newsreels of the emperor and imperial family should be separated from the rest of the program, "not mixed up with the other pictures," and that they should be presented without musical accompaniment. The curtain was to be lowered before and after the showing of the imperial family, and films of them were to be projected by hand, "at a speed that ensures that the movements and gait of those represented on the screen does not give rise to any comment."[13]

To publicize and associate himself with the great accomplishments of the dynasty, Nicholas encouraged the production of historical films. He personally approved the release of two productions to mark the tercentenary—Alexander Khanzhonkov's "The Enthronement of the Romanov House, 1613–1913," and Alexander Drankov's "Three Centuries of the Ruling House of the Romanovs, 1613–1913: Historical Pictures." Khanzhonkov's film depicted the last years of the Time of Troubles and Michael's election.[14] Only the first quarter of Drankov's footage was devoted to 1613; the remaining sections presented an overview of the principal events of the subsequent three centuries.[15] Both films consisted of a succession of tableaux vivants. Their format, like that of many other motion pictures of the time, conformed to the structure of the cheap popular *lubok* literature circulated among the people: the actors struck conven-

[12] "Po voprosu tsenzury kinematograficheskikh snimkov s izobrazheniem Vysochaishikh Osob," RGIA, f. 472, op. 49, d. 988; N. N. Kalinin and M. A. Zemlianichenko, *Romanovy i Krym* (Moscow: Rurik, 1993), 83.

[13] Audiences went to the theater, Tsivian writes, to see an entire program, a show consisting of a series of short subjects, and "the impression made by one picture imposed itself involuntarily on the next." Tsivian, *Early Cinema in Russia*, 127.

[14] The film apparently concluded with a scene, which has not survived, of Michael's anointment. "Votsarenie Doma Romanovykh, 1613–1913," RGAK (Rossiiskii Gosudarstvennyi Arkhiv Kinofotodokumentov), I–12890.

[15] "Trekhsotletie tsarstvuiushchego Doma Romanovykh, 1613–1913: Istoricheskie kartiny," RGAK, I–22645.

tional heroic poses from popular prints, *lubki*, to illustrate particular historical events.[16]

The semilegendary context of the *lubok* permitted imaginative portrayals of tsars by actors. The censors accepted the dramatic portrayal of Michael Romanov on the screen, played by the actress S. Goloslavskaia in Khanzhonkov's production and by Michael Chekhov in Drankov's, as well as the presentation of eighteenth-century monarchs in tableaux vivants of eighteenth-century courts. But the censors were less tolerant about the portrayal of more recent rulers. Nineteenth-century emperors had to be presented with care and dignity, for their memory as persons had not faded, and therefore they could not properly be portrayed by actors. Drankov used busts to represent Alexander I and Nicholas I, and portraits for Alexander II and Alexander III. Their images alternated with tableaux of the great moments of their reigns, such as the struggle with Napoleon, the emancipation of the serfs, and the court reform of 1864. Nicholas II appeared at the end of the film himself, in a succession of clips of ceremonial occasions—the coronation, the dedication of the Petersburg monument to Alexander III in 1909, Nicholas with his troops and at the Borodino celebrations. Setting Nicholas in sequence with images of the foremost of his predecessors associated him with their glory and achievement. Showing him at major celebrations recalled the moments of exaltation that confirmed the popular backing of the monarchy.

These films, however, affronted conservative sensibilities. A Prince Kudashev wrote to *Moskovskie vedomosti* that he found Khanzhonkov's presentation of the siege of the Trinity Monastery, which showed the portals as well as the icons painted on the walls, "frightening and unusual." "A place, which as a shrine is dear to the people, . . . has been turned into a stage set for the film to be performed." Kudashev not only deplored the showing of the pectoral cross but was also appalled that actors were dressed up as monks "on this very spot," and that one was actually permitted to play Patriarch Hermogen, whom the people worshiped as a saint.[17]

"The Crowned Toiler"

The most important means of popularizing the tsar and the monarchy during the celebrations was the printed word. At the end of 1905, the

---

[16] Many of the authors of *lubok* tales in the penny newspapers became screenwriters at this time: S. S. Ginzburg, *Kinematografiia dorevoliutsionnoi Rossii* (Moscow: Iskusstvo, 1963), 114–18; and Jeffrey Brooks, *When Russia Learned to Read: Literacy and Popular Literature, 1861–1917* (Princeton: Princeton University Press, 1985), 109.

[17] *Moskovskie vedomosti*, March 3, 1913: 1.

leaders of the government and Nicholas himself had resolved to create newspapers that could reach the people and argue the government's program against the opposition. The government dispensed large sums to support more than thirty newspapers across Russia. Under the aegis of the Ministry of Internal Affairs, the newspaper *Rossiia* was established as a private organ supported by the government—what was called *ofitsioz*.[18] The ministry's newspaper for the peasants, *Sel'skii vestnik* became an independent periodical, the change symbolized by the replacement of the former "manager" of the newspaper by an editor who received leeway to make the newspaper more appealing to a mass readership.[19] But, like other government-supported organs, neither of these attracted large numbers of readers.[20] Assistant Minister of Interior S. E. Kryzhanovskii explained the failure of official organs in terms of "the complete absence of people prepared for journalistic activity. This is not surprising since newspaper work was the province of oppositional circles that had at their disposal large staffs, mainly of Jewish origin."[21]

The official organs achieved far greater success in their publication of brochures and books. *Rossiia* and *Sel'skii vestnik* circulated brochures in the millions.[22] The peasants, Jeffrey Brooks pointed out, were unaccustomed to newspapers but liked to read chapbooks and popular journals. Moreover, in the words of one student of peasant attitudes, S. A. Rappaport (An-skii), for the peasants, "printed means it is true, printed means it is just."[23] With the help of Peter Stolypin, *Sel'skii vestnik* acquired a printing press and storehouses. It published books on such practical matters as agriculture and law and set up outlets at towns along the Trans-Siberian Railway. During the Borodino and tercentenary celebrations, the editors expanded their lists to include books on history and patriotic studies.[24]

These celebrations provided the occasion for a vast expansion and distribution of monarchist literature in the countryside. In 1911, *Sel'skii vest-*

[18] On the official press during and after the revolution of 1905, see A. V. Likhomanov, *Bor'ba samoderzhaviia za obshchestvennoe mnenie v 1905–1907 godakh* (St. Petersburg: Rossiiskaia natsional'naia biblioteka, 1997).

[19] James H. Krukones, *To the People: The Russian Government and the Newspaper Sel'skii Vestnik ("Village Herald"), 1881–1917* (New York: Garland Publishing, 1987), 190–204.

[20] In 1906, the numbers of copies circulated of *Rossiia* ranged from 1,037 to 7,217. Likhomanov, 110–11. Circulation of *Sel'skii vestnik* fell from over 100,000 before 1905 to less than half of this. By 1912, it had risen to only 47,500 and was increasing only slowly in 1913. Krukones, *To the People*, 204. This compares to close to 4 million for *Novoe vremia* in 1912 and close to 300,000 for *Russkoe slovo*. Louise McReynolds, *The News under Russia's Old Regime: The Development of a Mass Circulation Press* (Princeton: Princeton University Press, 1991), Tables 5 and 8.

[21] S. E. Kryzhanovskii, *Vospominaniia* (Berlin: Petropolis, n.d.), 101–2.

[22] Likhomanov, *Bor'ba samoderzhaviia*, 112–13; Krukones, *To the People*, 209–10.

[23] Brooks, *When Russia Learned to Read*, 31–32.

[24] Krukones, *To the People*, 208–13.

nik entered into an agreement with the house of Ivan Sytin, the commercially successful publisher of the newspaper *Russkoe slovo*. Sytin commanded a vast distribution network in the provinces. Books and pamphlets were also distributed through the Trusteeships of the People's Temperance, libraries, schools, the Church, and the military. During the Borodino jubilees, the books and pamphlets published by *Sel'skii vestnik* jointly with Sytin reached 2,860,000 copies. Portraits of the imperial family and war heroes numbered 700,000.[25] According to Sytin, his house published 3.8 million copies of books and pamphlets for the tercentenary, while *Sel'skii vestnik* reported 2.9 million books and 1.9 million portraits.[26]

Sel'skii vestnik also promoted and distributed the "Tercentenary Icon," which the Synod had approved in December 1912. The icon was painted with pictures of all the saints whose names were borne by rulers of the Romanov house. It came in large versions suitable for churches, schools, and state and public institutions, and small ones for private use. The kiot, the icon case, could be of wood, marble, or silver.[27] The editor of *Sel'skii vestnik*, P. P. Zubovskii, claimed that it was the most popular of the bric-a-brac sold for the tercentenary. Zubovskii wrote, "The Russian people know how to pray and enjoy praying for what they love."[28]

The very scope of official publications and other items associated with the ruling house confirmed the belief in the popularity of the monarchy held by Nicholas and many of his advisors. Such literature made known the tsar's person and life, showing the qualities they thought would strengthen the bond between him and the people. This was the goal of the unprecedented authorized account of the life of a reigning tsar, *The Reign of the Sovereign Emperor Nicholas Aleksandrovich*, published under the auspices of *Sel'skii vestnik*. The author, Professor and Major-General Andrei Georgievich Elchaninov, was a member of Nicholas's suite.[29]

[25] Ibid., 213; On Sytin, see Charles A. Ruud, *Russian Entrepreneur: Publisher Ivan Sytin of Moscow, 1851–1934* (Montreal: McGill-Queens University Press, 1990).
[26] Brooks, *When Russia Learned to Read*, 314; "Ob izdanii redaktseiu *Sel'skogo Vestnika* knigi General-Maiora A. El'chaninova, 'Tsarstvovanie Gosudaria Imperatora Nikolaia Aleksandrovicha,' " i podnesenii ee Ego Imperatorskomu Velichestvu," RGIA, f. 472, op. 49, d. 1187, ll. 56–57.
[27] *Sel'skii vestnik*, January 18, 1913: 4.
[28] Krukones, *To the People*, 214.
[29] Prof. A. El'chaninov, *Tsarstvovanie Gosudaria Imperatora Nikolaia Aleksandrovicha* (St. Petersburg: Sel'skii vestnik, 1913). The intermediary between the editor and the tsar was Prince Michael Andronikov. "Ob izdanii redaktseiu *Sel'skogo Vestnika* knigi General-Maiora A. El'chaninova," passim. El'chaninov was a major-general in the tsar's suite and a professor of military art at the General Staff Academy. He had written specialized books on fortification and cavalry, a biography of the eighteenth-century military hero Alexander Suvorov, and a commemoration of the three-hundredth anniversary of the siege of the Trinity Monastery during the Time of Troubles. *Novyi entsiklopedicheskii slovar'*, 29 vols. (St. Petersburg: Brockhaus-Efron, 1911–16), 17: 474.

Elchaninov's book was released in early 1913, before the beginning of the February celebrations, and appeared in excerpts or installments in many major newspapers during and after the events.[30] French and English translations followed in 1914.[31] Elchaninov presented Nicholas to the Russian people and to Russia's allies as a tsar expressing the needs and advancing the interests of his people—a democratic ruler on the Russian throne.

Elchaninov organized his text to permit the broadest possible dissemination in newspapers. The book comprises twelve brief chapters. The themes are set forth in the first chapter, but repeated throughout so that the chapters could stand on their own. The prose is simple, but elevated in tone like a panegyric. But it is a realistic panegyric devoid of extended metaphor or allegory. The author depicts Nicholas as a virtuous, exceptionally able, and feeling human being on the basis of considerable detail from the tsar's personal life and recent history. He gives his account a patina of verisimilitude, even if the idealization of his subject deprives the text of credibility. The mixture of panegyric and journalism clearly favors the former.

The book presents a unique statement of how Nicholas himself understood his office and wished himself to be perceived. Elchaninov gathered considerable material about Nicholas's personal life from observations and impressions of those close to the tsar, who clearly acted with Nicholas's consent.[32] The personal detail prompted the court censor to express misgivings about the book's "intimate character." "Similar publications have not been authorized until now," he observed. When Nicholas reviewed and corrected the page proofs in January 1913, he made one very significant change, which affirmed his absolute unwillingness to cooperate with the Duma. He insisted that Elchaninov delete the sentence, "In his work, the Sovereign Emperor considers his closest assistants in legislative work the reformed State Council and the State Duma, which he has summoned to life."[33] He also requested the removal of sentences de-

---

[30] For example, *Novoe vremia, Moskovskie vedomosti, Russkoe slovo, Grazhdanin, Kopeika,* and *Zemshchina* printed one or more excerpts from the book. An article in the *New York Tribune* that summarized the sections on the tsar's family life was headlined, "Intimate Details of the Czar's Daily Routine Given in a Book by a Well Known Professor Reveal Him as a Kindly Man of Family," *New York Tribune,* April 13, 1913: 9.

[31] The English version was entitled *The Tsar and His People* (London: Hodder and Stoughton, 1914), the French version *Le règne de S. M. l'Empereur Nicholas II* (Paris: Hachette, 1913). Grand Duke Pavel Aleksandrovich wrote to Nicholas on May 29, 1913, that his wife Ol'ga Pistolkors had decided to translate the book into French "so that foreigners, and especially the French, had a correct idea of Russia and her tsar, a country that is a friend and ally." V. P. Semennikov, *Nikolai II i velikie kniazia* (Leningrad: Gosizdat, 1925), 58.

[32] El'chaninov remarks in the last lines of Chapter 1 that the reader should thank not "my humble and unworthy self" but "all those who, standing in close proximity to the throne, have honoured me with their confidence and enabled me to give to the world their observations and impressions." *Tsarstvovanie,* 16; *Tsar and His People,* 9.

[33] "Ob izdanii redaktseiu *Sel'skogo Vestnika* knigi General-Maiora A. El'chaninova," 2, 4, 8. The deleted sentence was on page 97 of the proofs.

scribing prayers for the recovery of the heir, which placed undue emphasis on Alexei's recent illness.[34]

The text of Elchaninov's book therefore can be read as an exposition of Nicholas's conception of his own mythical role, and it functioned, like previous panegyric, to confirm to the tsar the truth of his idealized image. In this respect, Elchaninov extols the qualities of heroic self-sacrifice to duty and to the people, characteristic of Nicholas's predecessors. Nicholas's dedication, Elchaninov emphasized, came from his personal designation by God during his coronation. The book opens at the moment after his investiture when the tsar kneels before the congregation and begs God to help him "in his high service to order all for the good of his people and the glory of God." Nicholas's every word and deed, Elchaninov wrote, was occupied with this "mission, which cannot be compared with any obligation of our own."[35] Heeding his coronation vow, Nicholas is "the true father of his people," who thinks and works only for them. "He never lays down his work, on week days, and weekends, resting only during his short period of sleep, offering in small things, as in great, a lofty example of 'loyalty in the performance of his duty.' "[36]

The conscientious, diligent, and able performance of his duty became the principal sign of the tsar's title to rule. His dedication set him apart from his subjects but also revealed him laboring like them: he is "the crowned toiler" (*ventsenosnyi truzhenik*) who, "following the precept of the founder of the dynasty, Tsar Michael Fedorovich, ceaselessly devotes himself to serving his people."[37] Like other authors expressing Nicholas's view of the tercentenary, Elchaninov makes Michael's self-sacrifice for his people the central act of 1613.[38] The synchronic mode of the myth is reflected in the persistence of this ethos as the characteristic distinguishing all members of the dynasty.

The title of the first chapter, "The Sovereign Helmsman of the Russian Land" (*Derzhavnyi kormchii russkoi zemli*), sets Nicholas on this timeless plane: Pushkin's image of Peter the Great as helmsman is juxtaposed with the initial designation of Russian unity in the chronicles, "the Russian

---

[34] "Ob izdanii redaktseiu *Sel'skogo Vestnika* knigi General-Maiora A. El'chaninova," 8. These deleted passages were on pages 34 and 45 of the proofs.

[35] *Tsarstvovanie*, 7–8; *Tsar and His People*, 1–2. The vow or supplication was introduced at the coronation of Anna Ioannovna in 1730. See Richard Wortman, *Scenarios of Power*, Volume 1: *From Peter the Great to the Death of Nicholas I* (Princeton: Princeton University Press, 1995), 101–2.

[36] *Tsarstvovanie*, 8; *Tsar and His People*, 3.

[37] *Tsarstvovanie*, 16; *Tsar and His People*, 9.

[38] See, for example, I. Bazhenov, "Prizvanie Mikhaila Feodorovicha k prestolu," *Iubileinyi sbornik kostromskogo tserkovno-istoricheskogo obshchestva* (Kostroma, 1913), 58–59; *Moskovskie Vedomosti*, February 22, 1913: 3; P. G. Vasenko, ed., *Boiare Romanovy i votsarenie Mikhaila Feodorovicha* (St. Petersburg: Komitet dlia ustroistva praznovaniia, 1913), 142–52; S. A. Toluzakov, *Podvig 300–letnego sluzheniia Rossii gosudarei Doma Romanovykh* (St. Petersburg: Iakor, 1913), 3–4, 312.

Land." Nicholas is endowed with Peter's traits of absolute control, will, and sense of direction: he acts on behalf of the Russian land, the nation. But the concept of nation was not present in the legislation or manifestos of Peter's time. Peter had directed his energies to the organization and strengthening of the Russian administration, the very institutions that now eluded Nicholas's influence and control. Elchaninov gives a picture of one who is sure of himself and is in absolute control of the government. This is clearly an answer to the widespread conception at the time of Nicholas as passive and distant from state affairs.

Like Drankov's film, Elchaninov sets Nicholas in a historical frame with his illustrious forebears, associating him with their glories and heroism. At the conclusion, he draws explicit parallels between the crisis of the early twentieth century and the troubles faced by Romanov tsars in the early seventeenth, eighteenth, and nineteenth centuries. Each had triumphed by uniting with the people. Michael had received his power from the people and then "with a gentle but firm hand, in unity with his people, led his country back to the path of glory and greatness." Peter had brought Russia out of the chaos left by "the Empress Sophia." Russia was "raised to a greater height than ever before by 'the unity of the people with the Tsar.' " When Napoleon had taken Moscow, "the people with one accord offered their soul, full of love and devotion, to their Tsar, and by a united effort, with the aid of the army repulsed the terrible invasion and soon planted their standards on the walls of Paris." In all three cases, "as soon as the people responded to the Tsar's summons to unite with him, the sun once more shone on the Russian Land!"[39]

Elchaninov places Nicholas within the recurring motif of triumph of tsar and people. He shows Nicholas as leader of his people, taking initiative in the political, agrarian, and military reforms of his reign. He presents tragedies and defeats as minor setbacks on the path to national unity and resurgence. The Khodynka massacre at Nicholas's coronation is mentioned only as an occasion for a show of Nicholas's pity and largesse to the suffering. The Russo-Japanese war is passed over with the assertion: "In spite of the unfortunate war with Japan, our country's international position is stronger than ever before, and all nations vie with one another in seeking to secure our friendship."[40]

Elchaninov's detailed description of Nicholas at work brings out the tsar's dedication and self-discipline. Chapter Two, "The Crowned Toiler," takes us through Nicholas's workday.[41] By nine in the morning the tsar finishes his breakfast, "a simple frugal meal in keeping with his whole way of

[39] *Tsarstvovanie*, 132–34; *Tsar and His People*, 145–48.
[40] *Tsarstvovanie*, 14–16; *Tsar and His People*, 6–9.
[41] *Tsarstvovanie*, 17–31; *Tsar and His People*, 9–28.

living," and is at work in his study. From ten to eleven, he takes walks, alone or with the tsarevich, but usually he forgoes this to receive reports from high officials of the imperial court, ministers, or other "less exalted personages." At eleven, he tastes the soldiers' rations from His Own Infantry Regiment and the Imperial Escort, usually with the tsarevich. From twelve to two, he takes lunch, ample but simple, then holds audiences from three until four. From five to six he has tea with the family, though sometimes this hour too is devoted to business. At free moments, he would exercise—walking, bicycling, or canoeing—often with his children. He works from six until dinner at eight, sometimes giving audiences to officials. At 9:30, he returns to work until he retires at 12 or 12:30, "and often much later." According to the author, the tsar spent ten to twelve hours working each day.

Following the image of helmsman, Elchaninov shows Nicholas taking charge of everything personally. He gathers information himself and reads all correspondence. Nicholas trusts no one to make decisions, delegates no responsibility, and does not even allow a secretary to help him. This section makes clear Nicholas's complete independence from the institutions of state—the ministries and the Duma. Thus he remains true to the myth of all-competent absolute monarch, without concession to the complex demands of modern leadership. In most cases, the tsar thinks through a problem by himself, grasps its import, and composes the answer. When the tsar needs assistance, he turns not to government officials but to "heads of the various departments of the Palace, members of the Imperial suite, and others." He attentively studies the bills submitted to him by the State Council—more than nine hundred in 1909–11. The tsar annotates reports in his own hand, and the author cites several of his notes. For example, "I am persuaded of the necessity of a complete reform of our law statutes to the end that real justice should at last reign in Russia."[42]

Much of the tsar's time is spent attending audiences, with ministers, ambassadors, officials, and private individuals. He holds these frequently, sometimes receiving several hundred people in his day. "Courteous, attentive, and with a full and exact knowledge of every subject dealt with, the Tsar goes straight to the heart of the question, with a rare skill in anticipating a speaker's train of thought."[43] Private audiences last three to four minutes, those with ministers and ambassadors longer, but the tsar quickly understands the thread of all conversations and treats each according to his merits. All feel the tsar's proverbial charm. He gives pecuniary aid justly to supplicants. He knows exactly what to say, speaks con-

---

[42] *Tsarstvovanie*, 25, 31, 123–31; *Tsar and His People*, 18–21, 28, 133, 141–44.
[43] *Tsarstvovanie*, 24; *Tsar and His People*, 17.

cisely but always finds sympathetic things to say, and is informed about the life and work of all those he speaks to. He makes no distinction according to status. "The humblest person is honored by the Tsar's knowledge of his past and services and by his inquiries after his family and relatives." Elchaninov presents a tsar who both displays his concern for his people and serves as a model for them. The chapter ends with Nicholas's own words, "I do the work of three men. Let every one learn to do the work of at least two."[44]

Three of the twelve chapters of the book are devoted to Nicholas's family life. Elchaninov makes it clear that the family is a separate and even superior field of the tsar's virtue. Nicholas is a model father. He has few friends. The family is Nicholas's favorite company. Nicholas, the worker-tsar (*tsar'-rabotnik*) does not like "worldly pleasures" and "raises His Family in this spirit." "Entertainments at the Palace are comparatively rare. Great balls and processions are presented only when necessary, as a duty of service. A modest, frugal way of life is evident here too."[45]

The imperial family is an enclosed sphere, completely separate from court and state. The members are united by love and a sense of the significance of every detail of their life, giving the sense of a domestic novel, much as Queen Victoria had been presented in the last decades of the nineteenth century.[46] In this respect, Nicholas II's elevation of the family was quite different from his great-grandfather's. Nicholas I had made his family the symbol of the state, the center of the court and the bureaucracy; Nicholas II kept his family apart from these institutions.[47]

One of the three chapters is devoted to the vigorous outdoor recreation preferred by the imperial family. They enjoy swimming, hunting, tennis, rowing, horseback riding, bicycling, motoring, and picking mushrooms and berries. The text dwells on their automobile rides in the Crimea and their walks and berry collecting on the Finnish archipelagoes (*Fig. 2*). The involvement of parents and children alike with family life is most strikingly reflected in their passion for photography. "All the Tsar's family have cameras and bring back from every visit numbers of excellent photographs." These are pictures to be shown not to the public but to themselves and to friends. The imperial family shares the self-absorption of the middle-class family, one of the features that has made them so much more appealing to posterity than they were to their contemporaries.[48]

---

[44] *Tsarstvovanie*, 29, 31; *Tsar and His People*, 28.

[45] *Tsarstvovanie*, 50, 54; *Tsar and His People*, 47, 51. The word *tsar'-rabotnik* in the original is not translated directly in the English edition.

[46] Thomas Richards, *The Commodity Culture of Victorian England: Advertising and Spectacle, 1851–1914* (Stanford: Stanford University Press, 1990), 102–3, compares the life at the court of Victoria to a domestic novel.

[47] On Nicholas I's conception of the family, see Wortman, *Scenarios of Power*, 1: 325–42.

[48] *Tsarstvovanie*, 41–44; *Tsar and His People*, 37–41.

Figure 2. Nicholas and daughters in the Crimea. From A. Elchaninov, *The Tsar and His People.*

The recreations present Nicholas as an ordinary man, enjoying the pleasures of nature and sport. But as a Romanov he also must do things better than anyone else. In swimming "he has no equals amongst his suite; he is able to dive and remain under water for minutes together"(*sic*). He is extremely proficient at billiards. But the greatest attention is bestowed on Nicholas's hunting excursions, which are described in great detail and with illustrations *(Fig. 3)*. "Given his excellent marksmanship and his cool self-possession, it is not surprising that the Tsar should generally make the largest bag."[49]

Nicholas also has broad cultural interests. He loves opera, particularly Russian opera, but also the works of Richard Wagner. His favorite newspapers are *Novoe vremia*, the mass circulation conservative nationalist daily, *Russkii invalid*—the military newspaper—and among foreign periodicals, *Figaro* and *L'Illustration*. Nicholas's great passion, however, is for history, and he believes that history is the source of Russia's greatness. "The Tsar brings to the consciousness of Russian society the sense that only that state is strong which respects the heritage of its past and he himself is the first to honor that heritage." Nicholas studies old manuscripts and follows the work of the Alexander III Historical Society. He eagerly studies history, "paying special attention to the reign of the most tranquil

[49] *Tsarstvovanie*, 36–38, 50–52, 54–55; *Tsar and His People*, 33–34, 49, 52. Nicholas from youth prided himself on his triumphs in these sports and gladly heard flattery about his prowess. He wrote to his father on June 24, 1887, his first year on maneuvers at Krasnoe Selo, about his victories in billiards and boasted that he was considered the best player in his division. "Pis'ma V. Kn. Nikolaia Aleksandrovicha k Aleksandru III," GARF, f. 677, op. 1, d. 919, l. 110.

Figure 3. Nicholas in a Convoy Cossack uniform, "after a shoot." A. Elchaninov, *The Tsar and His People.*

Tsar Alexei Mikhailovich." He recites to his children the old Russian folk epics (*byliny*) and tells them tales of the exploits of heroes like the great Russian general, Alexander Suvorov. The breadth and precision of his knowledge is "astonishing."[50]

He has an especially great knowledge of Russian literature. His favorite writers, whose works he reads to his family, are Nikolai Gogol and I. F. Gorbunov, a theatrical monologist who delivered and published sketches from the life of the people. The family also enjoys Cossack songs and dances accompanied by balalaikas. The tsar is partial to Russian foods, particularly borsch, kasha, pancakes, and the monastery kvas, the recipe for which came from the Sarov Monastery. "Only Russian champagne is drunk in the Palace."[51] The palace servants are "for the most part Russians." Nicholas is "careful to notice and support every unique Russian initiative, every manifestation of the Russian national genius. Similarly he likes to have the country's affairs directed by Russians."[52] Such tastes associated Nicholas and the other members of the imperial family with the Russian people as distinguished from other nationalities making up the empire.

[50] *Tsarstvovanie*, 34, 54; *Tsar and His People*, 31, 34, 51–53.
[51] *Tsarstvovanie*, 38, 55; *Tsar and His People*, 34; 52–53.
[52] *Tsarstvovanie*, 26, 38; *Tsar and His People*, 22, 34.

The Orthodox religion, Nicholas believed, brought him closer to the Russian people. Elchaninov's chapter "The Orthodox Tsar" describes the imperial family's intense devotion—their attendance at all services and observances of fasts.[53] The tsar's rooms are hung with sacred icons; he loves the old chants and ceremonies, and when he meets priests, he kisses their hands. The church and clergy, however, play a minor role since Nicholas is convinced that he has a direct relationship to God. "In all his work, he seeks the instruction and support of God, from whom he derives his power as 'the Lord's anointed.' " Nicholas's religious observance expressed the bonds he felt between himself and God and between himself and the people, not between himself and the clergy. Much of the chapter is dedicated to his appearance in July 1903 at the canonization of Serafim of Sarov, which he and Alexandra promoted with little support from the church hierarchy. "The worshipers were deeply impressed by the sight of the Emperor and Empress in their midst as simple pilgrims, unattended by any suite or high officials." A photograph shows Nicholas carrying relics of Serafim at the Sarov observance. The tsarevich Alexei, who was conceived soon after the visit, also loves to read the saints' lives, particularly Serafim's, we are told.[54]

Elchaninov briefly describes the warm and helping relationship between emperor and empress and gives details of his daughters' education and tastes. But it is the tsarevich who is at the center of the tsar's attention. "The Tsar's relations with his son are extremely touching, their love for one another is extraordinarily deep and strong." Nicholas takes Alexei with him when he reviews the troops and when possible "spends three or four hours a day with him in healthy outdoor work."[55]

To the emperor and the empress, the tsarevich of course represented the continuation of the dynasty within the family. The next year a luxury edition of a book on the childhood and upbringing of Russian emperors was published to mark Alexei's tenth birthday. The cover carries an inset of Alexei in Russian hat and early Russian costume. At the sides are griffins from the Romanov coat of arms, holding shields.[56] Elchaninov presents the heir as a symbol of the rejuvenation of the Russian army and nation, "the future hope of the Russian people." Alexei is described as "thoroughly proficient in rifle exercises (with a wooden gun), skirmishing order, the elements of scouting, the rules and requirements of military discipline and performs the exercises correctly and smartly." He "delights in gymnastic exercises," and participates in the activities of the *poteshnye* in

[53] The chapter title is misleadingly translated "The Tsar and the Orthodox Church."
[54] *Tsarstvovanie*, 66–72; *Tsar and His People*, 62–69.
[55] *Tsarstvovanie*, 36; *Tsar and His People*, 31–32.
[56] I. N. Bozherianov, *Detstvo, vospitanie, i leta iunosti Russkikh Imperatorov* (St. Petersburg, 1914).

the Crimea, made up of soldiers' sons.[57] Alexei appears in eleven of the forty-seven photographs in the volume, more than any member of the family except the tsar himself. We see him selling flowers in Yalta, and held by his father, who is wearing "the full military outfit of a soldier of low rank"[58] (Fig. 4). He stands at his father's side on the yacht Standard, and in the ranks of his unit of poteshnye (Fig. 5).

Russian emperors were traditionally presented as paternalistic defenders of all estates of the realm and Elchaninov does not fail to characterize Nicholas in this manner. But he devotes little space to the tsar's relations with the nobility and the merchantry, and the new classes of Russia—the professions and the industrial workers—are ignored. These groups, along with other nationalities, clearly do not fit his image as people's tsar. For Nicholas, the Russian peasants are the Russian nation.[59] Elchaninov writes, "The emperor devotes much attention and care to the welfare and moral improvement of the weakest of the estates in their economic condition, if also the most numerous—the peasantry." To demonstrate this point, he describes Nicholas entering peasant huts "to see how they live and to partake of their milk and black bread."[60] He enumerates the agricultural reforms that the tsar presumably initiated on their behalf—the abolition of mutual responsibility for taxes in 1903 and of corporal punishment in 1904, and in 1906 the abolition of redemption payments and civil disabilities such as those connected with the passport system. The list concludes with statutes introduced by Stolypin to permit the dissolution of the peasant commune and to create a class of independent peasant proprietors, though there is no reference to Stolypin in this context. The tsar, Elchaninov emphasizes, is a "firm upholder of the new system of land tenure" and has introduced it on his Peterhof estate. A photograph shows Nicholas examining a new model of plow at Peterhof.[61]

The lower ranks of the Russian armed forces were made up of peasants, and Elchaninov emphasizes the tsar's personal rapport with the common soldiers. Nicholas, he asserts, feels particularly close to the "Rifles of the Imperial Family," which comprised peasants from the imperial estates; and he preferred to wear their uniforms, particularly when traveling abroad. Elchaninov also cites the details of a highly publicized episode of the tsar hiking with the weight of the backpack of the rifleman of the Sixteenth Rifle Regiment. He goes on to point out that Nicholas not only

---

[57] Tsarstvovanie, 14, 60; Tsar and His People, 7, 56–57.

[58] Tsarstvovanie, 45; Tsar and His People, 38.

[59] This theme is captured better in the English title The Tsar and His People than in the Russian The Reign of the Sovereign Emperor Nicholas Aleksandrovich.

[60] Tsarstvovanie, 76–80; Tsar and His People, 73–78.

[61] Tsarstvovanie, 80–82; Tsar and His People, 79–81.

Figure 4. Nicholas II in soldier's uniform holding Alexei. A. Elchaninov, *The Tsar and His People.*

Figure 5. Tsarevich Alexei in the ranks of *poteshnye*. A. Elchaninov, *The Tsar and His People*.

takes "every opportunity of seeing the army at close quarters" at reviews and maneuvers, but also on such occasions "converses personally with the men, gives them fatherly advice, thanks them for their service, praises them for their smartness, and gives them monetary or other rewards." Nicholas displays the same concern for the lower ranks of the navy. In photographs, he tastes the sailors' rations on the *Standard (Fig. 6)*, and kisses, chats with, and decorates Sub-Ensign Shepel for bravery in the Russo-Japanese War.[62]

Through these descriptions Elchaninov tries to give Nicholas the features of Peter the Great as he was presented in the popular literature—"as a Westernized gentleman, but also as a good comrade who does not recognize class distinctions."[63] Nicholas, like Peter, is portrayed as a military leader and reformer. The opening sentence of the chapter on the armed forces states that the tsar "personally directs all military affairs." Elchaninov attributes recent reforms of the military to him, among them increases in pay and pensions, the reform of the General Staff Academy, and other improvements in the recruitment and education of the rank and file. Nicholas, he claims, also promoted the production of airplanes, the construction of fortresses, and the rebuilding of the the Baltic, Black Sea, and Pacific fleets.[64]

[62] *Tsarstvovanie,* 92, 96–102; *Tsar and His People,* 97–98, 103–08.
[63] Brooks, *When Russia Learned to Read,* 79.
[64] *Tsarstvovanie,* 87–92; *Tsar and His People,* 91–97.

Figure 6. Nicholas II tastes sailors' rations on board the yacht *Standard*. A. Elchaninov, *The Tsar and His People*.

The lasting bond between tsar and the Russian peasantry is revealed most vividly at national celebrations, which are mentioned throughout the book and treated in a separate chapter as well. Elchaninov describes Nicholas's conversations with peasants at Poltava, Chernigov, Grodno, and Borodino, and their tearful exclamations when they hear his simple and kind words. He cites their speeches of gratitude at length, as expressions of the feelings of the people as a whole. For example, at Chernigov, a peasant from Liubech by the name of Protsko, proclaims, "We have come to you our Father, not alone, but with our children, 'poteshnye,' future heroes and defenders of Tsar and country, and to bless your future exploits." Protsko then presents the tsar with an icon of "the first Russian monk" St. Antony of Pechera, who came from Liubech. He continues, "In Your reforms we see the prosperity of Russia. Follow bravely in the footsteps of your ancestors, the Tsar-Liberator, Alexander II of blessed memory, and the Tsar-Peacemaker, Alexander III, of blessed memory; fear no foe—God and Russia are with you."[65]

At meetings with the peasants, Nicholas shows that he is one of them, sharing common Russian traits and interests. They need no deputies to voice their point of view, for the tsar has a special, abiding rapport with them. They have given their assent not at the ballot box, but at celebrations, where they reveal the unspoken ethnic, personal bonds, "the invisible threads," which link them to him.

> Thousands of invisible threads center in the Tsar's heart which is, as in the words of the Scripture, "in the hand of God"; and these threads stretch to the huts of the poor and the palaces of the rich. And that is why the Russian people always acclaims its Tsar with such fervent enthusiasm, whether at St. Petersburg in Marinskii Theatre, at the opera "A Life for the Tsar," or at the dedication of memorials to Russian glory at Borodino, or on his way through towns or villages.[66]

This bond with the people allows Elchaninov to minimize the importance of the State Council and the State Duma, which stand between tsar and people. He presents the establishment of representative institutions as the tsar's own initiative, and the institutions themselves as extensions of the imperial will. As evidence of the tsar's early constitutional intentions, Elchaninov cites the evasive manifesto of February 26, 1903. In the spring of 1905, Nicholas decided that over the years following the emancipation of the serfs, "the Russian people had become educated up to and accustomed to dealing with public and political affairs." This conclusion had moved him to "revive in all its original force the custom, practised by the

---

[65] *Tsarstvovanie*, 82–83; *Tsar and His People*, 82–83.
[66] *Tsarstvovanie*, 115; *Tsar and His People*, 121.

first Tsars of the Romanov dynasty, of allowing the people, through their representatives, to examine matters of State and to investigate the needs of the State." The revolutionary turmoil of 1905 ostensibly played no role in Nicholas's decision.

Portraying the tsar as the creator of the Duma, Elchaninov describes Nicholas's reception of the deputies of the first Duma in the Winter Palace and cites his speech welcoming "the best people" of the land. But the ensuing "troubles" showed the tsar that the Duma deputies were not the best people and convinced him to change the electoral law on June 7, 1907. The new electoral system sharply curtailed the number of deputies of the nationalities, particularly in the outlying areas of the empire. "Aliens" [*inorodtsy*], Nicholas II declared, should not "settle questions that are purely Russian." Elchaninov does not indicate that the new law also reduced representation of the urban population, especially workers and professionals.[67] He emphasizes Nicholas's great concern for peasant deputies, without mentioning that many of them belong to oppositional parties. At the tsar's reception for the Duma deputies in December 1912, Elchaninov remarks, the peasants were placed in the rear, but Nicholas "marked them out for special attention, beyond the greeting he gave to all the members."[68]

Like all his forebears, Nicholas inhabited a realm of myth, validated by ceremonial performances of homage and adulation. As in the past, symbolic agency was invoked when the monarch's preeminence was challenged, and the devices of myth reshaped the appearances of reality to vindicate the tsar's self-image. But Russian institutions and society had changed drastically by 1913. The establishment of the Duma and the expansion of a mass circulation press, which after 1905 thrived under relaxed censorship restrictions, had introduced new competitors for the attention of the Russian public. Nicholas, viewing himself as a democratic tsar, vied with the political parties through the media of publicity.

Alexander II had also claimed the love of the people, but his representations had been directed principally at the elite and sought to elevate him above his subjects by his supreme benevolence and beneficence. Nicholas addressed the masses directly. He vied with the Duma, and in so doing relinquished the Olympian superiority to politics that had been fundamental to the imperial myth. By bringing his life and rule into a public dialogue, he abandoned the monologic self-sufficiency characteris-

---

[67] *Tsarstvovanie*, 116–22; *Tsar and His People*, 123–32. On the expanded use of the term *inorodtsy* in this period, see John W. Slocum, "Who, and When, Were the Inorodtsy? The Evolution of the Category of 'Aliens' in Imperial Russia," *The Russian Review* 57, no. 2 (April 1998): 186–90.

[68] *Tsarstvovanie*, 80; *Tsar and His People*, 78.

tic of a myth that allowed no response but affirmation in elevating the absolute power of the Russian emperor.[69] At the same time, the modern genres of publicity demeaned his image and associated him with the everyday and ordinary. Such devices may have helped to popularize Victoria's homey grandmotherly character, but she was not a ruler seeking grounds to restore absolute monarchy.[70] Nicholas's image assumed traits of the European monarchs whose modus vivendi with parliamentary institutions Russian monarchs had vowed to avoid.

Indeed, Elchaninov's book, with its uncertain genre, veering between grandiloquent panegyric and democratic propaganda, typified the contradictory goals of tsarist representation in 1913. On one hand, Nicholas is the all-competent monarch, performing prodigiously. On the other, the excess of detail about Nicholas's daily life could only further diminish the superhuman image of the Russian emperor. On one hand, he is the epitome of elegant Western royalty, the aficionado of tennis, yachting, and fancy automobiles, the recreations of Western high society. On the other, he is the "crowned toiler" sharing a hard life of work with peasants and soldiers. The resulting image lacks coherence and is so at variance with well-known facts that it could hardly have gained the credence of contemporary readers.

The main importance of *The Reign of the Sovereign Emperor Nicholas Aleksandrovich*, however, was not its influence on the Russian public but its effect on the tsar himself. The publication of the book presumed a positive response and showed his involvement with the masses of the Russian people. It was self-validating, reinforcing Nicholas's idealized conception of himself. It reflected and magnified his belief in his virtues as father and Christian, as well as his capacities as ruler and military commander. It sustained his sense of calling to rule the state and to command the army following the tradition of his forebears, Peter the Great and Alexander I. Elchaninov narrowed the mythical reality of the Russian sovereign to the personal world of the all-competent monarch isolated from the institutional and social realities of Russia. He glorified Nicholas apart from the institutions of the Russian state. This image distinguished him from all his predecessors, who identified their own supremacy, to a greater or lesser degree, with the supremacy of the state.

The tercentenary celebrations convinced Nicholas that he had the support of the vast majority of the Russian people. Elchaninov's book confirmed his sense of prowess and destiny. In late 1913, Nicholas began to act on his convictions and sought, though unsuccessfully, to curtail the

[69] See *Scenarios of Power*, 1: 7, on the epic and monologic character of the imperial myth.
[70] On the publicity and marketing of Victoria's image, see Richards, *Commodity Culture*, 73–118.

powers of the Duma. During World War I, he continued this struggle by refusing to compromise with the Duma, thereby precluding a unified government to cope with the military emergency. In 1915, he realized his fatal dream and assumed the position of commander in chief of the Russian armed forces. In this respect, Nicholas utilized the genres of modern publicity to preserve his own mythical construction of reality and the belief in his historical mission to restore autocratic rule in Russia.

CHAPTER FIVE

The Silent Movie Melodrama: Evgenii Bauer Fashions the Heroine's Self

LOUISE MCREYNOLDS

Millions of Russians flocked to enjoy the dramatically new entertainment medium, the motion picture, at the turn of the twentieth century. As the tsarist empire struggled to become a modern industrial state, the movies offered both a respite from the burdens of that struggle and a glimpse into the potential of a modern future. Yet these ordinary moviegoers have long been overshadowed by the political elite of the era, the restive intelligentsia.[1] The complex capacity of the movies to influence how modernization took shape disappeared into the social critics' denunciations of manipulation and their accusations of the political escapism so often associated with mass culture. Contemporary theory, though, is redrawing the picture of a passive audience being molded by culture, allowing the masses to recover some of the agency that the elites had denied them. This permits a return to imperial Russia to watch the movies afresh.[2] A technological marvel, the motion picture provided the inarticulate and often illiterate an unprecedented opportunity to refashion them-

I thank Stephanie Sandler and Joan Neuberger for comments on an earlier draft of this paper. At the University of Hawai'i, Linda Engelberg of Sinclair and Pat Polansky of Hamilton Library procured many of these films and other materials for me. IREX and the Kennan Institute provided invaluable funding for my research, for which I am grateful.

[1] Even the best books to date on the prerevolutionary cinema—Yuri Tsivian, *Early Cinema in Russia and Its Cultural Reception* (New York: Routledge, 1994), and Neia Zorkaia, *Na rubezhe stoletiii* (Moscow: Nauka, 1976)—regard the movies from the perspective of the intelligentsia. Only the Futurist movement proved capable of appreciating the movies.

[2] Tsivian, *Early Cinema,* 104, discusses this. See also James Hay, Lawrence Grossberg, and Ellen Wartella, eds., *The Audience and Its Landscape* (Boulder: Westview Press, 1996).

selves—or, with reference to the title of this volume, to tell themselves stories about themselves.[3]

The contributions of movies to the positive creation of identity went unremarked at the time. Many would have echoed fledgling journalist Maxim Gorky's lament on the fate of characters in the black-and-white celluloid stories as "condemned to eternal silence and cruelly punished by being deprived of all of life's colours."[4] Himself an artist in the medium of print, and steeped in radical politics, Gorky preferred the descriptive realism of the word, whether spoken on stage or recorded in literature. For him, the "happy, laughing, working girls" on screen were "out of place," contrasting sharply to the "victims of social mores" he found seated around him.[5] Ever the astute social observer, Gorky measured the distance between life on the screen and in the crowd.[6] But like so many of his successors, he allowed his personal agenda to distort that measurement.

Explaining the distance between silver-screen personality and isolated viewer became the linchpin of the critique of narrative film from its inception. Social critics feared that audiences, particularly the female element, would close the gap with a reckless speed, eager to see the screen as a mirror. These women constitute the focus group for this essay because of their centrality to film audiences, which gave them a unique role in the development of narrative cinema.[7] Rendered vulnerable by the social circumstances that denied them a niche in the power structure, women supposedly flocked to movies in order to retreat into a melodramatic fantasy world, a deceptive celluloid paradise that lulled them into a false sense of security about their place in patriarchal society.[8] Gorky would have no doubt endorsed feminist film critic Molly Haskell's wry indictment of such viewings as "wet wasted afternoons."[9]

---

[3] On the relationship between movies and modernity, see Leo Charney and Vanessa Schwartz, eds., *Cinema and the Invention of Modern Life* (Berkeley: University of California Press, 1995).

[4] Quoted in Tsivian, *Early Cinema*, 2.

[5] Ibid., 36.

[6] Berthold Brecht's better-known theory of theatrical "distanciation" derived from his artistic and philosophical concerns about reminding the audience to keep itself separate from what they were watching.

[7] See Miriam Hansen, *Babel and Babylon: Spectatorship in American Silent Film* (Cambridge, Mass.: Harvard University Press, 1991), especially chapter 2, "Early Audiences: Myths and Models," 60–89. See also L. A. Handel, *Hollywood Looks at Its Audience* (Urbana: University of Illinois Press, 1950). Although these are studies of American audiences, it is commonly held that all national film industries targeted females.

[8] For an excellent survey of film theory as it has dealt with female viewers, see Tania Modleski, *The Women Who Knew Too Much: Hitchcock and Feminist Theory* (New York: Routledge, 1988), Introduction, 1–15.

[9] Ibid, 8.

Wet with tears, perhaps, but wasted for whom? Although it is widely held that the genre of melodrama gave silent movies one of their first essential narrative structures, this has been more readily interpreted as a negative rather than a positive influence. As theory returns agency to the audience, though, it must also reconsider the foci of their entertainments, including melodrama. Peter Brooks, a seminal figure in the rehabilitation of this genre, has argued that it developed in response to the limited capacities of tragedy and realism to convey the post-Enlightenment world destabilized by increasing secularization and an industrial revolution.[10] Tragedy, for example, depends for dramatic tension upon the fates, forces that individuals cannot control, whereas melodrama frames actions within contemporaneous social circumstances.[11] And despite their common grounding in the readily familiar and secular influences, melodrama distinguishes itself from realism by emphasizing emotionalism. Form and content depend upon each other for meaning, evident in melodrama's deliberately antirealist aesthetics. By trafficking in feelings lying beneath the surface reality, melodrama employs nonverbal means to convey what words, so critical to realism, were inadequate to tell.

Influenced also by romanticism's fetishization of the occult, and the secrets in Gothic novels that threatened on every page the uneasy facade of harmony, melodrama illuminates what Brooks termed "the moral occult," which resembled "the unconscious mind," the hiding place of "our most basic fears."[12] Melodrama anticipated Freud, and the discourses of sexual repression and desire that underlay psychoanalysis became especially manifest in silent movies. Psychoanalysis became further entangled with melodrama when it became a prominent tool for analyzing mass culture, of which melodrama remains a favorite genre because it deals with repression, both personal and social.[13] This connection to both the popular and the psyche, usually presented as a form of hysteria, has underscored melodrama's traditional secondary status as female-oriented culture. By the same token, however, it has highlighted the genre's ability to expose the threat of the repressed female to the male-dominated social order. For example, melodrama has been criticized as fundamentally conservative because when characters surrender to their lot they are assumed to be accepting the status quo; when repressed sexuality enters this formula,

---

[10] Peter Brooks, *The Melodramatic Imagination* (New Haven: Yale University Press, 1976).

[11] As R. B. Heilman pointed out, "Tragedy is concerned with the nature of man, melodrama with the habits of men." Quoted in Laura Mulvey, "Notes on Sirk and Melodrama," in Christine Gledhill, ed., *Home Is Where the Heart Is: Studies in Melodrama and the Woman's Film* (London: British Film Institute, 1987), 77.

[12] Brooks, *Melodramatic Imagination*, 5.

[13] For a discussion of how this affected film theory, see David Bordwell, *Making Meaning: Inference and Rhetoric in the Interpretation of Cinema* (Cambridge, Mass: Harvard University Press, 1989), especially chapter 4.

though, "restoration" really means "repression" rather than "resolution," so the status quo has by no means been made stable.[14]

When it arrived in movie houses, the melodrama had long suffered the same reproaches to which the custodians of culture had subjected the motion picture upon its appearance. Traditionally, melodrama depended upon threats to the status quo, the bourgeois patriarchal order, for dramatic energy. The moral core around which the action centered recreated the virtues of repressing impulsive behavior and restoring domestic stability. A morality tale for women and workers, melodrama championed the equilibrium offered by the bourgeois patriarchy. The bourgeois nucleus provided aesthetic as well as thematic inspiration for melodramas, with bric-a-brac and other bourgeois tropes dominating visual reproductions of the home as surely as sexual virtue provided the moral center. Yet for all of its presumed simplicity about virtue triumphant, melodrama as a medium of cultural expression had lost its "primitive integrity" by 1913,[15] as the genre found itself obligated to mediate between desire and expectation in an increasingly complex world. Melodrama offered "a heightened and expressive representation of the implications of everyday life,"[16] not neat resolutions.

The "implications of daily life" at the turn of the twentieth century differed remarkably from many of those of the nineteenth. Even if class and gender were still the primary markers used to identify the audience, those categories themselves had changed, as had the nature of the bourgeois patriarchy. The movies epitomized the key to this transformation: mass consumption. Emerging at a specific point in the evolution of consumer capitalism, movies constructed a place for pleasure away from "the 'real,' from the world of work and dreary production."[17] They offered constant spectacle, generated constant desire; by their very nature they functioned to integrate their audiences into consumption, which provided the dominant cultural discourse of the industrialized world early in the twentieth century.[18] Like consumerism, melodrama was propelled by desires, often unspoken, so it offered a natural medium for negotiating the new ways. Moreover, desire shattered the integrity of the bourgeois patriarchy because the middle classes, who pocketed most of the money produced by

[14] David N. Rodowick, "Madness, Authority, and Ideology: The Domestic Melodrama of the 1950s," in Gledhill, ed., *Home*, 268–80.

[15] Frank Rahill, *The World of Melodrama* (University Park: Pennsylvania State University Press, 1967), xiii.

[16] Patrice Petro, *Joyless Streets: Women and Melodramatic Representation in Weimar Germany* (Princeton: Princeton University Press, 1989), 34.

[17] Quoted in E. Ann Kaplan, "Mothering, Feminism, and Representation: The Maternal in Melodrama and the Woman's Film, 1910–40," in Gledhill, ed., *Home*, 123.

[18] As Miriam Hansen pointed out, "Besides turning visual fascination itself into a commodity, the cinema generated a metadiscourse of consumption . . . a phantasmagoric environment in which boundaries between 'looking' and 'having' were blurred." *Babel*, 85.

mass production, wanted freedom from the old pious confinements. The bric-a-brac that identified the domestic economy on screen also celebrated its conspicuous consumption.

Melodrama proved to be an especially effective medium for late imperial Russian audiences, stuck in an anachronistic political system yet trying to adapt to the social and cultural pressures that followed in the wake of the rapid industrialization of the 1890s. Russians were happy to embrace mass consumption, flocking to the fancy new department stores in the big cities, yet they still found many of their ambitions constrained by the moribund autocracy and antiquated system of social estates.[19] The contradictions generated by this situation could not be easily understood, much less articulated. Viscerally as well as cerebrally, audiences spirited themselves back and forth between seat and screen. The movie melodramas gave them a space for experimentation, not a retreat from reality. Identification with characters on screen would be partial, contingent. Each individual viewer might experience the story differently, but collectively they recognized the present, however exaggerated for dramatic purposes. Left alone to script themselves into, or out of, the action, they could explore alternatives to their *selves.*

The primary escort for Russian viewers through these melodramatic journeys was director Evgenii Bauer, 1865–1917, an *auteur* too long forgotten whose contribution to the evolution of narrative film compares well with that of his more famous contemporaries, American D. W. Griffith and Frenchman Louis Feuillade.[20] Bauer, a product of the commercial boom that accompanied Russia's industrialization, saw how the socially disruptive capacity of melodrama could be made all the more potent by the seductive aesthetics of consumerism. Within the dual context of the evolution of narrative film and the development of mass consumption, Bauer's films recapture the era rather like a childhood memory recovered on an analyst's couch.

Sex, psyche, and self: Bauer tapped into all three as he supplied a needed relevance to Russia's motion pictures. In an attempt to prove their cultural worth, Russian studios in 1913 were producing movies either based as loosely as a few reels would allow on such literary classics as Aleksandr Pushkin's "The Queen of Spades" or the seemingly infinite number of nationalistic plots that put actors in boyar and peasant costumes. Bauer changed this by developing the narrative properties possible through the techniques of *mise-en-scène*, that is, of accentuating the

[19] On the development of commercial consumption in imperial Russia, see especially "Cultural Transformation in Late Imperial Russia," in Catriona Kelly and David Shepherd, eds., *Constructing Russian Culture in the Age of Revolution, 1881–1940* (New York: Oxford University Press, 1998), 57–224.

[20] S. S. Ginzburg, *Kinematografiia dorevoliutsionnyi Rossii* (Moscow: Iskusstvo, 1963), 306–7, pays short Soviet shrift to the "formalist" Bauer.

Figure 7. Evgenii Bauer, 1865–1917.

spaces within his shots to tell stories through lighting and set design. His work makes plain the crisis of modernity from which many Russians were suffering, and he offers neither simple solutions nor an ideological panacea to those he implicates in his torrid plots. Bauer's lasting influence was to develop a uniquely Russian cinema characterized by its preference for psychological rather than action-oriented stories.

The future director had come to movies from the world of bourgeois extravagance and its commercialization of culture. The son of a musician and brother of two operetta stars, Bauer grew up in theater, but originally studied architecture with F. O. Shektel', the foremost designer of private homes for Moscow's newly moneyed merchants.[21] The key requirements of Shektel''s designs reemerged in Bauer's settings, from the central stair-

---

[21] German director Fritz Lang, 1890–1976, who became the king of sophisticated comedies in exile in Hollywood, also began his artistic career in architecture, an influence evident in such silent films as *Metropolis*.

case that rearranged private and public spaces to the different lighting arrangements necessary to illuminate the interior and the open spaces for display of acquisitions that allowed the bourgeois home to replicate the department store. Bauer left architecture for theatrical odd jobs, working also as a portrait photographer and master set designer for Moscow's most prestigious nightclub, the Aquarium—coincidentally the site of the first showing of a motion picture in Russia.[22] Bauer's sets, with the imaginative lighting and positioning strategies he had mastered as a photographer, became his film signature.[23] As veteran actor / director Ivan Perestiani said of him, "A beam of light in his hands was an artist's brush."[24]

Glamor and melodrama characterized Bauer's most important movies, and this heightened their appeal to female audiences: women constituted both the subjects and the objects of a Bauer film, the heroines and the consumers. Bauer's heroines were identifiably "new" women, that is, women whose circumstances were urban and who enjoyed opportunities to make choices previously unavailable to their sex. His melodramas accentuate the emergence of female subjectivity in Russia between the Revolutions of 1905 and 1917; his heroines are hopelessly entangled in the issues of the day. The nascent commercial capitalism that drove both the movie industry and the new woman kept the audience in touch with the heroine.[25] As Rita Felski argued, "The pleasures of consumerism may hold a particular allure for women, given that female fantasies of self-transformation have historically been linked closely to the charismatic power of the commodity."[26]

The female on the Bauer screen embodied contemporary struggles, which she accented through purposeful exaggeration. Bauer's brief movie career spanned the tumultuous interrevolutionary era, when festering national political and social problems were exacerbated by disastrous participation in World War I. The discourses his heroines "performed" included: the rapid industrialization that had precipitated modernity; the rise of a distinctively female-centered culture industry, headed by popular novelist Anastasiia Verbitskaia, who dramatized her works for the screen; and contested notions of femininity, especially dur-

[22] Biographical information about Bauer comes from Yuri Tsivian et al., *Silent Witnesses: Russian Films, 1908–1919* (London: British Film Institute, 1989), 546–50.

[23] Ginzburg, *Kinematografiia*, 16.

[24] Quoted in Tsivian et al., *Silent Witnesses*, 548.

[25] See Barbara Klinger, "Digressions at the Cinema: Commodification and Reception in Mass Culture," in James Naremore and Patrick Brantlinger, eds., *Modernity and Mass Culture* (Bloomington: Indiana University Press, 1991), 117–34.

[26] Rita Felski, *The Gender of Modernity* (Cambridge, Mass.: Harvard University Press, 1995), 124.

ing the war years when women began entering the public sphere through the back door of the workforce.[27]

Bauer played upon the ambiguous allure of the new ways in his directorial debut, *The Twilight of a Woman's Soul* (1913). The opening shot presented a readily recognizable trope of new money: tropical plants, as though straight from the dining room at the Aquarium, adorn a ballroom.[28] Conflict comes quickly: not everyone is enjoying the party. In a remarkable shot for that era, the camera moves the audience into the heroine's bedroom, through the gossamer curtain that separates her symbolically from the real world. Bauer implicated viewers in the heroine Vera's intimate life by drawing them surreptitiously into her bedroom and letting them observe, unknown to her, her private emotions.[29] He orchestrated the story through an intricately designed set, skillfully using curtains and other props to create depth on an otherwise flat surface: the room is white, with two large vases in the foreground, the bed ominously in the background. Bauer's experience in portrait photography is evident in his framing of Vera in a profile shot, head in hand, surrounded by the white furniture that reflects her troubled innocence.[30] Deciding to join the party below, she first walks through the light curtain and draws back a heavy drape to let in the sunlight. Positioning and lighting thus portend the action and provide the basis of Bauer's cinematographic syntax, his structuring of the story through visuals.[31]

A simple plot becomes nuanced at Bauer's touch. To mollify her daughter, Vera's mother, a countess active in charities and therefore a familiar figure in late imperial society, takes her daughter on her rounds among the poor. Bauer establishes social hierarchy, and in the process he gives the audience inside information about the supposed beneficiaries of Vera and her mother's good will. The audience first sees men drinking vodka and playing cards, and then a deep-space camera angle shows them to be in a basement, with the legs of the approaching do-gooders visible

---

[27] This model is borrowed from the introduction to Gledhill, ed. *Home,* 3.

[28] Svetlana Boym, *Common Places: Mythologies of Everyday Life in Russia* (Cambridge, Mass.: Harvard University Press, 1994), 5–10.

[29] Brooks, *Melodramatic Imagination,* 28, describes enclosed spaces as *topoi* characteristic of melodrama.

[30] Bauer's background in photography generated a degree of controversy about his use of actors, the critiques usually based on others' expectations of what the cinema should be. V. Khanzhonkova, "Iz vospominanii o dorevoliutsionnom kino," *Iz istoriia kino,* no. 5 (1962): 126–27.

[31] As Jean Mitry argued, "It was Griffith's role to define and to stabilize—we would say, to codify—the *function* of these different procedures in relation to the filmic narrative, and thereby unify them up to a certain point in coherent 'syntax' (Mitry does not use this word). . . . Thus, it was in a single motion that the cinema became narrative and took over some of the attributes of language." Quoted in Tom Gunning, *D. W. Griffith and the Origins of American Narrative Film: The Early Years at Biograph* (Urbana: University of Illinois Press, 1991), 34.

through the windows at the top of the frame. The men notice the charity ladies in time to change their demeanor, feign humility, and accept their gifts; they laugh at the joke to which the audience was also privy after the women leave. Bauer often took full advantage of the scopophilic potential of the camera to give viewers inside information on the characters, thus encouraging the sort of sympathy or repulsion—depending on the situation—that comes with the intimacy that movies allow.[32]

For the ladies' next visit Bauer uses the same techniques of inside knowledge for the audience, but rather than repeating the use of the basement, now Vera and her mother must climb to the attic to help another of society's unfortunates, Petrov, a worker who pretends to have been assaulted so that Vera will bandage his arm. That night, in another cinematic device that Bauer will make great innovative use of, the dream sequence, the heroine relives her happy day of philanthropy. Bauer appreciated as few others the revolutionary capability of movies to disrupt temporal and spatial sequences, to carry spectators around as if on some magic carpet not just through time and space but also through the characters' conscious and unconscious.

While Vera lies asleep, happy in the melange of translucent arms of those whom she aided reaching out to her, Petrov also recalls the day's activities. Stroking his bandage, he plots to bring Vera back to his garret. He writes a note telling her that he is dying, thanking her for her kindness. Climbing up to her window, he leaves it by the heavy drape so that she will find it when she opens the curtains the next morning. When Vera runs back to help him, Bauer again uses a camera angle more effectively than a script: from an overhead shot the audience sees Vera below in the courtyard, watching her from Petrov's predatory angle. Her ascent to the attic thus foreshadows a descent: once he has her alone, Petrov rapes her. While he is sleeping it off, she struggles free, grabs a trowel, and buries it in her molester. Disheveled and shaky, she climbs back down.

Calm soon returns. Vera meets and falls in love with a handsome prince. When he proposes marriage and moves forward to kiss her, though, she visualizes Petrov's face. This leads to a nervous breakdown, Vera once again in her bedroom, but this time no gossamer curtain signals her chastity. Her nerves recover. Vera agrees to marry the prince, and tries several times to tell him her secret, but circumstances always prevent disclosure. On their wedding day, finally alone together, she tells him the story. Vera sits centrally, on the couch, a fireplace to her left. A source of artificial light, the fireplace breaks the theatrical convention of uniform lighting and creates an ambiance of distorted angles and shadows. Vera speaks, the prince paces, the fireplace illuminates their conflicted senti-

---

[32] Hansen, *Babel,* 80, refers to this capacity as a means of "omniscient narration," which gives "the viewer an epistemological edge over characters, thereby encouraging emotional involvement and identification."

ments.[33] The prince blames her for her lost innocence, but Vera has been fortified by adversity. Gazing at her husband with a mixture of pity and contempt, she picks up her coat and walks out.

The disconsolate prince begins to search for her. The audience learns that she has become an opera star under an assumed name, but she still keeps a photograph of her estranged husband on her dressing table. Bauer uses the various spatial arrangements in a theater to create the deep-space shots that permit those sitting in a movie theater to feel that they are also spectators at this performance of *Traviata*. This unique positioning of spectators watching a show within a show paradoxically helped to destroy any remaining notions that the movie frame should simply replicate the proscenium arch of the legitimate stage. The prince watches Vera on stage through binoculars, and in another example of scopophilia, the camera closes in as though looking through his eyes. He sends his card backstage; she agrees to see him. But she cannot forgive his moral cowardice, and he returns home, takes a pistol from his desk drawer and fires a bullet through his heart.

In the melodramatic mode, this resolution satisfies the requirements of the genre. Vera has overcome the serious physical and emotional abuse exerted by men and pulled herself out of a meaningless, shallow life, finding personal fulfillment through art and altruism. The essence of melodrama is not so much that it rewards virtue as that it exposes evil in the moral universe constructed by daily life; as Brooks argued, "melodrama has the distinct value of being about recognition and clarification."[34] The evil in Vera's life came from the extreme ends of the social system, the undeserving poor and the morally deficient nobility. In both cases, however, it was male, which reflected a distinct lack of confidence in the patriarchal order. Vera's own noble birth was irrelevant to her sense of the important things in life, and she struggled successfully to free herself from the private world represented by her bedroom and move into the public world of charity and then the theater. Virtue triumphs in the form of Vera achieving selfhood, precisely because she does not return to the vacuous life offered by the prince.

Before reading too much celebratory feminism into Vera's actions, though, she must be returned to her turn-of-the-century context. Socially ruined by her rape, Vera has reclaimed her personal worth by a life on the stage. Had she wanted to return to her former life of privilege and benevolence, she would have found the doors closed. Yet Vera cannot be described as abandoned to the fates; she represents what Janet Staiger has

---

[33] In a review of the American movie melodrama *The Wife*, the critic observed that "the room is lighted only by the reflection from the fireplace. The spectator's vision seems to actually penetrate the privacy of domestic life." Quoted in Gledhill, ed., *Home*, 365.

[34] Brooks, *Melodramatic Imagination*, 206.

Figure 8. ". . . a man lies dead at the end of a Bauer film." *Child of the Big City* (1915).

identified as the New Bad Woman, that is, one who exercises agency, makes choices, and can desire as well as be desired.[35]

Bauer often used melodramatic heroines as a discursive strategy for positioning this New Bad Woman at the heart of social strife, with gender a deeper dividing line than class. Two of his next important movies, *Child of the Big City* (1914) and *Silent Witnesses* (1914), both feature heroines from the lower classes, the first a seamstress and the second a maid in a wealthy household. Both young women try to use men to escape their tedious lives; the seamstress succeeds where the maid does not. The vivacious ex-seamstress steps lively over the corpse of her suicidal lover as she and her friends head off to dinner at Maxim's at the end of *Child of the Big City*. The maid, whose life Bauer has brilliantly juxtaposed with her seducer's in upstairs / downstairs actions that mirror each other, is back upstairs dusting furniture as her seducer leaves with his fiancée, presumably also on their way to Maxim's.

Despite the difference in their fates, Bauer painted the women with the same melodramatic brush. The seamstress had been pursued initially because of her innocence, which her seducer equated with her lowly social

[35] Janet Staiger, *Bad Women: Regulating Sexuality in Early American Cinema* (Minneapolis: University of Minnesota Press, 1995).

station. He had grown tired of—or intimidated by—the sophisticated New Bad Women and hoped to cure his problems by finding someone he could make over into his own fetish. The seamstress, however, with a view of the urban kaleidoscope from her window in the sewing shop, had long desired to become a part of the glitter and took him for what he was. Neither was the maid an ingenuous working girl; she had manipulated the servant who loved her while she chased the wealthy "sir" upstairs, knowing that he loved another. Nor did the maid's seducer escape scot-free; his beloved is carrying on behind his back with a baron, *his* social superior.

Bauer's films did not project the blunt social message that could be easily read into these tales of working-class girls seduced by men from the upper classes. On the contrary, they implicated women far more deeply in the transformation of late imperial society than could be essentialized in the crude vocabulary of class conflict. His critics longed to read a critique of social exploitation in his movies, which permitted them to forgive the actions of the seamstress and the maid because "the big city, perhaps everyday life, maims and destroys innocent, pure souls, celebrating over our indifference and egoism."[36] But this attitude betrayed their place as members of the intelligentsia and therefore deeply suspicious of the popular commercial culture Bauer was producing, which had in fact more serious implications for Russia's modernization than they could recognize. In the search for class they overlooked the essentiality of gender, especially important because of the extent to which the latter related to consumption in this era.[37] Material culture posed a far greater threat than noblemen, and when innocent girls gave into its seduction, the ambivalent resolutions offered no conclusive moral lesson.

Movies, melodrama, and consumerist ideology converged most specifically in the person of Vera Kholodnaia, 1893–1919, tsarist Russia's first genuine movie star. Her multitude of fans idolized her, sending postcards with scenes from her movies, or dancing to the "Vera Kholodnaia Waltz." Discovered by Bauer, she is most closely identified with him even though they made only seven films together. With no previous training for the stage, she did not bring any baggage of preset notions about acting. Bauer saw immediately that the camera would adore her. Born Vera Levchenko, her married name "Kholodnaia" ironically implied frigidity. Kholodnaia depended on her expressive face, especially the great dark eyes inevitably embellished with heavy makeup.

[36] This quotation is in a review of *Child of the Big City*, quoted in Tsivian et al., *Silent Witnesses*, 216. In the same vein, *Silent Witnesses* was "produced in tones of strict realism, with complete sincerity and artlessness. The image of the maid, Nastia, is constructed splendidly, the silence of the suffering young woman, mocked so cruelly by life." Ibid., 230.

[37] As Kelly and Shepherd point out, working girls spent more of their salaries than did their male counterparts on clothes, eager to dress according to the new fashions. *Constructing Russian Culture*, 111.

Figure 9. A postcard of silver-screen icon Vera Kholodnaia, 1893–1919.

Kholodnaia's stardom derived primarily from her ability to present a fundamentally new style of performance. Heretofore, Delsartism, the gesture-oriented technique developed by the French mime, had influenced melodramatic acting. In addition, those who came to the screen from the legitimate stage had problems adapting to the increased spatial possibilities offered by cameras. Bauer realized that the camera, which could bridge the distance between actor and audience, was particularly sensitive to exaggeration. Not only her economy of gestures but also her playing to the camera rather than to the perceived audience put Kholodnaia rightfully in the company of Asta Nielson, Mary Pickford, and Lillian Gish, women who became stars by cultivating a unique style appropriate to the new medium.[38]

Stylistic changes in acting were as decisive as technology to the success of narrative films, and once again the genre of melodrama proved pivotal. As Simon Shepard has argued, melodrama requires the body not only to express the emotions that cannot be vocalized but to do so with a kind of control that clarifies the plotlines, such as causality and ramifications, for the audience.[39] Kholodnaia was all eyes and heavy breathing, desire incarnate. Her internalized angst worked as a constant reminder that she was powerless to act against her instincts, even when she knew them to be wrong. Kholodnaia on the screen recalls Gloria Swanson's classic line about her own silent film career in *Sunset Boulevard*: "We didn't need dialogue. We had faces."[40] Kholodnaia's fans did not need a voice, which could not have articulated more eloquently the intensity of her glance, her frozen pose on the corner of a couch. She became a heroine for her dreams, for always wanting something better than she had.[41]

The first movie Bauer and Kholodnaia made together, *Song of Love Triumphant*, has not been preserved, but their second, *Children of the Age* (1915) has. Bauer's *mise-en-scène* polarizes Kholodnaia's social worlds, the modest one she inhabits with her bank-clerk husband and their baby, and the one of wealth and privilege enjoyed by her husband's boss. The cramped apartment is juxtaposed to both the defining central staircase of the bourgeois house and the enormous windows in the sitting room looking out over the estate. Kholodnaia cannot help herself; she leaves the clerk for the rich man, who tries to buy off the husband. Although capable of leaving her husband, she cannot abandon her child. With the old school chum who encouraged her to pursue the good life in the first place, she goes back to snatch the baby while her husband is out. In one of the few instances when Bauer used parallel editing to generate suspense, he cuts speedily back and forth between the women after the baby and the husband return home. The women just barely spirit the child away, and when the husband realizes his loss, he puts a bullet in his forehead. As in *Child of the Big City*, it is the man rather than the woman who

[38] B. B. Ziukov, comp., *Vera Kholodnaia* (Moscow: Iskusstvo, 1992). This collection includes a short biography, numerous reviews, photographs, and correspondence from and about her.

[39] Simon Shepherd, "Pauses of Mutual Agitation," in Jacky Bratton et al., eds., *Melodrama: Stage, Picture, Screen* (London: British Film Institute, 1994), 27.

[40] Billy Wilder, dir., and Charles Brackett, prod., *Sunset Boulevard* (Paramount Pictures, 1950).

[41] See, for example, Teresa de Lauretis, *Alice Doesn't: Feminism, Semiotics, Cinema* (Bloomington: Indiana University Press, 1984); Mary Anne Doane, *The Desire to Desire: The Woman's Film of the 1940s* (Bloomington: Indiana University Press, 1987); and Petro, *Joyless Streets*.

idealizes the domestic economy. The mother returned for the child, true, but only after having forsaken the home for the mansion. Yet another woman has had a sexual encounter beyond the bounds of matrimony in a Bauer film, and yet another man lies dead for her having taken this step.

The most famous coupling of Bauer and Kholodnaia, in *A Life for a Life* (1916), introduced another future star, Lidiia Koreneva, whose respected work at the intellectually elite Moscow Arts Theater did not prepare her to hold the camera initially, and her style contrasts tellingly to Kholodnaia's.[42] More significant, though, the two women played sisters, and Bauer cast Kholodnaia as the one who deceives the other, hence at first blush the less sympathetic of the two. This movie was rightfully heralded as Russia's equivalent to the large-scale international productions, as Bauer at last had a budget that could fund his luxuriant visuals. In addition to Kholodnaia and Koreneva, the cast included three other big draws in the Russian cinema, Perestiani, Vitol'd Polonskii, and Ol'ga Rakhmanova.

A Life for a Life reconstructed one of melodrama's most basic formulas: the contrast between noble decadence and bourgeois morality.[43] Koreneva and Kholodnaia play daughters of the wealthy Rakhmanova, who manages her own factory. Kholodnaia, however, is adoptive and without a dowry, so she lacks Koreneva's marriage prospects. Both fall in love with a gold-digging prince, played by Polonskii, who marries Koreneva for her money but seduces Kholodnaia, who has been forced to marry businessman Perestiani, who is as kindly and wealthy as he is older than she. In an enchanting flight of fancy, Kholodnaia imagines herself and Polonskii as lovers in ancient Rome, Bauer again using his magic carpet. The haughty Polonskii also steals from Perestiani, and when his sins are discovered, he contemptuously throws his behavior in Rakhmanova's face, confident that the mother will do nothing to the man both daughters love. On the contrary—she pulls a gun from her desk and shoots him dead, then arranges the scene to look as though he had committed suicide. He must die for his transgressions, whereas Rakhmanova is permitted to cross the line of the legal order to punish crimes against the home.[44] Once again, a man lies dead at the end of a Bauer film.

[42] V. T. (Valentin Turkin, the preeminent film critic who wrote often on Kholodnaia), "Zhizn' za zhizn'," *Pegas*, no. 5 (May 1916): 49–52. Zorkaia, *Na rubezhe stoletii*, 285, quotes a review that points out "We remember her more than Koreneva. . . . It's the beginning of a new art." To be fair, Koreneva is much more expressive and stationary in her later films for Bauer.

[43] The original Ohnet novel was entitled *Serge Panine* after the prince whose name was changed in the movie. Bauer followed Ohnet's skeletal plot, but his *mise-en-scène* established differences in focus. One aspect lost in Bauer's transition was the *Russianness* of the royal cad, whose nationality would suggest something different to French readers than to Russian viewers.

[44] This theme, of a mother justified in killing a scandalous son-in-law, also played on the American screen with *Three Women* (Warner Brothers, 1923), starring Mary McAvoy.

Figure 10. Bauer's innovative use of *mise-en-scène* helped to construct his narratives. *A Life for a Life* (1916).

A Life for a Life, subtitled even more ominously, *A Drop of Blood for Every Fear*, made an especially direct connection between material culture and desire, both aesthetically and thematically. The opening scene, a dress ball, established the opulence and was shot with the multiplane effect that drew the audience into the scene. A sitting area in the foreground, for example, permitted a three-dimensional effect by allowing actors to move to and from the dance floor in such a way as to give the audience the sense that they were seated in the foreground. The various characters can move back to and fro, from the party into the sitting area / audience, where the marital fates of the two daughters are being decided. Polonskii makes his first overtures toward Kholodnaia here, close to the viewers.

From this opening shot Bauer's *mise-en-scène* takes over the narration; the bigger budget he enjoyed for this film did not simply make it more lush, but increased his narrative options. Although using furniture as a metaphor for social estate was fairly standard, Bauer's visual contrast between Rakhmanova's overstuffed bourgeois household and Polonskii's starkly modernist noble apartment is unusually striking. Again he uses a fireplace to cast shadows on the nobility's concept of morality. The pathetic Koreneva feels out of place in this setting, and Bauer highlights their incompatibility by dwarfing her in one of Polonskii's oversized, throne-like chairs, the groom towering over her, the fireplace in the background offering the unhappy bride no domestic warmth. Perestiani's office, like Rakhmanova's home, is simultaneously cluttered and spacious, open spaces supported by columns, as in a department store, but also with desk and table surfaces covered with bric-a-brac.[45] Tropical plants ornament *their* rooms, but not Polonskii's.

Bauer also used the scopophilic camera to track Koreneva as she spies on Polonskii and Kholodnaia. When she catches them together, she staggers away instead of announcing her presence. The audience, watching through Koreneva's eyes, enjoys inside information on Kholodnaia: her own sister now realizes that she has betrayed her. The heroines Kholodnaia played invariably left victims in their wake, and her tremendous popularity suggests that fans preferred her in roles where she indulged her fantasies and desires, regardless of how destructive they were for herself and those closest to her.[46]

The heroes betrayed by Kholodnaia and her ilk raise an important issue about spectatorship, the male in the audience. Because viewing experiences are as fundamentally gendered as is the audience itself, and because the female viewers were measuring their identities in relationship to men as well as to other women, a look at how Bauer treated the male element will increase our understanding of his rendering of his times.[47] A man viewing a Bauer film would find himself confronted with the same ambiguities about consumption, but his role models lack Kholodnaia's opportunities to make choices, not to mention to indulge in her gratifications. In one of his last major films, *The Dying Swan* (1917), Bauer flipped his formula and a woman lay dead in the last scene, the casualty of a man's fetish.[48] The male protagonist, though, had murdered the heroine as a result of his psychologically imbalanced obsession with her, so this protagonist was ultimately as morally weak as any of the cads and suicides who preceded him. And again the female character is the star. Bauer cast Vera Karalli, a prima ballerina who had left

[45] In point of fact, Bauer was making clever technical use of these props, using the columns to support lighting fixtures that allowed him to backlight his characters, and the tall plants with their broad leaves hid other lights.

[46] This contrasts sharply with America's silent film heroines, who had to pay a high social price even when led unwittingly down the primrose path. Sumiko Higashi, *Virgins, Vamps, and Flappers: The American Silent Movie Heroine* (St. Albans, Vt.: Eden Press, 1978).

[47] The literature on the gendered nature of spectatorship, too expansive to include here, began with Laura Mulvey's highly controversial "Visual Pleasure and Narrative Cinema," *Screen* 16, no. 3 (1975): 6–18, in which she argued that classical narrative cinema had been structured according to a specifically "male gaze."

[48] Some ideas and techniques used in *The Dying Swan* were ones that Bauer had first experimented with in *Daydreams* (1916), notably the insane, obsessive, and murderous male protagonist.

Figure 11. Vera Kholodnaia, desire incarnate.

the Bolshoi for the silver screen, as a mute dancer. Although the trope of muteness might seem excessive in a silent film, Bauer used her silence as a theatrical mechanism to explore her unconscious and to privilege her gaze over her voice.[49] The dancer needs her body offstage, too, to express her emotions.

The *Dying Swan* was filmed in the Crimea, where the crew could escape the social unrest of revolutionary Moscow. Bauer made a grandiose and uninhabited estate his set. Able to shoot much outdoors with natural lighting, he concentrated now on spatial contrasts to create an ethereal ambiance. Karalli falls in love with a lawyer, played by Polonskii. Stealing over to visit him, outside his house and pressing herself against a stone wall, she watches him from below, with another woman. Throughout the movie, Bauer avoids frontal shots, often positioning the characters in the sides of the frame rather than in the center, or at slightly different levels with regard to one another. Here Bauer was experimenting with visual rather than social realism, filming in the way that the eye actually sees, the world at angles rather than on a flat stage. Thus he found yet another

[49] Brooks, *Melodramatic Imagination*, 57, argued that muteness can be a meaningful artistic device in melodrama because the latter "is about expression."

way to insinuate spectators into the construction of the narrative, forcing them, like Karalli, to spy and eavesdrop in order to piece together the action.

Karalli runs away and becomes a professional ballerina specializing in one virtuoso scene, the dying swan, made famous by Anna Pavlova. Able to express her mood only through her dance, Karalli is chanced upon by a local artist, played by the popular actor Andrei Gromov. This character is possessed by death, dark in complexion, dress, and studio, where he paints skeletons. In the silent dancer he sees his consummate model. He sends her a jeweled diadem, hoping she will pose for his portrait of death, which she consents to do because she has found a soulmate who finds "life stranger than death." The diadem, however, is an omen. That night in a dream sequence, a woman in white leads Karalli through open spaces and then proclaims, "That's my crown! I died because of it!" The dancer then finds herself being swarmed by figures in black. This nightmare, however, does not deter her from posing. Before the swan's portrait is complete, though, Polonskii tracks Karalli down and begs her to marry him. This changes her mood to rapture, which confounds the artist because he is painting her depressed essence rather than her body. He strangles the now-buoyant dancer, then finishes his painting by gazing at her corpse. The final shot blurs the portrait with the murdered ballerina, art with reality, as the cinema itself does.

Just as women were identified with consumption, so were men with production, which underscored how the two sexes played different social roles in modernization. Developing capitalism called for restraint and mastery over emotions among the male element, a positive trait found only in Bauer's peripheral characters, such as Perestiani in *Life for a Life*. The dominant discourses of masculinity during Bauer's reign would include both the political impotence felt by those who had demonstrated for participatory democracy in 1905 and, especially, the millions called up to fight the Great War from 1914 onward. Bauer's male viewers, as caught up as the females in the complications of developing a modern identity, experienced through his protagonists the crippling frustrations of their situations. It is tempting to recall here Siegfried Kracauer's enormously influential study of the silent cinema in Weimar Germany, *From Caligari to Hitler*, which interpreted the same type of characters found repeatedly in Bauer's melodramas—the weak-willed male authority figures—as Oedipal tropes that foreshadowed the rise of fascist youths to kill their fathers; in Bauer's day, many were loudly sounding the death knell for their tsar-father. Russian capitalism offered them no alternative safe haven of domesticity to which to retreat. Pleasure came from acting on one's instincts, but men paid a far greater price for their inability to master their passions than women did in a Bauer film. Patriarchal but not yet bourgeois, the status quo was hardly worth restoring.

Bauer did not provide escape to compliant women and emasculated men but rather offered confrontation on a higher plane. His melodramas portrayed males who could not control females, the subtext of which re-inforced the extent to which aristocratic rule had lost its certitude. In the world he depicted, social and gender relationships were critically askew, endangering the status quo. However much his critics might have wanted otherwise, social estate did not in itself provide the defining characteristic either of virtue or power: workers could exploit as well as be exploited, the largely dissolute nobility could still furnish emblems of the moral or-der, and the bourgeoisie could destroy as well as produce. Behind it all, though, lurked the destabilizing possibilities inherent in mass consump-tion. Yet Bauer was no harbinger of commercial doom: his heroines were rewarded more often than punished for their desires, even while tripping cheerfully over their victims.[50] Contradictory gender roles suggested a fe-male bisexuality, not so much deriving from amorous inclinations as from contestation over social roles.[51] These characterizations show both class and gender identity to be essentially negotiable, however dependent upon the dominant cultural norms for the origins of their respective definitions.

Bauer's lavish settings reflected the ambitions of modernity, and his aesthetics the prelude to an expressionism that would invest little faith in surface reality. Through dream sequences, visualizations of the re-pressed, he revealed the anxiety arising from the failure of the secular machine age to produce the freedom it had promised. His movies were about private lives rather than public issues, and they pulled the multi-tude of isolated spectators into the experience portrayed on the screen. At a critical point when so many Russians were struggling to find a place for themselves in a changing world, Bauer helped them to see their options.

[50] Hansen, *Babel*, 112, commented on the "tensions, contradictions, and ambiguities" at the "intersection of cinema and consumer culture" in the contemporaneous United States.

[51] Although the theoretical debates on the bisexuality of the female viewer lie beyond the purview of this essay, for more on this subject, see Modleski, *Women Who Knew Too Much*, 5–8.

Filmography

We are fortunate that Evgenii Bauer's most important films have been at least partially preserved.

Bauer films available on video from the British Film Institute:

Daydreams
Silent Witnesses
A Life for a Life
For Happiness
The Revolutionary
The 1002 Ruse

Bauer films available at the Library of Congress:

The Twilight of a Woman's Soul
Children of the Age
Leon Drei
Iurii Nagornyi
The Dying Swan
The King of Paris
Cold Showers

CHAPTER SIX

Girl Talk: Lydia Charskaia and Her Readers

SUSAN LARSEN

Secret Pleasures and Public Acts

At the time I was secretly engrossed in reading Charskaia, I also read Verbitskaia. On account of those books I even developed a friendship of sorts with a girl about two years older than me, but still in our class. Her name was Lelia T. . . . Once—for some reason in a whisper—I asked Lelia whether she believed in God, and she nodded her head. Then she removed her Pioneer scarf, unbuttoned her blouse and showed me a small gold cross. . . . All this . . . felt like a secret, a secret that Lelia for some reason entrusted to me. . . . I knew that Mama would have practically killed me if she'd seen what I was reading. But I liked Charskaia's heroines, especially Nina Dzhavakha. . . . Sometimes I even tried on Nina Dzhavakha as an image for myself, because when I looked in the mirror, I thought I saw a resemblance.[1]

Elena Bonner elaborates no further on the resemblance she glimpsed in her mirror in 1935, but the story she tells about the consequences of her secret friendship with Lelia T. offers a vision of her twelve-year-old self that reflects the values Lydia Charskaia's first readers defined as central to their own identification with their favorite heroines in the eighty-odd nov-

I am grateful to Jehanne Gheith, Helena Goscilo, and Stephanie Sandler for their thoughtful and provocative comments on earlier drafts of this paper. Travel grants from the Committee on Research of the Academic Senate at the University of California, San Diego, provided vital support for my research.

[1] Elena Bonner, *Dochki-materi* (New York: Chekhov Publishing, 1991), 217–19. My translation of Bonner's memoir is adapted from *Mothers and Daughters*, trans. Antonina Bouis (New York: Vintage Books, 1992), 203–4.

els for children and adolescents that the phenomenally popular Charskaia published between 1902 and 1918. Respondents to a 1906 questionnaire on young people's reading habits, for example, repeatedly listed Charskaia's heroines' "courage," "boldness," and ardent friendships to explain her status as their favorite writer.[2] Although Bonner's clandestine friendship with Lelia never achieves the emotional intensity of Charskaia's schoolgirls' passionate attachments and elaborate conspiracies, Bonner portrays their meetings as equally alluring in their simultaneous evasion of and challenge to adult authority. And Bonner is as courageous as any of Charskaia's heroines in defense of the secret she shares with Lelia. When Bonner's Party-member mother finally discovers the "garbage" her daughter is reading, she demands to know its source, but the young Elena refuses to betray her secret friend, and—like Charskaia's many unjustly accused heroines—she remains heroically silent as her mother slaps her, "painfully," in the face.[3]

This may seem an inconsequential episode, only a few pages in a long memoir, yet as she recalls the incident in the late 1980s Bonner concludes, "I might have been different and my whole life might have been different if I had only told Mama about Lelia instead of protecting 'our secret.'" In apparent illustration of this comment, Bonner shifts from her recollections of Lelia to an account of her midnight interrogations by the NKVD in 1937, several months after both her parents had been arrested. As she had protected Lelia in defiance of her mother, here, too, Bonner defies her interrogator's threats and refuses to speak. The juxtaposition of these two stories—Bonner's covert passion for Charskaia and her first defiance of the "secret" police—suggests a fundamental connection between Bonner's early image of herself as Nina Dzhavakha and her vision of herself and the choices she made as an adult. "I might have been different and my whole life might have been different."[4]

I am not arguing here that Elena Bonner modeled her whole life, or even her memoir, after that of Charskaia's heroines, but this story demonstrates the influence that books often regarded as pernicious trash may have on the lives of women—like Bonner—who might seem to have little in common with authors like Charskaia, once reviled by Kornei Chukovskii as a "genius of vulgarity" whose "mangy immortality" Viktor

[2] The questionnaire was distributed to subscribers of *The Soulful Word for Older Children* (*Zadushevnoe slovo dlia detei starshego vozrasta*), the journal in which all of Charskaia's most famous novels first appeared. Responses to the questionnaire were numbered and published consecutively, four or five to an issue, on the back covers of *The Soulful Word* 42, nos. 2–52 (1906). The "courage" and "boldness" of Charskaia's heroines are cited in responses 1, 19, 28, 33, 46, 71, 79, 89, 96, 101, 107, 112, 132, 179, 181, 187, 186, 191. The importance of "love for a girlfriend" and "girls' friendships" are cited in responses 19, 21, 58, 60, 96, 172, 161, 168, 179, 193. Similar praise for Charskaia's heroines recurs throughout readers' letters to *The Soulful Word* between 1902 and 1918.

[3] Bonner, *Dochki-materi*, 218–19.

[4] Ibid., 221–23.

Shklovsky likewise deplored.[5] Bonner's subsequent career—as a prominent Soviet dissident, human rights activist, and partner in her husband Andrei Sakharov's political activities—is unique, but the story she tells about her shared, secret reading of Charskaia is not. Thousands of Russian girls "tried on" Charskaia's rebellious heroines as models for themselves, and, like Bonner, their interpretation of Charskaia's works was profoundly influenced by the situations in which they read her books and the companions who shared that reading with them.

This essay explores the circumstances and debates surrounding Charskaia's emergence as Russia's most popular writer for children and adolescents from 1902 until 1918, when both Charskaia and *The Soulful Word for Older Children* (Zadushevnoe slovo dlia detei starshego vozrasta), the weekly journal that created her reputation, went abruptly out of print. It examines the novels Charskaia published annually in serial form in the *The Soulful Word for Older Children* and the comments on her work in readers' letters to the journal's "Mailbox" pages.[6] In these letters Charskaia's readers conducted an ongoing conversation about her work that shaped Charskaia's celebrity and determined the kinds of resemblances that other girls would look for in stories that they persisted—despite the opprobrium of highbrow critics like Chukovskii—in reading as images of themselves.

Creating Charskaia: The Writer as Commodity

L. A. Charskaia (the stage and pen-name of Lydia Alekseevna Churilova, *née* Voronova, 1875–1937) achieved—as even her harshest critics admitted—unprecedented success among Russian children and adolescents. As one Russian historian of children's literature noted in 1909, "If one is to measure a writer's popularity by the number of books sold, then L. A. Charskaia must be acknowledged as the most popular children's writer at the present time."[7] Charskaia's fame among young readers blossomed almost overnight. Her first novel for adolescents,

---

[5] Kornei Chukovskii, "Lidiia Charskaia," *Sobranie sochinenii v shesti tomakh* (Moscow: Khudozhestvennaia literatura, 1965–69), 6: 158; Viktor Shklovskii, "O pishche bogov i o Charskoi," *Literaturnaia gazeta*, 5 April 1932: 1. I am grateful to Glen Worthey for providing me with the Shklovskii reference.

[6] The number of letters printed each year in the journal's "Mailbox" ["Pochtovyi iashchik"] section ranges from 178 to almost 400. These letters give some sense of the social origins and geographic distribution of the journal's readers, who span the social spectrum from "princes" and "countesses," to entire classes of orphans. They write from large cities, small towns, country estates, and railway stations throughout the Russian Empire. Between 1884 and 1918 *The Soulful Word* was published in separate editions for older and younger children. Charskaia was an equally frequent contributor to *The Soulful Word for Younger Children* (Zadushevnoe slovo dlia detei mladshego vozrasta), but this essay focuses on her work for *The Soulful Word for Older Children*, addressed to readers between the ages of nine and fourteen. All references to *The Soulful Word* (Zadushevnoe slovo) refer to the edition for older children.

[7] N. Chekhov, *Detskaia literatura* (Moscow: Izdatel'stvo "Pol'za," 1909), 141.

Figure 12. "The author of *Notes of an Institute Girl* at age 10 (during her life at the institute)." From *The Soulful Word for Older Children* 42, no. 45 (1902): 715.

Notes of an Institute Girl (Zapiski institutki, 1902), was so popular among the readers of *The Soulful Word* that the journal sold out three editions of an issue containing a "Biographical Note on the Author of *Notes of an Institute Girl*."[8] This "Note" featured large photographs of Charskaia—

[8] Viktor Rusakov, "Avtor 'Zapisok institutki.' Biograficheskaia zametka," *Zadushevnoe slovo* 42, no. 45 (1902): 715–17; "K piatiletiiu 'Zapisok institutki,' " *Zadushevnoe slovo* 46, no. 44 (1906): 692. Throughout this essay, I date Charskaia's novels by the year of their serialization in *Zadushevnoe slovo*. The journal's publisher, M. O. Vol'f, subsequently released most of these novels in luxuriously bound and lavishly illustrated separate volumes, many in multiple editions.

Figure 13. "The author of *Notes of an Institute Girl* at work. (Photograph taken by the writer's father.)" From *The Soulful Word for Older Children* 42, no. 45 (1902): 716.

as a ten-year-old schoolgirl in her institute uniform, as a young author at her desk, and in a standard head-shot. The photographic and narrative emphasis on Charskaia's childhood years in the "Note" transforms her biography into a story that asserts a similarity between the author, her heroines and, implicitly, her readers' aspirations for themselves—they are all ten years old, gifted, and "universal favorites" among their peers.

Until Charskaia's appearance in the pages of *The Soulful Word*, readers' letters usually referred to favorite books by title alone, without mentioning the author. By 1904 it is rare to find a reader's letter discussing a work by Charskaia that does not mention her name. Charskaia became, in effect, *more* than the sum of her works to her readers, who showered her with letters, poems, needlework, paintings of her heroines, and even waltzes dedicated to their "dear, beloved" writer. The journal recorded and thereby perpetuated this process: it printed the waltzes and poems, listed the gifts sent, and regularly made space for Charskaia's thank-you notes to her admirers.[9] Charskaia's fans borrowed the forms of their adulation in part from her novels' frequent depictions of the institute tradition of "adoration" (*obozhanie*), in which a younger girl strives to win the affection and attention of an older student or teacher via gifts, lavish praise, and heroic deeds. The journal provided a forum for Charskaia's fans to display their "adoration," but the readers themselves played the leading role in the formation of her cult as they vied with one another to compose a longer waltz, a better poem, a more ecstatic tribute. As they increased her visibility among their peers, Charskaia's fans also made themselves visible. Charskaia's fandom benefited her publishers insofar as it increased the demand for her books and for subscriptions to *The Soulful Word*, but "fan culture" also rewarded the fans themselves, as they basked in the glow of the celebrity they helped create.[10] Charskaia's phenomenal popularity resulted from the not quite spontaneous combustion of her texts with the needs and interests of both publishers and readers. These were shaped in turn by the particular historical and cultural conditions of early twentieth-century Russia when celebrity had market value in and of itself.[11]

It might seem logical to discuss the serial publication of Charskaia's four-volume pseudo-autobiography in *The Soulful Word* as the culminating point in the commodification of her celebrity.[12] Yet letters about the first

---

[9] "Pochtovyi iashchik," *Zadushevnoe slovo* 43, nos. 6, 26, 42 (1903); 44, nos. 11, 28 (1904); 46, nos. 40, 42 (1906); 47, nos. 22, 50 (1907); 48, no. 25 (1908).

[10] On "fan culture," see Constance Penley, "Feminism, Psychoanalysis, and the Study of Popular Culture," in *Cultural Studies*, ed. Lawrence Grossberg, Cary Nelson, and Paula Treichler (New York: Routledge, 1992), 479–500.

[11] On the commodification of female celebrities in Russia at the turn of the century, see Holmgren, "Gendering the Icon: Marketing Women Writers in Fin-de-Siècle Russia," in *Russia–Women–Culture*, ed. Helena Goscilo and Beth Holmgren (Bloomington: Indiana University Press, 1996), 321–46, and Louise McReynolds, "The 'Incomparable' Anastasiia Vial'tseva and the Culture of Personality," in Goscilo and Holmgren, *Russia–Women–Culture*, 273–94.

[12] The tetralogy, which takes its heroine only to the start of her writing career around age twenty-three, consists of *Za chto? Moia povest' o samoi sebe* (1907); *Bol'shoi Dzhon* (1909); *Na vsiu zhzizn': Iunost' Lidy Voronskoi* (1912); and *Tsel' dostignuta: Tri gody zhizni Lidy Voronskoi* (1913).

installment in this series, *Why? My Tale about Myself* (Za chto? Moia povest' o samoi sebe, 1907), indicate that by 1907 Charskaia's image was so solidified in her readers' minds, that many of them had trouble accepting her autobiographical but not very well-behaved heroine, Lida Voronskaia, as "the real thing." As one disillusioned reader wrote late in the serialization of *Why?*, "Reading L.A. Charskaia's *Notes of an Institute Girl, The Second Nina, Liuda Vlassovskaia,* and others, I fell in love with the author of these tales and was convinced that Mme Charskaia was the best, kindest woman in the world. But in the tale *Why?*, Mme Charskaia represents herself in her youth as bad-tempered, neurotic, and intolerable. How can one reconcile what she writes about herself with the impression created by her tales?"[13]

Charskaia's initial representation of her "self" in fiction did not measure up to the standards set either by her own carefully orchestrated public persona or by her previous heroines. Many letter writers phrase their comments in ways that suggest that Charskaia's fictional heroines were more "real" to them than the heroine of her "tale about herself." Implicit in these readers' comments is the assumption that even stories from "real life" must adhere to established norms for the coherent presentation of an ideal self. Charskaia's fans understood that stories offer models for behavior, and many shared the opinion of the reader who wrote, "I find [*Why?*] interesting, true, but it doesn't inspire emulation."[14] Readers' resistance to Charskaia's deviations in her "tale about herself" from the norms her previous works had established suggests that Charskaia was both queen and captive of her own celebrity.

Creating a Community of Readers: Soulful Words and Soul Mates

In addition to fanning the blaze of Charskaia's popularity, readers' letters to *The Soulful Word* also shaped the ways in which her works were read, as her fans developed a "girl's own" interpretation of Charskaia's works and the cultural values inscribed within them. This interpretation in its turn influenced the letter writers' reading of and aspirations for their own lives. Many letter writers express sentiments similar to those of twelve-year-old Mania Oblesimova: "[If you asked me] 'Whom would you most like to resemble?' I would answer—Princess Dzhavakha."[15] All

---

[13] "Pochtovyi iashchik," *Zadushevnoe slovo* 47, no. 52 (1907). Similarly negative evaluations of *Za chto?* may be found in "Pochtovyi iashchik," *Zadushevnoe slovo* 47, nos. 38, 39, 40, 42, 45, 47, 51 (1907).

[14] "Pochtovyi iashchik," *Zadushevnoe slovo* 47, no. 40 (1907).

[15] "Pochtovyi iashchik," *Zadushevnoe slovo* 44, nos. 9, 44 (1904); 48, no. 28 (1908).

of Charskaia's principal heroines whom the readers describe as "brave" and / or "daring" evoke similar responses.[16]

The ongoing dialogue among letter writers in the pages of *The Soulful Word* created a community of readers who were connected to one another through their shared fascination with reading in general, and with Charskaia's books in particular. This community perceived itself as chiefly, though not exclusively, female. Letters discussing Charskaia's works were not only written primarily *by* girls, but were also addressed primarily *to* girls. Many letters begin with the phrase "Dear girl friends" or "Dear girl readers."[17] Other letters are addressed to a specific correspondent with whom the writer agrees or disagrees, often in vehement terms, as is the case in the following letter about the relative merits of several characters in *Liuda Vlassovskaia* (1904):

> Dear Lilia Pototskaia! I disagree with your opinion of Nora Trakhtenberg (in L. A. Charskaia's novel). I think she acted wrongly in betraying Marusia Zapol'skaia [as the author of a prank that backfires]. After all, not only Marusia, but all the girls were involved in the prank. . . . Marusia was not the only guilty one; all the girls were guilty, the whole class; so Nora was wrong when she betrayed Marusia alone. If you, Lilia, are a student in a school of some kind and if you have ever been involved in such a story and had to stand up for the honor of the entire class, then you will undoubtedly understand me.—Lipa Sokolova.[18]

The author of this letter judges both Charskaia's characters *and* the character of her addressee by their adherence to a set of "community standards," for which the community of record consists of actual girls, Charskaia's heroines, and the girls' collective sense of those heroines' relative merits. The hundreds of similar letters published in *The Soulful Word* between 1902 and 1918 allowed their authors to circulate cultural values that they ascribed to Charskaia's texts but which, in fact, they themselves articulated in their epistolary conversations with one another.

The process of formulating such "community standards" had value for its participants in and of itself. Some girls formed special "circles" devoted to reading Charskaia: one letter in 1910 reports on a group of girls who take turns purchasing Charskaia's works in order to assemble a collective

---

[16] Charskaia's more conventionally feminine heroines are much less frequently cited as models. As one letter writer explains, "The life of the proud Caucasian princess, filled with endless dangers, is more interesting than the calm life of the modest Ukrainian landowner's daughter" ("Pochtovyi iashchik," *Zadushevnoe slovo* 44, no. 11 [1904]).

[17] Given the age of the letter writers, I have translated "chitatel'nitsy" throughout this paper as "girl readers," rather than the more literal "female readers." Unless otherwise specified, all letters cited are written by girls.

[18] "Pochtovyi iashchik," *Zadushevnoe slovo* 50, no. 2 (1910).

"library," while another describes a group of girls who are too poor to purchase her works even in this fashion. So, as the writer reports: "Each of us in turn obtains one of her works and reads it; then we meet and the girl who has read the book tells everyone its contents, and also—the impression it made on her. This is very interesting, especially when it happens that several people have read the same novel. Then we have passionate arguments."[19]

The formation of such small "circles" and of the larger circle of readers in the pages of *The Soulful Word,* created a community of girls that resembled in some respects those Charskaia celebrated in her fiction. In perhaps unconscious imitation of all those "soulful" discussions late at night in the institute dormitory, Charskaia's readers came to revel in their own "passionate arguments" and epistolary debates.

Creating a Canon: Girlhood Genres

Why did Charskaia's works evoke such intense and extensive responses from her readers? What drew girls, in particular, to her novels?[20]

In the first place, the narrative form and the girl-centered plots of Charskaia's novels encouraged her readers to see themselves in her books, and, as they often wrote, to "live together with" their beloved heroines. As one such reader explains, "I myself am a girl, consequently, everything that [Charskaia] writes is so close to me, so familiar and easy to understand."[21] Charskaia's novels not only took girls' experiences as their subject; they were also written in girls' voices. Ten of the seventeen novels that she published in *The Soulful Word for Older Children* are first-person stories by girls between the ages of ten and twenty-two, a narrative voice that clearly appealed to her readers. Another reader reports, "In the magazine for younger children I really liked [Charskaia's] *Notes of an Orphan,* and I rejoiced when I saw that the one for older children also publishes *Notes,* since I like such notes most of all." At least some readers thought that *Princess Dzhavakha* (Kniazhna Dzhavakha, 1903) might "really" have been written by Princess Nina herself at the age of eleven and were ready to be

---

[19] "Pochtovyi iashchik," *Zadushevnoe slovo* 50, nos. 44, 46 (1910). For descriptions of other circles of readers, see "Pochtovyi iashchik," *Zadushevnoe slovo* 50, no. 16 (1910), and Z. Maslovskaia, "Nashi deti i nashi pedagogi v proizvedeniiakh Charskoi," *Russkaia shkola,* no. 9 (September, 1911), Part 1, 104.

[20] I focus here on girls' responses to her works, but boys also rated Charskaia highly. *Notes of an Institute Girl* was the work most praised by both boys *and* girls in *The Soulful Word* 42 (1902), with positive mentions in 31 of 70 letters by boys (44%), 69 of 102 by girls (68%), and 2 of 6 by writers of unknown gender.

[21] "Pochtovyi iashchik," *Zadushevnoe slovo* 54, nos. 17, 27 (1914); 47, no. 6 (1907).

impressed. "If that's the case," writes one such fan, "How surprising—it's so marvelously written!" Other letters report that their authors, "like Nina," have started keeping a diary.[22] This is a simple point, but an important one: Charskaia's heroines speak for themselves and, in so doing, present her readers with a voice they can recognize and claim as their own.[23]

Secondly, Charskaia's works are set in environments that are simultaneously familiar and exotic. The state-supported institutes for girls of noble birth and the daughters of military officers in which many of her works take place were the least accessible forms of "public" schooling for girls and had a special charm as a result.[24] The institute setting also enables Charskaia to represent a community of girls isolated from the everyday world of parents and siblings, but it remained a place most girls could imagine inhabiting.[25] Charskaia also puts a new twist on the "institute tale" by combining it with the Russian equivalent of American stories of "cowboys and Indians"—the adventure story set in the Caucasus. The popularity of both types of stories among girls may be judged by the results of *The Soulful Word*'s 1906 survey of subscribers' reading habits, which included the question: "What sort of works do you prefer—from what sort of life, what sort of environment—and what engages you most in these various works?"[26] In response to this question, twenty-three girls (but no boys) listed *both* works based on institute (or, in a few instances, gymnasium) life *and* works based on life in the Caucasus as their favorites. This is the most frequently mentioned combination of themes in responses to the 1906 questionnaire. Twenty-four girls (and three boys) listed works from institute life alone as their favorites. Combined, these two groups of readers constitute almost one-quarter of the respondents to the 1906 questionnaire—an indication of the extent to which Charskaia's work had come to define her audience's literary tastes only five years after her debut in *The Soulful Word.*

---

[22] "Pochtovyi iashchik," *Zadushevnoe slovo* 43, nos. 3, 29, 30 (1903); 48, no. 28 (1908).

[23] Female readers of *The Soulful Word* increasingly report that they are either keeping a diary or ask for advice on how to keep one ("Pochtovyi iashchik," *Zadushevnoe slovo* 46, nos. 35, 52 [1906]; 48, nos. 25, 26, 28 [1908]; 54, nos. 17, 23, 24, 28, 30 [1914]). The publication of other memoirs of girlhood in this period (i.e., those of Mariia Bashkirtseva, 1892; E. A. D'iakonova, 1904–5; A. A. Verbitskaia, 1908–11; E. N. Vodovozova, 1908–1911) may also have heightened girls' interest in the diary form.

[24] Charskaia's rosy portraits of institute life differ significantly from many other accounts, which represent institute girls as at worst ignorant and vicious and at best well-intentioned but ridiculously naive. For a survey of the evolution of the institute girl's image, see A. F. Belousov, "Institutki v russkoi literature," in M. O. Chudakova, ed., *Tynianovskii sbornik: Chetvertye tynianovskie chteniia* (Riga: Zinatne, 1990), 77–99.

[25] For a related argument, see Beth Holmgren, "Why Russian Girls Loved Charskaia," *Russian Review* 54, no. 1 (January 1995): 99–100.

[26] "Pochtovyi iashchik," *Zadushevnoe slovo* 46, no. 1 (1906).

Mapping Girlhood, Taming the Caucasus: Can Wild Girls Be Good?

This marked preference for tales of both the "wild" Caucasus and the "civilizing" institute may seem incongruous, yet the frequency with which Charskaia's heroines traverse the boundaries between various forms of "wildness" and "civilization" suggests that it is an essential component of the narrative structure and cultural codes embedded in her works. The second, third, and fourth novels in the Dzhavakha series—*Princess Dzhavakha, Liuda Vlassovskaia,* and *The Second Nina* (Vtoraia Nina, 1906)—are divided into two parts, each half of which takes place either "Within the institute's walls" or "Under the skies of the Caucasus." These geographical pointers subtitle the two parts of *Liuda Vlassovskaia* and inscribe an opposition between girls' confinement within the institute and the freedom they experience "beneath Caucasian skies."

Even the first novel in the Dzhavakha series, *Notes of an Institute Girl,* which takes place entirely within an institute, incorporates this opposition in its portrait of Nina Dzhavakha's death as the inevitable result of tuberculosis and homesickness for the Caucasus—the same combination of ailments that killed her Tatar mother. The latter's "fatal illness" is also equated with a terminal longing for home—the Tatar mountain village she abandoned together with its Muslim religion to accept Christianity and the marriage proposal of a Georgian general serving in the Russian army. Despite the Dzhavakha novels' ostensible advocacy of tolerance for religious and ethnic differences, divided cultural loyalties usually result in tragedy in these works. Nina Dzhavakha, as the daughter of a Russified Georgian general and the Tatar maiden whose people he conquered, is doomed before she ever leaves the Caucasus.

Further accentuating the apparent opposition between the worlds of the institute and the Caucasus is the association of particular types of characters with particular environments. Liuda Vlassovskaia—the model institute girl, who travels throughout the Caucasus with her "good conduct" medal—is repeatedly praised by readers for her "kindness," "love for her friend," "capacity to forgive insults," and "selflessness." By contrast, readers admire the Caucasian princesses for their "bravery," "nobility," and "boldness."[27] These daring heroines are also marked by their defiantly boyish behavior. Nadia Durova [*sic*], the transvestite heroine of *A*

---

[27] These characterizations are drawn from readers' responses to *The Soulful Word*'s 1906 questionnaire that asked readers to name their favorite literary character and justify their choice. On Liuda's all-around goodness, see "Voprosnyi listok," *Zadushevnoe slovo* 46 (1906), responses 9, 11, 24, 32, 33, 42, 58, 60, 61, 73, 82, 96, 104, 132, 112, 183, 187, 190. Only one respondent, a boy, praises Liuda for her "daring," as well as her "love for her girlfriends." On Nina's bravery, see "Voprosnyi listok," *Zadushevnoe slovo* 46 (1906), responses 1, 15, 16, 19, 46, 89, 96, 101, 107, 112, 132, 141, 181, 191. Only two of these responses, both from girls, cite Nina for her "kindness" as well as her bravery.

Daring Life (Smelaia zhizn', 1905) is not the only girl in Charskaia's *oeuvre* who prefers male attire. Both *The Wood Sprite* (Lesovichka, 1907) and *The Second Nina* open with scenes in which the heroine is mistaken for a boy—by both the reader and the other characters in the novel. And when Charskaia's most famous heroine, Princess Dzhavakha, runs away from home disguised as a minstrel boy, his clothes give her the freedom she lacks.

Despite what seems like a fairly clear-cut opposition between these two imaginary realms and the characters who inhabit them, the letters published in *The Soulful Word* suggest that many of Charskaia's readers perceived—or wanted to perceive—the values represented by the institute and the Caucasus as existing in an unsteady but necessary equilibrium within the heroines they most admired. Many of these letters suggest that girls, while they relished the images of Charskaia's bold heroines, were troubled by the moments in which their heroines' "courage," "daring," "nobility," and "unruliness" seemed to verge on "vainglory," "willfulness," "excessive pride," and "disobedience." Charskaia's readers consistently oppose these two groups of qualities in their discussions of heroines like the "second Nina," Lida Voronskaia of Charskaia's pseudo-autobiographical tetralogy, Ksania the "wood sprite," and Dania Larina of *The Dzhavakha Nest* (Dzhavakhovskoe gnezdo, 1910). The details of this opposition evolve gradually, but its seeds are evident in early descriptions of Charskaia's heroines as "daring, courageous, and, *moreover*, kind and warm-hearted little girls," or as "daring, proud, *and at the same time* kind" (emphases added).[28] The letter writers' assertions that the heroines they admire for their daring are also "kind" suggests a need to defend them from charges of ungirlish self-centeredness.

A central point of contention in later debates about the behavior of Charskaia's heroines is their "wildness" (*dikost'*), its origins, pleasures, and dangers. The first extended discusion of this issue breaks out in the pages of *The Soulful Word* in 1907 as the result of a short letter about *The Second Nina* that states, "I personally like Liuda the best for her kindness and love of Nina. But I don't like Nina because of her wild character. Who shares my opinion?"[29] This letter triggers two related arguments—one that centers on the second Nina's "wildness" and another that questions Liuda's "goodness" and her treatment of the second Nina.[30]

---

[28] "Pochtovyi iashchik," *Zadushevnoe slovo* 46, no. 2 and 50 (1906); no. 10 (1910). For letters with similarly equivocal phrasing, see "Pochtovyi iashchik," *Zadushevnoe slovo* 50, nos. 9, 10, 23, 24, 35 (1910).

[29] "Pochtovyi iashchik," *Zadushevnoe slovo* 47, no. 1 (1907).

[30] The "second Nina" is Nina bek-Izrael, a cousin of the original Nina Dzhavakha. The following discussion refers to the second Nina by first name only; references to the original Nina will include her surname.

In the ensuing debate Nina's supporters outnumber her critics, but only two of her defenders reject the charge of wildness outright. Unable to deny Nina's wildness and uncomfortable celebrating it, most of Nina's admirers try to redefine it: six of these attribute Nina's alleged "wildness" to what they variously label her "Caucasian," "Southern," "Oriental," or "mountain" origins.[31] One reader, for example, absolves Nina of blame for a "base" trick she plays on a classmate on the grounds that "she was seeking revenge . . . ; after all, the mountain people are very vindictive." Another, writing in response to a letter that criticized Nina for tearing her hair and ripping her clothes "in a moment of despair" like "uncivilized wild men from an Indian tribe," cautions:

> Don't forget—she is a native of the Caucasus, and she has a character that is hot-tempered, but kind, proud, a little frivolous, yet resistant to influence. It was very difficult to reeducate her, since she was accustomed to freedom, to obeying only her own desires, and she never let anything stop her. It's not surprising that she couldn't resist giving in to such an expression of sorrow in a moment of despair. In fact, she could have been a well-behaved young lady, if she had been taught from her earliest childhood, and if she hadn't had such a passionate character. But then I wouldn't have liked her. Then she would have been just an ordinary girl, the kind you can find anywhere. But Nina was a *special* girl, the kind you don't meet often, and it is just *what you call "wildness"* that I like in her (emphasis added).[32]

This is not the only letter that celebrates Nina's "specialness" yet resists naming her special difference as "wildness"; this resistance, I think, points to readers' discomfort with the term and its connotations for "good girls." The prevalence of "ethnic" explanations of Nina's so-called "wildness" suggests that many readers may have seen such behavior—however attractive—as tolerable only if it can be justified as innate, not willed or chosen. Nina's ethnic "otherness" also makes it possible for the letter writers to admire her behavior without accepting it as a possible model for their own.

At stake in all these letters is the writers' sense of which heroines it is permissible to admire and therefore emulate. *The Second Nina* was particularly troubling to readers in its representation of recurrent conflicts between an already-acknowledged heroine and role model, the always-demure Liuda Vlassovskaia, and her young adopted sister, Nina bek-Izrael, who resents and actively resists all Liuda's attempts to turn her into a

---

[31] "Pochtovyi iashchik," *Zadushevnoe slovo* 47, nos. 16, 21, 37, 38, 39, 50 (1907). Of the twenty-two readers who enter the debate about Nina's "wildness," seven agree with the original letter or offer further criticisms of Nina for her impetuousness, excessive pride, hot temper, and uncivilized behavior, while fifteen defend Nina's character ("Pochtovyi iashchik," *Zadushevnoe slovo* 47 [1907], nos. 1, 11, 12, 34, 42, 50 [readers against Nina]; and nos. 14, 16, 17, 21, 22, 30, 31, 32, 34, 36, 37, 38, 39 [readers for Nina]).

[32] "Pochtovyi iashchik," *Zadushevnoe slovo* 47, nos. 39, 34, 38 (1907).

"proper young lady" with the aid of corsets, French verbs, and long dresses. Readers offer two competing interpretations of Liuda's treatment of Nina: two letters claim that Liuda is too "strict" and "persecutes" Nina; two others insist that Liuda was "not persecuting" Nina, but "trying to check" her "unbridled character" and "hot-tempered impulses."[33] Others try to claim that the two "types" are equally admirable, yet incompatible due to their different ethnic origins, as the following letter indicates:

> Liuda and Nina are two completely opposite types—Liuda is the embodiment of Christian kindness, unselfishness, and humility, while Nina is all fire, irrepressible whirlwind, boldness, pride, and originality! . . . Both these types are deeply appealing, both are identically interesting and attractive. I like them both and I simply don't understand what makes Liuda better than Nina. And what is "wild" in the character of the young princess Izmail-bek [sic]? You, dear Shura, simply don't know southerners, if you can make such a statement. How is Nina "wild"? She and her character show only the imprint of the free, ardent, unbending, magical Caucausus. Liuda Vlassovskaia, a Poltava Ukrainian, of course, could never be like that.[34]

This explanation of "wildness" in terms of national origin is not unique to readers' interpretations of *The Second Nina*, but migrates from one novel to another and becomes a model defense for favorite characters who have been criticized for behaving improperly. The particular nationality invoked is irrelevant. One reader defends a mischievous schoolgirl nicknamed "Redhead" (in *Liuda Vlassovskaia*) from charges of wildness as follows: "It's [her] *Russian* nature, broad and deep, which does not fit within the bounds of propriety and good breeding, which always preserves within itself something spontaneous and lively. You look at Redhead too one-sidedly, and see in her actions only bad breeding and wildness, and don't pay attention to anything else (emphasis added)."[35]

A later debate about the "wildness" of Ksania the "wood sprite" takes a similar turn, as another reader argues that Ksania is just like Princess Dzhavakha because "Ksania is just as much a southerner, just as proud and beautiful, and loves her forest just as much as Princess Dzhavakha loved her Caucasus."[36] While the novel never specifies precisely where Ksania's very northern-seeming forest is located, nothing suggests that it is anywhere "south" except in the imaginary geography of Charskaia's readers—for whom "south" is a state of mind, not a place on a map.

---

[33] "Pochtovyi iashchik," *Zadushevnoe slovo* 47, nos. 17, 24, 31, 37 (1907). The language of these letters indicates how well Charskaia's readers understood the many beloved half-wild horses in her works as alter egos for her wild heroines—passionate equestriennes all.

[34] "Pochtovyi iashchik," *Zadushevnoe slovo* 47, no. 21 (1907).

[35] "Pochtovyi iashchik," *Zadushevnoe slovo* 47, no. 35 (1907).

[36] "Pochtovyi iashchik," *Zadushevnoe slovo* 48, no. 25 (1908).

How *are* these girls wild? The letter writers almost never specify a particular "wild" act—except for the "moment of despair" when Nina bek-Izrael tears at her hair and clothing—yet the word is clearly loaded with meaning for both critics and advocates of the so-called wild girls. The readers' resistance to the term also seems odd since Charskaia's heroines often describe themselves and their behavior as wild and take pride in the fact. Insofar as the wild girls are usually compared—both favorably and unfavorably—with characters who are "well-brought up," "calm," "even-tempered" young ladies, their wildness consists in their defiance of culturally sanctioned norms of girlish behavior. They don't fit in and are, in fact, constantly on the verge of breaking out—of their corsets, their filial obligations, and the institute. What drives these wild girls—and what agitates their admirers and critics alike—are their "unbridled" desires: for adventure, affection, admiration, and, most of all, autonomy.

To be a wild girl is to want too much—and to want the wrong things. The "second Nina," for example, wants to be a boy. Her wildness is—as the readers' letters indicate—particularly marked, and I want to examine it in some detail in order to clarify how Charskaia's novels simultaneously seduce and caution their readers with images of girls who refuse to be good. What sets the second Nina apart from earlier and later wild heroines in Charskaia's immense *oeuvre* is the ferocity and inchoate nature of her desire. She is constantly plunging into one abyss—literal or metaphorical—after another. She is rescued from her first near-fatal tumble by the notorious mountain bandit Kerim, who exchanges gifts with her (her dead horse's saddle for his dagger) to mark their new friendship, escorts her home, and tells her to expect a visit from him—despite the price on his head and the fact that Nina's adoptive father is a Georgian general in the Russian army. At this point in another novel, the reader might expect a romance to develop, but Nina bek-Izrael does not want to "have" Kerim, she wants to "be" him—or at least she thinks she does. As she exclaims repeatedly throughout the first half of the novel: "O glorious and fearless Kerim! How I long to be even a little bit like you! Why am I not a boy! Not a man! If I were a man! Oh! I would rip off these girl's clothes, chop off these black braids without regret and, dressed like a *dzhigit*, would flee to the mountains, to Kerim."[37]

For this Nina, femininity is inextricably linked with Russification, as she makes clear when she questions her Dagestani parents' conversion from Islam to Christianity and wonders, "What appealed to them in the life of the Russians? I don't understand. If I had my way, I would cast off this delicate, cloudlike ball gown and replace it with the coarse *beshmet* of the Lezgin mountain warriors. . . . I would start walking like the boys and no

---

[37] L. A. Charskaia, *Vtoraia Nina* (St. Petersburg: Ellips, Ltd., 1994), 32.

one would recognize the highborn young lady, doomed to memorize French verbs."[38]

Nina not only wants to walk the mountain boys' walk, however, she also wants to dance the mountain girls' dance—the *lezginka*. Although Nina relishes the admiration her solo performance evokes at the ball thrown in honor of her fifteenth birthday, she wishes she had a partner—" a true son of the Dagestan mountain village"—who would dance the *lezginka* her way. She rejects her father's Cossack lieutenants as "too theatrical" and "officer-like" in their dancing and chooses instead a mysterious, handsome "Persian." As Nina closes her eyes, "intoxicated, [her] strength sapped by the dance," the mysterious stranger's "hot breath flow[s] over" her cheek . . . and Nina realizes she is dancing with her hero, Kerim. Chaos ensues when the notorious bandit casts off his Persian disguise and Nina, overwhelmed "by ecstasy and fear simultaneously," cries out his name to the assembled spectators. Kerim challenges Nina's father to honor Eastern codes of hospitality and treat him as a guest, not a criminal, but Nina's father rejects the notion that this guest could be "sacred"—proving his own thorough Russification.[39] Kerim escapes unharmed only because of Nina's hysterical interference in her father's pursuit. This is the "moment of despair" to which the letter writers referred:

> I writhed on the dew-damp grass, tore at my dress and hair, cursing my involuntary fault. I don't know if my fit lasted long, but I came to myself only when someone's strong hand placed itself on my shoulder.
>
> My father stood before me. . . .
>
> No, not my former father—the affectionate and indulgent, all-forgiving father, the kind and always benevolent Georgii Dzhavakha. . . .
>
> No. This grey-haired awe-inspiring general with his proud bearing, sternly knitted brows and somber look could not be a father to me—only a judge.[40]

This passage demonstrates the extent to which Nina's passionate attachment to Kerim is a transgression that *confounds*—in every sense of the word—gender norms, sexual propriety, paternal authority, and civic duty.[41] Charskaia's readers labeled the scene of Nina's hysteric fit "wild," because they understood it—correctly, I think—as a public expression of that "subversive attitude toward norms" which some feminist critics have

---

[38] Ibid., 47.
[39] Ibid., 56, 58, 61.
[40] Ibid., 61.
[41] My reading of this scene is informed by Stephanie Sandler's "Pleasure, Danger, and the Dance: Nineteenth-Century Russian Variations," in Goscilo and Holmgren, *Russia–Women–Culture*, 247–72.

identified as the origin of the hysterical symptom.[42] Wanting both to ride and to dance with outlaws, Nina not only challenges the social norms that make a mountain bandit an improper partner for the daughter of a Russian general; she rejects the order that defines identity in terms of sexual difference.[43] Her fit may be read as one of simple sexual frustration, but at the heart of the ball scene is Nina's right—or lack thereof—not only to choose the object of her desire but also to constitute herself as a desiring subject.

Nina's dance and her defiant claim that she will "not allow" anyone to hurt her partner are attempts at a public display of cultural authority unsanctioned by the social and civic order her father is sworn to uphold. The consequences of Nina's defiance were not encouraging for girls who might have wanted to follow her example. Her father refuses to "see" her until she tells him the "whole truth" about Kerim; Nina becomes, in essence, invisible in the eyes of the law as embodied by her father, whom she sees again only after his death from an injury sustained while trying to tame a wild horse (a surrogate for his equally unruly daughter). Too late, Nina vows "to reform, to do everything possible to become like other girls . . . to try to harness [her] wildness" out of love for her father. Nina is convinced that God is punishing her for her "wildness, evil temper, laziness, and bad character," and the novel offers no evidence to the contrary.[44] Consigned by her father's will—more powerful in death than in life—to live with distant relatives of his until her majority, Nina narrowly escapes a forced marriage to a villainous hypocrite and finds her only legal refuge in the institute where Liuda and Princess Dzhavakha were once students. Nina's inability to control her own destiny after her father's death suggests the impossibility of a girl—even a wild one—finding a place outside the law—or in the Caucasus. The institute offers freedom *from* interference by the outside world, but very little freedom *to* set and pursue goals independent of the larger legal and social system that limits the choices girls can make about their own lives. Charskaia's institutes do offer the image of a powerful girls' society, as Beth Holmgren has noted, but it is an image—or illusion—of power that her heroines themselves are schooled to renounce.[45]

Only in their passionate friendships with "good" girls—like Liuda Vlassovskaia—are Charskaia's "wild" heroines—like the two Ninas—able

---

[42] This phrase belongs to Ellie Ragland-Sullivan, "Hysteria," in *Feminism and Psychoanalysis: A Critical Dictionary*, ed. Margaret Whitford (Oxford: Basil Blackwell Ltd., 1992), 164–65, as cited in Diana Fuss, *Identification Papers* (New York: Routledge, 1995), 130.

[43] I rely here in part on Stephen Heath's discussion of hysteria in "Difference," in *The Sexual Subject: A Screen Reader in Sexuality* (New York: Routledge, 1992), 50–52.

[44] Charskaia, *Vtoraia Nina*, 116, 114.

[45] Holmgren, "Why Russian Girls Loved Charskaia," 99–100.

to bridge the otherwise separate spheres of public bravery and private affection. In Charskaia's novels, the almost constant tension between girls' duty to be "good" and their powerful desire for heroic self-display is resolved primarily in girls' struggle to win the approval and affection of their chosen soul mates. Schoolgirls' tumultuous relationships are the principal sources of conflict within her institute tales, which often conclude with the principal heroine's dramatic reconciliation with a beloved but estranged girlfriend.

The reconciliation of duty and desire in girls' passionate friendships—in ways that both affirm and challenge cultural norms—is exemplified in the conclusion to Charskaia's most popular novel, *Princess Dzhavakha*. A long-standing quarrel between the timid Liuda Vlassovskaia and the bold Princess Nina is resolved only when Liuda takes the blame for a prank Nina has committed but refused to confess. As the innocent Liuda faints from the shame of her public punishment, Nina finally recognizes that she "alone is guilty of everything," and she stabs herself with a penknife—in "atonement" for the sins of which she only now repents and in order to join Liuda in the institute's infirmary. Reunited with Liuda and full of self-reproach, Nina ends her story as follows:

> We fell into each other's arms. . . . Only now did we realize that we couldn't live without each other. . . . Yes, I loved her, loved her terribly. . . . My lonely little soul had languished in anticipation of a real, genuine friend. And she had appeared. . . . We cuddled close to each other, happy in our friendship and reconciliation. . . . Liuda and I sat quietly, silently. . . . Everything had been said and discussed . . . but our silent happiness was so great, so quiet, that a deep silence expressed it better than any words, empty and unnecessary.[46]

It may not be accurate to identify this profoundly silent happiness with the "love that dare not speak its name," but this is the language of passion—and a girl-centered passion at that.

Within Charskaia's works these passionate female friendships fulfill another function as well—they compensate the wild heroines from the Caucasus for their loss of freedom within the institute walls. This is clearest in the case of the "second Nina," who is just barely prevented from fleeing the institute "to freedom" in the Caucasus when proud Lidiia Ramzai intervenes, offering her friendship and explaining that "you have to know how to be patient." Only at this point does Nina realize that the primary cause of her unhappiness within the institute had been the apparent hostility of this "wonderful, long-beloved girl," and she gives Lida a

---

[46] L. A. Charskaia, *Kniazhna Dzhavakha* (St. Petersburg: Book Chamber International, 1990), 332, 334, 335–36.

"warm" kiss, then allows her new friend to lead her back inside the dormitory. The novel ends as follows: "Neither of us slept that memorable night. Our ardent, friendly conversation continued until dawn. In that night the blue sky, groves of plane trees and gigantic moutains [of Nina's native Dagestan] seemed to fade into the background—as did my Petersburg impressions. Everything was displaced by the delicate figure of a young girl with surprising, sparkling green eyes."[47]

In passages like these Charskaia offers her readers an emotional substitute for the Caucasus that most of them will never visit, the horses most of them will never ride, the adventures most of them will never have. The institute—and the larger institutions of authority for which it is a metonym—tames and domesticates even the wildest girls in Charskaia's works, making it possible for the would-be wild girls among her readers to accept the cultural limitations placed on their own behavior as both inevitable and necessary.

Girls and Their Secrets

Early twentieth-century critics of Russian children's literature were increasingly disturbed by the phenomenal popularity of Charskaia's heroines, and many couched their criticism in terms that suggest they read other stories between the lines of her heroines' extravagant endearments and passionate kisses. As N. Fridenberg warned in 1912, "The most blatant pornography is less dangerous . . . than the works of Charskaia," arguing that her works catered to adolescent girls' excessive "self-love" and "self-delight"—*samoliubie* and *samouslazhdenie*.[48] These words lack the sexual connotations of their English equivalents, but in a cultural tradition that placed self-sacrifice and self-effacement among the cardinal feminine virtues, "self-love" and "self-delight" could not help but seem unhealthily self-centered and perverse.

In every case, Charskaia's critics single out her heroines' passionate friendships for particular, if indirect criticism. Fridenberg's polemic against Charskaia's influence concludes, for example, with a call for the expansion of coeducational schools in order to "root out all the evil fostered by old [single-sex] schools," although the article never specifies the forms this "evil" takes.[49] In similarly cryptic fashion, Z. Maslovskaia footnotes her 1911 critique of "adoration" in Charskaia's works with a reference to the "chapter on friendship" in a 1904 study of St. Petersburg pros-

[47] Charskaia, *Vtoraia Nina*, 266–67.
[48] N. Fridenberg, "Za chto deti liubiat i obozhaiut Charskuiu?" *Novosti detskoi literatury*, no. 6 (February, 1911–1912): 5–6.
[49] Ibid., 6.

titutes.[50] This treatise claims that many prostitutes modeled their friendships after the schoolgirl practice of "adoration," but that in their "de-
grading circumstances" this "ideal feeling" often assumes what the author
elliptically terms "a different character."[51] Charskaia's novels themselves
represent their heroines' friendships as entirely asexual, yet her critics
persistently hint at the potentially sexual subtext of the girlish intimacies
they so deplore.

The most virulent of Charskaia's critics was Kornei Chukovskii, who
railed against Charskaia's beloved institute in an article saturated with disgust for what he calls the "eroticism" of her heroines' relationships with
one another. In contrast to young letter writers' readings of the institute
as a place that cools the fiery temperaments of spoiled girls or domesticates wild Caucasian princesses and other "noble savages," Chukovskii in-
dicts Charskaia's institute as "a little nest of vileness, a torture chamber
that cripples children's souls." He makes hilarious fun of her heroines'
weekly fainting fits and daily bouts of hysteria, but he concludes his article
with a hysterical fit of his own as he denounces "the notorious institute
practice of 'adoration,' which sends Charskaia into such raptures," and
laments that her schoolgirl heroines "adore people indiscriminately. It
could be Kuz'ma the cook. . . . And the kisses, the kisses! Cheap, sniveling
[kisses]. Just try to count the kisses in *Liuda Vlassovskaia*."[52] The notion
that girls might adore and therefore kiss "indiscriminately"—not just a
cook, but also each other—lies at the heart of Chukovskii's attack on the
"eroticism" of Charskaia's works. Chukovskii may have been particularly
troubled by the illustration of two girls giving one another "a strong,
warm kiss" in the 1904 publication of *Liuda Vlassovskaia* in *The Soulful
Word.*

Charskaia's publishers took these attacks seriously. In 1913, a year after
Chukovskii's critique appeared, *The Soulful Word* released a brochure, *Why
Do Children Love Charskaia?*, which devoted the last ten of its forty pages to
citing and refuting Charskaia's critics.[53] And Charskaia herself, in a novel
that began to appear in *The Soulful Word* in the fall of 1913, responds directly to the most serious accusations leveled against her works—that her
kissing heroines were parading secrets better left untold. This novel, *Se-r-i-
te* (T-a i-ta), differs significantly from Charskaia's usual "institute" tales,
most obviously in its principal heroine's rejection of "adoration" as "abnormal" and "ridiculous" and her acceptance of a marriage proposal at
the novel's conclusion; all but one of Charskaia's previous schoolgirl

[50] Maslovskaia, "Nashi deti," 116.
[51] B. Bentovin, "Torguiushchie telom (Ocherki stolichnoi prostitutsii)," *Russkoe bogatstvo*,
no. 12 (December, 1904): 165.
[52] Chukovskii, "Lidiia Charskaia," 160, 163.
[53] Viktor Rusakov, *Za chto deti liubiat Charskuiu?* (St. Petersburg: M. O. Vol'f, 1913), 30–40.

Ориг. рис. В. А. Табурина.

Figure 14. "We gave each other a strong, warm kiss." Illustration by V. A. Taburin for the serialized publication of Charskaia's *Liuda Vlassovskaia* in *The Soulful Word for Older Children* 44 (1904): 135.

heroines either die tragically or choose a celibate life of service to others.[54] This novel's title also invites a different, less literal reading than Charskaia's previous works had demanded, as it challenges its readers to fill in the blanks and solve the mystery of "Se-r-i-te," an abbreviation for "The Secret of the Institute" (*Taina instituta*). *Se-r-i-te* thus foregrounds the elusive—and literally elliptical—quality of the girls' secrets it takes as its subject, even as it denies them any sexually subversive power. A careful

---

[54] The exception is Charskaia's pseudo-autobiographical heroine, Lida Voronskaia, whose marriage is a brief episode in *Na vsiu zhizn'*.

reading of the novel suggests, however, that Charskaia may have been playing with the very secrets her novel initially appears to disavow.

The novel's title refers to one particular "secret," the five-year-old orphan Glasha whom the graduating class has covertly adopted as their common "daughter" and nicknamed the "Secret of the Institute," although they refer to her—for greater security—as either "Secret" or "Serite" in the notes they pass one another in class. This proliferation of names—Glasha / Secret / Serite—confused at least one of Charskaia's readers, who wrote early in the novel's serialization, "It seems to me that "Serite" refers to Glasha, but why is she called that? After all, the schoolgirls named her Secret."[55] This reader's query is simple, but indicative of the way in which *Se-r-i-te* opens up the possibility—unusual in Charskaia's works—that words and their referents may not always exist in an absolute one-to-one correspondence. Just as Glasha has multiple secret names, so, too, does her chief protectress, Nika Baian, have multiple secrets.

Nika's other secret is her "adoration" of a younger girl, Princess Zaria Ratmirova, whom she has nicknamed "Fairy Tale" (*Skazka*). *Se-r-i-te* places Nika's two secrets in conflict throughout the novel, as Zaria grows increasingly jealous of Nika's attention to Glasha. All of Charskaia's heroines quarrel frequently and often suffer agonizing pangs of jealousy, but these disagreements typically result from temporary misunderstandings and conclude with renewed avowals of passionate friendship. In *Se-r-i-te*, however, Nika finds it impossible to remain friends with Zaria. Each encounter between the two is punctuated by Nika's increasingly emphatic rejection of "adoration" as the basis for girls' friendship.

The pivotal quarrel between the two girls is provoked by a handsome doctor who whirls Nika onto the dance floor at a school party and into the world of heterosexual romance. As they dance, the doctor persuades Nika that her sulky "Fairy Tale" looks more like a "gloomy tale," or a "poem in prose," and he insists that her name, Zaria, "reeks of Mohammed." The doctor claims to "see nothing" in Zaria, despite Nika's defensive assertions that Zaria reflects the trace of "something otherworldly, something special, unique and beautiful, like a fairy tale."[56] At the conclusion of this fateful waltz, Nika feels "different, as if [her] eyes had been opened," and she abruptly denounces "adoration" as "ridiculous," "abnormal," and "wild." Nika eventually abandons the secret world of "uncivilized" (and implicitly "unchristian") girls' friendship altogether in exchange for entry into a different fairy tale—one that begins when the princely doctor offers to "settle your Secret and get you all out of trouble." "Getting you all out of trouble" entails providing a new, legitimate home not only for Glasha, but for

---

[55] "Pochtovyi iashchik," *Zadushevnoe slovo* 54, no. 19 (1914).
[56] L. A. Charskaia, *T-a i-ta* (Petrograd: M. O. Vol'f, 1916), 190.

Nika as well. When the doctor proposes marriage, Nika accepts, certain that in her new life she will be "happy the way only people in fairy tales can be happy."[57] In contrast to the otherworldly "Fairy Tale" Nika saw in Zaria, however, this is a lower-case fairy tale that, for the first time, rewrites Charskaia's characteristic story of girls' exalted same-sex love with a mundane heterosexual happy ending.

The novel wants its readers (at least some of them) to believe that Nika's more "natural," maternal concern for Glasha leads to Nika's rejection of Zaria as her secret fairy tale. Yet as the secret daughter of a self-appointed all-female "family"—with a tomboy "father" and that tomboy's ultra-feminine best friend for a "mother"—Glasha embodies in even more subversive ways the fairy tale of Amazonian utopia in which heterosexuality is only an option, not a mandate.[58] The similarity between Nika's two secrets—her secret daughter, Glasha, and her former secret soul mate, Zaria—is suggested in a scene in which Zaria threatens to reveal Nika's "revolting Secret, the one you call Serite," if Nika continues to reject her friendship. As Zaria boasts with "malevolent joy" that she "know[s] everything," Nika collapses in "despair" at the thought that "their Secret was no longer a secret. . . . Zaria had found out all about it, and with her, perhaps, their whole class."[59] Nika's abject terror in this scene is incommensurate with the threat posed by Zaria's knowledge of her innocent "Secret," but because the two girls never mention Glasha by name, the precise identity of Nika's "revolting Secret" remains strategically open to other, less innocuous interpretations. As Eve Sedgwick has noted, "by the end of the nineteenth-century, . . . knowledge meant sexual knowledge, and secrets sexual secrets."[60] In this scene, *Se-r-i-te* dares its author's critics to read the secrets elided in its title as sexual (i.e., the love that dares not "write" its name), while it insists on its heroine's innocence of the "abnormal" sexual knowledge imputed to Charskaia's previous heroines—and their fans—by her critics.

The novel's dramatic tension thus derives less from the nature of the girls' shared secret than from its openness to both discovery and misinterpretation. The girls flaunt their Secret throughout the novel, yet it remains thoroughly inaccessible to adult eyes, even when, at Easter, all

---

[57] Ibid., 194, 278, 283.

[58] Glasha's fate in Charskaia's next novel for *The Soulful Word, Deli-Akyz* (1915), confirms this point. Neither placed in an institute nor adopted by Nika, Glasha is dispatched instead to an orphanage in the Caucasus run by two confirmed bachelorettes, the second Nina and her longtime companion, Liuda Vlassovskaia.

[59] Charskaia, *T-a i-ta*, 197. No English translation can do complete justice to the double entendres of this passage, since the pronoun translated here as "it" may refer either to a female person or to the Russian word for "secret" (*taina*), which is grammatically feminine.

[60] Eve Kosofsky Sedgwick, *Epistemology of the Closet* (Berkeley: University of California Press, 1990), 73.

thirty-five girls in the class confess to "concealing a certain Secret from the institute authorities," thereby baffling the institute's priest but preserving the sanctity of both sacrament and Secret.[61] At another point the girls bring Glasha out of hiding and introduce her to their teachers as Nika's cousin, "little princess Serite," but their instructors still fail to recognize the girls' Secret, even as she stares them in the face. The girls' ingenious dissimulations are matched in number and variety by the institute authorities' equally improbable hypotheses to explain their pupils' frequent visits to the watchman's room where Glasha is concealed: secret drinking; an improper interest in the watchman; a morbid fascination with ghosts; and, finally, "political secrets" and "conspiracies."[62]

The equation of the girls' Secret with "political secrets" reveals the extent to which this novel acknowledges public anxieties about the potentially subversive power of any "plot," however well-intentioned, that is initiated and executed by a group of girls without benefit of "institutional" authority. In the novel's conclusion, Nika conceals Glasha in an empty trunk, where she almost suffocates while Nika refuses to hand over the key to institute authorities, who are certain the trunk conceals stacks of seditious literature. Although Glasha is eventually revived, the novel pulls out all the stops to convince the reader that Nika has, in fact, killed her. Nika collapses with a "hopeless, soul-rending shriek" after she is forced to open the trunk, while the assembled grown-ups exclaim in horror, "A little corpse! A dead little girl!" as they peek in to see "a frozen little face— twisted in convulsions of unbelievable suffering."[63]

Se-r-i-te presents its readers with at least two potentially dead girls in this scene, as if to underscore the dangers of keeping secrets—and secret passions—pent up too long, whether in a politically suspect trunk or an unruly student body. But which of the institute's multiple secrets are most endangered here? In this scene, the novel's seemingly opposed secrets merge in Glasha's almost lifeless body, for the Secret and Fairy Tale that Glasha and Zaria represent are most closely linked in the violence of Nika's denial that they exist. Nika denounces her former passion for Zaria with the same ferocity as that with which she defends Glasha against discovery by the institute's authorities, with near-fatal consequences for both. Nika's first words when she revives from her faint are telling, as she cries: "I killed her! . . . I am her murderer!"[64] Glasha, of course, is not dead, but Nika's murderous terror has another victim here: the story of

---

[61] Charskaia, *T-a i-ta*, 268.

[62] Early in the novel's serialization, readers' letters acknowledge the impossibility of keeping a secret long in such a fashion, as they predict that Glasha's presence will be discovered "soon" ("Pochtovyi iashchik," *Zadushevnoe slovo* 54, nos. 24, 27, 37 [1914]).

[63] Charskaia, *T-a i-ta*, 294.

[64] Ibid., 297.

girls' secret love for each other, a story Nika has to smother if she is to survive within the master narrative of heterosexuality.

No evidence exists that any of Charskaia's young readers comprehended the dangers of the secrets from which this novel struggled to deflect their attention.[65] It might be more accurate, in fact, to identify a passion for secrets, rather than secret passions, as the source of both Charskaia's appeal to her readers and the anxieties her works provoked in their adult critics. For Charskaia's critics, her heroines' shared secrets necessarily constituted a "plot" against the innocence of her readers. For her fans, these same shared secrets marked Charskaia's heroines as extraordinary and admirable in their "wild" defiance of parental and pedagogical authority.[66] Although the secrets of Charskaia's schoolgirls are always revealed and defused at novel's end, her characters become heroines in large part because of their ability to create secret identities for themselves—whether of passionate friendship, transvestite adventure, or covert parenthood. Charskaia's critics stigmatized her heroines' unconventional behavior with sexualized rhetoric, but what is really at stake in her institute tales is girls' autonomy, their attempts to love and take delight in themselves as the subjects of their own stories. These attempts were fraught with dangers—as *Se-r-i-te* so melodramatically illustrates. But the risks that Charskaia's heroines courted were essential to the seductive, unsettling pleasures her stories offered their fans. Her schoolgirls' elaborate mystifications proclaim that they have something worth hiding, and their secrets grow in value as the threat of their discovery increases. Charskaia's exotic settings and mysterious institutes offered her heroines and her readers an arena for self-fashioning and self-display that was gratifyingly public, yet safely secret—open to the admiring gaze of other girls but closed to adult surveillance and interference.

In their impassioned debates, Charskaia's readers thrilled in their ability to explain behavior that remained comically and sometimes dangerously mysterious to the adult characters in Charskaia's works. Girls' letters to *The Soulful Word* suggest that their shared reading of Charskaia united her community of readers in the same ways that shared secrets united her heroines. As they confessed their anxieties and ambitions about the possible resemblances between themselves and their favorite heroines,

---

[65] For accounts of lesbian activity in an institute setting, see Anastasiia Verbitskaia's autobiography, which characterizes "those [girls] to whom all secrets were revealed" as "undoubtedly *tribades*," in her *Moemu chitateliu. Avtobiograficheskie ocherki* (Moscow: Tipografiia I. N. Kushnerev, 1908), 236, and Laura Engelstein, "Lesbian Vignettes: A Russian Triptych from the 1890s," *Signs* 15, no. 4 (Summer 1990): 824–31.

[66] I am indebted here to D. A. Miller's analysis of secrecy as a "subjective practice" in *The Novel and the Police* (Berkeley: University of California Press, 1988), 207, as cited in Sedgwick, *Epistemology of the Closet*, 67.

Charskaia's readers united, as did her heroines, in efforts to determine for themselves both who they were and who they might become.

Secret Legacies

Charskaia was unable to publish anything under her own name after 1918, but young Soviet readers continued to list her works among their "very favorites" through the mid-1930s, even as critics added new charges to the prerevolutionary indictment of Charskaia's works, shifting the focus of their accusations from her novels' unhealthy "eroticism" to their alien class politics.[67] Although the changed historical circumstances altered the terms in which Charskaia's works were read, both her fans and her critics in the 1930s acknowledged the role of secrecy as a source of her enduring appeal. The critic Elena Dan'ko argued, for example, that banning Charskaia's books would simply force them "underground," making them "even more seductive," and she advocated reading Charskaia's works out loud as the best means of combating their pernicious influence. When read aloud in large groups, contended Dan'ko, the melodramatic speeches of Charskaia's heroines evoked only laughter or revulsion among young readers, rather than the tears and admiration they reported when reading her by themselves.[68]

Elena Bonner's mother, however, takes the opposite approach when she confiscates her daughter's "vile" book and refuses to return it until she reveals its source. Rather than disarming Elena's secret, Bonner's mother reaffirms its danger and importance when she places it in an already loaded hiding place—the locked drawer where Bonner's father keeps his " 'weapon.' " The seductive threat of secrets in general, and the subversive power of girls' shared secrets in particular, is exemplified by Bonner's account of her desperate attempt to recover the forbidden book. To protect Lelia and their common secret, Bonner resolves for the first time in her life to break into her father's locked drawer, despite her profound terror of guns. The forbidden book lies atop a thick manuscript in her father's hand, and beneath them Bonner uncovers her father's small and utterly mysterious arsenal. She does not even know, she reports, the proper names for the weapons she carefully removes from their cases, examines "with trembling hands," then replaces, leaving, however, indeli-

---

[67] For a perturbed response to surveys of young readers' recidivist preferences in the 1930s, see Elena Dan'ko, "O chitateliakh Charskoi," *Zvezda*, no. 3 (1934), 124–40. On Charskaia's fate after 1917, see Evgeniia Putilova, "Tri zhizni Lidii Charskoi," in M. Sh. Fainshtein, ed., *Russkie pisatel'nitsy i literaturnyi protsess v kontse XVIII–pervoi treti XX vv.* (Wilhelmshorst: Verlag F. K. Gopfert, 1995), 169–86.

[68] Dan'ko, "O chitateliakh," 124, 138–39.

ble traces of her crime on the drawer's broken lock.[69] Bonner's foray into her father's dangerous yet fascinating secret drawer indicates the power of girls' reading—and girls' secret loyalties—to inspire at least some girls to defy both their own fears and adult authority. As she insists on her right to keep her own secrets, Bonner also asserts her resemblance to Charskaia's most daring heroines, who were equally persistent in their rejection of adult claims to know and control girls' secret pleasures.

The ultimate fate of the secrets contained in the locked drawer also suggests, however, the limitations of defiant secrecy as a strategy for both self-fashioning and self-protection. Bonner looks into her father's drawer only one other time in her life—on the day after his arrest in 1937 and the police search of their apartment. The drawer is open and no longer contains either her father's " 'weapon' " or his manuscript, but only "for some reason, Mama's beige pumps, which later became my 'going out' shoes."[70] One might read this conclusion to the story of the locked drawer as indicating—like the conclusions to Charskaia's novels—that even the most rebellious girls must ultimately relinquish their dreams of picking up their fathers' weapons and settle for stepping into their mothers' hand-me-down shoes. Bonner's memoir, *Mothers and Daughters* (Dochki-materi, 1991) is devoted to her recollections of her strong-willed mother and grandmother, however; and the larger story it tells of everyday female heroism in the Stalin era suggests that a mother's legacy of courage—hidden in plain sight, rather than kept under lock and key—may prove a more effective weapon than a father's gun when a girl goes out into a world patrolled by an increasingly aggressive secret police. The shifting contents of the Bonner home's single locked drawer—trashy book, Papa's weapons and unpublished manuscript, Mama's shoes—also reminds us that secrets, as Charskaia's novels and their shifting interpretations reveal, are mutable, but their psychic effects—the threat of exposure and the thrill of dangerous knowledge—are not. The legacy of the secret-filled drawer—like that of Charskaia's secret-filled novels—lies not only in what is found there but also in the memory of having broken its locks.

---

[69] Bonner, *Dochki-materi*, 219–21. The book in question is not one of Charskaia's but "Danilevskii's *Mary Magdalene*," which Bonner skips school to finish reading, although she declares that "it wasn't interesting at all." The title and content of this book, presumably Gustav Danilovskii, *Mariia Magdalena*, 4th ed. (Leningrad: Biblioteka vsemirnoi literatury, 1927), are almost irrelevant to Bonner's story, which centers on the structure and significance rather than the content of girls' secrets.

[70] Bonner, *Dochki-materi*, 221.

CHAPTER SEVEN

The Russian Myth of Oscar Wilde

EVGENII BERSHTEIN

Oscar Wilde remains, to the present day, one of the first foreign writers a Russian reader encounters in his or her life. The catalogues of the National Library in St. Petersburg list hundreds of editions of Wilde's work in Russian translation, many of them aimed at children and adolescents. In educated families, parents read Wilde's fairy tales to their kindergarten-age children. In their school years, children are expected to read *The Picture of Dorian Gray*. Wilde's major society plays, such as *The Importance of Being Earnest* and *An Ideal Husband*, are made into popular movies shown often on television. When Russians learn English in secondary schools or colleges, their reading lists inevitably include Wilde's works. Students of Russian literature acquaint themselves with classic translations of Wilde's poetry made by celebrated Russian poets such as Konstantin Bal'mont ("The Ballad of Reading Gaol") and Nikolai Gumilev ("The Sphinx"). From the first years of this century until today, Wilde has been one of the main aesthetic influences of West European modernism on Russian culture. This influence is a rich topic for literary scholarship, but it will not be addressed directly in the present essay.

To explain the reasons for this omission, I will have to make a detour of a personal nature. In the 1970s, when I was a Leningrad schoolboy, I duly received an education in Wilde of the kind that I have just described (my first English book was *The Happy Prince*). However, when I recollect my im-

I wish to thank Olga Matich, Eric Naiman, Irina Paperno, Hans Sluga, and Roman Timenchik for their discussions of the earlier versions of this essay. I am also grateful to Laura Engelstein for her valuable editorial suggestions and to Nikolai Bogomolov, who shared with me a number of yet unpublished archival materials.

pressions of reading Wilde in my early teens, the memory that stands out in my mind is of my father's embarrassment and evasiveness when I asked him why "they" had sent Wilde to prison. The question was provoked by the vagueness the book's introduction acquired when it came to presenting the end of Wilde's life. I remember that it referred to "the hypocrisy of bourgeois society," the "tragedy," and the "debtors' prison." In addition, there was an aura of something morbid and unnamable. This aura of tragic mystery is, I will argue, a relic of the widespread, powerful and formative cultural mythologies that surrounded the persona of Oscar Wilde and his life story in Russian culture at the end of the nineteenth century and the beginning of the twentieth.

In the English-speaking world, Wilde is a cultural symbol. He is emblematic of flamboyance, effeminacy, and, by extension, the modern type of homosexuality (the crime for which Wilde was sentenced in 1895 to hard labor). As the British critic Alan Sinfield notes in his recent book *The Wilde Century*, "our stereotypical notion of male homosexuality derives from Wilde, and our ideas about him."[1] Wilde the dandy, Wilde the fashion plate, Wilde the queen—those very aspects of the British writer's persona that became central to his reputation in the Western world remained marginal in Russia. The Russian picture of Wilde was drawn in the tragic colors of rebellion, suffering, and saintliness. Even his physical appearance underwent a bizarre metamorphosis: the Russian critic Nikolai Abramovich gave the following description of Wilde in his 1909 book: "Wilde was healthy with the beautiful health of a beast of prey."[2] There is nothing in Wilde's looks to support this passage (in photographs, he appears a chubby, somewhat awkward eccentric). Instead, it is determined by the idiosyncratic Russian discourse on Wilde, popularized mostly by Russian Symbolists and near-Symbolist writers. That discourse, its genesis, structure, and cultural consequences, will be the focus of this essay.

Oscar Wilde's Trials and Prince Meshcherskii's Trumpeters

In the spring of 1895, the Marquis of Queensberry, angered by the public relationship between his son Lord Alfred Douglas and the writer Oscar Wilde, left his card with an insulting inscription "For Oscar Wilde posing Somdomite" (as spelled in the original) in one of Wilde's London clubs. The marquis had been looking for a confrontation for some time and had

[1] Alan Sinfield, *The Wilde Century: Effeminacy, Oscar Wilde, and the Queer Moment* (New York: Columbia University Press, 1995), vii.
[2] N. Ia. Abramovich, *Religiia krasoty i stradaniia. O. Uail'd i Dostoevskii* (St. Petersburg: Posev, 1909), 15.

at last found it. Instigated by Lord Alfred, Wilde filed a defamation suit against Queensberry. He lost, was immediately arrested, and was soon tried on the charge of "gross indecency" (the nineteenth-century legal euphemism for homosexuality). The first jury could not bring in a verdict. The case was retried, and on May 25, 1895, Wilde was found guilty and sentenced to two years of hard labor.[3] The horrible conditions of the prisons where Wilde served out his sentence ruined his health. His plays were taken off the stage; his name became unmentionable in the press. Unable to write, he spent the last three years of his life in self-imposed exile in France, where he died in poverty in 1900.

Before the moment of his catastrophe, Wilde had reigned on the British stage, was widely read in Western Europe, and was the toast of the London and Paris beau monde, which considered him one of the most fashionable people of the time. This was why his scandalous trials turned into a major sensation in the European press. In the words of Elaine Showalter, Wilde's spectacular downfall, following the accusations of his having engaged in commercial sex with numerous male acquaintances from the lower classes, shocked the public by its "revelations of the gross materiality of homosexual liaisons."[4] "Open the windows! Let in the fresh air," the London *Daily Telegraph* exclaimed in reaction to the verdict.[5]

At the time, Wilde was practically unknown in Russia. Like other European cultural and literary fashions, "aestheticism," which proclaimed Wilde as its prophet, arrived in Russia after a delay, reaching full strength only in the early 1900s. Russian newspapers nevertheless followed the example of their West European counterparts, covering the trials extensively. In particular, the major national daily *Novoe vremia* (New Time), published by A. S. Suvorin, devoted the incredible number of eighteen reports to the court proceedings. One of Russia's most influential papers, *Novoe vremia* essentially created the Wilde trials as a news event for the Russian public. The questions of how and why Suvorin's newspaper did this deserve consideration.

The structure of this news event as presented in *Novoe vremia* was quite peculiar. Because only five of the eighteen reports were received by telegraph, and the rest brought by mail, which usually took eight days, the narrative was serialized in a curious way: the telegrams provided the reader with previews of the story and the outcome of the various trials;

---

[3] On the history of Oscar Wilde's trials, see H. Montgomery Hyde, *The Trials of Oscar Wilde* (New York: Dover, 1962); Michael S. Foldy, *The Trials of Oscar Wilde: Deviance, Morality, and Late-Victorian Society* (New Haven: Yale University Press, 1997).

[4] Elaine Showalter, *Sexual Anarchy: Gender and Culture at the Fin-de-Siècle* (New York: Penguin Books), 177.

[5] Cited in Richard Ellmann, *Oscar Wilde* (London: Penguin Books, 1987), 450.

somewhat later, longer articles clarified psychological and factual details. At the end of this "soap opera," the paper published the only signed article on the topic, giving an overview and analysis of the preceding trials. The first telegram, datelined March 25, London, explained how Wilde had come to stand trial "for actions offensive to public morality." It concluded with the story of Wilde's arrest and reports of the rumor

> that the arrest of Lord Douglas will follow, as well as that of others among Wilde's friends, mostly from the ranks of servants, grooms, trumpeters, and persons repeatedly convicted in the past.
>
> Theaters have stopped performing Wilde's plays, the magazine that Wilde has been publishing has been canceled. All of London is despondent over the exposure of the way of life and the character of one of England's most brilliant writers.[6]

Novoe vremia published subsequent reports in the international news section. The March 27 item provided a detailed account of the first day of the trial and the full translation of the major piece of evidence against Wilde, his love letter to Lord Alfred Douglas. It also included the observation that "Wilde . . . 'poses' a lot" and reported that the court had heard "very compromising facts."[7]

The March 28 issue contained the text of prosecutor Carson's interrogation of Wilde almost verbatim and described the heartbreaking family drama that accompanied the reading of the insulting telegrams which the marquis and his son exchanged: "The eyes of the marquis, directed at [his] son, clearly communicated contempt and hatred. The young lord, pale, emaciated, with dim eyes and thick blond hair, was trying to meet his father's eyes, but broke down and turned away."[8]

While evoking the atmosphere of extreme tension that permeated the audience, the next report emphasized the gravity of the offense: "In English law, the crime of which Wilde is accused stands only one step below murder. Therefore, if Wilde's guilt is proved, he may be sentenced to a very severe punishment—hard labor for ten years or even for life. He is also at risk of the same punishment, although for a term from three to ten years, if he is found guilty only of the attempt to commit the said crime."[9]

In its reports on the next two trials, *Novoe vremia* followed the same principle: the flashy psychological characterization complemented the narrative line and the scandalous details.

[6] *Novoe vremia*, no. 6851 (March 26 / April 7, 1895): 1.
[7] Ibid., no. 6852 (March 27 / April 8, 1895): 2.
[8] Ibid., no. 6853 (March 28 / April 9, 1895): 2.
[9] Ibid., no. 6854 (March 29 / April 10, 1895): 2.

The second witness, a certain Atkins, a nineteen-year-old youth, tells how he met Wilde by chance on the *trottoir* . . . . Wilde started to receive Atkins in his flat, during his spouse's long absences.[10]

During this time a big change took place in Wilde himself. His old self-confidence all but evaporated. When he was taken into the "dock," that is the cage for defendants, his former friends and acquaintances could not recognize the writer who had previously been self-confident and somewhat of a fop. Pale, his hair undone, unwashed and dressed sloppily, Wilde was, indeed, hard to recognize.[11]

After describing the proceedings of the third trial and reporting the jury's guilty verdict, the paper published the news analysis by its London correspondent G. S. Veselitskii-Bozhidarovich, writing under his usual pen name Argus. In "Oscar Wilde and Oscar-Wilde-ism" ("Oskar Uail'd i oskar-uail'dizm"), Argus made two main points. First, he stressed the gravity of Wilde's offense ("unprecedented trial, more horrible, as the judge who pronounced the sentence said, than the most horrible murder"). Second, the correspondent concluded that "This trial . . . has extremely serious and deep significance. I see it not simply as a trial of individuals, but as one of England's blood aristocracy."[12]

The last point was more than the expression of the writer's personal opinion. It reflected Suvorin's political line as publisher and ideologue.[13] In the field of international politics, *Novoe vremia* took a strongly anti-English and pro-French position. In the field of the Russian Empire's internal affairs, it opposed aristocratic exceptionalism, exalting the figure of the monarch as the center of national statehood to which Russians of all social classes were entitled to contribute (except *inorodtsy*, for the paper was expressly anti-Semitic).

One of Suvorin's important ideological opponents and his main competitor in the struggle for influence in governmental spheres was Prince Vladimir Meshcherskii, the publisher of the daily *Grazhdanin* (Citizen). Meshcherskii's diplomatic line was Francophobic and Anglophile, and his ideology was aristocratic. According to Meshcherskii, it was the gentry that formed the true basis of monarchy in Russia. While Suvorin's paper was an incredibly successful commercial venture, Meshcherskii's *Grazhdanin* was secretly subsidized by the government on the order of Alexander III, during whose reign Meshcherskii enjoyed enormous influence at the court (ministerial appointments were allegedly decided at his

---

[10] Ibid., no. 6859 (April 5 / 17, 1895): 2.
[11] Ibid., no. 6867 (April 13 / 25, 1895): 2.
[12] Ibid., no. 6907 (May 24 / June 5, 1895): 2.
[13] On Suvorin's *Novoe vremia*, see I. Solov'eva and V. Shitova, "A. S. Suvorin: portret na fone gazety," *Voprosy literatury*, no. 2 (1977): 162–99.

"Wednesdays").[14] Alexander died in 1894, and it took Meshcherskii several years to restore his authority with Nicholas II. In 1895 Meshcherskii's standing appeared quite shaky, Nicholas expressing squeamishness about his personality and unwillingness to employ his publication as a mouthpiece for conservative views.

During the two months of covering the Wilde trials, *Novoe vremia* constantly returned to its polemic with *Grazhdanin*.[15] The subject provided a direct link to Meshcherskii, who was a notorious homosexual. Memoirists agree that no educated person in St. Petersburg was unaware of Meshcherskii's taste for young men.[16] E. K. Pimenova, a *Grazhdanin* staff member in the 1880s, wrote in her memoir, "everyone in the newspaper knew about his [Meshcherskii's] vices." Then she crossed out "in the newspaper."[17] In the 1880s satirical poems played on the name of Meshcherskii's periodical, claiming that its publisher was "the citizen of Sodom" (*grazhdanin Sodoma*).[18] Vladimir Solov'ev wrote a whole series of epigrams depicting Meshcherskii as a proud and shameless Sodomite.[19] The scandals related to his private life were numerous and loud.

In putting Oscar Wilde and his "offence against morality" in the limelight, Suvorin may have had two goals. First, by publishing a long psychologized narrative on sexual vice, he pleased his readers; second, by alluding to Meshcherskii and *his* vice, he could deliver a political blow to the competitor, also implicating both the latter's aristocratic ideology (it was hinted that this vice was aristocratic) and his Anglophilia (because the scandal came from England).[20]

[14] The career, reputation and personality of Prince Meshcherskii are analyzed in W.E. Mosse, "Imperial Favourite: V.P. Meshchersky and the *Grazhdanin*," *The Slavonic and East European Review* 59, no. 4 (October 1981): 529–47.

[15] See, for instance, the editorials on the role of the aristocracy in Russian society in *Novoe vremia*, no. 6907 (May 24 / June 5, 1895) and on Meshcherskii's Francophobia in *Novoe vremia*, no. 6904 (May 20 / June 1, 1895).

[16] *Vospominaniia E. M. Feklistova: Za kulisami politiki i literatury, 1848–1896*, ed. Iu. G. Oksman (Leningrad: Priboi, 1929), 247.

[17] E. K. Pimenova, "Dni minuvshie," OR-RGB, f. 1000, l. 2, no. 1054, p. 59.

[18] The anonymous epigram, entitled "To His Highness Prince Meshcherskii," found in the collection of manuscripts of the National Library, St. Petersburg (fond 391, no. 81), puns on the word *grazhdanin* (citizen), claiming that the addressee is the *grazhdanin Sodoma* (the citizen of Sodom). It also refers to the publisher's sodomitical relationship with another editorial staff member, the poet A. N. Apukhtin. See also the recently published archival materials on homosexuality in St. Petersburg in the 1880s, in which Meshcherskii figures prominently: Konstantin Rotikov, "Epizod iz zhizni 'golubogo' Peterburga," *Nevskii Arkhiv: istoriko-kraevedcheskii sbornik* (St. Petersburg: Atheneum-Feniks, 1997), 449–66.

[19] Vladimir Solov'ev, *Stikhotvoreniia i shutochnye p'esy*, ed. Z. G. Mints (Leningrad: Sovetskii Pisatel', 1974), see p. 148 ("Znamenitomu grazhdaninu" [1887]) and pp. 255–60 ("Dvorianskii bunt," a satirical play [1891]).

[20] Michael Foldy notes that the British press interpreted Wilde's transgression as an unfortunate consequence of French cultural influence (Foldy, *The Trials of Oscar Wilde*, 53).

The insulting and politically damaging parallel between the compromised English writer and the Russian political journalist who had just fallen out of favor might, however, have escaped the attention of contemporaries, not to mention that of later scholars, if *Novoe vremia* had not included direct allusions to the best-known of Meshcherskii's sex scandals in its first telegram on the Wilde case. This telegram described Wilde's friends as drawn "from the ranks of servants, grooms, trumpeters, and persons repeatedly convicted in the past." There were no *trubachi* (trumpeters) among those of Wilde's acquaintances whose testimonies Queensberry solicited. Neither were there *trubochisty* (chimney sweeps, the word linguistically related to the former and more appropriate in the context of listing lower-class vocations). However, an 1887 scandal that compromised Prince Meshcherskii was caused by his amorous relationship with a trumpeter from the Infantry Batallion of the Guards. The soldier "visited" Meshcherskii at his St. Petersburg home, where he was caught by his superior, Colonel Keller. The soldier was then reprimanded and further visits to Meshcherskii were banned. Meshcherskii responded in *Grazhdanin* with what memoirists call a smear campaign against the colonel. As a result, Keller was first dismissed, then, upon investigation of the story, recalled to service. While *istoriia s trubachem* (the trumpeter story) is mentioned by several memoirists, Count Sergei Witte recounts it in some detail in his memoiristic essay on Meshcherskii.[21]

Apparently, Meshcherskii's *Grazhdanin* could not afford to omit mention of the Wilde trials. Long after *Novoe vremia* started its coverage, *Grazhdanin* published several Reuters telegrams, all very short, about the trials. Curiously, these telegrams contained not the slightest hint as to the character of Wilde's crime.[22]

Unlike in England and Germany, where the fin de siècle was marked by homosexual scandals that included legal prosecution and the participation of the press, in Russia no such thing happened. In the words of Laura Engelstein, "on the [Russian] public stage, homosexuality never served as a vehicle for symbolic politics, as it did in England and Germany during the same period."[23] She adds that "one obvious candidate to become the Russian Eulenburg was Prince Vladimir Meshcherskii."[24] If Suvorin's coverage of the Wilde scandal was an attempt to draw legal attention to the moral corruption in upper governmental spheres, he did not succeed. That would have required greater development of such institutions of

[21] S. Iu. Vitte, *Vospominaniia* (Moscow: Izdatel'stvo sotsial'no-ekonomicheskoi literatury, 1960), 3: 582.

[22] *Grazhdanin*, no. 113 (April 26, 1895); no. 128 (May 11, 1895); no. 132 (May 15, 1895). See also the articles in the weekly *Nedelia* (no. 15 [April 9, 1895] and no. 18 [April 30, 1895]).

[23] Laura Engelstein, *The Keys to Happiness: Sex and the Search for Modernity in Fin-de-Siècle Russia* (Ithaca: Cornell University Press, 1992), 58.

[24] Ibid., 58n.

civil society as an independent press and an independent legal system. In Russia, Meshcherskii's case as well as others like it were settled quietly at the tsar's discretion. However, Suvorin's most likely design was to hurt Meshcherskii's already tainted political and journalistic credibility. It seems that with the means available to him, Suvorin was creating his own epigram on Meshcherskii, as many others had done.

A Nietzschean Life

The search for the ideological interpretation of the Wilde scandal started in Russia right after the trials. It would continue for two decades. No Russian newspaper named Wilde's actual transgression but, except for *Grazhdanin*, they all found indirect ways to communicate its nature. The conventions of "decency" adopted by the Russian press did not, however, prevent the name of Wilde from turning into the standard euphemism for modern homosexuality. The common use in fin-de-siècle Russia of the expressions "the tastes of Oscar Wilde" and "Oscar Wilde's inclinations" reminds one of the nineteenth-century Russian evocation of the name of Jean-Jacques Rousseau to designate masturbation, another sexual "transgression." Indeed, Dostoevsky's formulation "the sin that Jean-Jacques Rousseau confessed in his *Confessions*," takes the same form as the later references to Wilde.[25] It also places the transgressive sexual practice in the West. Thus a cultural role for a Russian Rousseau or a Russian Wilde was created, and in the case of the latter, this role was assigned, as I will show, to at least one cultural figure—and consciously tried on by others.

In 1897, when Wilde was still serving his prison term, and while his name was still taboo in the English press, a journalist of the St. Petersburg weekly book review *Knizhki nedeli* (Books of the Week), signing himself "N. V.," noted: "the sad story that interrupted the literary activities of Oscar Wilde did a service to his fame."[26] This was particularly true in Russia, where the scandal unleashed a flood of publications on the previously unknown writer and his work.[27]

Zinaida Gippius's society tale "Oxeye" (Zlatotsvet), published in *Severnyi vestnik* (Northern Herald) eight months after the trials, provides a lively satirical picture of the St. Petersburg artistic circles that had started discussing Wilde's writing and creating his reputation. The story's main

[25] F. M. Dostoevskii, *Polnoe sobranie sochinenii v 30–ti tomakh*, vol. 11 (*Besy*) (Leningrad: Nauka, 1974), 14.

[26] N. V., "Oskar Uail'd i angliiskie estety," *Knizhki nedeli* (June, 1897): 5.

[27] See Tat'iana Pavlova's highly informative article for a review of the Russian translations of Wilde and critical reaction to his work: Tat'iana Pavlova, "Oskar Uail'd v russkoi literature (konets XIX–nachalo XX vv.)," *Na rubezhe XIX i XX vekov. Iz istorii mezhdunarodnykh sviazei russkoi literatury: sbornik nauchnykh trudov*, ed. Iu. D. Levin (Leningrad: Nauka, 1991).

character, the decadent Zviagin, presents a paper on Wilde's aesthetic theory (apparently based on Wilde's collection of articles *Intentions*) to a circle of wealthy literary dilettantes. His talk provokes opposition in Pavel Vasil'evich Khamrat. With the ill-grounded pathos of a true philistine, Khamrat throws himself against Wilde's "aestheticism": "I categorically disagree," he starts, "that such a person as Oscar Wilde can be considered only from the point of view of his literary opinions, without touching on his persona. What an incomplete, incomplete picture!" But the expected analysis of Wilde's persona never follows. "Gentlemen, we are in the company of ladies—I don't have the opportunity to touch upon certain subjects," says Khamrat—and he never does. Instead, as the sarcastic narrator reports, "Pavel Vasil'evich . . . forgot Wilde and started a long, passionate, even raging debate and censure of the most modern themes."[28]

According to Khamrat, the discussion of "certain subjects" relevant to Wilde's persona was not fit for ladies' ears, and therefore such a discussion was unbecoming. This argument underscores the paradoxical side of the early perception of Wilde in Russia—for almost a decade it was precisely the persona of Wilde that enjoyed renown, not his writings, yet the public transgression that made Wilde famous could be discussed in print only in the most equivocal terms.

This persona was organized around the analogy between Wilde and Nietzsche. In Europe as well as in Russia, both supporters and opponents of Wilde and Nietzsche took notice of their ideological kinship. Max Nordau in his voluminous pamphlet *Degeneration*, popular all over Europe in the late 1890s, put Wilde next to Nietzsche in a subcategory of modern degenerates which he called "Egomaniacs."[29] In his treatise "What Is Art?" (1897–98), Lev Tolstoy also invokes Wilde side by side with Nietzsche, a "prophet" of the false, that is, immoral attitude toward art: "Decadents and aesthetes of Oscar Wilde's sort choose the rejection of morality and the lauding of depravity as the theme of their works."[30] André Gide mentions in his memoirs, published in 1905, five years after Wilde's death, that when he started to read Nietzsche, he was "astonished less" because he had already heard similar ideas from Wilde.[31]

Severnyi vestnik, the voice of modern artistic movements, was the first periodical to stress the parallel. Akim Volynskii, its editor, reviewed Wilde's *Intentions* for the Russian public in December 1895, half a year after

[28] Zinaida Gippius, "Zlatotsvet," *Severnyi vestnik*, no. 2 (1896): 229–30.
[29] Max Nordau, *Degeneration*, translated from the second edition of the German work (Lincoln: University of Nebraska Press, 1993 [Originally published: New York: D. Appleton, 1895]), 442–43.
[30] Lev Tolstoi, *Polnoe sobranie sochinenii* (Moskva: Gosudarstvennoe izdatel'stvo khudozhestvennoi literatury, 1951), 30: 172.
[31] André Gide, *In Memoriam (Reminiscences). De Profundis*, trans. Bernard Frechtman (New York: Philosophical Library, 1949), 15.

Wilde's last trial. In his review he outlined the connections between Wilde's theories and Nietzsche's philosophical discourse. He did not hide the enormous impression made on him by Wilde's spectacular downfall: "All of a sudden, his life, glamorous from the outside, but containing inner sores, played itself out in a depressing drama [*razygralas' v gnetushchuiu dramu*] with a repulsive criminal finale."[32] The notion of a play evokes the Nietzschean ideal of creating one's life as a work of art, so consonant with Wilde's own aesthetic statements. Transposed from the realm of aesthetic and philosophical thought into biographical analysis, the Nietzschean concepts of "play" as the artistic creation of life and "morality" as the inferior human majority's tool of subjugation gave Volynskii a key to understanding Wilde's fate.

In September 1896 Volynskii published an article in *Severnyi vestnik* in which he mobilized his sarcasm against the hypocrisy of the English judicial system and a society that kept Wilde at hard labor. In the article, Volynskii mocks the liberal intelligentsia's ideal of equality before the law. There could not be any doubt that Volynskii's antiliberal and pro-Wildean stance was Nietzschean in its ideological roots.[33]

> The immoral Wilde is imprisoned, and thus moral people have punished a vice soiling the reputation of English society, which of course consists entirely of highly moral people. Wilde, untidy in his personal life, is to be ostracized. To trample and spit on him before the whole world is to show one's own moral infallibility. To torture him with the strictest regime is to sow terror in the hearts of those who may be inclined to turn off the road of virtue. There should be no doubt that the law, which deals severely with any moral sin, could not treat Wilde differently. To subjugate people, it must be merciless. . . . Some naive people submitted to the English minister of the interior numerous petitions asking to mitigate the prisoner's fate. What an inexcusable indifference to the law! What an absence of fine juridical feeling for law and order! What a shameful lack of understanding of one's own duties to the powerful state. Wilde's health has deteriorated. How could it be otherwise? Do you think that the English prison must serve as an Eldorado for those who broke the moral law as it is understood by the English parliament? . . . Imprisoning its criminals, the English government will not think of their nerves, their health and their literary talent. . . . *Fiat justitia!* For Wilde— sickly, nervous, pitiful in his helplessness—no mitigation has followed. At the height of its juridical grandeur, the English law is deaf and dead to the insane pestering of people who don't think finely.[34]

---

[32] Akim Volynskii, "Oskar Uail'd," *Severnyi vestnik*, no. 12 (1895): 312–13.
[33] See Volynskii's articles on Nietzsche published in *Severnyi vestnik* in that same period: "Apollon i Dionis" (no. 11 [1896]: 232–55) and "Literaturnye zametki" (no. 10 [1896]: 223–55). A large part of Lou Andreas-Salomé's biography of the German philosopher was published in three issues of the journal (nos. 3–5 [1896]).
[34] Akim Volynskii, "Oskar Uail'd," *Severnyi vestnik*, no. 9 (1896): otdel 2, 57–58.

In Volynskii's accounts, the once-glamorous Wilde is made to seem pitiful by his severe punishment and resulting illness. The expectation that "the sickly, the nervous, and the pitiful" will utter the final truth is quite in the spirit of the Russian literary tradition. It was not by chance that *Severnyi vestnik* started its campaign to introduce Nietzsche to the Russian public by publishing Lou Andreas-Salomé's biography of the German philosopher, where his sufferings, caused by debilitating disease, were described in vivid detail.[35] As many Russian followers of Nietzsche later contended, his sufferings put the stamp of truth on his writings and gave him a moral right to preach amorality. The pain he had undergone sanctified both his philosophy and his persona. Russian Symbolists clearly perceived Nietzsche as a Christ-like figure.[36]

Wilde's perceived "Nietzscheanism," a peculiar combination of amorality and saintly "superhumanness," was gradually becoming commonplace in turn-of-the-century Russian literary discourse. Moreover, the Nietzschean associations outgrew the persona of Wilde; critics started to attach them to homosexuality as such. The philosopher Lev Shestov thus noted in his 1898 book *The Good in the Teaching of Count Tolstoy and F. Nietzsche*:

> The opinion that O. Wilde is justified and made into an ideal by the philosophy of Nietzsche can be heard everywhere. Moreover, all kinds of people, tempted by Wilde's amusements, find it possible now to engage in their trade with a conviction that they are the precursors of the *Übermensch*, and therefore, the best workers in the field of human progress.[37]

The first years of this century saw a great rise in Wilde's popularity in Russia.[38] The focus of public discussion, however, remained constant: as before, the persona of Wilde, rather than his creative writing, dominated the debate. Konstantin Bal'mont, the major Symbolist poet, translator and popularizer of Wilde, laid the foundation for a Symbolist interpretation of Wilde. Bal'mont's 1903 lecture "The Poetry of Oscar Wilde" produced a noticeable scandal and was soon printed in the first issue of the main Symbolist journal *Vesy* (Libra). Its position, following Briusov's manifesto "The Keys of Mysteries," reflects Wilde's stature in the hierarchy of

---

[35] Lu Andreas-Salome, "Fridrikh Nitsshe v svoikh proizvedeniiakh," *Severnyi vestnik*, nos. 3, 4, 5 (1896), passim.

[36] Lev Shestov made clear the connection between Nietzsche's painful illness and his "sacred right to say what he has said"(Lev Shestov, "Dobro v uchenii gr. Tolstogo i F. Nitsshe," *Sochineniia* [Moscow: Khudozhestvennaia literatura, 1992], 57, and 57–61 on the meaning of Nietzsche's illness). See also Andrei Bely on Nietzsche as a new Christ (Andrei Belyi, "Fridrikh Nitsshe," *Arabeski* [Moscow: Musaget, 1911], 69–90).

[37] Shestov, "Dobro v uchenii gr. Tolstogo i F. Nitsshe," 140.

[38] See Pavlova, "Oskar Uail'd v russkoi literature."

literary authorities recognized by the Russian Symbolists. Bal'mont refuses to talk about Wilde's work, however; by "the poetry of Wilde" he understands "the poetry of his persona, the poetry of his fate."[39] Bal'mont
equates Wilde's life with that of Dorian Gray. "Beauty" was given to Wilde,
and it was "Beauty" that he pursued all his life, but "like all true gamblers,
he miscalculated his odds, and had to make sure personally that it was the
Devil who presided over the games of luck."[40]

Most importantly, Bal'mont reinforces the parallel between Wilde and
Nietzsche. He sees in Wilde's *life* the phenomenon analogous to
Nietzsche's *writing*:

> In the sense of being an interesting and original person, he cannot be com-
> pared to anyone except Nietzsche. However, while Nietzsche's personality
> marks the absolute impetuosity of literary work, combined with the asceticism
> of personal behavior, the reckless Oscar Wilde is as chaste as air in his artistic
> work . . . , but in his personal behavior, he went so far from the commonly ac-
> cepted rules that he spent two years at hard labor despite all his enormous in-
> fluence, despite all his fame.[41]

It was in the numerous responses to Bal'mont's article that Wilde's story
became completely mythologized. Russian critics now considered his life
as a failed superhuman effort to overcome morality; and in his attempt to
create life artistically, they saw a revolt doomed to punishment.

A Latter-Day Raskol'nikov

The selection of Wilde's works first translated and widely discussed in
Russia contributed to such an interpretation of his life story. These were
not his sophisticated early poems that had earned him in England the
reputation of a major poet, nor the witty society plays that made him famous. In Russia's Silver Age, Wilde's two texts written in prison and right
after his liberation were the most important: first, his tragic *Ballad of
Reading Gaol*, translated by Bal'mont (his programmatic lecture on Wilde
accompanied the translation); second, Wilde's book-length letter to Lord
Alfred Douglas, written in Reading Gaol. The fragments of this letter
made up a book published posthumously in 1905 under the title *De
Profundis*. It was immediately translated into Russian by E. Andreeva and
printed in the March issue of *Vesy* in the same year, with a sympathetic editorial introduction.

[39] Konstantin Bal'mont, "Poeziia Oskara Uail'da," *Vesy*, no. 1 (1904): 25.
[40] Ibid., 25.
[41] Ibid., 37.

In the part of the letter omitted in early editions, Wilde repeatedly reproaches Lord Alfred for the irresponsibility and selfish behavior that were the main reasons for Wilde's fall. In the letter's published part, Wilde admits that in his life before the trial he was misled by the constant pursuit of pleasure, in particular "perverse" and "pathological" pleasure. As a result, he continues, he did not understand the importance of suffering, which he realized only later in prison. "Suffering—curious as it may sound to you," he writes to Lord Alfred, "is the means by which we become conscious of existing."[42] He speaks at great length about Christ, of whom he claims to have approached an understanding while in prison.

By 1905, when Wilde's Nietzscheanism appeared to be a proven fact in Russia, the discovery of his later Christian inclinations caused an enthusiastic response in Russian modernist circles. Having always suspected a Christian, if not Orthodox, basis to Nietzsche's preaching of suffering, Russian culture now found its material confirmation in the Nietzschean life of Wilde. Presenting a mystical and philosophical interpretation of Wilde's *Salomé*, the Symbolist writer Nikolai Minskii saw that in this drama, while "still being a prophet of demonic aestheticism, Wilde had already had the presentiment of the new light that revealed itself to him at the depth of his ostracism and suffering."[43]

Perhaps the most peculiar feature that Wilde's life story acquired in Russia was the aura of self-sacrifice added to his actually illogical behavior immediately before and between the trials. Grigorii Petrov, a religious activist and journalist writing in the newspaper *Russkoe slovo* (Russian Word) under the pen name V. Artaban, turns Wilde into a latter-day Raskol'nikov:

> He [Wilde] feels that he is a criminal and he sends himself to hard labor; he executes himself. One can say with confidence that the horrors of Reading Gaol where Wilde did two years of hard labor were no more dreadful for him than the torture that he bore inside at the end of his life, long before the trial.[44]

Petrov entitled his article, devoted to Nietzsche and Wilde and Bal'mont's lecture, "The Rotten Soul," and built it around the metaphor of "the apple of Sodom." By this, Petrov explained, he meant a particular fruit that grew in Palestine at the place where Sodom had stood. That fruit looked quite beautiful from the outside but was rotten inside. Such, in his opinion, was the persona of Wilde. Though Petrov's view of Wilde is clearly

---

[42] Oscar Wilde, *De Profundis and Other Writings* (London: Penguin Books, 1986), 113.
[43] Nikolai Minskii, "Smysl Salomei," *Zolotoe runo*, no. 6 (1908): 56.
[44] V. Artaban, "Gnilaia dusha," *Russkoe slovo*, no. 43 (February 12, 1904): 1.

negative, he nevertheless persists in describing Wilde, on the model of Raskol'nikov, as somewhat Christ-like.

In February 1906, in the midst of revolutionary upheaval in the country and soon after the publication of *De Profundis*, the official journal of the St. Petersburg Theological Academy, *Khristianskoe chtenie* (Christian Reading), printed Vasilii Uspenskii's article "Oscar Wilde's Religion and Contemporary Asceticism" ("Religiia Oskara Uail'da i sovremennyi asketizm"). Uspenskii, an Orthodox priest and member of the St. Petersburg Religious Philosophical Meetings, believed that there was a religious meaning in the call for tragic pleasure, emblematized in contemporary culture by Wilde and Nietzsche. Comparing Wilde to a saint, Uspenskii describes the writer's suffering as "great and profound—and not only because of the external circumstances of his life. He knew more horrible, internal tortures. His blood merged with those streams of blood through which mankind acquired profound religious thought."[45]

The critic Nikolai Abramovich, known for repeating the commonplaces of contemporary criticism,[46] wrote an entire book in a similar vein. In his *The Religion of Beauty and Suffering: Oscar Wilde and Dostoevsky*, Abramovich notes that "by admitting the living meaning of suffering, Wilde closely approached Dostoevsky."[47] According to Abramovich, Wilde's Nietzscheanism was pregnant with Orthodox Christianity.

Most Russian critics focused on Wilde's life during and after the trials and interpreted it as the apotheosis of voluntary suffering. Common was the opinion that "Wilde sent himself to hard labor." The critic Zinaida Vengerova echoed: "Now, amidst the tortures of the legal proceedings, his spirit was overwhelmed with joy, for . . . fate gave him the opportunity to incarnate the tragic truth of being, the law of suffering."[48]

However, even in suffering Wilde appeared ambiguous—Christian with a distinct pagan aura. The pagan overtones were reminiscent of Dionysian orgies. In *The Birth of Tragedy*, Nietzsche presented and propagated the Dionysian element in Greek art as a symbol of the tragic liberation from the control, responsibilities, and moral restrictions imposed by the world of fixed forms. The leading ideologue of Russian Symbolism, Viacheslav Ivanov, saw an absolute, metaphysical principle in Nietzsche's distinction between the Dionysian and Apollonian elements. As a scholar of antiq-

---

[45] Vasilii Uspenskii, "Religiia Oskara Uail'da i sovremennyi asketizm," *Khristianskoe chtenie* (February, 1906): 225.

[46] On Abramovich, see Petr Pil'skii, "Vodevili literaturnoi bor'by," in his *Problema pola, polovye avtory, i polovoi geroi* (St. Petersburg: Osvobozhdenie, [1909]),132–33. See also A. V. Chansov's biographical article: "Abramovich, N. Ia.," *Russkie pisateli: Biograficheskii slovar', 1800–1917*, vol. 1 (A-G), (Moscow: Sovetskaia entsiklopediia, 1989), 13–14.

[47] Abramovich, *Religiia krasoty i stradaniia*, 60.

[48] Zinaida Vengerova, "Sud nad Oskarom Uail'dom," *Novaia zhizn'*, no. 11 (1912): 174.

uity, he concentrated on the study of the cult of Dionysus and finally arrived at the conclusion that the Greek religion of the suffering god was, along with Judaism, a major source of early Christianity.[49]

This philologically argued hypothesis had major consequences for the philosophical foundations of Russian Symbolism: it proved that the Dionysian element, with its always implied "unbridling of sexual drives"[50] and the Christian ideal of suffering were not mutually contradictory.[51] By extension, the orgiastic, or Dionysian, side of Wilde's reputation only complemented his saintliness. As Ivanov annnounced in his 1909 article "Two Elements in Contemporary Symbolism": "the whole life of the noble singer and humble martyr of Reading Gaol has turned into the religion of the universal Golgotha."[52]

In the beginning *Novoe vremia* made Wilde's story as familiar to the public as the contents of a best-selling novel. Taken as a fictional or mythological narrative, Wilde's life contained striking contrasts: celebrity and infamy, wealth and poverty, pleasure and suffering, beauty and ugliness. These and other antinomies made it extremely attractive for myth creation and for sentimentalization in popular culture. Highbrow literature and criticism may have emphasized Wilde's similarity to Christ, but the public wanted to know more about the orgiastic excesses of the English poet's transgression. While such exposés were not fit for print in the 1890s, after the revolution of 1905 and the following liberalization of the laws regulating censorship, they became a regular occurrence.

Soon after Wilde's trials and again after his death, the European publishers of scandal books produced numerous biographies of the disgraced writer, along with the unofficial transcripts of the court proceedings. A number of them—their seriousness varying—were translated into Russian. The sensationalist *Trial of Oscar Wilde*, by Oscar Sero, complemented more respectable biographies such as Halfdan Langgaard's *Oscar Wilde: His Life and Literary Work* and Hedwig Lachmann's *Oscar Wilde: Biography and Characterization.*[53] The 1908 collection *People of the Intermediate Sex*, the first

---

[49] Viacheslav Ivanov, "Ellinskaia religiia stradaiushchego boga," *Novyi put'*, nos. 1–3, 5, 8–9 (1904); Viacheslav Ivanov, "Religiia Dionisa," *Voprosy zhizni*, nos. 6,7 (1905).

[50] Viacheslav Ivanov, "Nitsshe i Dionis," in his *Sobraniie sochinenii*, ed. D. V. Ivanov and O. Deschartes (Brusselles: Foyer Oriental Chrétien, 1971–87), 1: 720.

[51] Explaining and extending the specifically Orthodox notion of *sobornost'*—a communal spiritual unity, Ivanov even made the statement: "*Sobornost'* is sex" (Sobornost' est' pol). Quoted in S. V. Trotskii, "Vospominaniia," *Novoe literaturnoe obozrenie*, no. 10 (1994), 53.

[52] Viacheslav Ivanov, "Dve stikhii v sovremennom simvolizme," *Sobranie sochinenii*, 3: 564–65.

[53] Oscar Sero, *Protsess Oskara Uail'da*, translated from German by A. N. Osipov (St. Petersburg: Tipo-litografiia I. Iudelevicha, 1909); G. Langgaard, *Oskar Uail'd. Ego zhizn' i literaturnaia deiatel'nost'*, translated from German (Moscow: Sovremennye problemy, 1908); G. Lakhman, *Oskar Uail'd. Biografiia i kharakteristika*, translated from German (St. Petersburg: Izdatel'stvo Aktsionernogo obshchestva tipografskogo dela, 1909). The original German publications: Oscar Sero, *Der Fall Oscar Wilde und das Problem der Homosexualität: ein Prozess und ein Interview* (Leipzig: Spohr, 190?); Helfdan Langgaard, *Oscar Wilde: Die Saga eines*

Russian homosexual almanac of sorts, featured the essay on Wilde's trials, translated from the French. Written by Wilde's personal enemy, Marc-André Raffalovich, this essay (known as "L'affaire Oscar Wilde" in the French publication) was rich in scandalous detail and hostile in tone.[54]

The reverberation of the Wilde story all around Europe was so strong that, as Eve Kosofsky Sedgwick has noted in a different context, "from our twentieth-century vantage point . . . the name Oscar Wilde virtually *means* 'homosexual.' "[55] This statement and the reverse ("homosexual" *means* Oscar Wilde) would also be true from the point of view of early Russian modernism. Almost all its homosexual literary characters bore some similarity to Wilde. The most famous of them, Shtrup from Mikhail Kuzmin's *Wings* (Kryl'ia, 1906) and Edgar Stark from Evdokiia Nagrodskaia's *The Wrath of Dionysus* (Gnev Dionisa, 1910), were dandified aesthetes, half-English by origin. (In Nagrodskaia's novel the very name of the protagonist refers phonetically to "Oscar Wilde"; the author obviously wanted to make sure that even a not-too-bright reader could catch the hint).

The orgiastic image of Wilde even reached early Russian cinematography, although only at the pre-production stage. The Russian Archive of Literature and Art (RGALI) has preserved a film script by Georgii Ustinov written around 1910 and based on Wilde's life. Entitled "The King of Life" ("Korol' zhizni"), the unfinished manuscript gives a rather graphic, although sympathetic picture of Wilde's fictional erotic adventures. Some of its descriptive clichés come from the biographical materials available in Russian, but most of them appear to be sheer fruit of the imagination.[56]

The three-part film was to present Wilde at the zenith of his fame—and through the story of his downfall. It starts with Wilde walking the roads of Oxford, followed by hordes of admirers: "As Wilde approaches, the crowd of passersby whisper to one another and gaze at him with admiration. Many men take off their hats. Wilde responds to them with a reserved elegant bow. The ladies present Wilde with flowers. Having walked away, he gives them to beggars."[57] As the story develops, other main characters make their appearances. The beautiful young Lord Harry is in love with the writer. The Girl (*Devushka*) is also enamored with him. Captions render the dialogue between Wilde and Lord Harry:

Dichters (Stuttgart: Juncker, 1906); Hedwig Lachmann, *Oscar Wilde* (Berlin: Schuster und Loeffler, 1905).

[54] See Part 6 ("Protsess Oskara Uail'da") in P. V. Ushakov (psevdonim), *Liudi srednego pola* (St. Petersburg: Pushkinskaia knigopechatnia, 1908). The French original: Marc-André Raffalovich, "L'affaire Oscar Wilde," *Uranisme et unisexualité: Etude sur differentes manifestations de l'instinct sexual* (Paris: Masson, 1896), 241–78.

[55] Eve Kosofsky Sedgwick, *Epistemology of the Closet* (Berkeley: University of California Press, 1990), 165.

[56] Georgii Ustinov (1888–1932), a writer and a Party journalist, a friend of Sergei Esenin. Apparently, Ustinov wrote the script in his youth. RGALI, f. 341, l. 1, no. 744.

[57] Ibid., l. 1r.

"I am having a holiday today, along with all of Oxford, Mr. Wilde. The King has come to visit us—the King of Life—"

"I would like to kiss you, young man."

Wilde kisses Harry. The Girl looks at the young man with envy.[58]

In the second part, Wilde invites the Girl to be the Queen of his "bachelors' dinner party."

Wilde's study. Enter Wilde and the Girl wearing white.

[Captions:]

"I am so weak that I am afraid to die of weakness—"

"You know, White Lily, I love to pick flowers— Aren't you afraid?"

"My wonderful, fairy-tale Prince, each woman who gives herself to you becomes a Queen."

Wilde puts her on the sofa. A prolonged kiss. The Girl disheveled in the throes of passion. Aperture.[59]

The dinner party goes on and a little later, as the script states boldly, "the orgy begins."[60] Against the backdrop of Wilde's orgiastic life an evil intrigue develops. A certain Mrs. Beignal, Wilde's nemesis, follows him secretly and watches his debauches with the apparent intention of making her knowledge public. Unfortunately, the conclusion of the manuscript has not been preserved. The beginning, however, hints at the trials and imprisonment, the central episodes of Wilde's life story as it was absorbed in Russia.

Creation of Life

Historians of sexuality have repeatedly noted that since the 1870s, the numerous medical, legal, and social discourses developed in such a way that they formed in European cultures the idea of a coherent homosexual identity. As Michel Foucault famously phrased it, "the sodomite was a temporary aberration; the homosexual was now a species."[61] The timing and scale of the Wilde scandal predetermined his role as a semantic center for this new discourse. The newly discovered homosexual identity was pronounced Wildean—and the competing interpretations of Wilde's life reflected the competing views of homosexuality. This process of discursive reorganization affected Russia, too.

[58] Ibid., l. 6r.

[59] Ibid., l. 8v.

[60] Ibid., l. 9.

[61] Michel Foucault, *The History of Sexuality*, vol. 1, *An Introduction*, trans. Robert Hurley (New York: Vintage Books, 1990), 43.

Indeed, for certain modernist artists in Russia, the meaning of the Oscar Wilde story had important personal significance. Thus, one day in the summer of 1906, Oscar Wilde became the theme of a heated debate at Viacheslav Ivanov's St. Petersburg apartment on Tavricheskaia Street, known as the *Bashnia* (Tower), the very heart of the Russian Symbolist movement. Besides Ivanov and his wife Lidiia Zinov'eva-Annibal, there were three other men present in the Tower, the poet Mikhail Kuzmin and the young artists Konstantin Somov and Leon Bakst, friends of Kuzmin and the Ivanovs. Everyone in attendance belonged to Ivanov's inner circle, that is, to the so-called Hafiz society which had been launched at the Tower several weeks earlier.[62]

In his diary Kuzmin reported the "huge argument" about Oscar Wilde: "V[iacheslav] I[vanovich / Ivanov] places this snob, hypocrite, bad writer, and most fainthearted man, this man who dirtied the very thing he was tried for, side by side with Christ—this is downright horrible."[63] A week later the same dispute was repeated in the same setting, as Kuzmin noted briefly in his diary: "Talked about Wilde again. Somov doesn't believe him either."

Ivanov's pronouncement belonged to the very core of Symbolist discourse on Wilde, and Ivanov rephrased it later in his published work. However, it was its context that made this exchange so passionate and fraught with symbolic significance.

The Friends of Hafiz first assembled at the Ivanovs' in May 1906 and continued to meet until November. The Society included several of Ivanov's close friends who were homosexual (Mikhail Kuzmin, Konstantin Somov, Walter Nuvel') and several other young men, talented and handsome, among them the philosopher Nikolai Berdiaev, the poet Sergei Gorodetskii, and the writer Sergei Auslender. With the exception of Zinov'eva-Annibal, the group consisted exclusively of men. The location of the apartment near the Tauride Garden ("the Tauride" in the slang of that time) added in the eyes of Kuzmin's friends to the attractiveness of these gatherings: the Tauride was St. Petersburg's central area for homosexual cruising, and several members of the Society had the habit of checking out its paths before or after the meetings, at which their reports of recent "escapades" featured prominently.

---

[62] On the Hafiz society, see the pioneering work of Nikolai Bogomolov, "Peterburgskie gafizity," *Mikhail Kuzmin: Stat'i i materialy* (Moscow: Novoe literaturnoe obozrenie, 1995), 67–99. On Kuzmin circa 1906, see John E. Malmstad and Nikolay Bogomolov, *Mikhail Kuzmin: A Life in Art* (Cambridge, Mass.: Harvard University Press, 1999), 92–124.

[63] Quoted in Nikolai Bogomolov, *Mikhail Kuzmin: Stat'i i materialy*, 84–85. Nikolai Bogomolov and Sergei Shumikhin have prepared the diary of Mikhail Kuzmin, preserved in RGALI (fond 232), for publication. Whenever I cite the parts of the dairy not yet printed, I use the manuscript kindly provided by Professor Bogomolov. In these cases, I only indicate the dates when Kuzmin made entries.

During the gatherings, the participants immersed themselves in what was perceived as the Dionysian: they drank wine, dressed up, played flutes, flirted, and kissed. They also read their diaries, as well as poetry written on the topics that interested the "Hafizites" (Ivanov's coinage—*gafizity*). If Ivanov took the mystical side of the Hafiz society quite seriously, Kuzmin and some other members seemed rather to be enjoying the appealing social scene. Berdiaev finally found its erotic ambiance inappropriate and distanced himself from the Society. In a later letter to Ivanov (June 22, 1908), he expressed his disapproval of the bygone Hafiz:

> I have never shared your mystical hopes, your *personal* hopes—others did not seem to have them—in this kind of social interaction. . . . some tendencies which appeared in this socializing displeased me. Then I withdrew and soon the whole thing broke up by itself.[64]

As for the Hafizites' conversations, Eros was the main topic. In these talks, Ivanov formulated his views on homosexuality, as recorded in his diary:

> [Kuzmin] is a sort of pioneer of the coming age when, as homosexuality grows, humanity will not be uglified and crippled anymore by the present-day ethic and aesthetic of the sexes understood as "men for women" and "women for men." This aesthetic of savages—with its tacky *appas* for women and the aesthetic nihilism of the male brute—makes it impossible for a "normal" person to see half of humanity and cuts off one-half of his individuality in favor of the continuation of the genus. Homosexuality is indissolubly tied to humanism, but as a one-sided principle that excludes heterosexuality, it also contradicts humanism, turning into the *petitio principii* in regard to the latter.[65]

The question of homosexuality was far from purely theoretical for Ivanov. His affair with the young poet Sergei Gorodetskii took place that very summer. Ivanov conceptualized that relationship as mystical and Dionysian, and it was supposed to clear the way to the superhuman for both participants. Also, from its very beginning, Ivanov expected his love for Gorodetskii to be "tragic" in the Nietzschean sense of high illuminating suffering.[66]

For his part, around the summer of 1906, Kuzmin was entering the elite cultural and literary circles of St. Petersburg. His programmatically homosexual novel *Wings* was not published until November 1906, in a special is-

---

[64] Published (in French) in Andrej Shishkin, "Le banquet platonicien et soufi à la "Tour" pétersbourgeoise: Berdjaev et Vjačeslav Ivanov," *Cahiers du monde russe* 35, nos. 1–2 (January–June 1994). I had at my disposal the text of the Russian original.

[65] Ivanov, *Sobranie sochinenii*, 2: 750.

[66] See Evgenii Bershtein, "Western Models of Sexuality in Russian Modernism," Ph.D. diss., University of California, Berkeley, 1998, 40–57.

sue of *Vesy*. However, by the summer, it was already being read widely in manuscript. The common critical and public opinion of Kuzmin as a Russian Wilde was one that he, as his diary shows, found most irritating. Ivanov, for one, did not share this opinion, stating in print that it was a mistake to see in Kuzmin "a Petersburger in Wilde's raincoat" (*peterburzhets v Ual'dovom plashche*), a pun paraphrasing the line "a Muscovite in Child Harold's raincoat" from *Eugene Onegin* (*moskvich v Garol'dovom plashche*).[67] Not that Kuzmin disliked the artistic work of Wilde. As Mikhail Rathaus has noted, "in other, more balanced periods of his life, Kuzmin's attitude towards Wilde was more tranquil."[68] But the Russian cultural mythology of Wilde prescribed for the homosexual an inclination for Nietzschean revolt and mystical suffering, which was deeply alien to Kuzmin.

Nikolai Bogomolov has shown a close connection between the choices that Kuzmin made in his sexual and his artistic lives.[69] One of the entries in Kuzmin's diary helps illuminate his rejection of the Wildean mythology and the influence of this mythology on how he and the homosexual artists of his circle conceptualized the social repercussions of their own sexual behavior. On September 15, 1906, Kuzmin depicts what was apparently his first sexual experience with more than one partner. The two in this case happened to be a young man, Pavlik Maslov, Kuzmin's lover at that time, and the artist Konstantin Somov, Kuzmin's close friend. After a rather detailed description of the sexual encounter, Kuzmin remarks in his diary:

> What an unexpected event. I was asking K. A. [Somov]: "Is it possible that our life will not remain for posterity?"—"If these terrible diaries are preserved—then it will remain, and in the next epoch, we will be considered Marquises de Sade." Today I understood the importance of our art and our life.[70]

In suggesting that posterity will liken them to the Marquis de Sade, Somov refers to the first line of the Russian translation of *De Profundis*: "My place would be between Gilles de Retz and the Marquis de Sade. I dare say it is best so. I have no desire to complain."[71]

[67] Viacheslav Ivanov, "Proza Mikhaila Kuzmina," *Apollon*, no. 7 (1910): 46.

[68] Mikhail Ratgauz, "Kuzmin—kinozritel'," *Kinovedcheskie zapiski*, no. 13 (1992): 68. This article, one of the best examples of Kuzmin scholarship, treats several of the questions I discuss below.

[69] Bogomolov, *Mikhail Kuzmin: Stat'i i materialy*, see especially the chapter "Kuzmin osen'iu 1907 goda," 99–116.

[70] Kuzmin's conviction that the way he performed sex had historic significance is noteworthy. Recording the sexual scene in the diary served as a guarantee of being forever remembered by posterity. Moreover, by acting it out, he reached the desired unity of life and art, related to the Nietzschean ideals of amorality and of treating life as the main object of creative effort.

[71] Wilde, *De Profundis*, 135. Russian translation: Oskar Uail'd, "De profundis," *Vesy*, no. 3 (1905): 5.

The figure of Wilde, with the looming shadow of the Marquis de Sade behind it, symbolized to Kuzmin and Somov the unbridgeable clash between society's accepted values and their own sexual practices. Wilde had fallen victim to this clash, and had done so without grace, dirtying "the very thing he was tried for." Wilde's fall pushed this "thing" from the periphery of culture to its center, thus making possible Kuzmin's discourse, in which his homosexuality played a far from marginal role. Kuzmin's and Somov's refusal to trust *De Profundis* could not cancel out the profound effect this text and the related mythology had on them. Even in confronting the mythologized persona of Wilde, Kuzmin could not but recognize its extreme relevance.

Kuzmin presented the erotic ideal in *Wings* as a serene and harmonious pre-Nietzschean image of Greece, represented in the modern world by the homosexual connoisseurs of classical languages. In the era of *The Immoralist* and *Death in Venice*, this ideal was old-fashioned. In contrast to Ivanov's notion of the superhuman homosexual passion doomed to suffering, Kuzmin—as his diaries show—persistently constructed a psychologically comfortable homosexual niche in everyday life and culture. The strangely heroic mask of Oscar Wilde did not suit him; he could not stay unaffected by the modern (and modernist) discourse on homosexuality, but he could and did reject the role it prescribed for him, the role of a saintly sufferer.

The explanation for the remarkable vitality of Oscar Wilde's Russian mythologies seems to be in the easy adaptability of Wilde's life story to the discursive resources of Russian culture. Particularly relevant is the Russian nineteenth-century novelistic model of a hero's "remaking his own essence," to use Yuri Lotman's expression, through moral crisis, self-sacrifice and suffering.[72] Rooted in mythology, this model kept kinship with Orthodox theological thought and influenced the modern and modernist conceptualization of sexuality. The absorption of Wilde's life story in Russia shows that, besides providing a forum for discussing sexuality, literary discourse influenced the forming of sexual identities. The discursive mechanisms of this formation appear comprehensible in the case of Russian Symbolists, thanks to the fact that they made "life creation" a focal point of their art.[73] A fortuitous political expediency helped introduce the Wilde narrative in Russia. Through it, the all-European modern theme of homosexuality received its Russian interpretation, in which the symbolic meaning of "Oscar Wilde" was preserved, although this symbol was loaded with specifically Russian cultural meanings.[74]

[72] Iurii Lotman, "Siuzhetnoe prostranstvo russkogo romana," *Izbrannye stat'i* (Tallinn: Aleksandra, 1993), 3: 102.

[73] On "life creation," see Irina Paperno and Joan Delaney Grossman, eds., *Creating Life: The Aesthetic Utopia of Russian Modernism* (Stanford: Stanford University Press, 1994).

[74] On the meaning of the Oscar Wilde story in Europe, see Sinfield, *Wilde Century*, and Ed Cohen, *Talk on the Wilde Side: Toward a Genealogy of a Discourse on Male Sexualities* (New York: Routledge, 1993).

CHAPTER EIGHT

Hysterical Episodes: Case Histories and Silent Subjects

CATHY POPKIN

I have not always been a psychotherapist. Like other neu-
ropathologists, I was trained to employ local diagnoses and
electro-prognosis and it still strikes me myself as strange that
the case histories I write should read like short stories and that,
as one might say, they lack the serious stamp of science. I must
console myself with the reflection that the nature of the subject
is evidently responsible for this, rather than any preference of
my own. The fact is that local diagnosis and electrical reactions
lead nowhere in the study of hysteria, whereas a detailed description of mental processes such as we are accustomed to find
in the works of imaginative writers enables me, with the use of a
few psychological formulas, to obtain at least some kind of insight into the course of that affection. Case histories of this
kind are intended to be judged like psychiatric ones; they have,
however, one advantage over the latter, namely an intimate
connection between the story of the patient's sufferings and
the symptoms of his illness—a connection for which we still
search in vain in the biographies of other psychoses.
                    —Sigmund Freud, ostensibly on Fräulein
              Elizabeth von R., but more manifestly on himself

Freud has been relegated to an epigraph here because the consummate storyteller and his psychoanalytic narrative strategies remain emphatically beyond the purview of the case histories penned by his Russian
counterparts during the heyday of hysteria. And yet Freud's insistence on
the reconstruction of a story that would restore the self to itself posits a

I am grateful to Edyta Bojanowska for her invaluable assistance in locating and obtaining
many of the documents used in this study.
    Epigraph is from *Studies on Hysteria: The Standard Edition of the Complete Psychological Works of
Sigmund Freud*, trans. James Strachey (London: The Hogarth Press and the Institute of
Psycho-Analysis, 1955), 2: 160–61.

narrative practice against which we might instructively position Russian psychiatric writing during the last two decades of the nineteenth century and the first few years of the twentieth. Also instructive is the fact that Freud's characterization of his distinctive case histories of hysterics reads like a confession: with the hindsight bestowed by conversion ("I have not always been a psychotherapist"), Freud's defense of storytelling proceeds through a confession of error to a profession of faith. And although Freud insists that the need for narrative arises from "the nature of the subject ... rather than any preference of my own," his account begins, in good Augustinian fashion, by looking for truth by looking into himself.

The early Russian psychiatric writers, as we shall see, differ markedly from Freud on both counts—in their determined neglect of narrative and in their minimal display of self-consciousness. At the same time, though, they greatly outdo Freud in making their case histories a study in their own professional development. Evidently more powerful than either the "nature of the subject" or any "preference of [their] own" is the nature of their own position as practitioners in a developing field and forgers of a new discourse. What we see in the Russian case histories, rather than a profession of faith, is an anxious faith in the profession. Somewhat short on Freud's "detailed description of mental processes," late nineteenth-century Russian psychiatric writing documents most tellingly the urgencies of professionalization.

Hysteria

In Russia, as elsewhere in the 1880s and 1890s, much of the clinical writing centered around the problem of hysteria. High-strung ladies and neurasthenic young men were succumbing to the affliction in droves on both sides of the Atlantic, and the medical community's preoccupation with the curious disease was equally prodigious. This international absorption in hysteria and its manifestations was triggered first and foremost by neurologist Jean-Martin Charcot's pioneering and well-publicized studies of hysterical patients at the renowned Salpêtrière clinic in Paris between 1878 and his death in 1893. Charcot's public lectures and exhibitions of hysterical women in contorted positions, along with his published photographs of his patients' dramatic poses, made hysteria a matter of public curiosity as well as a professional challenge. These same years mark Freud's above-mentioned transition from neuropathologist to psychotherapist—chiefly on the basis of his professional encounters with hysterical women—as he moved from his apprenticeship to Charcot (1885–86) to his collaboration with his mentor Josef Breuer. Between 1886 and 1905 he published a whole series of studies on the disorder, most notably the seminal *Studies on Hysteria* (with Breuer, 1895), featuring the case studies of Anna O. and several other hysterics, and his own book-length case history of the famous Dora (*Fragment of an Analysis of a Case of Hysteria*, 1901). Other prominent physicians, such as Carl Friedrich Westphal, Pierre Janet, and Hippolyte Bernheim, challenged Charcot's assumptions and exposed his errors, establishing rival schools of thought (Bernheim's "Nancy school," Westphal's Berlin group) that moved French and German clinicians similarly toward a more psychological understanding of the disease, giving rise to lively and long-standing polemics that kept hysteria very much in the spotlight of medical writing. In every major European language, the 1880s and 1890s produced an explosion of scholarly pieces, polemical exchanges, and, above all, individual case histories of hysterical patients.

In Russia the same two decades are notable for the rise of the medical and psychiatric periodic press. *The Physician* (*Vrach*), the weekly newspaper that played such a pivotal role in the process of professionalization of Russian physicians, rapidly became the central organ for zemstvo medicine after its inception in 1880. As the most general forum, *The Physician* had the largest circulation, and it in no way lagged behind the specialized journals in its engagement with the conundrum of hysteria.[1] The first Russian psychiatric journals began publication in 1883, ranging from the *Bulletin of Clinical Psychiatry and Neuropathology* (Vestnik klinicheskoi psikhiatrii i nevropatologii), written by and for specialists, to *Archive of Psychiatry, Neurology, and Forensic Psychopathology* (Arkhiv psikhiatrii, nevrologii i sudebnoi psikhopatologii), conceived more for the general practitioner and widely accessible to the intelligentsia at large.[2] Each of these new publications contributed to the development of a professional and public psychiatric discourse in Russia; each individual case history also performed the double task of conceptualizing a disorder while it depicted a particular disordered self.

The disorder in question here, hysteria, is most interesting for how it has been imagined. Today hysteria refers to a wide array of psychogenic symptoms involving mental, sensory, motor, or visceral dysfunction. Most widely discussed, thanks to Freud, is "conversion hysteria," the psychic transformation of anxiety into actual physical symptoms, such as blindness, deafness, and paralysis (or lesser versions thereof, like blurred vision

---

[1] For a consideration of the importance of *The Physician*, see Nancy Mandelker Frieden, *Russian Physicians in an Era of Reform and Revolution, 1856–1905* (Princeton: Princeton University Press, 1981), 113–17.

[2] For details on these and other new organs that played a major role in the dissemination of psychiatric findings and the establishing of professional credentials, see A. M. Shereshevskii, "Razvitie periodicheskoi psikhiatricheskoi pechati v Rossii v kontse XVIII–nachale XX stoletiia," *Obozrenie psikhiatrii i meditsinskoi psikhologii im. V. M. Bekhtereva*, no. 1 (1991): 88–96.

and numbness). "Major hysteria" (*hysteria maxima*), the syndrome described by Charcot, presents as an attack lasting anywhere from a few minutes to a half hour and consisting of several stages: (1) a subjective sensory stimulus, usually a strange sound or smell (the "aura"), followed by (2) convulsions; (3) tonic and clonic spasms; (4) eccentric and dramatic behavior; and ending finally in (5) delirium.[3]

In the four thousand years since its first appearance in medical records, hysteria has been perceived in terms of four basic paradigms. The earliest and yet most persistent has been the gynecological model, which chalks hysteria's otherwise unmotivated symptoms up to wandering wombs in urgent need of repositioning. The second paradigm, more pernicious but no less imaginative, emerged courtesy of the Christian era, which identified hysteria's characteristic convulsions, anesthesias, muteness, and blindness as signatures ("stigmata") of the devil. If wandering uteruses could only be redirected by the application of local pressure and the administering of emetics, the demonological understanding of the disease called for exorcisms at best, torture and even executions at worst. Fortunately, the seventeenth-century mind produced a rudimentary neurological model of the disorder, theorizing hysteria as a matter of brain and nerve dysfunction rather than the manifestation of evil. It also ecumenically admitted male sufferers to the ranks of hysterics. Finally, around the turn of the twentieth century, the paradigm shifted again to a psychological conception of hysteria that attributes its symptoms to psychic / emotional disturbance rather than physiological / organic causes and that inspires another form of treatment altogether and a radically different descriptive discourse.[4]

Our period falls right on the cusp between the neurological and psychological perceptions of the disease, and as even a cursory examination of the titles of the Russian journals might suggest, the Russian psychiatric arena, like the European medical establishment in general, still leaned more toward the former than the latter.[5] The case histories themselves betray a strong somatic bias, especially in terms of their therapeutic prac-

---

[3] *Stedman's Medical Dictionary*, 26th ed. (Baltimore: Williams and Wilkins, 1995), 843.

[4] In fact, the four views are not strictly sequential and have recombined in numerous ways to produce the most curious pictures and stories. See Mark S. Micale's superb treatment of the history and historiography of hysteria, *Approaching Hysteria: Disease and Its Interpretations* (Princeton: Princeton University Press, 1995). I am indebted to his chapter, "A Short 'History' of Hysteria," for the above synopsis (19–29).

[5] Even a decade or more after the debut of the *Bulletin of Clinical Psychiatry and Neurology* and the *Archive of Psychiatry, Neurology, and Forensic Psychopathology* in the early 1880s, the predilection for neurology is evident: *Neurological Bulletin* (*Nevrologicheskii vestnik*, 1893); *Problems of Neuropsychic Medicine* (*Voprosy nervno-psikhicheskoi meditsiny*, 1896); *Review of Psychiatry, Neurology, and Experimental Psychology* (*Obozrenie psikhiatrii, nevrologii i eksperimental'noi psikhologii*, 1896); and the *S. S. Korsakov Journal of Neuropathology and Psychiatry* (*Zhurnal nevropatologii i psikhiatrii im. S. S. Korsakova*, 1901).

tices and their attachment to the kind of "local diagnosis" shunned by Freud. And yet their explanatory strategies begin to gesture toward a semiotics of suffering that recognizes the etiologic force of psychic / emotional trauma and its translation into physical pain. In an early issue of *The Physician*, I. R. Pasternatskii, one of the leading Russian practitioners in the treatment of hysteria, undertook to define the disease and enumerate its characteristic manifestations. With due homage to the advances made by Charcot, Pasternatskii acknowledges that the pathological-anatomical process that produces hysterical symptoms is still not understood. What we do know, however, he continues, is that "this disorder is the expression of suffering [*vyrazhenie stradaniia*] of the patient's entire nervous system."[6] The retention of urine, the bouts of anesthesia and hyperesthesia, the contractions, and the epileptoid fits associated with hysteria were all "expressions"—signifiers—of suffering (albeit of a nervous system rather than of a self). Noteworthy is how the clinicians came to read these expressions—and how they chose to write them.

If the relative newness of the field and its organs—new, in fact, throughout Europe—sparked a concerted effort on the part of late nineteenth-century psychiatrists to establish them*selves* as practitioners, their discourses as scientific, and their object as legitimate, this final mandate was especially fraught in the case of hysteria (*la grande simulatrice*), the symptoms of which ape those of somatic illnesses and the emotional basis of which marked sufferers, as often as not, as shirkers. If the patients are fakers, their disease a sham, what can possibly be the status of the doctors who treat them?

Perhaps because of this awkwardness, the emphasis in early Russian case histories of hysterics remains firmly on the visible—and verifiable—manifestations of the disease rather than on its emotional underpinnings. Perhaps for similar reasons, writing about hysteria in the Russian scientific press reveals a marked preference for concrete detail and an almost complete lack of theoretical speculation; citations to conceptual pieces are almost exclusively to French, German, and occasionally British authors. What we find instead are specific inspections of observable symptoms; virtually every published piece is entitled some variation of "A Case of Hysteria" ("Sluchai isterii"). Russian physicians and psychiatrists confirmed their object of study case by case, empirically, as it were, with a high premium placed on objectivity and an obvious investment in the "serious stamp of science" wanting in Freud's "stories." As repositories of the psychiatrists' own anxieties about science and professional status, the early case histories of hysterics can be read not only as a reflection of late nineteenth-century intellectual culture's preference for objectivity and

---

[6] I. Pasternatskii, "Istero-epilepsiia" ("Hysteria Maxima"), *Vrach*, no. 3 (1881): 49.

materiality, but as a product of the era's underlying nervousness about its predilections.

With some differences in format from journal to journal, the formulaic nature of the psychiatric case study, at least its late nineteenth-century Russian variant, serves well the purposes of its practitioners: the "subject"—that disconcerting subjectivity of the sufferer—is conveniently taboo. Virtually every case history begins with a brief introductory section (often no more than a paragraph) situating the present case in terms of the "state of the art" of hysteria studies, frequently recapitulating what is generally held and proposing to confirm a hypothesis or to elucidate an unresolved issue in hysteria. This is followed immediately by the account of the case itself, invariably set in smaller, closer type, as if to suggest that this is unadorned, even undigested, data, unalloyed by speculation or commentary and uninfluenced by any unsightly subjectivity on the part of the observer. The small print itself is customarily divided into (1) the *anamnesis* (an "act of remembering"; the medical history of the patient); (2) the *status praesens*, which enumerates the patient's (primarily physical) symptoms upon entering treatment and records in detail the results of the initial examination (temperature, measurement of skull, chemical content and quantity of urine passed, and so forth); and (3) the *decursus morbi* (*techenie bolezni*), which, depending on the length and the purpose of the particular case study, provides a daily, or, more often, a fairly compressed chronicle of the course of the ailment during hospitalization / observation and the progress of the treatment; this segment is sometimes omitted altogether. The shorter newspaper accounts in *The Physician* dispense with the three subsections and subtitles (and even the paragraph breaks) but follow essentially the same outline. Finally, having faithfully presented his data, the author then reappears in larger type to conclude by summarizing the outstanding features of his case, explaining its significance, and most often, weighing in on the considerable diagnostic challenges presented by hysteria, either humbly acknowledging the pitfalls in all attempts to diagnose hysteria with any degree of certainty or, more often, congratulating himself warmly on having successfully overcome these daunting obstacles to arrive at a definitive identification of the disease.

The recognition experienced here, in other words, is not the patient's but the doctor's, and it is a recognition not of the connection between symptom and story (Freud's linking of the symptoms of the illness to the life story of the patient) or even between symptom and suffering (Pasternatskii's promising "expression of suffering"). Nor is it a tale of a self coming back to its recognizable self. The case studies document chiefly the recognition of a contested disease by a medical professional seeking his own recognition.

This professional urgency manifests itself most transparently in the large-print, self-congratulatory wrap up to each case report, where absolute certainty reigns, and the results "eliminate all doubt" that we are in the presence of hysteria. Here, in the most egregious cases, the physician's self comes unabashedly to the fore, while the patient, who has at best been "my patient" and "the patient seen by me," disappears altogether in the rhetoric of what the doctor begins to refer to proprietarily as "my case."[7] More interesting than the patent self-promotion, though, is the effect this need for legitimation has on the small-print segments of the case histories. The pervasive anxiety about scientific reputability seems to undermine the very genre of the case history, minimizing in the story of an individual hysteric anything that is individual and short-circuiting any impulse to story at all.

Anamnesis

If here we seek Freud's stories or, closer to home, the narratives that inspire the present volume, we will be sorely disappointed. "Acts of remembering" notwithstanding, there is very little reminiscing or recovery of a personal past discernible in most of the accounts of these patients' medical "histories." Anamnesis, it turns out, is important principally in establishing *nasledstvennost'*: what in the patient's past—or rather *who*—can be used to document a genetic proclivity toward nervous disorders. One detects palpable satisfaction in this "raw" data when the investigation turns up an epileptic sibling or a parent who was prone to fainting. Organic explanations take clear precedence over emotional ones, neurology continues to edge out psychology, and since, as Freud notes, psychological speculations make much more engaging stories than do neurophysiological observations, especially when the neurological basis for a complaint is not self-evident, narrative content is at a minimum here.

The preference for physiological fact over personal narrative nicely eliminates the professional ambiguities presented by case histories that "read like short stories and . . . lack the serious stamp of science." And yet the reconstruction of a narrative sequence necessitated by the *recollection* of emotional suffering and its *reconnection* with present symptoms is, by definition, the only prospect for any authentic recognition of a physical ailment rooted in experience. Nevertheless, connections (other than family ones) are perversely disregarded in the anamnesis. The section is "nar-

---

[7] M. B. Bliumenau, "Redkie sluchai muzhskoi isterii. I. Isteriia ot udara molnii. II. Isteriia, pokhodivshaia na zabolevanie mozzhechka" ("Rare Cases of Male Hysteria: I. Hysteria From Being Struck by Lightning. II. Hysteria Resulting From a Disease of the Cerebellum"), part 2, *Vrach*, no. 19 (1895): 527–30. Once the doctor warms to the topic of his achievement in diagnosing hysteria, the patient is literally never mentioned again.

rative" insofar as it proceeds in chronological order, but it makes little effort to discern progressions from one state to another, to craft connections between "episodes," or to link "then" and "now." Above all, there is no correlation drawn between the "stories" of these patients and their regrettable "symptoms," Pasternatskii's eloquence about the "expressiveness" of hysteria notwithstanding.

The understanding of hysteria as an expression of suffering implies a connection between the manifest signifier and the hidden signified. Yet in all the medical literature I examined, only one case history established that connection, demonstrating in the process that the connection is meaningful, the form of the symptoms not arbitrary but precisely expressive. Not surprisingly, the case reads like a very good story.

In this impressive exception to the non-narrative rule, we learn of a private in the Bendersky regiment who is experiencing grave difficulty breathing and is sent to the Kiev military hospital for a possible tracheotomy. The soldier is unable to speak, suffering from sharp pain in his larynx, and indicates by gesturing that there is something caught in his throat that prevents him from drawing a proper breath or producing so much as a whisper. When all attempts to locate the foreign body prove unsuccessful, a specialist in "nervous" disorders is invited in, and the latter determines that the attack is hysterical in nature. Only once the symptoms have subsided and the soldier has regained his ability to breathe and speak does it come to light that he had quit smoking several months earlier, vowing at the beginning of Lent never again to succumb to that "sinful and blasphemous habit." Just before the onset of the attack, however, he had accepted a cigarette from a friend, the result of which was this intense sensation of suffocation. Having identified the requisite genetic predisposition to hysteria (a younger brother who suffers from fits in which he loses consciousness, and a history of headaches in the soldier himself), the author of the study emphasizes that this case "leaves no doubt" as to its hysterical origins—not only because of the absence of organic causes, the quick recovery with no lasting consequences, the disappearance of the muscle spasms during sleep, and the sudden onset of the attack in response to a powerful "psychic disturbance" (*dushevnoe volnenie*), but also because of the imaginative *connection* between the symptoms and the "agent provocateur" that stimulated them. This is not a question of the harmful effects of tobacco itself, the author stresses, but of the soldier's (unconscious) anxieties about how he has sinned through the throat. The body actually expresses the unrecognized nature of the suffering, as Freud's—or even Pasternatskii's—formulation might lead us to expect.[8]

[8] P. Gubarev, "Sluchai isterii" ("A Case of Hysteria"), *Voprosy nervno-psikhicheskoi meditsiny* 3 (1898): 398–403.

Dr. Gubarev's conviction (expounded in the "large print" conclusion) that the power of self-suggestion (*samovnushenie*) is enormous leads him to read his patient's episode as part of a life story: a meaningful incident in the private's psychic life "created" his disease. It is the author's ability to operationalize his essentially semiotic insight—that hysterical symptoms graphically register emotional experience—that produces this nice little story.

Despite its undistinguished title, though, "A Case of Hysteria" is exceptional. The reconstruction of this unusually compelling cause-and-effect sequence is facilitated by two circumstances: (1) the aphasiac soldier spontaneously recovers his power of speech and can supply the pertinent details known only to himself; and (2) the doctor is inclined to consult (or just listen to) his newly vocal patient. The result is a diagnostic process and report perhaps less defensive about scientific probity, based on the voice of the nonprofessional expert in the case, whose coauthorship is essential to this particular story.

More typical—and much less interesting—is the non-narrative extreme in which the anamnesis is given as a mere summary of "pertinent" facts: "The anamnesis indicates that. . . ." The author of one study, who details the case of Elena B. in order to demonstrate that high fever can be of hysterical origin, argues vehemently (in the large print) that psychic events may produce vascular changes (think, he avers, of blushing!), but he misses his chance in the small print that conveys the "history" of the feverish Elena to narrate, to infer, or evidently even to inquire about any such events in her own psychic life. He limits his disclosure (what is "indicated" in the anamnesis he conducted but neglected to record) to a one-sentence notation about the nervous constitution of her extended family.[9] Significantly, the lack of narrative interest here is problematic not in itself—the object, after all, is not entertainment—but as an index of the failure of the anamnesis to serve its purpose of reminiscence, to work toward recalling the "psychic event" that precipitated the fever and thus to contribute meaningfully to diagnosis, description, and treatment.

In some cases a lengthier chronological account is supplied, but it most often simply enumerates in the space of a sentence a few public, biographical facts about the individual, beginning the narration only at the onset of the *disease.* In the case of the twenty-four-year-old peasant woman from Kazan Province who is suffering from a protracted hysterical episode of astasia-abasia (the inability to walk or stand), we are told, beyond her age, class, and geographical origins, only that she is married, comes from a family with no history of mental or nervous complaints, and that she has

<hr>

[9] E. E. Foss, "K ucheniiu ob istericheskoi likhoradke" ("Toward a Study of Hysterical Fever"), *Zhurnal nevropatologii i psikhiatrii im. S. S. Korsakova* 4, no. 4 (1904): 634–46.

been employed in a candle factory for twelve years. It is here that the story begins:

> A year ago she began to suffer from persistent headaches that did not, how-
> ever, impede her working life. One day about four months ago, she felt a
> sharp pain in her head, went home from work early, and when her husband
> returned he found her in a deep sleep that lasted a day and a half and out of
> which they barely managed to awaken her. For seven weeks thereafter she re-
> mained in a state of constant drowsiness; each time it took great effort to
> wake her and feed her. Sometimes, though, the patient would rouse herself
> from her somnolence, start to scream, and utter a series of unconnected
> phrases, failing to recognize those around her. Sometimes she would try to
> get out of bed but would immediately fall down. After seven weeks the sleepi-
> ness suddenly disappeared, the patient resumed full consciousness, an-
> nounced that she had no more headaches and felt fine in every way, but she
> could not sit up, let alone stand and walk, and at the very first attempt fell
> powerlessly to the floor. In this condition she was taken to "Pokrov" hospital,
> and this is the condition in which she still finds herself, except that now she
> can more or less hold herself in a seated position.[10]

In other words, while we hear in considerable detail about the days leading up to her hospitalization, we are told nothing about the woman herself (except the striking fact—probably not even very striking for a peasant woman—that she has held down a job roughly since puberty). Nor, despite the author's subsequent insistence that the physical symptoms are neurotic in origin rather than organic, does he provide any narrative space for the neurotic self to unfold (or degenerate). Dr. Popov even produces the patient herself to establish his authority before his students, but though her capacity to speak is unimpaired, she is never once consulted about possible sources for her neurosis, a matter on which she can be the only possible expert, however inchoate her recollections may be. Clearly the psychiatrist's agenda lies elsewhere than in unraveling the story of his immobile patient; his most impassioned argument involves the appropriateness of the name of her *syndrome* ("Charcot-Blocque"). For while his story begins with "suffering," it is suffering ex nihilo, and the narrative breaks off equally sharply once the symptoms reach full bloom. The remaining nineteen pages of the "history" are markedly ahistorical. They exhibit the patient from every possible angle (with abundant illus-trations;[11] see figures 15–21), and correlate her symptoms with other known cases, but she is never allowed to *become* this exhibit, nor do we ever hear of the subsequent resolution of her suffering (or its failure to re-

[10] N. M. Popov, "Simptomokompleks Charcot-Blocq'a" ("Charcot-Bloque Syndrome"), *Nevrologicheskii vestnik* 6, no. 2 (1898): 76.
[11] Ibid., 77–85.

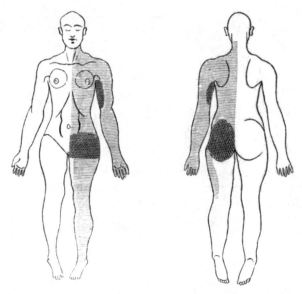

Схема распространенія нечувствительности къ прикосновенію.

Figure 15. "Diagram of the distribution of insensitivity to touch"

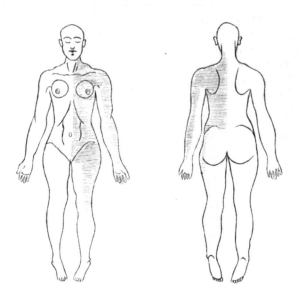

Схема распространенія нечувствительности къ болевымъ раздраженіямъ.

Figure 16. "Diagram of the distribution of insensitivity to pain"

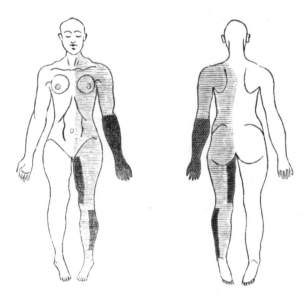

Схема распространенія электрокожной нечувствительности.

Figure 17. "Diagram of the distribution of insensitivity to stimulation by electrical impulses"

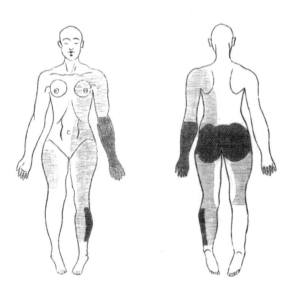

Схема распространенія нечувствительности къ холоду.

Figure 18. "Diagram of the distribution of insensitivity to cold"

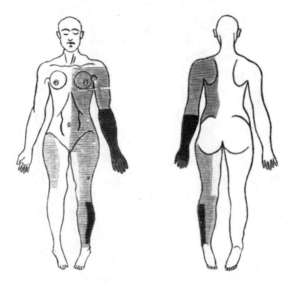

Схема распространенія нечувствительности къ теплу.

Figure 19. "Diagram of the distribution of insensitivity to heat"

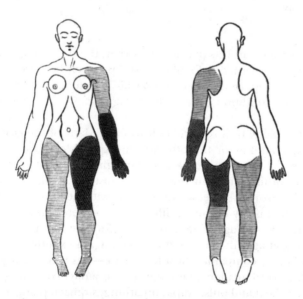

Схема распространенія нечувствительности къ давленію.

Figure 20. "Diagram of the distribution of insensitivity to pressure"

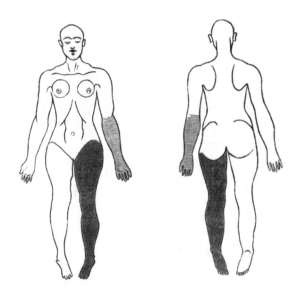

Схема распространенія мышечной анэстезіи.

Figure 21. "Diagram of the distribution of muscular anaesthetization"
Figures 15 through 21 are from N. M. Popov, "Simptomokompleks *Charcot-Blocqu'a*," *Nevrologicheskii vestnik* 6, no. 2 (1898): 77–85. Courtesy of The New York Academy of Medicine Library.

solve). No thread connects the candle worker, the screaming sleeper, and the paraplegic presented as Exhibit A. And precisely because her attack is envisioned and reported not as an "episode" in an ongoing story but as a self-contained "condition," the neurotic significance of her symptoms is lost.

Not that etiology is disregarded altogether. Many of the case histories do seek explanations for the otherwise inexplicable symptoms they describe. In some cases the causes are imaginative insofar as they correspond to nothing given in the medical history: V. Sh.—a twenty-two-year-old "girl" from an intelligentsia family with healthy parents and no known genetic history of mental illness, who suffered from a prolonged intermittent fever at age nine and scarlet fever at age fourteen, began menstruating at age fifteen and at eighteen again experienced a bout of fever, this time accompanied by a toothache—has recently begun to experience hysterical incidents (as many as four a day) consisting first of an elevated heartbeat and pulse, rapid breathing, stomach pain, and the classic *globus hystericus* (the sensation of a sphere that lodges in the throat); then of rapid, almost uncontrolled motion; then of dramatic, static, poses; followed by a period of strange, immodest speech and the repetition of single phrases for as long as a quarter-hour at a time. The author of this study manufactures a previously undiagnosed case of malaria to account for his patient's strange behavior (though the explanatory value of malaria strikes one as every bit as mysterious as the original symptoms).[12] Other cases similarly favor a physiological explanation, especially when it can be clinched by the invocation of genetics.[13] Having posited a "cause," albeit an organic one, for the illness of V. Sh. rather than contructing a temporal (narrative) sequence of event and aftermath that would contextualize and make sense of her present suffering, Dr. Dokhman expends his considerable energies identifying *mini*-sequences within the current attacks, dividing them into regular, recognizable phases, treating them as an isolated and infinitely iterative phenomenon in which the hysterical features only reproduce each other rather than reflecting anything else. As such, the *globus*, the movement / immobility sequence, and the period of provocative verbal behavior are utterly divorced from the nine-, the fourteen-, the eighteen-, and even the twenty-two-year-old self that produces them (much as the diagrams of "insensitivities" make off with the candle worker's anaesthetized skin).

And yet some case histories do make room for the self and its internal events by tempering physical facts with emotional content. Even in the face of a severe physical trauma, argues one physician, "it is less the injury itself than the powerful destabilizing effect of that injury on the psyche that is paramount in producing hysteria." Despite his best intentions, though, this particular author is unable to resist the temptation to capitalize on his patient's truly dramatic accident (he has been struck by lightning) rather than allowing his emotional story to unfold.[14] Somewhat more successful in this regard is the case of the eighteen-year-old leather worker who reported to work in perfect health but returned home two hours later and collapsed, unable to speak, swallow, or move his right leg. Initially, the author confesses, the sheer biographical and medical facts seemed to militate against the diagnosis of hysteria: "I was

---

[12] A. Dokhman, "Ob odnom sluchai isterii" ("On One Case of Hysteria"), *Vrach*, no. 10 (1881): 153–54. The malaria diagnosis is not quite as arbitrary as it appears; it is based on the patient's positive response to quinine, as detailed in the later *decursus morbi*. (The author's particular ax to grind involves innovative drug treatments for hysterical symptoms.) The explanation thus arises out of the course of the disease rather than the course of the life.

[13] See, for instance, M. A. Aristov, "Sluchai chistoi dvigatel'noi afazii" ("A Case of Pure Motor Aphasia"), *Arkhiv psikhiatrii, nevrologii i sudebnoi psikhopatologii* 22, no. 1 (1893): 96–102, where, despite the apparently psychological nature of the ailment, the doctor comes up with an embolism to explain the patient's symptoms.

[14] Bliumenau, "Rare Cases of Male Hysteria: I. Hysteria From Being Struck by Lightning," part 1, *Vrach*, no. 18 (1895): 497. Notice that Bliumenau even manages to smuggle the lightning, which he swears is of secondary importance, into his title.

simply skeptical that a young, blooming lad like this, a worker who had practically never tasted the fruits of civilization—that principal factor in the development of the nervousness of our age—could possibly suffer from hysteria." Fortunately, despite his assumptions about class and his conviction (characteristic in the literature just after the turn of the century) that nervous ailments are a reflection of a broader social malaise, the doctor can also point to the evidence of the worker's mother who spent the last two years of her life in a state of extreme fear, characterized by the paralysis of one hand and the complete inability to speak. More interesting than the predictable weight given to heredity, however, is the additional notation in the medical history that the patient had been in a gloomy frame of mind for two days preceding the attack and had even expressed the wish to die. His depressed state was the manifestation of a "powerful psychic disturbance" (*sil'noe dushevnoe potriasenie*), and the hysterical attack must therefore be read as an *expression* of this emotional distress.[15] Unfortunately, the nature of the upset is left unexplored, the patient's aphasia complicit with the general lack of psychiatric inclination to probe in this direction, and the connection of the depression to the specific symptoms remains obscure. But the potential for a coherent, personal story is there.

Indeed, even the earliest Russian case histories seem to recognize that hysteria may be triggered by "powerful psychic depression," but organic factors still loom largest. As in the case of the eighteen-year-old girl whose hysterical symptoms emerged on the heels of the death of her beloved mother, such symptoms almost invariably arise "when the organism has been radically weakened by anemia and exhaustion." And emotional in origin though her attack might be, it is nevertheless regulated by means of firm pressure on the left ovary. Still, this anamnesis does tell a rudimentary story (including sleepless nights and selfless devotion to the terminally ill parent), and the author even crafts a dénouement with some emotional content, prescribing, in addition to local ovarian pressure, the removal of the patient from her upsetting family milieu for several months.[16]

Even the isolated case histories that identify a rudimentary sequence connecting life experience to subsequent symptoms tend to truncate the anamnesis rather than developing the potentially illuminating insight. Kl. K-o, a nineteen-year-old peasant woman who first entered the hospital at age sixteen and continues to suffer dramatic convulsive attacks (along

---

[15] S. I. Syrkin-Shklovskii, "K kazuistike isterii u muzhchin" ("On the Origins of Hysteria in Men"), *Vrach*, no. 25 (1901): 799–800.

[16] M. V. Savel'ev, "Sluchai istericheskogo pripadka, prervannyi davleniem na levyi iaichnik" ("A Case of a Hysterical Attack Arrested by Pressure on the Left Ovary"), *Vrach*, no. 45 (1881): 759.

with a number of circulatory and respiratory disturbances and heightened sensitivity to pain), owes her hysteria to the hereditary factors outlined in her anamnesis and her "story" to the inclusion of the simple fact
that her first attack followed an incident in which she was questioned
about a theft. The hysteria was "called forth," summarizes the large print,
later, by this "powerful moral upset" (*sil'noe nravstvennoe potriasenie*).
Rather than exploring this shattering affront to the patient's sense of self,
the author summarily invokes heredity and proceeds rapidly to the presentation of the status praesens, which clearly interests him much more.[17]
L. M., a soldier suffering from debilitating hysterical attacks, is given an
anamnesis typical in its survey of his neurasthenic relatives, but of particular interest in its conclusion: "About three years ago during a rafting trip
on the Dnieper, the raft capsized and the patient fell into the water. He
was not so much injured as frightened. He considers this the beginning of
his illness."[18] A trauma like this not only has explanatory value, but as an
event (no less startling than the bolt of lightning), it is the sine qua non of
narrative. Importantly, the potential for story here arises from the doctor's alertness to what the patient himself "considers" the beginning of his
illness, an incident that scared him to death. But even in "storied" cases
such as this one that do connect hysterical symptoms with personal suffering and even specify the nature of the suffering, the nature of the subsequent *symptoms* (except in the matter of the penitent smoker) is never correlated with the story of the self.

Perhaps most interesting in this regard is the double anamnesis supplied in the case of Evfrosin'ia P-na, thirty-three years old, another peasant woman from Kazan Province, whose two-part anamnesis does inadvertently provide the material for this sort of analysis. Her medical history /
life story is first obtained from her husband for the simple reason that her
attack has rendered her able to pronounce only six words: *znaiu* (I know),
mechtat' (to dream), *Bugul'ma* (town due west of the southern reaches of
the Ural Mountains), *da* (yes), *vse* (everything), and *zoria* (dawn). As such
accounts go, the husband is relatively forthcoming. We learn that the patient has been:

> married for sixteen years, had seven children, of whom four are still living,
> the youngest of whom is only eleven months old. Each of the other three died
> of a different serious childhood illness. All her pregnancies went to term and
> all her children were born fully developed. In her family there has never
> been a single case of nervous or mental disturbance, though her father did

[17] V. S. Iakovenko, "Ob istericheskoi likhoradke" ("On Hysterical Fever"), *Zhurnal nevropatologii i psikhiatrii im. S. S. Korsakova* 5, nos. 3–4 (1905): 613.
[18] B. S. Greidenberg, "Sluchai isterii u muzhchiny" ("A Case of Hysteria in a Man"), *Vrach*,
no. 14 (1887): 296.

drink. In the past whenever the patient became very agitated she would have some kind of attack in which she would throw herself on the floor and tear her clothing. The present illness began on January 16, 1897. On the morning of that day, the patient got angry about something and beat her children very badly. The whole day after that she was in low spirits and disgusted with herself for what she had done. In the evening she set to work at the spinning wheel and spun until 10:00, then unexpectedly shuddered, went red in the face, for some reason ran out to the entranceway, then returned from there and stopped dead in the middle of the hut. In the words of her husband, she stood there immobile for a half-hour, staring fixedly at one spot. Her face was very red. Then she began as if to straighten up the hut, randomly moving things from one place to another, gathering up clothes, throwing them into the hall, saying that they had to go to the hospital to cure the children of their beatings. In the course of this quasi-cleanup she talked a lot, but in vain, for it was impossible to understand what she wanted to say. Her husband finally persuaded her to stop cleaning and go to bed; she assented but could not fall asleep all night. The next day her speech was already noticeably disturbed—the patient sang, spoke disconnectedly, and the only thing one could understand was that she regretted her treatment of the children. Excessive blood flow to her face was very evident. By the 19th the patient had lost the ability to say anything but two or three words, absolutely incomprehensible to those around her, but was no longer behaving strangely. This whole time the patient ate little and slept practically not at all. In this condition she was brought to the hospital.[19]

The husband is neither a bad observer nor a poor storyteller. The account of the onset of the attack is vivid, he evinces a real sense of cause and possible effect (the inclusion of the child-beating episode), and he supplies what he considers to be relevant prehistory—the birth and loss of children and a tendency to go off the deep end in the face of strong emotional disturbance. Perhaps the narrative genius here is the doctor, who no doubt had some role in eliciting the above information. We have no way of knowing what was volunteered as opposed to supplied in answer to a query. In any case, it is the doctor who has chosen what to include in this relatively lengthy summary.

And yet that it is lacking something becomes apparent when, after approximately a week at the clinic, Evfrosin'ia P-na regains her power of speech. Having listened to the story told by her husband during her enforced silence, she immediately moves to retell it. Since the doctor's account has already progressed beyond the anamnesis, through the status praesens that details the symptoms, into the decursus morbi that gives us the progress of the disease, this second pass at the anamnesis comes in

[19] V. I. Zhestkov, "Sluchai istericheskoi afazii" ("A Case of Hysterical Aphasia"), *Nevrologicheskii vestnik* 5, no. 3 (1897): 121–22.

"part three": curriculum vitae interrupts historia morbi and handily up-
stages it. Since the patient's revisions also double the account in length, I
won't transcribe it in its entirety. But note that she begins much earlier
and selects a different sort of data out of which to construct a narrative
about herself:

> From the age of ten the patient lived in the city, first taking care of children,
> then working as a cleaning lady. During this entire period she felt healthy
> and had no serious illnesses. At seventeen she married a peasant and moved
> with her husband to the village. In her husband's home she was put to work
> immediately: she had to prepare dinner for the whole family and care for the
> livestock. The work was completely unfamiliar to her, much was beyond her
> strength, and she had to learn how to perform a good deal of it. More than
> once the patient heard either reproaches from her mother-in-law that she
> didn't know anything or the latter's complaints to her son that he had mar-
> ried a shirker. Already at approximately a year into the marriage she began to
> feel unwell, each remark upset her, and when it was extremely insulting it
> provoked an attack. The attacks consisted of a sensation of irritation rising in
> her throat like a lump and she felt her throat constricting. In order to rid her-
> self of that unpleasant sensation she would begin to tear at the collar of her
> dress and throw herself on the floor. There were no convulsions and she re-
> mained conscious throughout.[20]

The patient goes on to describe her "normal" pregnancies as progressively more difficult until the last delivery when her weakness from loss of
blood was so extreme that she was forced to remain bedridden. We also
hear from her how she felt preceding the attack that brought her to the
hospital, how heartsick she was about her treatment of the children she
loves very much—how miserable she was about the fact that she was unable to control herself and how angry at her husband that he did not intervene. She is able to explain why she did certain otherwise inexplicable
things during her earlier attacks, as well as what she meant to say in her incomprehensible ravings and how it felt not to be able even to utter her
children's names.

In short, Evfrosin'ia herself is permitted to provide the material that
leads to a "large print" diagnosis of hysterical aphasia caused by the difficult, unaccustomed circumstances of her marriage and especially the oppressive emotional conditions (the reproaches, insults, and remarks). Of
course, the loss of blood associated with her labor didn't help matters, not
to mention her prolonged breastfeeding; the impulse to reach for organic explanations is always at hand. But the patient's self-study provides
remarkable material. In fact, though no one there seems to notice this,

[20] Ibid., 124–25.

the account makes clear the connection between past life and present symptoms. The original "objective" description provided by her husband—that "in the course of this quasi-cleanup she talked a lot, but in vain, for it was impossible to understand what she wanted to say"—as it turns out, applies equally well to her daily married life: while she makes frantic and all-consuming efforts to shoulder the burden of the housework, nobody there understands her. Thus her extraordinary attack only dramatizes her more chronically debilitating plight. And the patient alone is the repository of this knowledge. Indeed, even at the height of her aphasia, the one thing she can (and does) articulate again and again is "I know, I know, I know everything" ("Znaiu, znaiu, vse znaiu").[21] This is the only case study that gives us such a corrective, informed, and informative anamnesis, however delayed. The physical fact of aphasia (coupled with the circumstance that this patient, like so many others, is illiterate and thus fully silenced by her suffering) only makes concrete the status of the patient's "history" as set forth in the typical anamnesis: it is not the patient's own. The plight of the aphasiac patients only concretizes the plight of them all. Strikingly, even the "secondary revision" supplied by the newly vocal patient in this case is rendered in the third person. Never in these accounts (or with the rarest of exceptions) do the voices of patients themselves sound. Never, except to demonstrate disturbed speech, does a doctor quote a patient directly. And despite the frequently articulated intuition that hysterical symptoms "express" psychic injury, rarely in these accounts of selves (and their emotional traumas) do we hear what counts to the self. The hysterical self is thus doubly effaced and silenced: first by the disease and its fits and aphasias, secondarily by the discourses that diagnose it.

And yet not even the formulaic genre of the case history makes the eclipse of the hysterical self inevitable, only its deformation by practitioners who refuse to do the anamnesis justice, thus suppressing all traces of *becoming* hysterical.[22] What is noteworthy is that the genre of the case history, the explicit record of an individual's affliction rather than a textbook survey, makes the history of suffering so non-narrative. Where a story is told, it is more often the story of a disease coming into being than the tale of a person coming into a disease; and where it is the history of a self, the "act of remembering" is an exclusively third-person affair.

Identity itself falls victim to the show of empirical rigor. Virtually every anamnesis opens with "identifying" marks: "Young soldier of the 104th Ustiuzh regiment K. Z., twenty-one years old, from Kazan Province,

<hr>

[21] Ibid., 123.

[22] Detailed instructions to medical students on how to conduct interviews and examinations and construct an anamnesis are provided in S. A. Sukhanov, *Semiotika i diagnostika dushevnykh boleznei (v sviazi s ukhodom za bol'nymi i lecheniem ikh)*, part 1 (Moscow, 1904).

Orthodox."[23] "K. Z.," like all the other patients mentioned above, is specified quite a bit, but more for the purposes of authentication than for identification. Anonymity, after all, is essential, and patients' privacy must be protected even when their stories are made public. Pseudonyms are commonly employed for this reason: "Anna O." and "Dora" have become famous under their Freudian stage names. But the use of names—or rather, tantalizing fragments of names—is particularly striking in view of the story-less selves and self-less stories in the Russian context. For one thing, unlike Dora and her compatriots, who live, love, hate, and suffer as "Dora" and company, K. Z., Kl. K-o., and Evfrosin'ia P-na retain their truncated identities only as long as it takes to read the first sentence of the anamnesis; from there on in they became universally "the patient" (*bol'noi*, an infirm male, or, more frequently, *bol'naia*, an infirm female; gender is the one identifying mark that, thanks to Russian grammar, does not drop out of sight). Yet there is something curiously novelistic about the form of disguise applied to these names, reminiscent of the ubiquitous "Prince N**" of nineteenth-century fiction. Ironically, though, whereas in fiction the abbreviated name is a prelude to a fully delineated characterization, in the case history this conventional truncation instead pointedly corresponds to the incompleteness of the depiction to follow.[24]

Status praesens

In keeping with what we already know about the anamnesis, the clinical report of the patient's symptoms is not a record of "what ails you?" any more than the anamnesis answers the question "how did this come about?" What drives the status praesens is hysteria, not the hysterical patient. Primary is the list of classic symptoms; the patient may or may not fit these criteria. What sets the clinical agenda (the protocol for the examination) is not what the individual exhibits but what the disease stipulates,

---

[23] Bliumenau, "Rare Cases of Male Hysteria," part 1, 496.

[24] Interestingly, one of the few truly "storied" case histories actually calls attention to the practice of naming and its fictional antecedents: in "Sluchai polovoi manii vo vremia mesiachnykh i zhenskogo sadizma" ("A Case of Sexual Mania During Menstruation and Female Sadism"), *Vrach*, no. 8 (1898): 219–21, V. N. Peskov constructs an extraordinarily suspenseful and involving (and mildly pornographic) narrative, making himself a breathless character ("I could not wait!" "I ran right over!" "She asked me to touch her genitals") and, remarkably, quoting the patient herself verbatim at her most passionate. After setting the opening scene in the lexicon of "a strange, strange thing happened," Dr. Peskov introduces the provocative "Mrs. NN" and appends an immediate footnote to the effect that "I received permission to describe the following case from Mr. NN and his wife only under the condition that I use neither their surname nor their given names nor even their first initials." So scurrilous is the content (so worth reading?) that they feared the revelation of their identities even as the obscure Mr. and Mrs. NN. Surely the footnote is not necessary to protect their privacy—the obvious disguise already does that. But it heightens the suspense (what could be so scandalous?) and propels the reader in. And it draws attention to the fictional device.

and what is recorded is rather the presence or absence of each element in the given case. Admittedly this is standard diagnostic procedure, but it becomes extreme in this context in which the most pressing agenda is to attest to the very diagnosability of hysteria and thus to affirm the legitimacy of the medical / psychiatric enterprise that diagnoses it. What is attempted is less the identification of the specific pathologies that prevent the patient from resembling him- or herself than the painstaking identification of the disease that resembles so many others.

The physical examination typically looks for (and finds in an infinite number of combinations): irregularities in build; genital abnormalities (in women); asymmetries of the head, facial features, muscles, and extremities; inadequate subcutaneous fat; muscular distress; discoloration of mucus; paleness / redness of skin; joint dysfunction; insensitivity (or heightened sensitivity) to pain, cold, warmth, pressure, and electrical impulses, usually confined to one half or one quadrant of the body; narrowed field of vision; excessive accumulation of urine; slowness to bleed when skin is punctured; disturbed reflexes—muscular, salivary, vascular, etc.; paralysis; inability to recognize physical position in space; loss of speech, hearing, sense of taste or smell; impeded breathing; elevated heartbeat; convulsions; muscle spasms; lethargy; irritability; presence of *globus hystericus,* and much, much more. Obviously no single patient exhibits all these symptoms, or even a significant percentage of them. The examination is not tailored to individual patients, whose "present status" refers less to how well they are than to how well they fit the bill: is the patient a bona fide hysteric, or not?

The status praesens of the aphasiac F. Z., for instance, dispenses quickly with the patient's height and weight and proceeds directly to an examination of features obviously dictated by something other than the individual's inability to speak: his subcutaneous fat (normal); the coloration of his fingertips (mildly cianotic); his physiognomy (one side of nose and lips more sharply delineated); lids (normal); eyes (right wider); field of vision (left narrowed); grip (normal); gait (normal); sensitivity to pain (normal, except left shoulder); and so on, though we do at least hear about his tongue (which trembles slightly when stuck out, but does not fall to the side). Eventually the doctor characterizes the patient's disturbed speech as well, but the patient-specific examination is so clearly subordinated to the general grid of hysteria-identified symptoms as to submerge the individual's silent suffering beneath an avalanche of related and not-so-related data.[25]

The examination thus really is an "objective investigation"; the status praesens admits no suffering subject. The patient (whose name has by

[25] Aristov, "A Case of Pure Motor Aphasia," 97.

now receded into oblivion) is scanned, placed on a grid, and his or her disease is charted to see whether it qualifies as hysteria. Connections are fully severed here not only between symptoms and story but also between symptoms and self. In this virtual erasure of the individual bearer of symptoms in favor of a virtuoso display of empiricism, the "status" at stake is most certainly the physician's.

This pursuit of objectivity is an earmark of the late nineteenth-century investment in science in general, but it is also one of the many legacies of Charcot, whose influence on the development of Russian psychiatry was enormous.[26] Charcot's famous "clinico-anatomic method" is pure nosology; in his "objective demonstrations" of hysteria Charcot worked to classify observable symptoms into clearly delineated archetypes. As for the patients who fall into these categories, "something about them makes them all the same." Even conceding the emotional origins of hysteria, Charcot took no interest in what his patients had to say, relying solely on the visible stigmata of hysteria (*stigmates hystériques*).[27] His patients were as devoid of subjectivity as his own procedure, which was rooted in an empiricism that divides physician and patient into omniscient observer and passive, eminently available object.[28]

Charcot's fascination with visual records in particular was unparalleled. In fact, he appears to have been more committed to photographing his patients than to talking to them. He proudly established the first section of medical photography in his Salpêtrière clinic, the product of which is the famous *Iconographie photographique de la Salpêtrière*. These icons of pathology stood as irrefutable testimony to the visuality of hysterical disturbance.[29]

Charcot's Russian admirers closely followed his perceptual lead. Pasternatskii's early defining piece on the nature and forms of hysteria makes explicit reference to the invaluable resource provided by Charcot's photodocumentation. In fact, the editor of *The Physician* himself takes the opportunity to append a footnote here, agitating for the institutionaliza-

---

[26] V. M. Bekhterev, Russia's most eminent psychoneurologist, himself a student of Charcot's, eulogized the latter in the opening pages of the newly minted *Neurological Bulletin* as not only the creator of modern neuropathology, but as "friend of mankind in the true meaning of the word." As a "herald of progress and the bearer of the best ideals," he avers, Charcot is one of those individuals who ought never to have been allowed to die. "Pamiati prof. Sharko" ("To the Memory of Professor Charcot"), *Nevrologicheskii vestnik* 1, no. 3 (1893): v–vi. On Bekhterev and Charcot, see also David Joravsky, *Russian Psychology: A Critical History* (Oxford: Basil Blackwell, 1989), 83.

[27] Jean-Martin Charcot, *Charcot, the Clinician: The Tuesday Lessons*, trans. Christopher G. Goetz (New York: Raven Press, 1987), 104, 109–10.

[28] See the treatment of Charcot in Stephanie Kiceluk, "The Patient as Sign and Story: Disease Pictures, Life Histories, and the First Psychoanalytic Case History," *Journal of Clinical Psychoanalysis* 1, no. 2 (1992): 342–44.

[29] Charcot, *Charcot, the Clinician*, 107, 113–16.

tion of medical photography, that "absolutely essential component of clinical procedure, which enables us to preserve in graphic pictures everything instructive that is encountered in the clinic. The late A. Dubovitskii recognized this clearly," continues the loquacious editor, "spending large sums of money to supply the M. Kh. Academy with photographic equipment."[30] (Alas, like Charcot, the visionary Dubovitskii seems to have met his Maker and the fate of his expensive photographic installation is unknown.)

With less access to actual photographs, the Russian case histories are more often accompanied by drawings or engravings (though many journals also do without these). Bekhterev's *Neurological Bulletin* leads the league in its enthusiasm for illustrations, as in the proliferation of diagnostic diagrams that accompany the case of the patient with hysterical astasia-abasia (*figures 15–21*). The additional advantage of these schematic drawings over photographs of actual patients is that they are precisely schematic rather than personal. The patient is the female body rather than a particular self. There is even less here of the employee in the candle factory than there is in her anamnesis. But perhaps the most telling example of the predilection for the visual is the engraving that follows Bekhterev's own case study of "Irrepressible or Involuntary Laughter Associated with Palsy Caused by Brain Damage" (see *figure 22*).[31] While this picture of a seated naked man with a beard and a clenched fist does bear a distinct resemblance to the man Bekhterev describes in his case history, the point of the visual representation is unclear, since the "extraordinary symptom, without which the case would be of no particular interest,"[32] the patient's uncontrollable laughter, is not, and cannot be, *visible.*

Beyond the deployment of actual visual aids, the very language of the studies is predicated upon the assumption that diagnosis is a fundamentally visual (and hence one-sided) affair. It is conventional to speak of the "clinical picture" (*klinicheskaia kartina*), the spectacle of the disease perceptible to the observant clinician and awaiting exposure by him; the necessarily verbal descriptions of the clinical picture in the status praesens are themselves replete with ocular metaphors about "our observations" of the "stigmata," the visible signs of hysteria; the "features" that "strike the eye"; the "imprint" that is "observable"; the symptoms that "are exhibited incomparably clearly"; what one can readily "notice"; and corresponding rhetorical flourishes—"How should we view this?"[33] Paramount is not what you hear from the patient but what you see (or don't see) for yourself.

And yet the genre of the psychiatric (and especially psychoanalytic) case history as we know it today developed out of an effort to integrate two

[30] Pasternatskii, "Hysteria Maxima," 49.

[31] "Neuderzhimyi ili nasil'stvennyi smekh pri mozgovykh paralichakh," *Nevrologicheskii vestnik* 1, no. 3 (1893): 33.

[32] Ibid., 7.

[33] See, for instance, Popov, "Charcot-Bloque Syndrome," passim.

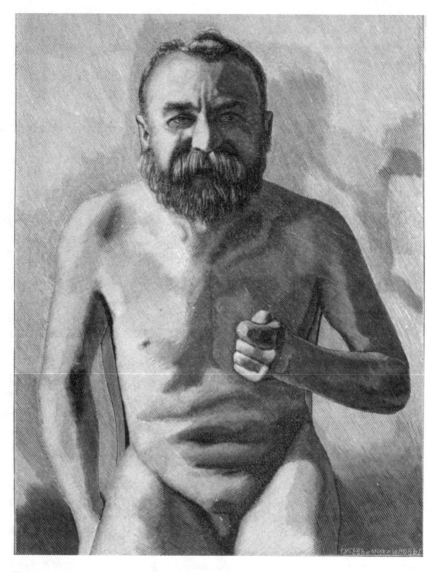

Figure 22. "From the article of Professor V. M. Bekhterev: 'Irrepressible or Involuntary Laughter Associated with Palsy Caused by Brain Damage' " ("Neuderzhimyi ili nasil'stvennyi smekh pri mozgovykh paralichakh"), *Nevrologicheskii vestnik* 1, no. 3 (1893):33. Courtesy of The New York Academy of Medicine Library.

modes of discourse: (1) the "pictorial," based on a cluster of visible, clinical signs that make diagnosis a matter of seeing and reconstituting a clinical *picture* (concretized in Charcot's photographs), and (2) the "narratological," a form of examination dedicated to eliciting a verbal account of what has befallen the patient and to reconstituting a clinical *story*. The latter method, which privileges plot over image, views the patient as a bona fide subjectivity with a story to tell and demands knowledge of that individual, not just a classificatory grid. It was Freud who fully succeeded in reconciling the two modes in his early studies of hysteria, treating hysterical symptoms as the visible manifestations of the part of the story the patient resisted telling (repressed). The body remembers (and makes visible) what the mind forgets (and silences). The connection between event (origin) and symptom, plot and picture, is then forged in the interpretive gesture of the case history. The patient's dissociation is ended and the "objectively" visible symptom is replaced by the reappropriation by the self of the explanation and the recognition of the self by the self.[34]

The trend in psychiatry in the last two decades of the nineteenth century has been characterized, like the transition from Charcot to Freud, as a shift from seeing to listening.[35] If Charcot collected photographs, Freud lets loose the "talking cure," and, appropriately, even that phrase itself was first turned by a patient.[36] In the ocular feasts published in *The Physician, Archive of Psychiatry, Neurology, and Forensic Psychopathology, Neurological Bulletin,* and *Problems of Neuropsychic Medicine* throughout the period in question, the patients may as well all have been aphasiac to the extent that their participation was required. And while Freud may have conceptualized his therapeutic method (and the resulting case histories) as a narrative procedure, a quest for the *mens sana in fabula sana,*[37] the Russian psychiatric press proceeded in a different discursive tradition. In the case histories I have read, the anamnesis is most often constructed as a sort of anti-story, and the status praesens aspires to be a virtual snapshot—or, given the numerous *missing* symptoms that are nevertheless invoked, even a photographic negative.

Decursus morbi

This is the section most often dispensed with, and given the constraints of space, I must give the depictions of the disease running its course correspondingly short shrift. In general, though, treatment is not the focus in these case histories, perhaps understandably, since the physical measures undertaken usually had minimal effect on hysterical symptoms and thus contributed little to the resolution of the disease. The decursus morbi, then, can hardly have been the most promising forum for credential building, and, considering the demands of professional affirmation,

---

[34] See Kiceluk, "The Patient as Sign and Story," 334–35, 362–63.

[35] Stephen Heath, *The Sexual Fix* (London: Macmillan, 1982), 37–38.

[36] One of Breuer's, actually, Anna O. herself.

[37] The clever phrase is Peter Brooks's, from *Body Work: Objects of Desire in Modern Narrative* (Cambridge, Mass.: Harvard University Press, 1993), 235.

its diminution makes substantial sense. Where a detailed chronicle of the course of treatment *is* provided, the overall lack of response (and, hence, lack of change) also produces nothing of narrative value, creating the illusion of a perptual present tense and eliding all traces of *becoming*. By and large the case histories begin without reconstructing an emotional past life, focus on the spectacle of the immediate present, and provide no dénouement in the form of resolution of suffering.

Given the unavailability of clinical success stories (a narrative paradigm with a beginning, middle, and end to suffering), the authors of the case histories sometimes capitalize instead on the *resilience* of the disease as an index of its authenticity (occasionally to the point of perversity, as when a doctor displays glee at having brought about a fresh attack—and renewed suffering—because it clinches the case for hysteria, or expresses regret that a patient's problem has abated to the extent that he can no longer exhibit it to his students).[38] The individual's persistent symptoms here are certainly meant to be seen as a sign of something—but not of "suffering," as Pasternatskii had led us to believe; they are read rather as a sign of the irrefutable reality of hysteria itself.

Self and Story

To be sure, case histories are written not to immortalize individual patients but to testify to broader medical facts. Their communicative purpose is *soobshchenie*—the dissemination of information, the augmentation of medical knowledge—not storytelling. And yet this determined abrogation of "the old Aristotelian prohibition" against "scientifically structured discourse about an individual"[39] calls very much to mind the narrative enterprise of nineteenth-century Russian realism, with its conviction that the "typical" could be discovered through astute observation of the particular. Indeed, revealing the general through the particular may be precisely what stories do best.

Particularity and universality aside, though—and the biases of a contemporary literary scholar notwithstanding—the very nature of hysteria as recognized by late nineteenth-century psychiatry makes the telling of individual stories essential to the clinical task. If, as the authors of these case studies argue, hysterical symptoms are signs of psychic suffering, diagnosis—the recognition of the disease—must entail the recognition of its particular logic in a particular case. The very fact of rooting symptoms in

[38] See, for example, Bliumenau, "Rare Cases of Male Hysteria," part 1, 498, or Bekhterev, "Irrepressible or Involuntary Laughter," 25.
[39] Michel Foucault, *The Birth of the Clinic: An Archaeology of Medical Perception*, trans. A. M. Sheridan Smith (New York: Vintage Books, 1975), xiv.

prior emotional disturbance necessitates a reconstruction of that experience and, hence, the use of narrative as a diagnostic, probably curative, and certainly descriptive tool.

What we find instead, though, in these case histories is a certain tension between **instinct** (that symptoms express something; that there's a story and a self behind them) and **procedure** (short-circuiting stories and silencing selves). This may be in part because of the distinct tension between **intuition** (that the "suffering" behind the hysterical expressions may not be visible even to the professional eye) and **agenda** (to establish beyond dispute the perspicacity and expertise of the professional / scientific self). Though the authors of these studies articulate a kind of "semiotics" of suffering that acknowledges the expressiveness of hysterical symptoms, their own needs seem to have impeded their ability to operationalize that insight by relinquishing their obsession with the visual and harnessing narrative, which would craft the connections—temporal and logical—that would make those symptoms "meaningful" and return them to the selves who produced them.

CHAPTER NINE

Weber *into* Tkachi: *On a Russian Reading of Gerhart Hauptmann's Play* The Weavers

REGINALD E. ZELNIK

"Read it, Semen, and don't show it to anyone else," he whispered to me.
　　　　　—Semen Kanatchikov, recalling his first exposure to
　　　　　The Weavers as a young apprentice pattern maker in 1896

I would like very much to look at *The Weavers.*
　　　　　—Lev Tolstoy, aging writer and social reformer, 1895

In 1892 Gerhart Hauptmann (1862–1946) published what soon became the most talked-about and controversial play on or off the German stage—*Die Weber.* A provocative and dramatic retelling of the story of the famous Silesian weavers' uprising of 1844,[1] *Die Weber* was intended by its author, the grandson of a weaver who took part in that event, to produce compassion (*Mitleid*) in the viewers and readers and prod them to take social and political action, however vaguely defined.[2] Apart from its obvious pro-worker sympathies, there was nothing particularly "Marxist" about the play, nothing, indeed, of a specific political or ideological character. The worker-protagonists were not "advanced" proletarians with nothing to lose but their chains, but protoindustrial handloom weavers—reli-

Research for this article has been supported by the University of California at Berkeley's Center for Slavic and East European Studies and by a UC Berkeley Humanities Research Grant. I am also very grateful to the organizers of and participants in the "Self and Story" conference, and especially to Laura Engelstein, a uniquely valuable critic. Thanks also to Grisha Freidin, Dan Orlovsky, Tony Swift, and the anonymous reviewers of this volume for their very helpful suggestions.

[1] The standard work on the events of 1844, and a major source for Hauptmann, was Alfred Zimmermann, *Blüthe und Verfall des Leinengewerbes in Schlesien* (Breslau, 1885).

[2] See Leroy R. Shaw, *The Playwright and Historical Change: Dramatic Strategies in Brecht, Hauptmann, Kaiser, and Wederkind* (Madison: University of Wisconsin Press, 1970), chapter 2, especially 36–37.

gious, lacking in "consciousness," sometimes dissipated, cowed by their bosses (until late in the action), protectors, when they finally are aroused, of a traditional way of life, which they defend not by forming militant unions or political alliances, but by engaging in wild acts of violence and destruction.

Yet despite this absence of Marxist political correctness, within only three years of the play's initial publication, a Russian version, *Tkachi*, had become an important propaganda tool of Russia's revolutionary Left, and of Marxists in particular. In late 1894 or early 1895, Anna Elizarova, Lenin's older sister, then a leading member of Moscow's Social-Democratic "Workers' Union" (*Rabochii soiuz*), had written a Russian version of the play that was surreptitiously circulated in hectographed form.[3] Shortly thereafter, still in 1895, another underground version appeared, this time translated by the Marxist and future Bolshevik Praskov'ia Kudelli (then a teacher at St. Petersburg's "Smolensk" evening school for workers).[4] This version (hereafter: the Kudelli version) was circulated under the imprint of the "People's Will Group" (*Gruppa narodovol'tsev*), the membership of which by this time, despite its Populist name, shared the political orientation of the Social Democrats. Elizarova was a collaborator in the group's illegal publication work.[5]

In the years that followed, both of Russia's main radical tendencies, Marxist and Populist (soon to become the RSDRP and the PSR, respectively), made propaganda use of *Tkachi*, mainly the Kudelli version.[6] The play was read by politicized workers in Russia's industrial centers, including a workers' circle from St. Petersburg's Thornton textile mill and groups of workers at the Sunday classes at Moscow's Prokhorov factory. In 1895–96 it was used by Marxists who were recruiting Petersburg workers at the famous Putilov works. In Moscow the apprentice pattern maker

[3] The illegal translation of works of the German Left (e.g., August Bebel's *Die Frau und Sozialismus* and the text of the Erfurt Program) was one of the Workers' Union's main activities. Iu. Z. Polevoi, *Iz istorii rabochei pechati: Ocherki literaturno-izdatel'skoi deiatel'nosti pervykh marksistskikh organizatsii v Rossii 1883–1900 gg.* (Moscow: Gospolitizdat, 1962), 150; see also S. I. Mitskevich, *Revoliutsionnaia Moskva, 1888–1905* (Moscow: Khudozhestvennaia literatura, 1940). Elizarova did much of this translating. Note: The hectographed edition of *Tkachi* was produced just before the appearance in Russia of the American mimeograph machine.

[4] V. A. Shelgunov, "Moi vospominaniia o voskresnykh shkolakh," in *V nachale puti: Vospominaniia peterburgskikh rabochikh, 1872–1897 gg.*, comp. E. A. Korol'chuk (Leningrad: Lenizdat, 1975), 339. Kudelli, who is warmly praised in the memoirs of Nadezhda Krupskaia (cited by Korol'chuk in ibid., 419n.), her fellow teacher at the Smolensk school, translated *Die Weber* in collaboration with M. G. Samokhinaia.

[5] On Elizarova's collaboration with The People's Will Group, see V. Bonch-Bruevich, "Moi vstrechi s L'vom Nikolaevichem Tolstym," in idem, *Vospominaniia* (Moscow: Khudozhestvennaia literatura, 1968), 86. (Thanks to Laura Engelstein for alerting me to "Moi vstrechi.") The quotation from Tolstoy in the epigraph of this essay is from ibid., 87.

[6] The Kudelli version was printed in an edition of 1,000; *Svodnyi katalog russkoi nelegal'noi i zapreshchennoi pechati XIX veka*, 1 (Moscow: Gosudarstvennaia Biblioteka SSSR, 1971), 121.

Semen Kanatchikov was shown the text in 1896, and he later recalled what a strong impression it had made on him. In 1897 *Tkachi* was found among revolutionaries who were propagandizing workers in Ivanovo and Tver. And in 1902 the Social-Democratic paper *The Spark* (Iskra) reported that at least one of Petersburg's underground workers' circles kept *Tkachi* (now available in the London edition discussed below) in its secret "library."[7]

It was the Kudelli version, somewhat modified, that became the basis for the first legally published edition of *Tkachi*, printed in London in 1902 by the highly respected, basically Marxist (though independent and ecumenical) journal *Life* (Zhizn'), which had recently been driven from Russia by government persecution. Edited by the writer-physician Vladimir Posse in close association with G. A. Kuklin and the future Bolshevik Vladimir Bonch-Bruevich, the journal enjoyed widespread support from Social Democrats of diverse tendency, but also from Socialist Revolutionaries, left liberals, and even hard-to-classify figures like Lev Tolstoy. Both in its earlier incarnation in Russia, when it published works by the likes of Gorky, Chekhov, and Gippius, and in its new position as part of Russia's "free press" abroad, *Zhizn'* published a wide variety of material. In England, free of censorship, it printed Russian translations of works by Kautsky, Bebel and other European socialists, translations of May-Day speeches, a chronicle of Russia's labor unrest, and illegally acquired government documents, much of this material destined for smuggling into Russia.[8] *Zhizn'*'s version of *Tkachi*, featured in its first London issue (April 1902) and soon followed by a separate printing in the series "Library of 'Life' " (Biblioteka "Zhizni"), quickly became *the* revolutionary underground version of the play.[9]

---

[7] F. M. Suslova, "Peterburgskii 'Soiuz borb'y za osvobozhdenie rabochego klassa' i gruppa 'Osvobozhdenie truda,' " in *Rasprostranenie marksizma v Rossii i gruppa "Osvobozhdenie truda," 1883–1903 gg.*, ed. S. S. Volk et al. (Leningrad: Lenizdat, 1985), 182, 183; V. F. Kut'ev, *Moskovskii "Rabochii soiuz"* (Moscow: Nauka, 1985), 144–45; *A Radical Worker in Tsarist Russia: The Autobiography of Semën Ivanovich Kanatchikov*, ed. and trans. R. E. Zelnik (Stanford: Stanford University Press, 1986), 33; *Rabochee dvizhenie v Rossii v XIX veke: Sbornik dokumentov i materialov* (hereafter *RD*), 4, pt. 1 (Moscow: Izdatel'stvo sotsial'no-ekonomicheskoi literatury, 1961), 33, 35, 319, 321, 680, 713; *Iskra*, no. 16 (February 1, 1902): 1. The citation from Kanatchikov in the epigraph is from *A Radical Worker*, 33.

[8] V. Iu. Cherniaev, " 'Khronika rabochikh volnenii i stachek' nelegal'nogo zhurnala 'Zhizn'' " i ee sozdateli G. A. Kuklin i V. A. Posse," in *Rabochee dvizhenie v Rossii. Sbornik statei i materialov dlia "Khroniki rabochego dvizheniia v Rossii v 1895–fevrale 1917 g.,"* ed. Iu. I. Kir'ianov and S. I. Potolov (Moscow: Akademiia Nauk SSSR, 1988), especially 170–78.

[9] Several "legal," censored versions of *Tkachi* did appear in the following years, first in 1903, as part of Hauptmann's *Sobranie sochinenii*, and later, thanks to the relaxed censorship after 1905, as separate publications. The most widely distributed and cheapest version (15 kopeks), that of 1906, came from "Labor" (*Trud*), the "semiparty" publishing house of S. A. Skirmunt, publisher of the earlier *Sobranie sochinenii*. A part of its "Inexpensive Library" (*Deshevaia Biblioteka*), *Trud*'s series of belles lettres for the poor, it was translated by L. Gurevich, with K. Bal'mont listed as editor. (A copy is in the New York Public Library.)

The play's appeal to Russians was very broad, its readership extending from Marxist revolutionaries to figures as far removed from revolution as Tolstoy. The excitement generated by the work, its nearly iconic quality, is nicely illustrated by a chance encounter in 1895 between Tolstoy and Bonch-Bruevich at the office of "The Intermediary" (Posrednik), the "people"-oriented publishing house of Tolstoy and Vladimir Chertkov. Tolstoy told the young Marxist that he wished to see a copy of Hauptmann's play. Starstruck by this encounter with the great man, Bonch-Bruevich agreed to bring him that "splendid work," which he discreetly concealed in a green dust jacket. Pleased to have the book in hand, Tolstoy began to leaf through it, admired how nicely it was produced, and respectfully acknowledged the danger its production must have entailed. Judging by the tone of Bonch-Bruevich's account, this encounter around *Tkachi* between two ideologically engaged Russians—a still little-known Marxist youth and a world-famous writer, men radically different in their moral and political philosophies—produced a kind of epiphany, as a special work, outlawed by their common foe, passed from one hand to the other. When the meeting ended, Bonch-Bruevich recalled, "Lev Nikolaevich [Tolstoy] got up, took leave of everyone, placed the little green book in the deep pocket of his overcoat, and, extending me his hand, said softly: 'Pay attention now, be careful! Please don't get in trouble.' " Five years later Tolstoy even thought about writing his own introduction to the play.[10]

The enthusiasm that *Tkachi* evoked along so wide an ideological spectrum of readers reinforces my point that, while emotionally radical in content, this was by no means a play with a rigid Marxist line. Wherever the reader may have stood on the other issues that divided educated society, there was ample sustenance in the play for a larger spectrum of champions of the poor and the downtrodden. In fact, on some of the most important and divisive of those issues, as we shall see, the play contained elements of plot that stood closer to the views of the Populists, the Marxists' main rivals on the Left, and elements of character that tolerated, and in some respects even valorized, the very personal traits and behaviors that Marxists were endeavoring to eradicate from Russia's still too

---

Nikolai Rubakin described Skirmunt's third edition of Hauptmann's complete works (Moscow, 1908) as the best Russian translation of Hauptmann (N. A. Rubakin, *Sredi knig* 1, pt. 1 [Moscow: Nauka, 1911], 106.) What could be called the first official Soviet version, translated by Zinaida Vengerova, was published by the Petrograd Soviet in 1918, the year it was first produced on the Petersburg stage. (The description of *Trud* as "semiparty" [*polupartiinoe*] is from V. D. Bonch-Bruevich, "Bol'shevistskie izdatel'skie dela v 1905–1907 gg.," in *Na barrikadakh: Vospominaniia uchastnikov revoliutsii 1905–1907 v Peterburge*, comp. T. P. Bondarevskaia and N. I. Primak [Leningrad: Lenizdat, 1984], 247n, and compilers' note, 394; see also Bonch-Bruevich, "Moi vstrechi," 93).

[10] Bonch-Bruevich, "Moi vstrechi," 91–92 (quotation from p. 92).

"backward" working class. And yet Bonch-Bruevich was no doubt correct when he wrote that the play was specially beloved by "our revolutionary Social Democracy."[11]

In what ways did Hauptmann's play violate the canons of Russian Marxism? To begin with, his weaver-protagonists, far from exemplifying the "advanced," "conscious" proletariat whose struggles would mark a new, heroic phase in the march of progress, belonged to a pre- or pro-toindustrial village community, and, like the characters in E. P. Thompson's epic study of English workers,[12] directed their energies not at overturning an already well-established, advanced capitalist system but at resisting the encroachments of a new and disruptive machine-based capitalism upon precapitalist modes of production and a traditional moral economy. Moreover, the weavers became rebellious under the influence of drink, used "wild," violent tactics, and, at times, acted with a kind of religious fervor and inspiration. Surely this scenario of resistance to industrialism was closer in spirit to the values of Populists and anarchists (and to some extent, excluding the tactics, even of conservatives) than to those of Social Democrats like Lenin, who in the polemics of the 1890s, notwithstanding all its manifest evils, welcomed industrial capitalism's rapid development and its inevitable victory over preindustrial modes of production.[13]

Particularly embarrassing to Marxists was Hauptmann's depiction of workers in a less than heroic mode, particularly in the early parts of the play. Although his weaver community finally does rise to the occasion, it does so under circumstances, including the powerful sway of alcohol and the influence of a religious impulse, that would have been absent from any propaganda work that *originated* in Russian Marxist circles. Hauptmann's fidelity to naturalism in portraying his workers with all their warts—passivity, cowardice, drunkenness, superstition—may augment the power of his work in our eyes, but it presented a serious challenge to his Russian Marxist interpreters. At a time when the real and future identities of the common folk (*narod*), the worker, and the "conscious" worker-activist, were still in heated dispute on the Left,[14] Marxists found themselves distributing a play that featured worker characters with traits from

---

[11] Ibid., 92.

[12] Edward P. Thompson, *The Making of the English Working Class* (New York: Vintage Books, 1963).

[13] See Andrzej Walicki, *The Controversy over Capitalism: Studies in the Social Philosophy of the Russian Populists* (Oxford: Oxford University Press, 1969), especially part 3.

[14] For many examples, see *Rabochie i intelligentsiia Rossii v epokhu reform i revoliutsii 1861–fevral' 1917*, ed. S. I. Potolov et al. (St. Petersburg: Izdatel'stvo "Russko-Baltiiskii Informatsionnyi tsentr BLITs," 1997); *Workers and Intelligentsia in Late Imperial Russia: Realities, Representations, Reflections*, ed. Reginald E. Zelnik (Berkeley: International and Area Studies Research Series, 1999).

which they would have preferred to avert their eyes, engaging in actions that Marxists often decried as counterproductive: machine-breaking, destruction of furniture, arson—all serious violations of the self-discipline Marxists now were urging on Russia's still inadequately proletarianized workers. In December 1895, the Workers' Union, the very Moscow group that had promoted Elizarova's translation, issued a short brochure, *Strikes, Their Significance for Workers*, in which it cautioned workers against the naive tendency to blame their sufferings on the character of their boss or on their machines; the brochure rejected violence and the destruction of property, that is, participation in a "riot" (*bunt*). Then, in a note, the authors actually cited Hauptmann's *Weavers* as illustrative of the kind of rioting they condemned![15]

A close reading of the Russian rendering of Hauptmann's unorthodox play can provide us with an opportunity to examine a limiting case of the notions on the Russian Left, particularly its Marxist wing, of what kind of worker identity was presentable and what kind of narrative could be used to convey that identity to a (potentially) militant audience. In this paper I focus on the widely used Kudelli-based version published in London by *Zhizn'*, a product of the very years in which the Marxist-Populist debate had been raging. By examining that text with some comparisons to the German original, I hope to show the extent to which Russian Marxists were able to accept, and in a sense were *compelled* to accept, a narrative about workers that conflicted with their political and intellectual preferences, a situation that may have represented in microcosm the larger cognitive dissonances produced by application of the Marxist model to Russian society in the conditions that prevailed at the turn of the century.

The German Background

Hauptmann began to think about researching *Die Weber* in 1888 and set to work in earnest in 1890. After several field trips to the Silesian location of the uprising (Peterswaldau, at the foot of the Eulenbirge), as well as intense historical research, he completed a final draft in early 1892, first

---

[15] "Takoi 'bunt' rabochikh, ne doshedshikh eshche do ponimaniia uslovii truda i zhizni, ochen' khorosho opisen v drame Gauptmana *Tkachi*." *RD*, 4:1, 75 (the entire brochure, *Stachki, ikh znachenie dlia rabochikh*, is on pp. 72–89). For a depiction of the kind of worker conduct that was worrying the authors of the brochure, see Daniel R. Brower, "Labor Violence in the Late Nineteenth Century," *Slavic Review* 41, no. 3 (1982): 417–31, followed by comments by Robert E. Johnson, Ronald Grigor Suny, and Diane Koenker, and a "Reply" by Brower (432–53). See also Theodore H. Friedgut, "Labor Violence and Regime Brutality in Tsarist Russia: The Iuzovka Cholera Riots of 1892," *Slavic Review* 46, no .2 (1987): 245–65, and Charters Wynn, *Workers, Strikes, and Pogroms: The Donbass-Dnepr Bend in Late Imperial Russia, 1870–1905* (Princeton: Princeton University Press, 1992).

with a Silesian dialect text, and then in more standard German, though still replete with dialect locutions.[16] Hauptmann read voraciously in primary sources, most notably the 1844 report of Alexander Schneer, secretary of the Breslau *Hilfsverein,* an organization of Prussian gentlemen who sympathized with the impoverished weavers.[17] As was typical of nineteenth-century noblemen, Schneer looked down on merchant manufacturers, rich commoners who mistreated the hapless poor and lacked the sense of social obligation claimed by gentlemen like himself. As a consequence, his report is filled with criticism of the manufacturers and compassion for the weavers, poor rural craftsmen who were being displaced by mechanization and by competition from more advanced factories. Here was a conservative perspective congenial to many leftist sympathizers, including Hauptmann himself.

While he of course reworked these historical materials for his own dramatic, polemical, and sentimental purposes (he wrote with great emotional commitment to his grandfather), Hauptmann strove to adhere to the record provided by Schneer and others and to information gathered during his own visits to the region, where he conducted interviews with survivors of 1844 and their children. So important was it to the "naturalist" writer to stay true to Schneer's account that he even retained some names of the actual participants.

And while his sympathies are crystal clear, Hauptmann allowed no narrowly defined political viewpoint to be elaborated or even referenced in the play. Instead, the action was organized around more fundamental conflicts: a raw and obvious conflict between poor, hungry families of weavers and the manufacturers who oppressed them; and a somewhat more complex internal conflict within the weaver community, sometimes in a single family, and even in a single individual, over whether to accept one's miserable fate or to join in acts of resistance. The relation between these two conflicts gives life to the story, for the weavers' misery serves as explanation of both the need to resist and the difficulty of doing so. In this respect the story was very true to life.

---

[16] See *Erläuterungen zu Gerhart Hauptmanns Die Weber,* Neubearbeitet von Dr. Karl Brinkmann, 12. Auflage (Königs Erläuterungen, Band 189, C. Bange Verlag: Holfeld / Obfr., n.d. [but late 1960s]); hereafter: *Erläuterungen.* The text of the dialect version, *De Waber,* may have been completed by the end of 1891.

[17] *Über die Noth der Leinenarbeiter in Schlesien und die Mittel ihr abzuhelfen* (Berlin: Veit und Comp., 1844). This work is discussed and evaluated in H. Schwab-Felisch, " 'Die Weber': ein Spiegel des 19. Jahrhunderts," in idem, ed., *Gerhart Hauptmann, Die Weber: Dichtung und Wirklichkeit* (Frankfurt / M: Verlag Ullstein, 1959), 73–113, especially 76–79. In addition to the text of the play and the above-mentioned article, this important collection contains many documents related to the play's publication history. Another of Hauptmann's essential historical sources was Alfred Zimmerman's *Blüte und Verfall des Leinengewerbes in Schlesien,* published in 1885.

As befit his naturalist assumptions, which he took to a more radical extreme than Emile Zola (one of his models), Hauptmann eschewed the "contamination" of his story with romantic intrigue. There are no love motifs in *Die Weber*, not even flirtations (though there is a scene that might qualify today as sexual harassment), and, as commentators were quick to note, there are no well-developed individual heroes (though there *are* poorly developed heroes, discussed below). Mainly, the weavers carry the action as a group, a crowd, though to some extent a differentiated one. In contrast to Zola's *Germinal* and *L'Assommoir*, the crowd, while sometimes fainthearted, sometimes violent, and (the males, at least) always prone to drink, is not vilified or presented with aversion, and certainly there is no Zola-esque notion that its deficiencies were biologically inherited or that families had degenerated.[18] But neither is the crowd greatly glorified, for the reader soon learns that poverty, overwork, and fear can destroy or damage one's self-respect. Hauptmann's naturalism represents the "masses" with blemishes. The question is: can they be removed? overcome? put to good use?

The subversive implications of Hauptmann's play were not lost on German censors. To be sure, because censorship was organized at the regional level (the *Land*), the crackdown was not concerted, nor was it experienced simultaneously in all *Länder*. Because different parts of Germany operated under different legal codes, there were *Länder* like Prussia where complicated litigation was involved, drawing even greater public attention to the play. This was particularly true in Berlin, the imperial capital, where performances of *Die Weber*, first staged in early 1893, were prohibited, then allowed to proceed, then again prohibited. None of this excitement was lost on Russia's ever-attentive political and cultural intelligentsia.

The Russian Background

Russia's intelligentsia, whether radical or liberal, was well attuned to developments in German cultural life. *Intelligenty* regularly read the German press or excerpts in the "thick" journals. Many educated young Russians studied in or, like the young Lenin, visited Berlin. In the summer of 1895, returning to Russia from his celebrated pilgrimage to Georgii Plekhanov in Geneva, Lenin stopped in Berlin, where he saw *Die Weber* performed. Having lived in Moscow with his sister just before his trip, certainly aware of Anna's interest in the play (her translation was finished well before his

---

[18] On Zola's perspective, see Susanna Barrows, *Distorting Mirrors: Visions of the Crowd in Late Nineteenth-Century France* (New Haven: Yale University Press, 1981), especially 69–72, 93–113.

departure), Lenin could hardly bypass the opportunity to view it on the stage. In August he wrote to his mother that he was unhappy with the progress of his spoken German and had trouble with the language of Berliners, who "pronounce so strangely that I cannot grasp the words even of a public lecture, whereas in France I understood almost everything." "On my third day here," he continued, "I went to the theater, where they were showing Hauptmann's *Weber.* Though I read the entire play in advance to help me follow the action, I was unable to catch all the words." Without commenting on the play itself, Lenin concluded by reassuring his mother that while he regretted not having studied German more thoroughly, he was not dejected.[19]

Russia's *intelligenty* also followed cultural trends in Paris, where *Les Tisserands,* the French version of *Die Weber,* was staged in May 1893, and with great success. A little later, in June, the play could be read in brief Russian summary in *Books of the Week* (Knizhki nedeli),[20] which may be where Elizarova first encountered it. By 1895 Hauptmann's name, if not a household word, was provoking controversy in Russian journals, as exemplified by an article in the December issue of the Populist-oriented journal *The New Word* (Novoe slovo). There, in a twenty-page essay, Evgenii Degen celebrated Hauptmann's naturalism, contrasting it favorably to the idealism of earlier German writers and to French decadence and symbolism, all of which he deemed escapist, out of touch with society's "living tasks." Clearly a man of the Left, Degen reviewed Hauptmann's earlier writings (at least one play had been staged in Russia), praising some, dismissing others, but treating *Die Weber* as by far his finest work, harbinger of the revitalization of German letters. Degen was pleased that Hauptmann could write about the poor and downtrodden without condescension, a talent he identified with Tolstoy and Dostoevsky, suggesting (correctly) their influence on Hauptmann's writings. And in keeping with the broadly Populist but nonpartisan nature of the journal in which he wrote, he was pleased that *Die Weber* was not cast in the mold of specific partisan politics.[21]

Russian censorship officials were no less aware than left *intelligenty*—whose sensitivity to literature's propaganda potential they shared—of the play's provocative nature. As early as December 1893, after reading a gov-

---

[19] V. I. Lenin, *Polnoe sobranie sochinenii,* 5th ed., vol. 55: *Pis'ma k rodnym, 1893–1922* (Moscow: Gosizdat, 1965), 11 (first published in *Proletarskaia Revoliutsiia,* no. 11, 1929). (Even in the nondialect version in which it was presented on the Berlin stage the play is full of difficult popular locutions; I saw it performed at the Schiller Theater in 1976.)

[20] N. Travushkin, "V. I. Lenin i 'Tkachi' Gauptmana (Po memuaram i dokumentam," *Volga,* no. 3 (1968): 148.

[21] Degen, "Gergard Gauptmann," *Novoe slovo,* no. 3 (December 1895): 36–56. *Novoe slovo* was taken over by Marxists in 1897; see Allan K. Wildman, *The Making of a Workers' Revolution: Russian Social Democracy, 1891–1903* (Chicago: University of Chicago Press, 1967), 24–25.

ernment agent's report, the Censorship Office pronounced the play "extremely tendentious" and prohibited its printing or staging in Russia.[22] For much the same reasons, Russian revolutionaries would be drawn to the play as a potential propaganda tool. The subject was suitable: exploited textile workers rising up against a rapacious employer, as they had begun to do in Russia (Nevskii strike of 1870, Kreenholm strike of 1872, Petersburg strikes of 1878–79, Morozov strike, Ivanovo-Voznesensk, of 1885). By 1895, Petersburg Marxists had a clear if still limited interest in local textile workers, an interest that grew rapidly the following year, when Russia's first protracted citywide strike erupted in the city's textile industry. Suffering weavers had also entered the repertory of Russian poetry and song, most notably in Sergei Sinegub's 1873 poem "A Weaver's Meditation" (Duma tkacha), still popular in the 1890s, and in the equally well known poem "Tkachi," authored in 1879 by two workers.[23]

And yet there were, as already suggested, serious problems with this play for a Russian Marxist. In contrast to the militant weavers of Russia, most of whom labored under a single roof in what for the times were modern, mechanized plants, the protagonists of Hauptmann's play were village handworkers in a traditional putting-out system, working in their homes with yarn supplied by a *Fabrikant*; their main complaint was hunger, brought about by piece rates that were driven down by competition with technically advanced enterprises. From a Marxist perspective, their struggle was "regressive," a tragic response to the cruel yet nevertheless *welcome* advance of capitalism that Lenin was cheering on in 1899 in *The Development of Capitalism in Russia*; this was material suited more for E. P. Thompson than V. I. Lenin.

To be sure, the play does end with the workers' apparent triumph, which may have been reason enough to invest it with propaganda value. Yet it was also well known, and was even suggested in the play itself, that the true story of the Silesian uprising was the story of its *defeat* in the face of hopeless odds, normally not the best means for urging workers to action or resuscitating an often-wavering labor movement. Russian weavers, by then sometime participants in strikes for three decades, needed no reminder of the combined power of their employers and the state.

Given these and other ideological anomalies, the Elizarovas and Kudellis had to have sensed something attractive in what was, as far as I

---

[22] Travushkin, "V. I. Lenin," 148–49 (based on RGIA, f. 776, op. 26).

[23] The two workers were Shtripan and Petr Moiseenko. Moiseenko was a leading figure in the strikes of 1878–79 and 1885, and was still active in the 1890s and beyond. Their poem begins: "S utra do nochi v zabote / My na fabrike v rabote / Chisto kak v adu." For the full text see *Pesni russkikh rabochikh (XVIII–nachalo XX veka)*, comp. A. I. Nutrikhina (Moscow: Sovetskii pisatel', 1962), 90–92; see also editor's note on 257–58. For Sinegub's "Duma tkacha" see *Agitatsionnaia literatura russkikh revoliutsionnykh narodnikov: Potaennye proizvedeniia 1873–1875 gg.*, ed. V. G. Bazanov (Leningrad: Nauka, 1970), 457–58, 492n.

know, the only instance of a work of fiction of any significant length (eighty-seven pages in the London version) that Marxists of this period saw fit to translate. Not plays or novels but the theoretical and polemical writings of the German masters were the true loves of their Russian disciples, who in these years were frantically translating Marx, Engels, Bebel, Liebknecht, Kautsky, and, to a lesser extent, their French epigones. This was equally true of Plekhanov (who translated the *Communist Manifesto*) and his Geneva-based "Emancipation of Labor group," which, though not without literary interests, had little time for novels or plays. That such people should involve themselves in the translation of Hauptmann's linguistically difficult text—even today's German editions include special glossaries for the German reader!—clearly indicates that the tale he told had something inspirational, however heterodox, to offer a Russian popular audience, at least from the hopeful perspective of the Marxist intelligentsia.

We will now examine *Tkachi* (the *Zhizn'* version) act by act, trying to imagine what the story, as it unfolded, might have meant to its Russian readers, and noting, where applicable, the changes, mostly quite nuanced, introduced by the translators. It should first be observed that the action still takes place in Germany, in the same location in Silesia, with references to the King of Prussia, local officials, place names, and the same German names of characters (minimally Russified in transliteration, e.g., "Jäger" = "Ieger," "Hilse" = "Khil'ze"). In other words, there is little attempt at the surface level to turn the play into a Russian story. True, there are concessions to the familiar, as when *Branntwein, Schnaps*, or *Fusel* are turned into *vodka* (drink was a leitmotif for Hauptmann, as it was for Zola), and an *Edelmann* becomes a *pomeshchik*, but the overall setting is pointedly German, suggesting—in contrast to some earlier Populist translations or reworkings of foreign literature for propaganda purposes—that the translators were prepared to present the reader with a foreign situation and let that situation speak for itself, hoping that its generalization to Russia would readily follow.[24] In principle, at least, Germany, or rather the

---

[24] An important example of a foreign book reworked by Populists in order to make it more familiar to an uneducated Russian is the propaganda brochure *Istoriia odnogo frantsuzskogo krest'ianina* (Geneva, 1873), an abridgment and revision of Emile Erckmann's and Alexandre Chatrian's long novel of the French Revolution, *L'Histoire d'un paysan* (1868). While the brochure does retain a French setting, it appeals to Russian peasants and workers by addressing them directly and providing them with revolutionary guidance by invoking the current situation in Russia. See B. S. Itenberg, *Rossiia i Velikaia frantsuzskaia revoliutsiia* (Moscow: Mysl', 1988), 100–104; V. F. Zakharina, "Roman Erkmana-Shatriana 'Istoriia krest'ianina' i ego peredelka v revoliutsionnoi narodnicheskoi propagande," *Russkaia literatura*, no. 2 (1964); idem, *Golos revoliutsionnoi Rossii: Literatura revoliutsionnogo podpol'ia 70-kh godov XIX v. "Izdaniia dlia naroda"* (Moscow: Mysl', 1971), 67–76.

German labor movement, was, after all, a positive model for Russian Marxists, the object of boundless admiration.

At the same time, the play had numerous elements that were familiar to a Russian worker, particularly a textile worker. In Act 1, we immediately meet a manufacturer, Dreisiger (double "s" in German) and his assistants, chief clerk (*kontorshchik*) Pfeifer and paymaster (*kassir*) Neiman (Neumann), in a context that a Russian weaver would easily recognize. The weavers are paid by the piece, as was then common in Russia, and, as was also common, the clerk devalues the quality of the work while the weaver insists that the real problem was the quality of the yarn. Workers complain about delayed wages, and here we encounter some liberties with the original German text in the service of darkening an already dismal atmosphere: whereas in the original a weaver complains of having to wait an hour or a day, in the translation he must wait a day or a week. Similarly, the factory office denounces the weavers as devils (*cherty*), absent from the German original (6/8).[25]

The overall mood of the opening scene is one of gloom and despair. Several workers complain of overwork, fatigue, and the hunger and disease that wrack their families, complaints that surely struck a chord among Russians at a time of recurrent crop failure, famine, and epidemic disease (1891–92, 1899). Most of the weavers appear sullen and bitter, beaten down and frightened, and like Geiber (Heiber), easily cowed by threats of dismissal if they beg for a small advance to make ends meet. Nevertheless, it is fair to say that Heiber is more obsequious and groveling than Geiber, a sign of the translators' reluctance to present too demoralizing an image of a worker's crushed spirit and lack of self-worth. Similarly, where in the original a key character, old man Baumert, laments that the weavers have no hope, this is omitted from the Russian, where he simply asks rhetorically (anticipating Lenin?): "Chto budesh' delat'?" (what is one to do?) (9/11). This distinction is minor, however, for quite early in the German story, as in the Russian, we begin to see some weavers arguing with the clerk and, however guardedly, asserting themselves by talking back (8/9). The weaver Bekker (Bäcker), soon to emerge as a rebel leader, even begins to speak defiantly (10/12), thereby blurring the textual distinctions noted above. There is a sharp contrast, at this point, between Bekker's defiance and old Baumert's desperation, symbolized here and later by Baumert's slaughter of a pet dog to feed his family.

[25] NB: Where I give two page numbers in this manner ("6/8"), unless the context indicates a different sequence, the first number is from the Russian version, the second from the German; and if I give only one page number it is because the context clarifies the reference. Note also that, because my chapter is mainly about the play's Russian version, where a Russian name differs in spelling from the German, I use the Russian, adding the German in parentheses the first time only.

This contrast sets the stage for the story line that follows, that is, for the closing of the gap between Bekker's self-confident defiance and Baumert's original defeatism, with Baumert and others eventually deciding to join forces with Bekker. If critics have called Hauptmann's play a drama without heroes, or else a play in which the hero is not an individual but a community, a hallmark of the author's naturalism, this is true only insofar as Hauptmann eschews the development of a single psychologically complex protagonist. Bekker, unlike Ieger (Jäger), the play's other agent of rebellion, is simply there, just the way he is, from the outset. He arrives on stage fully formed, a representative of the community's potential strength and manly courage, but with almost no indication of how he became—to borrow language absent from the play, but by then central to leftist discourse in Russia—"conscious" (*soznatel'nyi*), advanced, part of a weaver vanguard. The only hint of what might have made him special is that he is called a weaver from Bielau ("Das is a Bielauer Weber"), a place known for its troublemakers (10/12), but this reference would surely have been lost on a Russian audience. Nevertheless, Bekker *is* a hero in the simple sense that he represents the best qualities of the community, which, with Ieger, he will ultimately lead in heroic action.

Act 1 also introduces the reader to the manufacturer Dreisiger, to whom Hauptmann grants more complexity than he does to any weaver. Like other characters, Dreisiger reveals his main personal traits when first we meet him. He is, of course, stereotypically selfish and hard-hearted but also, as we quickly learn, insecure and fearful. What he seems to fear most is *singing*—specifically a song, often heard in the background, called the "Weavers' Song," "Dreisiger Song," or, most ominously and patently vengeful, the song of "Righteous Judgment" ("Pravednyi sud," in Russian, and the still more ominous "*Blut*gericht" in German). Whatever the song is called, when he hears it Dreisiger trembles (11/12).

Dreisiger is allowed just a faint trace of humanity when the collapse of an exhausted child moves him to words of sympathy (though only at Bekker's urging). But mainly the occasion moves him to a long self-serving speech in his own defense, and that of other manufacturers, blaming the workers' greed for the plight of their overworked children. How dare they sing that terrible song when, despite his own meager profits (a familiar employer's defense in Russia's early industrial conflicts), he does so much for his workers!—providing them with enough pay to keep from starving and even with money for "vodka" (*Fusel*). This is also the occasion for a display of the weavers' self-abasement, as their collective response to his query, "Am I really so hard-hearted?" is—"Net, net, gospodin Dreisiger!"—"Nein, Herr Dreissiger!" (16/15)

Dreisiger, then, already has his rationale worked out when first we meet him appealing for his workers' good will. Although the crowd seems cowed by his presence, the weavers' behavior in his absence (when he steps outside, they come to life "like schoolboys when the teacher leaves the classroom") bespeaks their volatility, while the sound of the "Blutgericht" signals an impending change.

Act 2 unfolds in the home of the weaver Anzorge (Ansorge), where the Baumerts rent their crammed living quarters (though payment has been impossible for months). In contrast to the centralized, mechanized mills of 1890s Russia, the home is also where the Baumerts do their weaving. In addition to old man and old woman Baumert, there are two daughters—aged fifteen and twenty-two—and the older daughter's four-year-old son, whose father has already succumbed to disease. The point of the action is to show us old Baumert's transition from a passive role to that of a man of action, signifying that the community's metamorphosis will not be confined to youthful hotheads.

An important new character is introduced, the ex-soldier Ieger, who serves as the immediate instrument of Baumert's transformation. If Ieger too is brought to us more or less "ready-made," we do learn more about his past than about Bekker's. Though a member of the weaver community, Ieger, having served in the army, has a military bearing. And he was not an ordinary soldier, but the orderly of his regimental commander. He is well-dressed and—a signifier of achievement with resonance among Russian workers—he sports a watch. He has learned to read and write and has become well spoken: he "red't wie de vornehmen Leute," as old Baumert puts it, admiringly; or in Russian, with more emphasis on his education, "govorit to on po obrazovannomu" (he speaks like an educated man) (23/22), all of which enhances him and sets him apart from his community. We also learn from the dialogue, though without much specificity, that as a soldier he had seen the world, including the big city ("Dogs live better in the cities than you do," he tells the weavers), hence he is a source of counsel to still-benighted weavers like Anzorge, who asks him, in view of Ieger's wide travels and knowledge of the outside world, whether life will be better for them in the future (26/25).

Even more than Bekker, Ieger is, in short, a rough counterpart of what Russian radicals by now were calling a "conscious" worker; like Antonio Gramsci's organic intellectuals, he comes from the workers' own midst yet can claim a new identity, one that distinguishes him from the rest. When old Baumert naively proposes to tell the king of Prussia of the weavers' plight (recalling a Russian peasant's traditional faith in the tsar), Ieger is right there with the precise message Marxists wished to press upon the Russian people: it will do no good, the king will never act against the rich (that is, "Don't forget to link the economic to the political struggle!"). Ieger thus embodies a partial solution to the chronic problem of the Russian Left (dating from the 1870s, well before Lenin hypostatized it in *What Is To Be Done?*): how a benighted *narod* (for Lenin, "the working class"), which cannot emerge from the blinding limitations of daily life if "left to its own devices," can be awakened to effective action by a more educated elite.

Yet it is only a partial solution, for Ieger, though more "advanced," still shares the weavers' love of drink, whereas the pernicious influence of drink on worker consciousness (almost a pun!) was a persistent theme of the Russian Left. With money to spare, he even likes to treat the other men to vodka, perhaps a "petty-bourgeois" gesture, but one that assures their devotion to him. Of course, the practice of treating workers to vodka was not unknown to Russian radicals, but it was usually viewed as a necessary evil or condemned as a capitulation to "backwardness."[26] There is no sign, however, that Hauptmann wished to condemn it.

At first Ieger's answer to Anzorge's question—will the future bring improvement to their lives?—is simply that he hopes so. But as the evening wears on, Ieger, his clarity of thought and purpose not visibly impaired, perhaps even enhanced, by alcohol, has a surprise up his sleeve that will raise the spirits if not the consciousness of his audience—the text of the "Weavers' Song." Wisely, he orders more drink before reading it aloud, presumably hoping that alcohol will sensitize his listeners to the message. The tactic works, at least on old Baumert, whose response amounts to a request that Ieger become their leader: "Tebe sledovalo-by o nashem dele pokhlopotat'!" / "Du sollt'st unsere Sache amal in de Hand nehmen dahier."

These words, along with old woman Baumert's sudden decision to abandon her belief that there must always be rich folk, bring Ieger to an agitational frenzy. He calls for solidarity against *manufacturers* (though *not* against *capitalism*), declaring that the people need neither government nor king. Speaking ever more "fanatically" (the stage direction in both versions), he denounces those who blame the weavers for their own fate and discloses—the first we hear of their conspiratorial ties—that he and "red" Bekker have vowed *over drinks* to keep singing the "Weavers' Song." ("Red," which alludes to Bekker's hair as well as his ideas, appears in German only, since the pun cannot be reproduced in Russian. Elsewhere we learn that Bekker is *ryzhevolosyi*.)

The magical effect of Ieger's reading of the verses, an emotional high point of the play, is designed to come across as a kind of religious experience. Old Baumert, now transformed, says that the verses speak the truth as in the Bible ("budto iz biblii vziato!"); it is only after hearing them that he and Anzorge declare their commitment to struggle. Here we have a rare hint that Russia's revolutionary and atheist Marxists, like some of

---

[26] See, for example, my "Workers and Intelligentsia in the 1870s: The Politics of Sociability," in *Workers and Intelligentsia in Late Imperial Russia*, 20–21.

their Populist predecessors,[27] were prepared to tolerate religion, or at least religious feeling, as a propaganda tool. (Note also that Bonch-Bruevich, known for his efforts to attract religious sectarians to the revolutionary cause, had an important role in the leadership of *Zhizn'*.)

Act 3, set in a local tavern, introduces new characters, including innkeeper Vel'sel' (Welzel) and his wife, their pretty daughter Anna, carpenter Vigand (Wiegand), ragpicker Khorning (Hornig), a traveling salesman, and a forester. Verbal interplay among these figures dominates much of the act, with the mid-act arrival of old Baumert and Anzorge, now converts to activism (thanks to Ieger and the song), linking the conversation more directly to the weavers' plight. The salesman is a semi-comic, almost grotesque figure, who makes crude remarks to and about Anna, one dramatic purpose of which is to tell us more about Dreisiger's background and introduce the theme of upward mobility, its attractions and its dangers. The salesman, concealing his wedding ring, teases Anna, urging her to exploit her looks by marrying upward. Her father, spokesman for the values of the community, rejects the idea, but her mother is tempted. In the course of these exchanges we learn that Dreisiger's grandfather was a poor weaver whose hard work and determined efforts had led to his grandson's social and economic success—a story that would have sounded a familiar note in the textile trades of Russia's Central Industrial Region, where Old Believer manufacturers were the descendants of serfs-turned-entrepreneur.

Here the translators manage to bring the story closer to Russia by using terms with Russian resonance. Anna's hypothetical marriage to a Silesian *Magnat* becomes marriage to a *pomeshchik*, and when the debate is joined by others, we hear protests that not only manufacturers but also *pomeshchiki* take advantage of weavers, who, since they are also villagers, are still burdened with obligations to the local lords on whose land they live. This reference to the weavers' dual status as obligated peasants and hired workers echoes (while not precisely duplicating) the situation of many workers in post-Emancipation Russia.

In this connection it is noteworthy that one of Elizarova's major writings was a pamphlet summarizing with a leftward spin statistician E. M. Dement'ev's controversial 1893 study of Moscow textile workers, which described their ties to the land but also stressed (and *exaggerated*, but that is another story) their transformation into a hereditary proletariat, whose ties to the village were mainly nominal. This was a development that Russian Marxists wished to document as part of their polemic against the

---

[27] See my " 'To the Unaccustomed Eye': Religion and Irreligion in the Experience of St. Petersburg Workers in the 1870s," in Robert P. Hughes and Irina Paperno, ed., *Russian Culture in Modern Times* (*California Slavic Studies* 17 [1994]): 49–82.

populist notion of narod, with its oneness of peasant and worker.[28] To that extent, the weaver's mixed identities was not a theme that Marxists would have wanted to underline. By leaving untouched Hauptmann's collapsing of worker and peasant, they were ceding some ground to their Populist rivals (and anticipating some future changes in the Bolshevik perspective).

Hauptmann, to be sure, is himself not very consistent on this point. For when he devises a heated argument between weavers and a peasant, and the peasant, bemoaning the weavers' laziness and drunkenness, blames them for their own poverty, the peasant is sharply rebuked by a weaver, who says categorically that "a Pauer bleibt a Pauer" ("muzhik ostaetsia muzhik"), and chides him for thinking "like a peasant." And another weaver goes so far as to accuse peasants of helping the landowner exploit the weavers (40–41/36).

The traveling salesman is also there to present the view that the weavers' misery is overstated. But when he cites a costly village funeral as evidence of the weavers' solvency, this is really a pretext for Hauptmann to assert the community's family values, as various speakers explain that family members, poor though they may be, are prepared to sacrifice for the honor of dead kinfolk. The poor folk of the region, says the village carpenter (in German using the awkward expression "die hiesige arme Bevölkerungsklasse," in contrast to the simplicity of the Russian, "bedniaki"), have their own way of thinking and are willing to go into debt to meet their obligations to the dead; and, he adds in the Russian version, summoning the specter of a still not forgotten serfdom, "they place themselves in bondage for life" ("oni zakabaliaiut sebia na vsiu zhizn'") (35/31–32).

By the time he enters the tavern, old Baumert, by now impassioned by song, is prepared for battle against the rich. When he launches into a tirade about the distinctions between petty and grand theft, the theme is echoed by other weavers, one of whom, in the Russian version, describes their excessive labor obligations as *barshchina* (a serf's work obligation, corvée). Anzorge adds that what the manufacturer fails to extract from the workers is taken by the *Edelmann* (in Russian, again *pomeshchik*). Another weaver complains, sounding like a Russian serf, that he must devote five days a week *na barshchinu* (to corvée), a detail not in the original (39–40/35–36).

[28] Dement'ev's widely cited *Fabrika, chto ona daet naseleniiu i chto ona u nego beret* was glossed in Elizarova's "Polozhenie rabochikh u nas po sravneniiu s polozheniem ikh v Anglii i Amerike" in 1895, at about the time she was translating *Die Weber*. Dement'ev's study was one of Lenin's sources in *Razvitie kapitalizma v Rossii* (1899). For thoughtful commentary on Dement'ev, see Robert Eugene Johnson, *Peasant and Proletarian: The Working Class of Moscow in the Late Nineteenth Century* (New Brunswick: Rutgers University Press, 1979), 35–37, 62–64.

When the salesman—who is put there by Hauptmann to introduce ideas for the protagonists to refute—asks why the local pastor allows his flock to squander its meager resources on burials, the carpenter, though a sometime defender of Dreisiger, uses the occasion to expose the clergy's cupidity, explaining that elaborate funerals enrich the pastor. This is not couched as an attack on *religion*, however, as Hauptmann maintains a distinction between anticlericalism and antireligion, one that many Russian radicals had learned to master after their stressful experience with pious peasants in the 1870s.

The arrival on the scene of Bekker, Ieger, and a noisy crowd of weavers is then anticipated by the sound of the song, now called a "Devil's Song" by the nervous innkeeper. Bekker and Ieger are clearly in charge, with ex-soldier Ieger's special ("professional"?) status accented by his use of the language of military command. The setting lets Hauptmann return to the alcohol theme, as Ieger, with Bekker's approval, treats the crowd to vodka (while the innkeeper's wife conceals the traveler for his own safety).

It is the drink, to the innkeeper's dismay (and perhaps to that of a Marxist reader), that gives the weavers the courage to resume their song, which in turn heightens their excitement. Bekker becomes sufficiently confident to propose a march on Dreisiger's home, while the village blacksmith talks not too coherently about the French Revolution. As the gathering attains a state of near-religious exaltation, as if preparing for a weavers' crusade, a wary old villager warns against blasphemy, predicts the coming of Judgment Day, yet adds that it is only those who live at the expense of the poor who will suffer God's vengeance (44–45/40). Like the ragpicker ("this may end badly"), the blacksmith, the carpenter, and others, he expresses confused and contradictory sentiments, capturing the continued ambivalence of part of the community. Nevertheless, the action does follow a single trajectory, as the weak-willed and hesitant move into the swelling ranks of the rebels. We already foresee that the *community* will eventually act as one, perhaps an attractive feature to Russian radicals, but surely more so to community-oriented Populists than to Marxists like Lenin or Elizarova, for whom communities could only be correctly understood when divided into opposing classes.

In Act 4, set in Dreisiger's home, we encounter some new characters, including his attractive wife (whose plebeian origins are betrayed by her speech), the pastor and his wife, and a nineteen-year-old student, Veingol'd (Weinhold). Veingol'd, son of a government official (*chinovnik*) and tutor to Dreisiger's children, is a type that resembles a Russian *intelligent*, but of the moderate, humanistic, "do-gooder," variety, not a revolutionary. When the pastor tries to disabuse him of his naïve ideals, such as the justice of the weavers' cause, the student defends their extreme actions on the grounds that they are ignorant and uneducated (German—

unwissende, Russian—the more suggestive *temnye*) (53/46). These exchanges are rendered increasingly tense by the ominous sound of the song (the spirited tavern crowd is approaching), the fearful interruptions of the pastor's wife, and the angry words of Dreisiger. Dreisiger's wife, perhaps revealing her humble origins, expresses sympathy (with just a hint of romantic attraction) for the tutor and pleads with her husband not to fire him, but in vain. (Later, as the revolt expands, she even wonders aloud if she wasn't better off in her former, lower station in life [62/53].)

Dreisiger, having by now called in the police, has them arrest the lead "singers" and leading troublemakers. (The arrest of a handful of *podstrekateli* or *zachinshchiki* so as to nip a strike in the bud was common in Russia, as elsewhere, but often led to escalation of the strike, with release of the prisoners emerging as a larger issue than the initial grievance.) After Ieger is arrested and brought to Dreisiger, we learn that the defiant rebel is flushed with excitement from drinking brandy (this time, in Russian, *vino*) (56/48).

As it turns out, the pastor knows Ieger well, having baptized him and brought him to Jesus, for which he now expects his gratitude. Ieger's response is interesting for what it tells us about Hauptmann's, and then his Russian translators', approach to questions of religion. In the original text "Jäger" responds defiantly: he is no longer a believer; he has become a Quaker! In Russian, by contrast, Ieger simply says that he has changed his faith. In the original, the pastor then challenges Jäger's statement: "Was, Quäker, ach rede doch nicht. . . . Das sind fromme Leute, nicht Heiden we du" (How can you call yourself a Quaker . . . They are pious people, not heathens like yourself). Since Quakers are not even mentioned in the Russian, the pastor's response can make no reference to them; he simply asserts that people *here* are "blagochestivye liudi, ne iazychniki kak ty" (pious people, not pagans like yourself) (57/49). In both cases, even though the translator does take other liberties, there is a reluctance to turn the rebel into a full-fledged atheist; he is a believer—in the German case of a specific denomination, while in the Russian case the faith is left vague, perhaps suggesting some kind of sectarian.

Shortly after being taken away by police, Ieger is freed by the crowd, which beats the policemen and chases them away. Hearing this news, the distressed pastor pronounces the word "revolution," heard for the first time in the play, thereby turning Hauptmann's work, at least momentarily, into something more portentous than a plea for humane treatment. The "R" word should not be taken too literally, however. There is never a plot to overthrow the government, and ideology in any formal sense remains absent. When asked by the pastor to describe the weavers' demands, a coachman who witnesses the burgeoning riot answers simply—

"additional wages" (61/52), a fairly accurate reply, even though the situation is obviously more complex.

What complicates it is that vengeance and destruction are becoming an end in themselves, the be-all and end-all of the weavers' activity (as warned against in *Rabochii souiz*'s brochure). The crowd, the "rabble" (*Gesindel / svoloch'*), as Dreisiger calls them (63/54), forces its way into his house, shaking the foundations, shattering windows, breaking down doors. A leading role is now played by the blacksmith, a waverer in the tavern, but by this time an axe-wielding belligerent, engaged in mortal combat. There is a moment of fascination with the luxuries of the rich, as men stand on chairs to scrutinize the Dreisigers' paintings and women are bewitched by their mirrors. But mainly there is destructive frenzy, with property shattered and much aimless rushing about.

Will any kind of revolutionary order or trade-union discipline be imposed on this wild movement? Will any genuine leadership emerge? The answer comes from Bekker (to the relief of many Marxist readers, no doubt), who gains control over the crowd, tells it that its mission of destruction at Dreisiger's is over (but not that it's *wrong*), and directs the crowd's attention to a factory in the nearby weaving center of Bielau (Bekker's home region). This generalizing of the protest, the spreading of the local movement to a neighboring settlement, was surely a plus from the viewpoint of revolutionary Marxists. The problem, however, was that Bekker now robustly declares a specific goal, one that amounted precisely to the Luddite position Marxists feared. Not only does he tell the crowd that their misery arose from the competition of modern factories like the one in Bielau, he specifically lays the blame on the factory's mechanized looms, which at this point in the original text the crowd targets for destruction. The Russian translators' solution to this dilemma was a simple one: to omit any reference to power looms at all.

Act 5 depicts the upheaval's spread to Bielau. The scene is the Bielau home of an old, religious, prayerful weaver, Khil'ze (Hilse). The action revolves around a bitter conflict within his hungry family over whether or not to cast their lot with the Peterswaldau weavers, whose actions are described to them by the ragpicker and a visiting medical man. Each member of the Khil'ze family occupies a different point on a continuum. At one end is the conservative old man (older people are less rebellious in the play, at least at first), never flinching from his opposition to the uprising; at the other end—his daughter-in-law Luiza (Luise), ever ready to back the rebels. The real drama is the struggle between Luiza and old Khil'ze for the soul of her wavering husband, Khil'ze's son Gotlib (Gottlieb), who begins by adopting his father's caution, though more from cowardice than conviction. His manhood is on the line, for Luiza quickly reveals that she cannot remain the loyal wife of a coward.

Gotlib has already encountered the approaching weavers, who, armed with cudgels, ask him to join their ranks, since he too is poor and hungry (*bedniak, golodnyi*). Hoping to win him over, they proclaim the dawning of a new day and reveal their vision of a new order—meat on Sundays, blood sausage and cabbage every holiday (74/62). Although to old Khil'ze these words represent the Devil's talk, they might well have been denounced as "economism" by Marxist *intelligenty*. That this language was retained in the translation, I would argue, is evidence of the superficiality of much of the "spontaneity v. consciousness" debate. In this respect, at least, the historical situation represented by Hauptmann, the melding of militancy with tangible economic goals, corresponded to the mood of major Russian textile strikes, with workers drawing no neat line between militant declarations of purpose and their immediate needs, between rebellion and hunger riot. The medical man, dismayed by what he sees and hears—the vandalism and plundering, the grisly song—captures this point when he describes the event in one breath as "Revolution" and "Rebellion," which in Russian comes out, even more tellingly, and still with no clear sense of contradiction: "Revoliutsiiu podniali, bunt!" (they have stirred up a revolution, a riot!) (72–73/61).

The arrival of the cudgel-wielding weavers (and the context for the play's dramatic resolution) is announced by the sound of the song. By now Luiza, having pointedly rejected old Khil'ze's prayers and "God talk," has abandoned her husband for the rebels, leaving poor Gotlib with the starkest of all-or-nothing choices. The character of the weavers' tactics is now more sharply defined (less "Marxist") than ever, as the ragpicker announces (this time the translation preserves the point): "They want to destroy the mechanized looms," which, "as even the blind can see," were destroying the handloom weavers.

It should be emphasized that despite Luiza's attacks on prayer and on Khil'ze's religious ranting, Hauptmann continues to present the rebellion in language with religious undertones, in effect defining it as a crusade. Referring to the marchers who summon the Bielau weavers from their homes, Gorning cries out: "Die Christen sein heut eemal im Zuge" (The Christians are now on the march). This may have been a bit too much for Russia's atheist translators, whose rendition eliminates "die Christen," simply stating that the weavers were "v samom razgare" (in full swing) (78/65).

When a group of weavers, Bekker and (a bit later) Ieger among them, enter the Khil'ze premises, they are inflamed by drink. Many of the hot-headed youths—"Whoever isn't with us is against us!"—want to torch the homes of the rich and beat up traitors like Khil'ze. But Bekker, now speaking in the voice of "consciousness," or at least of thoughtfulness (though he has never refused a drink himself), assures old Khil'ze that no one there will be harmed; clubs will be used only on the factory owner. Ieger even contributes to a widening of the rebels' perspective by calling for an attack on government officials (*Birokraten*), a hint of "conscious" linkage between the social and the political order.

But the most important rebel to enter the scene is neither Ieger nor Bekker, but old Baumert, who will now serve as a dramatic foil to Khil'ze, in a sense his mirror image. The two old men, both of whom had started out wary of rebellion, turn out to be old friends, providing Khil'ze with his last opportunity to convert to the weavers' cause. Baumert, in keeping with Hauptmann's naturalistic, "show-all-warts" portrayals, is drunk, wobbly on his feet, preoccupied with dreams of further drinking. Apparently decked in stolen clothes, he brags to Khil'ze that he looks like a count, expounds his vision of a happy future (now elevated from blood sausage and cabbage to roast rabbit and champagne!), and tries to win him over with—what else!—drink. When Khil'ze replies that he does not drink, Baumert is understanding but counters with the compelling argument that these are new times. Despite threats and pressure from Ieger and Bekker (who justifies theft in the context of a rebellion), and despite his own family's hunger, Khil'ze will not accept the stolen chicken Baumert offers him. Whatever the author's and translators' intent, Khil'ze's bold and principled stand turns him into a somewhat admirable figure, however briefly. There is almost a hint of moral equivalency. Then, when old Baumert, equally courageous, leaves to resume the struggle in the face of certain imprisonment ("a man has to breathe, if only for a moment"), he asks Khil'ze to pray for him!

In the end, however, it is not old Khil'ze's choice that will count, but that of the only young man in the play to have expressly rejected the rebellion, Khil'ze's son, whose manhood has been questioned by his wife. What forces Gotlib's hand is the inevitable arrival of army troops to quell the unrest (a familiar outcome in Russia, especially in remote areas like Ivanovo or Kreenholm, where regular police and gendarmes are outmanned). Gotlib is mocked by almost everyone, even in song, and by none more cuttingly than his wife, who now declares that she has no husband (83/68). Soon blood begins to flow outside—weavers attack soldiers, soldiers open fire, bullets fly. When Gotlib hears that his wife is braving bayonets, he can hold back no longer. Ignoring his parents' entreaties, he rushes to her assistance, axe in hand. As more people leave the house to join the fray, the intractable old Khil'ze is felled by a stray bullet.

With the soldiers in flight and the factory owner's home under siege, the play seems to conclude for the weavers on a note of triumph, adding to its effectiveness as galvanizing propaganda. Having suffered only light casualties, the defiant crowd is heard off stage marching on to liberate more villages. Of course, a more historically accurate version would have ended with their defeat, the actual fate of the Silesian uprising (and of most of Russia's pre-1905 textile strikes). But such a realistic ending, while transforming the play into a cautionary tale to discourage the rash, adventurous actions that Marxists warned against, would have defeated the courage-building purpose of revolutionary propagandists. For the translators to have tampered with Hauptmann's ending by calling excessive attention to the weavers' defeat would have made *The Weavers* a demoralizing story, with a chilling effect on potential mass action. Yet even Hauptmann's upbeat ending, retained in the translation, does gesture in the direction of realism by gently suggesting that some weavers know their efforts are fated to fail. One character is even permitted to speak of the hopelessness of the odds against them. There is nevertheless an irrepressible urge to act in the face of probable defeat, to continue the struggle for its own sake as an assertion of human values, a moral imperative, overcoming the shame of passivity and demonstrating the meaning of courage, of manhood, more in the spirit of the ethical idealism Lenin would claim to despise than of the scientific socialism he professed to love.

It would seem, then, that despite its partially triumphant ending, the play was far from being a harbinger of the crude, uplifting, socialist realism of the future, where defective characteristics are overcome, rather than being deployed in the battle, as they are in *The Weavers*. The play contained an "undialectical" core of existential rebellion, carried out by recognizably flawed human beings. The translation preserved the portrayal of the same "vices" that were so deplored elsewhere in the Russian Marxist literature, precisely the traits that Marxists wished to discourage in "advanced" or "conscious" workers: intoxication, religious sentiment, a passion for looting, personal acts of violence, arson, and Luddite machine-breaking. In the translation as in the original, these are not presented as deviations or side issues, but as central features of the weavers' movement, at times supported even by their more advanced, sophisticated leaders. Rather than being overcome, the ideological and behavioral imperfections of the workers are utilized in their struggle and absorbed into their heroism. This is almost the story of a peasant *bunt*, disguised as a workers' action. It was hardly a "strike" in the usual sense of the word (the term is avoided in the play), and the translators—who, as we have seen, while holding closely to the details of the plot, were prepared to take some liberties—even went so far as to introduce the Russian symbol of peasant arson, the red rooster (*krasnyi petukh*), a symbol that does not appear in the original. Yet the Russian Marxists chose this play, with all its contradictory moments, as their main contribution to the arsenal of translated propaganda literature for workers, believing quite plausibly that it would be successful enough to justify the time, risk, and expense of new editions, new translations, and secret performances. It was not only theory and practice that harbored contradictions but theory and literary representation. As Russian revolutionaries grasped, the categories of simple dramatic opposition were more powerful than the complexities of dialectical development. The heat and passion of drink and song, animal hatred and revenge, family and community loyalty could feed the common hunger for justice more powerfully than a correct class understanding of the forces and relations of production.

To be sure, this may have been made more palatable to a Leninist because the presence among the weavers of "vanguard" leaders, of a Bekker and a Ieger, would remind the reader that workers could not simply be left to their own devices; yet it cannot be ignored that these were leaders who fueled the passions of their followers with alcohol and vengeful song, raised their courage with feelings of religious exaltation, and, by their practice, taught them to reject industrial "progress." Could it be that these characteristics were always among the hidden wellsprings of Russia's evolving revolutionary movement, even accounting in part for its successes?

Writing a decade after the Bolshevik Revolution, Semen Kanatchikov, recalling his first youthful reading of *Tkachi* (which he finished in two sittings), wanted his readers to believe that the play had somehow failed to "satisfy" his needs, that in the end it made no contribution to the shaping of his "world outlook," or, we might add, to his notion of his adult self. But let doubters take note of Kanatchikov's own description of his immediate reaction, at the impressionable age of seventeen, to the text. We conclude with the words just preceding his expression of disappointment:

> The book made a rather strong impression on me. I soon learned the song of the weavers by heart and would recite it to the other apprentices of my age group in the workshop. The words kept echoing again and again in my ears. . . . The book had a very disturbing effect on me, stirring up my animosity toward the rich and my pity for the oppressed and awakening many new, previously unknown emotions.[29]

Postscript

With time, Hauptmann's plays would become a conventional offering in the repertory of Russian theater. In contrast to *Tkachi*, most of his plays were passed by the censors. Though daring and morally radical, the fact

[29] *A Radical Worker*, 33–34. Kanatchikov includes a stanza of the song where I have placed an ellipsis.

that Hauptmann would eschew such blatantly political and socially charged themes as were found in *Die Weber* helps account for the censors' tolerance of what appeared to be a "tamer" Hauptmann. This was especially true in the post-1905 years, when censorship became looser. By 1912 works of Hauptmann (excluding *Tkachi*) were even allowed into the repertory of a Petersburg acting ensemble targeted for workers and performed by workers, the choice of plays (in this case *Das Friedenfest*) now mimicking the repertories of Russia's state-sponsored and commercial theaters. At the same time the radical content of some of his earlier writings continued to generate heated debate, as in 1913, when members of another Petersburg workers' theater argued acrimoniously among themselves and then split over the issue of whether to sponsor pre-performance lectures by literary critics who failed to address the content of Hauptmann's works from a class perspective.[30]

[30] See Eugene A. Swift, "Workers' Theater and 'Proletarian Culture' in Pre-Revolutionary Russia," *Russian History / Histoire Russe* 23 (1996): 80–81, 86, 89.

CHAPTER TEN

Tolstoy's Diaries: The Inaccessible Self

IRINA PAPERNO

"God only knows how many diverse, captivating impressions and thoughts evoked by these impressions . . . pass in a single day. If it were only possible to render them in such a way that I could easily read myself and others could read me as I do" (1: 279 / 279).[1] This was the dream of the young Tolstoy: like Rousseau, he wanted to make himself into an open book.[2] Suspecting that "there is not enough ink in the world to write it, or typesetters to put it into print," he nevertheless embarked upon this project. A complete history of one day, the history of yesterday, remained unfinished. And yet, throughout his life, Tolstoy engaged in the continu-

The author is grateful to Laura Engelstein, Boris Gasparov, Boris Groys, Hugh McLean, William Nickell and Donna Orwin for their comments, suggestions, and editorial revisions. Unless otherwise indicated, excerpts from Tolstoy's diaries have been translated into English by John Randolph. For the Russian originals of Tolstoy's texts quoted in this essay, see a (fuller) version in the December 1999 issue of *Tolstoy Studies Journal* (vol. 11).

[1] From "Istoriia vcherashnego dnia" (1851). All references to Tolstoy's work are to the Jubilee edition, *Polnoe sobranie sochinenii v 90 tomakh* (Moscow: Khudozhestvenaia literatura, 1928–58). The English translation of "The History of Yesterday" is from *Tolstoy's Short Fiction*, ed. Michael R. Katz (New York: Norton, 1991), trans. George L. Kline. Here and below, the translation has been amended. The second number indicates the page in *Tolstoy's Short Fiction*.

[2] On Rousseau's project, see Jean Starobinski, *Jean-Jacques Rousseau: Transparency and Obstruction* (Chicago: University of Chicago Press, 1988), 182 and passim. Tolstoy's strategies of textualization of self were different than Rousseau's in his *Confessions*, but the original impulse could have come from Rousseau. Remembering this time later in life, Tolstoy claimed: "Many pages by him are so near to me, that it seems to me that I wrote them myself" (46: 317–18). Boris Eikhenbaum noted several parallels between the text of Tolstoy's early diaries and Rousseau's *Confessions* in his *Molodoi Tolstoi* (St. Petersburg: Grzhebin, 1922)—the first and most illuminating treatment of Tolstoy's early diaries (33–35).

ous narration of his daily history: he kept diaries.[3] The gigantic text of his diaries reflects Tolstoy's lifelong struggle with the constraints that narrative imposes on our ability to represent and know ourselves. It is believed that in his fiction Tolstoy succeeded in describing forms of human experience that had hitherto escaped representation: inner speech, subconscious processes, and dreams. In his diaries, the struggle continued on a daily basis; rooted in the mundane, it concerned his own self. This struggle became especially acute in his old age: the discoveries of Tolstoy the writer brought no relief. The despair that gripped the young diarist when he tried to capture his impressions and thoughts by "tracing letters on paper" (46: 65) remained with Tolstoy for life. This was more than a matter of rhetorical difficulty. Inherent in the structure of verbal narrative was a metaphysics of daily life—a philosophy that accorded linear temporal order a predominant role in shaping human life. This was a metaphysics of finitude. Ultimately, Tolstoy refused to accept that the self was limited to what could be told. In this sense, his dairies were a metaphysical quest.

Tolstoy's Early Diaries

Tolstoy's first diary, started in March 1847, at the age of eighteen, began as a clinical investigation launched under laboratory conditions: in the isolation of a hospital ward, where he was being treated for a venereal disease. A student at Kazan University, he was about to drop out for lack of academic progress. In the clinic, freed from external influences, the young man planned to "retreat into himself" (*vzoiti sam v sebia*; 46: 3). His introspection had a practical goal: the young Tolstoy planned to use his diary to exert control over his life. Keeping a diary was also a research project aimed at investigating the causes of events: the connection between external circumstances and inner states, and the relation between the physical and the moral. The goals were clear, but not the ways of attaining them. To begin with, the young diarist obviously found it difficult to sustain the flow of narrative. To fill the pages of his diary, Tolstoy gave an account of his reading (assigned by a professor of history)—Catherine

[3] Tolstoy (born in 1828) kept regular diaries between 1847 and 1857. Beginning in 1858 (soon after he started regularly producing fiction), Tolstoy neglected his diaries more and more. In the years 1858–65 he made only occasional notes; single notes were made in the years 1873 and 1878. The diary was resumed in 1881, when Tolstoy decided to abandon fiction writing, and maintained, with increasing regularity, until his death in 1910. Attention to the inverse relationship between writing diaries and writing fiction was drawn in Robert E. Gurley, "The Diaries of Leo Tolstoy: Their Literariness and Their Relation to His Literature" (Ph.D. Dissertation, University of Pennsylvania, 1979); Richard F. Gustafson, *Leo Tolstoy, Resident and Stranger: A Study in Fiction and Theology* (Princeton: Princeton University Press, 1986), 6–7, 88–89; and Donna Tussing Orwin, *Tolstoy's Art and Thought, 1847–1880* (Princeton: Princeton University Press, 1993), 218.

the Great's *Instruction* (*Nakaz*). This utopia of social order, which regulated relations of the future, and, especially, its philosophical foundation (happy is a man in whom will rules over passions and a state in which laws serve as an instrument of such control) appealed to the young Tolstoy. But with the account of *Nakaz* made on day two his diary came to an end.

Along with the first, hesitant diaries, for almost six months in 1847, Tolstoy kept a "Journal of Daily Occupations" ("Zhurnal ezhednevnykh zaniatii," 46: 245–61), whose main function was to account for the expenditure of time. In the journal, each page was divided into two vertical columns: one, marked "The Future," listed things he planned to do the next day; a parallel column, marked "The Past," contained comments (made a day later) on fulfillment of the plan. (The most frequent was "not quite," *nesovsem.*) There was no present. He also filled his notebooks with lists of rules: "Rules for Developing Will," "Rules in Life" (1847), "Rules" (1847 and 1853), and "Rules in General" (1850) (46: 262–76). With these journals Tolstoy created not a history, but a utopia of oneself: his personal *Nakaz*.

Yet another notebook, "Journal for Weaknesses" (Zhurnal dlia slabostei), or "Franklin journal," contained a list of moral weaknesses, arranged in columns (such as laziness, mendacity, indecision, sensuality, vanity), in which, in accordance with Benjamin Franklin's method, Tolstoy marked weaknesses that he exhibited each day by placing little crosses in the appropriate columns.[4] There was also an account book devoted to financial expenditures. On the whole, on the basis of these documents, it appeared that the condition of Tolstoy's moral and monetary economy was deplorable; yet another expenditure presented still graver problems: this was time.[5]

Between 1850 and 1857, Tolstoy kept regular diaries. Beginning in 1850, the time scheme of the "Journal of Daily Occupations" and the moral accounting of the Franklin journal were incorporated into one narrative. A day's entry was written from a specific reference point: yesterday's entry, which ended with a detailed schedule for the next day (under tomorrow's date). In the evening of the next day, Tolstoy reviewed what he had actually done, comparing the use of time to the plan made the previous day. He also commented on his actions, evaluating his performance on a general scale of moral values. The entry concluded with a

---

[4] On Franklin's method and its influence on Tolstoy, see Eikhenbaum, *Molodoi Tolstoi*, 26, and Viktor Shklovskii, *Lev Tolstoi* [1963], 2d ed. (Moscow: Molodaia guardiia, 1967), 73.

[5] Historians of private life have connected the practice of diary writing with anxieties about death. A companion of the account book, the diary was a means to stem the expenditure of life. See Alain Corbin, "Backstage," in *A History of Private Life*, ed. Michelle Perrot, vol. 4 (Cambridge, Mass.: Harvard University Press, 1990), 498–502.

plan of action and a time schedule for yet another day. The following entry (from March 1851) is typical for the 1850s:

> 24. Arose somewhat late and read, but did not have time to write. Poiret came, I fenced, and did not send him away (*sloth and cowardice*). Ivanov came, I spoke with him for too long (*cowardice*). Koloshin (Sergei) came to drink vodka, I did not escort him out (*cowardice*). At Ozerov's argued about nothing (*habit of arguing*) and did not talk about what I should have talked about (*cowardice*). Did not go to Beklimishev's (*weakness of energy*). During gymnastics did not walk the rope (*cowardice*), and did not do one thing because it hurt (*sissiness*).—At Gorchakov's lied (*lying*). Went to the Novotroitsk tavern (*lack of fierté*). At home did not study English (*insufficient firmness*). At the Volkonskys' was unnatural and distracted, and stayed until one in the morning (*distractedness, desire to show off, and weakness of character*).
> 25. [plan for the next day, written on the 24th] From 10 to 11 yesterday's diary and reading. From 11 to 12—gymnastics. From 12 to 1—English. *Beklemishev and Beyer* from 1 to 2. From 2 to 4—on horseback. From 4 to 6—dinner. From 6 to 8—read. From 8 to 10—write.—Translate something from a foreign language into Russian to develop memory and style.—To write today with all the impressions and thoughts it gives rise to.—
> 25. Awoke late out of *sloth*. Wrote my diary and did gymnastics, *hurrying*. Did not study English out of *sloth*. With Begichev and with Islavin was *vain*. At Beklemishev's *was cowardly* and *lack of fierté*. On Tver boulevard *wanted to show off*. I did not walk on foot to the Kalymazhnyi Dvor (*sissiness*). Rode with a desire to show off. For the same reason rode to Ozerov's.—Did not return to Kalymazhnyi, *thoughtlessness*. At the Gorchakovs' dissembled and did not call things by their name, *fooling myself*. Went to L'vov's out of *insufficient energy* and the *habit of doing nothing*. Sat around at home *out of absentmindedness* and read Werther inattentively, *hurrying*. (46: 55)

A plan for the future as much as an account of the present, this diary is prescriptive as much as descriptive. In the evening of each day, Tolstoy reads the present as a failure to live up to the expectations of the past and anticipates a future that will embody his vision. The next day, he again records what went wrong today with yesterday's tomorrow.[6] Wanting reality to live up to his moral ideal, he forces the past to meet the future.

In his attempt to create an ordered account of time (and thus a moral order), Tolstoy's greatest difficulty is capturing the present. Indeed, today makes its first appearance in the diary as tomorrow, embedded in the previous day. (In the plan for tomorrow, infinitive forms of the verbs are used.) On the evening of today, when Tolstoy writes his diary, today is al-

---

[6] The concept of "yesterday's tomorrow" was, of course, inspired by Reinhart Koselleck's *vergangene Zukunft*; in English, *Futures Past: On the Semantics of Historical Time*, trans. Keith Tribe (Cambridge, Mass.: MIT Press, 1985).

ready the past. (The past tense of the verbs is used.) His daily account ends with a vision of another tomorrow. (Since it appears under tomorrow's date, it masquerades as today, but the infinitive forms of the verbs point to timelessness.) In the diaries (unlike in the "Journal of Daily Occupations"), the present is accorded a place, but it is deprived of even a semblance of autonomy: the present is a space where the past and future overlap. It appears that the narrative order of the diary simply does not allow one to account for the present.

One of the notebooks that belonged to the adolescent Tolstoy contains the following excerpt, identified by the commentators as a language exercise: "Le passé est ce qui fut, le futur est ce qui sera, et le présent est ce qui n'est pas.—C'est pour cela que la vie de l'homme ne consiste que dans le futur et le passé et c'est pour la même raison que le bonheur que nous voulons posséder n'est qu'une chimìre de même que le présent" (1: 217). The problem that troubled the young Tolstoy was, of course, a common one, and had a long history. It was Augustine, in Book 11 of the *Confessions,* who first expressed his bewilderment: what is time? He argued: the future is not yet there, the past is no longer there, and the present does not remain. Does time, then, have a real being? What is the present? The day? But "not even one day is entirely present." Some hours of the day are in the future, some in the past. The hour? But the hour is itself constituted of "fugitive moments." In Augustine's words, "the present occupies no space." Augustine's solution was to place the past and the future within the human soul (or mind), as memory and expectation. As images "fixed in the mind like imprints," the past and the future lie within the present, which thus acquires a semblance of being.[7] For centuries philosophers continued to refine and transform these arguments. By the 1850s, after Kant and Schopenhauer, the theme of the being and nonbeing of time in its relation to human consciousness was a topic of language exercises that occupied adolescents. Since the late eighteenth century time—known through the mind of the perceiving individual—had also been a subject of narrative experiments undertaken by novelists. In his later years as a novelist, Tolstoy would play a decisive role in the neverending endeavor to catch time in the act. In the 1850s, in his personal diary he was designing his first, homemade methods of managing the flow of time by narrative means. Fixed in the diary, the past would remain with him; planned in writing, the future was already there. Creating a future past and a present future, the diarist relieved some of the anxieties of

---

[7] In formulating Augustine's views on time, I was aided by Henry Chadwick's translation (Oxford University Press edition of 1991) and Paul Ricoeur's analysis of Augustine's *Confessions* (Paul Ricoeur, *Time and Narrative,* 3 vols. [Chicago: University of Chicago Press, 1984–85], 1: 7–9).

watching life pass. But in one domain his efforts fell short of the ideal: not even one day was entirely present.

"The History of Yesterday"

In March 1851 Tolstoy embarked on a project he had long envisioned: to write a complete account of a single day, given from within. His choice fell on March 25 (Annunciation Day). An outgrowth of the diary, this account was entitled "The History of Yesterday" (Istoriia vcherashnego dnia); it was conceived as an experiment: where would narrative take him?

It turned out that after about twenty-four hours of writing (spread over a three-week period), Tolstoy was still at the start of the day. Having filled what amounts to twenty-six pages of a printed text, he abandoned his "History." By that time, Tolstoy could have known that the enterprise was doomed not only because of the physical limitations of the medium ("there is not enough ink in the world") but also because of to the constraints inherent in the nature of the narrative process.

"The History of Yesterday" starts in the morning: "I arose late yesterday—at a quarter to ten." What follows is a causal explanation that relates the given event to an earlier event, which happened on the day before yesterday: "—because I had gone to bed after midnight." At this point, the account is interrupted by a parenthetical remark which places the second event within a system of general rules: "(It has long been my rule never to retire after midnight, yet this happens to me about three times a week)." The story resumes with a detailed description of those circumstances which had led to the second event (going to bed after midnight): "I was playing cards" (1: 279 / 279). The account of action is interrupted by another digression—the narrator's reflections on the nature of society games. After a page and a half, Tolstoy returns to the game of cards. The narrative proceeds, slowly and painfully, tracing not so much the external actions as the webs of the protagonist / narrator's mental activity—reflections that accompanied the action and those that accompany the act of narration, fusing the two levels. After many digressions, the "History" follows the protagonist home and ends with an elaborate description of his dream, leaving the hero at the threshhold of "yesterday."

What, then, is time? In Tolstoy's "History," the day (a seemingly natural unit of time) starts in the morning, moves rapidly to the previous evening, and then slowly makes its way back, toward the morning. Time flows backward, making a circle. And in the end, Tolstoy wrote not a history of yesterday, but a history of the day before yesterday.

In Tolstoy's work, this pattern played itself out once again when, in 1856, he started working on a historical novel (the future *War and Peace*). As he later described it, Tolstoy's original plan was to write a novel about the Decembrists. He set the action in the present, in 1856: an elderly Decembrist returns to Moscow from Siberian exile. But before Tolstoy could move any further, he felt compelled to interrupt the narrative progression: "involuntarily I passed from today to 1825" (that is, to the Decembrist uprising). In order to understand his hero in 1825, he then turned to the formative events of the war with Napoleon: "I once again discarded what I had begun and started to write from the time of 1812." "But then for a third time I put aside what I had begun"—Tolstoy now turned to 1805 (the dawn of the Napoleonic age in Russia) (13: 54).[8] Timewise, the narrative did not progress, but regressed. In both a piece of personal history, "The History of Yesterday," and the historical novel *War and Peace*, Tolstoy turned the initial event into an end point of a chain of preceding events, locked in a causal dependency by the implications of the narrative order. Such was the inescapable logic of historical narrative.

In "The History of Yesterday," temporal refraction does not stop with a shift from the target day to the preceding day. In the very description of "the day before yesterday" time also does not progress: it is pulled apart to fit an array of simultaneous actions. The game of cards has come to an end. The narrator is standing by the card table involved in a (mostly silent) conversation with the hostess. It is time to leave, but taking leave does not come easily to the young man; nor is it easy to tell the story of leaving:

> I looked at my watch and got up. . . . Because she wished to end this conversation which I found so sweet, or to see how I would refuse, or because she simply wished to continue playing, she looked at the figures which were written at the table, drew the chalk across the table—making a figure that could be classified neither as mathematical nor pictorial—looked at her husband, then between him and me, and said: "Let's play three more rubbers." I was so absorbed in the contemplation not of her movements alone, but of everything that is called *charme*, which it is impossible to describe, that my imagination was very far away, and I did not have time to clothe my words in a felicitous form; I simply said: "No, I can't." Before I had finished saying this I began to regret it,—that is, not all of me, but a certain part of me. . . .
>
> —I suppose this part spoke very eloquently and persuasively (although I cannot convey this), for I became alarmed and began to cast about for arguments.—In the first place, I said to myself, there is no great pleasure in it, you

---

[8] From "Vstupleniia, predisloviia, i varianty nachal 'Voiny i mira' " (undated) (13: 53–55). On these aspects of the history of *War and Peace*, see Boris Eikhenbaum, *Lev Tolstoi: shestidesiatye gody* (Moscow: Khudozhestvennaia literatura, 1931), 208–9.

do not really like her, and you're in an awkward position; besides, you've already said that you can't stay, and you fell in her estimation. . . .

"*Comme il est aimable, ce jeune homme.*"

This sentence, which followed immediately after mine, interrupted my reflections.—I began to make excuses, to say I couldn't stay, but since one does not have to think to make excuses, I continued reasoning with myself: How I love to have her speak of me in the third person. In German this is rude, but I would love it even in German. . . . "Stay for supper," said her husband.—As I was busy with my reflections on the formula of the third person, I did not notice that my body, while very properly excusing itself for not being able to stay, was putting down the hat again and sitting down quite coolly in an easy chair. It was clear that my mind was taking no part in this absurdity. (1: 282–83/282–83)

Done from memory, in the past tense, this narrative nevertheless strives to imitate a notation of the immediate experience—something like a stenographic transcription of the human consciousness involved in the act of apprehending itself. As an external observer, Tolstoy can only guess at what goes on in his object's mind. As a self-narrator who describes "the behind-the-soul side of life in one day" (*zadushevnuiu storonu zhizni odnogo dnia*, 46: 279), he faces other difficulties: dealing with internal multiplicity—with splits between speech, thought, and bodily movement, with ambivalent desires, with a dialectical drama that stands behind a motive. There is yet another layer: the splitting of self into a protagonist and a narrator, who operate in two different times. Moreover, the narrator is involved in reflections not only on the process of narrating, but also on general (meta-) problems in the "historiography" of the self. And he keeps referring to the residue of that which cannot be expressed and explained.

All of this entails the most serious consequences for narrative time. In narrative representation, one event by rule follows upon another. Unbeknown to the young Tolstoy, Kant deplored this rule in *The Critique of Pure Reason*. Kant argued: "the apprehension of the manifold of appearance is always succesive"; "the representations of the parts" succeed one another. It does not follow, however, that what we represent is also in itself successive; this only means that we "cannot arrange the apprehension otherwise than in this very succession." This is the way "in which we are first led to construct for ourselves the concept of cause": succession suggests causality.[9] Unfamiliar with academic philosophy and its rules, the young Tolstoy attempted to stretch the temporality of his narrative to account for actions and processes that occur as if simultaneously.[10] As a re-

[9] *Immanuel Kant's Critique of Pure Reason,* trans. Norman Kemp Smith (New York: St. Martin's Press, 1965), 218–23. (*Kritik der reinen Vernunft,* II.3.B. [Zweite Analogie].)

[10] Discussing Tolstoy's "History of Yesterday," Shklovskii commented: "Time is pulled apart, broadened, lengthened, as it were" (*Lev Tolstoi,* 78).

sult, he extended time beyond the endurance of the narrative form: the story broke off. The narrator who describes his own being from within knows more than he can possibly tell. Is it humanly possible to give an account of even one day in one's own life?

There were, of course, cultural precedents. Tolstoy's narrative strategies were largely borrowed from Laurence Sterne, who, along with Rousseau, was among his first mentors.[11] Informed by Locke's philosophy, Sterne's narrative strategy was to make the protagonist / narrator's consciousness the locus of action. Unlike Augustine, Locke hoped that "time itself" could be captured. In his *Essay Concerning Human Understanding*, Locke derived the idea of time (that is, duration) and the sense of self (the duration of ourselves) from the perception that there was a train of ideas which constantly succeed one another in our minds.[12] Sterne followed suit by laying bare the flow of associations in the mind of the narrator.[13] But Sterne's "realistic" representation revealed flaws in Locke's argument: successive representation could not catch up with the manifold perceptions of a human mind; the narrative did not progress.

By mimicking Sterne's narrative strategy, young Tolstoy learned his first lessons in epistemology: the Cartesian shift to the point of view of the perceiving individual, the dualism of the outer and the inner worlds, and the dependence of personal identity on the ability to extend consciousness backward to a past action. Proceeding by way of a narrative experiment, Tolstoy also confronted the restrictions placed on our representations of time—limitations that he would continue to challenge throughout his life, even after 1869 when he read, and fully appreciated Kant.

In his early diaries and in "The History of Yesterday," Tolstoy discovered that there was no history of today. Even in a record that is almost concurrent with experience, there is no present. A history is a history of yesterday. Moreover, writing a history of the individual, a self-history, he was confronted with a need to account not only for the order of events but also for a whole other domain: the inner life. The opening up of the inner life led to further temporal refraction: from an inside point of view,

---

[11] Tolstoy's involvement with Sterne (in 1851, he translated *The Sentimental Journey* as an exercise in style) and the use of Sterne's techniques in "The History of Yesterday" were noted in commentaries to the Jubilee edition (1: 301 and 343). See also Boris Eikhenbaum, *Lev Tolstoi: Piatidesiatye gody* (Leningrad: Priboi, 1928), 54; also Peter Rudy, "Lev Tolstoj's Apprenticeship to Laurence Sterne," *The Slavic and East European Journal*, 15, no. 1 (1971): 1–21.

[12] Paraphrasing paragraphs 2 and 3 of Chapter 14, Book 2, of John Locke's *Essay Concerning Human Understanding.*

[13] On Sterne and his connection to Locke, see Ian Watt, *The Rise of the Novel* (Berkeley: University of California Press, 1957). (I used Watt's formulations on pp. 290–95 as well as Locke's formulations from Book 2, Chapter 14, paragraphs 2–4.) John Traugott, in *Tristram Shandy's World* (Berkeley: University of California Press, 1954), has challenged some of the established views on the philosophical origin and meaning of Sterne's rhetoric.

it appeared that behind an event or action there stood a whole array of simultaneous processes. This led to another discovery.

Let us return to the scene by the card table. Tolstoy indicates that the woman's remark, "*Comme il est aimable, ce jeune homme,*" immediately followed his statement "No, I can't," interrupting his reflections. A question arises: when (or, in spatial terms, where) did his lengthy reflections take place? The present seems to have an extension behind the scene. Since Augustine, it had been believed that the present has no duration or length; young Tolstoy found out that the present had depth: life has hidden recesses outside time and space.

"The History of Yesterday": The Dream

Tolstoy's investigation into the nature of time and consciousness continues in the representation of the dream. The narrator / protagonist observes and records the very process of the dissolution of his consciousness: the "I" abandons himself to sleep, writing as if from dictation; at the same time, the "I" makes self-observations and meta-remarks. Such narrative would seem impossible, and yet Tolstoy writes it. (If this is possible, it would also seem possible to leave an account of one's own death.) Here is the text of the dream:

"Morpheus, enfold me in your embrace." This Divinity whose priest I would willingly become. And do you remember how the lady was offended when they said to her: "Quand je suis passé chez vous, vous étiez encore dans les bras de Morphée." She thought Morphée was a name like André or Malapheé. What a comical name! . . . A splendid expression, *dans les bras;* I picture to myself so clearly and elegantly the condition *dans les bras,*—and especially clearly the *bras* themselves—arms bare to the shoulder, with little dimples and creases, and a white chemise indiscreetly open.—How wonderful arms are in general, especially that one little dimple!—I stretched. Do you remember, Saint Thomas forbade stretching. He looks like Diedrichs. We rode with him on horseback. What a fine hunting it was, how Gelke, riding beside the policeman, hallooed, and Nalyot was doing his best, even on the frozen mud. How vexed Serezha was! He is at sister's.—What a treasure Masha is—if only I could find such a wife! Morpheus would be good on a hunt, only he would have to ride naked, or else you might find a wife.—Oh, how Saint Thomas is tearing along—and the lady has already set off to overtake them all; only she shouldn't have stretched out, but then that wonderful *dans les bras.*—Here I suppose I went to sleep completely.—I dreamt that I wanted to overtake the lady, suddenly there was a mountain, I pushed it with my hands, pushed it again—it collapsed (I threw down the pillow) and I came home for dinner. Not ready yet. Why not?—Vasilii was swaggering loudly (it was the landlady behind the partition asking what the noise was, and the chambermaid answering her; I heard this, that is why I dreamt it). Vasily came in just as everyone wanted to ask him why it wasn't ready. They saw that Vasilii was in a frock coat and a ribbon across his chest; I became frightened, I fell on my knees, cried, and kissed his hands; it was as pleasant to me as though I were kissing her hands—even more so. (1: 291–92 / 291–92)

For Tolstoy, representing a dream is an opportunity to free the narrative from the rule of succession and implied causality: instead, the principle of association of words, memories, and bodily sensations rules the text. The starting point is a verbal formula related to the theme of dreaming: "Morpheus, enfold me in your embrace." The narrative unfolds through a series of associations with the initial idiom, *dans les bras*. The body then takes over the verbal consciousness: the next step is physical—an involuntary movement ("I stretched"). It evokes a memory of childhood: Tolstoy's tutor, St. Thomas, admonishing the boy ("St. Thomas forbade stretching"). The theme of horseback riding, with its obvious physicality, enters at this point and expands into a hunting theme, replete with erotic imagery. When the dream makes a circle, returning to the initial formula, *dans les bras*, the process of losing consciousness is complete: "Here I suppose I went to sleep completely." (However, the narrative continues.) In addition to the obvious associative connections, there is a subliminal layer: the image of St. Thomas has biographical underpinnings; the episode of kissing the servant's hands has a literary subtext (in Pushkin's *Captain's Daughter*). (These underpinnings have been revealed by Tolstoy's biographers.)[14] This order, akin to the one described in Locke's *Essay* and enacted in Sterne's prose, is radically different from the one described by Kant: the order allied by reason and used in traditional narratives.

In the second part of his dream narrative, Tolstoy goes beyond his predecessors: showing the ways in which consciousness deals with external impressions or physical stimuli ("I threw down the pillow," "the landlady behind the partition"), he suggests that the temporal / causal order known to us from logical narratives might be illusory. In sleep, freed from the constraints of common sense, human consciousness mixes external impressions and creations of the imagination, arranging them into plots. On several occasions, dream consciousness refigures physical time and causal order. This is how (further in his "History") Tolstoy described this type of dreams: "you have a long dream which ends with the circumstance

---

[14] Although Tolstoy gave no indication of this in the text, St. Thomas is an emotional knot connecting the dream lines: he was little Tolstoy's tutor, a Frenchman who wanted to marry a rich Russian lady; he offended the boy, threatening him with corporal punishment. Tolstoy kept returning to the memory of this episode throughout his life. See Shklovskii, *Lev Tolstoi*, 79. For information on appearances of St. Thomas in Tolstoy's writing, see commentaries to the Jubilee edition, 53: 453, n. 385.

that awakened you: you dream that you are going hunting, you load your gun, flush the game, take aim, fire—and the noise which you take for the shot is the carafe which you knocked onto the floor in your sleep" (1: 293 / 293). In physical time, the gun shot (an external occurrence) is an impulse that initiates narrative consciousness; in dream time, the gun shot concludes a whole sequence of events, constructed retroactively. Like time in "The History of Yesterday" as a whole, dream time moves from the present (the initial external event) to the past, and then makes its way back to the initial event, catching up with the present at the moment of awakening. The effect comes before the cause. Most importantly, since the moment of awakening is simultaneous with the initial impulse, in the dream, as in the conversation with the woman at the card table, the action occurs as if in some hidden recess of time.

The so-called "retrospective dreams" were known to psychologists and philosophers of Tolstoy's generation.[15] Perhaps the most famous of such dreams is Alfred Maury's vision of the French Revolution reported in his popular *Le sommeil et les rêves* (1861). In his dream Maury witnessed scenes of the Revolution, met Robespierre and Marat, and himself fell victim to the terror: condemned to death, he mounted the scaffold, put his head under the guillotine, and sensed how his head was separating from the body. At this moment he awoke—to discover that a section of the bed had fallen and struck him on the back of his neck. Also widely known was Napoleon's dream retold in A. Garnier's *Traité des facultés de l'âme* (1852). Asleep in his carriage, Napoleon dreamt that he was crossing the

---

[15] See the following books: L.-F. Alfred Maury, *Le sommeil et les rêves* (Paris, 1861) (it was preceded by excerpts in the medical journal *Annales médico-psychologiques* in 1848 and 1853); A. Garnier's *Traité des facultés de l'âme, contenant l'histoire des principales théories psychologiques* (Paris, 1852); Anonymous [Marquis d'Hervey de Saint-Denis], *Les rêves et les moyens de les diriger* (Paris, 1867), 110–11, 266–67, 386–403; F. W. Hildebrandt, *Der Traum und seine Verwertung für's Leben* (Leipzig, 1875) (37–39 of the 2nd, 1881 edition); and J. Volkelt, *Die Traumphantasie* (Stuttgart, 1875), 108. Carl Du Prel offered a metaphysical interpretation of retrospective dreams (an opening into the transcendental) in *Die Philosophie der Mystik* (Leipzig, 1885). At the turn of the century, reports of such dreams were challenged by scientists. See the 1894–95 debate in *Revue philosophique* (Jacques Le Lorrain, "De la durée du temps dans les rêves," vol. 38, 1894; Victor Egger, "La durée apparente des rêves," vol. 40, 1895; Le Lorrain, "Le rêve," ibid.). See also the dissertation by J. Tobowolska, *Etude sur les illusions de temps dans les rêves du sommeil normal* (1900). In his *Interpretation of Dreams* (1900), Freud discussed such dreams as specific distortions of thought processes (see *The Standard Edition of the Complete Psychological Works of Sigmund Freud*, vol. 4 [London: Hogarth Press, 1953], 26–29 and passim). Among philosophers who struggled with the linearity of time, Bergson wrote about retrospective dreams in *Le rêve* (1901) and, in Russia, Pavel Florensky in *Ikonostas* (1922). For Florensky, a twentieth-century scientist-mystic, dream time was an instance of relativity, testifying to the real presence of the transcendental in human life. (See Pavel Florenskii, *Sobranie sochinenii*, vol. 1 [Paris, 1985], 194–202.) (Florensky mentioned Du Prel, but did not acknowledge Du Prel's importance for his own ideas). For a present-day discussion of dream time, see B. A. Uspenskii, "Istoriia i semiotika (Vospriiatie vremeni kak semioticheskaia problema)," *Trudy po znakovym sistemam*, no. 22 (Tartu, 1988).

Tagliamento; at the moment when, in his dream, the Austrians started bombarding, he was awakened by a bomb explosion. Remarkably, it was history—and recent history, such as the French Revolution and the Napoleonic wars—that provided the material for the much-cited retrospective dreams. It seems unlikely, however, that young Tolstoy knew of these psychological studies in 1851; most probably, he discovered the reverse temporality and inverted logic of dream narratives from personal experience. This discovery held enormous potential for his experiments with narrative time (in later years, Tolstoy would use this discovery in his struggle with the metaphysics of finitude).

In the 1850s the young Tolstoy interpreted his discovery as a psychological phenomenon which had immediate implications for the task of representing reality. The dream narratives offered one representation of time; traditional narratives, another. Thus, in "The History of Yesterday" Tolstoy suggested that many a person, including himself, would be inclined to relate such a dream as a logically coherent structure with a linear temporal development. The reason lay in "being accustomed to continuity and to the form of time in which life manifests itself" (1: 293/293). While in the dream the mind seems instantly to invent—in retrospect—a whole sequence of events to explain the initial impression, in the act of remembering and narrating this dream the order of occurrences is regrouped in favor of sequential linearity.

Several years later, working on *War and Peace*, Tolstoy drew further conclusions from the discoveries made in "The History of Yesterday," which concerned not only psychology and narratology but also historiography. As he wrote in the preface to *War and Peace*, trying to find out how we represent historical events, he discovered that lying was inherent in the very act of verbal description. (He wrote of "the necessity to lie, stemming from the need to describe in only a few words the actions of thousands of people, spread over several miles.") A person who wants to find out "how things are" exchanges the "infinitely diverse and vague impressions" that formed inside him for "a deceitful but clear . . . representation" (16: 10–11). Some translate "infinitely diverse" impressions into logical, linear narratives; others provide retroactive justifications of events akin to the inverted logic of dreams. From his "observations on human psychology" Tolstoy concluded that what obstructs access to things "as they really are" is "the ability of man to retroactively and instantaneously fabricate an entire array of seemingly free deductions for every occurred fact" (16: 15).[16] In the novel itself, Tolstoy showed various forms of "false narratives" mis-

---

[16] As Shklovskii put it, in *War and Peace* Tolstoy returned "to a psychology of dreams, which 'fabricate causes' " (*Lev Tolstoi*, 292).

representing actual events.[17] He seems to suspect that histories (not only histories of individuals but also histories of nations), like retroactive dreams, are instant inventions of the past aimed at explaining the present. Thus, in *War and Peace* Tolstoy turned the self-analysis performed in "The History of Yesterday" into a philosophy of historical representation.

In their classical studies, Boris Eikhenbaum and Viktor Shklovsky presented the diaries of the young Tolstoy and his "History of Yesterday" as, first and foremost, laboratories that developed the techniques for his future works of fiction.[18] Other scholars have productively viewed Tolstoy's early and late diaries from this and other perspectives.[19] In this article, I view the whole corpus of Tolstoy's diaries as a project of independent value: an attempt to create not works of literature (and not private chronicles), but a book of life—to turn the whole of oneself into a book. The project was doomed, but the process proved to be fruitful. He found himself pursuing two strategies that alternated and competed with each other. In diaries and notebooks, the young Tolstoy subjects his life to a narrative, temporal, and moral grid, aimed both at ordering his life and capturing the ever elusive essence of experience. In "The History of Yesterday," he attempts to represent life as it is, transcending the limitations of narrative, such as the forms of sequential time and causal logic, the need for coherent meaning and closure, and the division between the subject and object. But in the end the ever-expanding flow of consciousness erodes the narrative. Moreover, what Tolstoy could not transcend were the constraints of consciousness itself: self-consciousness pursues the writer even into sleep, weaving a text. And yet the text of his diaries was more adequate to life and to self as we know them in experience: fragmented, inconsistent, and inevitably incomplete.[20] This text implied an al-

---

[17] On the variety of false historical narratives in *War and Peace*, see Gary Saul Morson, *Hidden in Plain View: Narrative and Creative Potentials in 'War and Peace'* (Stanford: Stanford University Press, 1987).

[18] See Eikhenbaum, *Molodoi Tolstoi*, 13; idem, *Lev Tolstoi: piatidesiatye gody*, 34–35; Shklovskii, *Lev Tolstoi*, 77–78; and idem, " 'Istoriia vcherashnego dnia' v obshchem khode trudovykh dnei pisatelia Tolstogo," *Khudozhestvennaia proza: razmyshleniia i razbory* (Moscow: Sovetskii pisatel', 1959), 421–25.

[19] Among (the not very numerous) works on Tolstoy's diaries, the unpublished 1979 doctoral dissertation of Robert E. Gurley, "The Diaries of Leo Tolstoy," which focuses on the "literariness" of the diaries, deserves special mention. (I am indebted to Gary Saul Morson for the opportunity to benefit from this little-known work.) Morson discussed Tolstoy's late diaries as a communicative act in his *Hidden in Plain View*, arguing that from the point of view of the genre's "presumption of privacy," Tolstoy's journals, which include "an audience of eavesdroppers," is a highly compromised document (29–32).

[20] Cf. Paul Ricoeur's observation on the narrative structure of psychoanalytic interviews: "a history that would remain inconsistent, incoherent, or incomplete would clearly resemble what we know of the course of life in ordinary experience" ("The Question of Proof in

ternative metaphysics of daily life as well as an alternative philosophy of history.

Tolstoy's Late Diaries

In 1881, after a long interruption, Tolstoy resumed a regular diary, maintained until his death in 1910. The diaries of Tolstoy's late years are written in view of approaching death. For no less than thirty years, beginning in the 1880s, Tolstoy expected death daily. This existential situation called for a special time scheme: in the late diaries, the account of a day usually ends not with a plan for tomorrow, but with a formula "*esli budu zhiv*" ("if I am alive," usually abbreviated "*e.b.zh.*"), which follows tomorrow's date. An account of tomorrow starts with a confirmation, "alive":

> [Written on 24 February.] 25 Feb. N[ikol'skoe]. 1897. *E.b.zh.*
> 25 February [1897]. Alive. Did not write much, but not as easily as yesterday. Went for a walk, twice. Read Aristotle. Today received letters with Serezha who came here. Unpleasant letter from S[onia]. Or rather I am in a bad mood. Yesterday, during a walk, prayed, and experienced a wonderful feeling. It was probably like the feeling that mystics evoke with the Jesus prayer: I felt solely my spiritual self, free, tied down by an illusion of the body.
> 26 F. 97. *E.b.zh.* (53: 141)

From his early years, Tolstoy's narrative utopia was to render life in its entirety. This involved writing one's life to its end. Concluding the account of "today," the formula *e.b.zh.* (under tomorrow's date) not only problematizes, but also posits a "tomorrow"—a point from which today appears as yesterday, that is, as "history." It would seem that the late Tolstoy aspired to produce a diary in which the account of each day—including the last day in his life—would be written as the history of yesterday. His personal history would thus be a total history of the evolving present.

The same diary entry that creates a grid fit to capture time in its entirety reveals an alternative, and competing, aspiration: to achieve the narrative-free and timeless consciousness of self—a different self—through an act akin to the mystical Jesus prayer.[21] The practice of the Jesus prayer ("internal prayer," or "wisdom act" [*umnoe delanie*]), which originated in the hesychast tradition of Orthodox spirituality, relied on the nonverbal. In

Freud's Psychoanalytic Writings," *Journal of the American Psychoanalytic Association* 25, no. 4, [1977]: 862.)
[21] Richard Gustafson, in *Leo Tolstoy: Resident and Stranger*, emphasized the importance of prayer for Tolstoy. Gustafson insists that Tolstoy was guided by the religious principles of Eastern Christianity, including the Jesus prayer (see 10–11, 326–37, and 416–17).

its basic form, the prayer is performed by perpetually repeating the name "Jesus." As one enters into a mystical state, the word loses its external form, its linguistic encasement; in silence, man unites with the divine (this state is accompanied by a vision of light). Tolstoy, it would seem, faced a dilemma: a total articulation of self or a total silence? In his late diaries, he fluctuated between the two goals, at times, in confusion, at times, in an attempt at reconciliation.

In his aspiration to provide a complete account of his "last day," Tolstoy also relied on cultural precedents. Along with some of his contemporaries, he was inspired by Victor Hugo's *Le dernier jour d'un condamné* (1829). A fictive diary of a man condemned to death, the story records the hero's feelings, thoughts, and impressions in the last day of his life. In *The Idiot* (1868), Dostoevsky extended Hugo's image into a metaphor of the human condition in the nineteenth century: a whole life, when lived in full awareness of one's finitude, becomes the last day of a *condamné*.[22] In his diary from 1909, Tolstoy used Hugo's image, as it was interpreted by Dostoevsky, to describe his personal situation: "In one's old age, one can and even should do this, although this is possible already in one's youth, namely, assume the condition not only of a man sentenced to death but of a man transported to the place of execution" (January 3, 1909; 57: 4). For Tolstoy, as for Dostoevsky, the situation of a condemned man provided a unique narrative potential: to give a transcription of completely authentic experience—a Heideggerian being-toward-death *avant la lettre*. In his late diaries Tolstoy meant to give exactly such an account. It could be that he hoped to do even more. Hugo's *Le dernier jour* stopped at the moment when the hero was about to climb the scaffold and face the guillotine. Unlike Maury in his famous dream, Hugo's condemned man did not relate the experience of how his head was separated from his body. But Tolstoy hoped to do so, as if asking himself: if self-consciousness were to pursue the writer even into death, what kind of text would he produce?

But first, what was to be done on one's last day? Starting his diary for the new year 1908 (in which he turned eighty), Tolstoy defined the agenda: "liberate one's soul" (56: 88). The account of his last day—which lasted some thirty years—reflects this process. In recording his routine occupations, the diarist documented not the course of his daily life but that of his daily struggle with his earthly self: bodily desires, habits, and, finally, consciousness itself.

[22] On the use of this metaphor by Dostoevsky, see A. L. Bem, "Pered litsom smerti" [1936], *O Dostojevském. Sborník statí a materiálu* (Prague, 1972), 168–69; Liza Knapp, *The Annihilation of Inertia: Dostoevsky and Metaphysics* (Evanston, Ill.: Northwestern University Press, 1996), 67–75 and 84–96; Irina Paperno, *Suicide as a Cultural Institution in Dostoevsky's Russia* (Ithaca: Cornell University Press, 1997), 128–31.

True to his task, Tolstoy faithfully—and joyfully—recorded signs of the deterioration of his body and the failings of his memory. It proved to be much more difficult to account for the workings of the soul, the inner life. In one entry (from March 1908) Tolstoy addressed this problem: "My internal labor, thank God, goes without stopping, better and still better. I want to write about what happens inside me and how it happens, about things I have never told anyone and about which no one knows." He proceeded, however, to give a summary account of his external life:

> This is how I live: I get up, my head is clear, good thoughts occur to me, and, as I sit on the pot, I write them down. I get dressed and I empty the contents of the pot with an effort but with pleasure. I go for a walk. On my walk I wait for the post from force of habit, although I don't need it. I often guess to myself how many steps it will take to get to such and such a place, and I count them dividing each into four, six, and eight breaths: one and a and a and a; and two and a and a and a. . . . Sometimes, from force of habit, I want to guess that if there are as many steps as I suppose, all will be well. But then I ask myself: what is "well"? And I know that everything is very well as it is, and there's no need to try and guess. Then, when I meet someone, I try to remember—though for the most part I forget that I wanted to remember—that He and I are one. It's particularly difficult to remember this during a conversation. (56: 109–10)[23]

This account reflects an ambivalence in Tolstoy's situation: striving to free himself from bodily constraints, he describes the ways in which the body asserts its habitual power over the soul (and the old habit of living for the future intrudes with an innocent game of guessing how many steps it will take to get to a place). Curiously enough, the inner life remains inaccessible to the author of *War and Peace* and *Anna Karenina*: in the end, Tolstoy gives an account of his daily routine.

Interspersed among accounts of quotidian chores were Tolstoy's philosophical reflections on the nature of the body, consciousness, time, and space. Like his beloved Schopenhauer in *Parerga und Paralipomena*, Tolstoy in his diary expressed personal preoccupations in the aphoristic language of metaphysics. Disgusted with his body, which provided evidence of man's perishable nature on a daily basis, Tolstoy toyed with a definition of self as the body: "Yes, I—the body—am such a disgusting chamber pot—just remove or open the lid of spirituality, and there's stench and abomination. Today I will try to live for the soul" (July 7, 1908; 56: 173). This metaphor is likely to have been prompted by experience: as Tolstoy mentioned in the inventory of his daily routine, he used to record

---

[23] English from *Tolstoy's Diaries*, ed. and trans. R. F. Christian (London: HarperCollins 1994), 412–13; translation has been amended.

his thoughts while sitting on a chamber pot. In the diary, the experiential and the metaphysical converged.

An obstacle in the process of liberation, the body gave obvious signs of deterioration (such as failures of the digestive system), but one thing seemed inescapable—consciousness. Tolstoy claimed to have known from personal experience that the "I" was not the body, but rather consciousness, forever locked in apprehension of itself:

> I remember how almost in childhood I was surprised at the appearance of this characteristic within me, a characteristic that still did not know how to find material for itself. I remember, I was always surprised that I could, being conscious of myself, be conscious of the self being conscious of itself, and, asking myself again, I was conscious that I was conscious of myself being conscious of myself. And from there: I am conscious of myself being conscious of myself being conscious of myself, and so on to infinity. (56: 128)

If we are to believe Tolstoy, in his childhood he rediscovered a concept from Fichte's philosophy: *Ich-an-sich*, the *I* not as an object of experience, but solely as the act of thinking about the *I*.[24]

Since Descartes, philosophers struggled with the concept of self as a subject that thinks, and thus continually relates to itself. One solution—suggested by Fichte—was to posit another type of consciousness, subjectless knowing (which Fichte associated with "light"), which can only be accomplished in action and cannot be grasped conceptually. Judging by several diary entries, Tolstoy seems to have built upon Fichte by positing a distinction between two types of consciousness, the lower (sensory or bodily) consciousness and a higher (spiritual) consciousness, which is beyond time, space, and body.[25] At the end of his life, he suffered acutely from a feeling of imprisonment within the sensory consciousness—in the Fichtean circle of one's consciousness of oneself. The self remained inaccessible; consciousness—inescapable. Indeed, one could liberate one's soul from the body, but was it possible to shed consciousness?

In his eightieth year, Tolstoy discovered that it was: he was now subject to *obmoroki*—episodes of loss of consciousness, followed by a temporary loss of memory. He interpreted this experience as a prefiguration of the complete oblivion to be gained in death. About his first fainting spell,

[24] From Fichte's *Versuch einer neuen Darstellung der Wissenschaftslehre* (1797); I have borrowed specific formulations from J. G. Fichte, *Introductions to the Wissenschaftslehre and Other Writings*, trans. and ed. Daniel Breazeale (Indianapolis: Indiana University Press, 1994), 13 and 107. Eikhenbaum noted that Tolstoy's familiarity with Fichte's concept of the *I* clearly reveals itself in the philosophical reflections recorded in his student years in Kazan (1: 226); see Eikhenbaum, *Lev Tolstoi: semidesiatye gody* (Leningrad, 1974), 214–15.

[25] See, for example, the diary entries for June 18, 1903 (54: 179–80) and April 29, 1910 (58: 42). For a detailed discussion of Tolstoy and Fichte, see an enlarged variant of this essay published in *Tolstoy Studies Journal* 11 (1999): 44–45.

which occurred on March 2, 1908, he wrote—with joy—in the March 10
entry: "About a week ago I got ill. I had a fainting fit. And it made me feel
very good. But the people around me make a fuss [English in the origi-
nal] over it" (56: 109).[26] During the next two such episodes (in April), of
which he made no record, Tolstoy felt the presence of his long-dead
brother Dmitri.[27] On May 12, 1908, Tolstoy described an episode of am-
nesia that occurred at the time of awakening:

> Something happened to me just now, something extraordinary, I don't know,
> if it's good or bad, probably good. . . . It happened that I awoke with a little
> headache and strangely having forgotten everything: what time is it? what am
> I writing? where to go? But—and this is a surprising thing—next to this I felt
> a special sensitivity to the Good: I saw a boy, sleeping on the ground—and felt
> pity; old women at work—I felt particularly ashamed. Passers by—not vexa-
> tion, but pity. So by all means it's not for the worse but the better. (56: 117)

He experienced the liberation from self-consciousness as being outside
time, and as a moral regeneration.[28]

Even apart from such episodes of complete oblivion, Tolstoy noticed
that his memory was diminishing. Taking this as another advance in the
process of liberation, he noted the progress of memory loss in his diary.
As was his habit, Tolstoy translated his observations on concrete experience into general principles applicable to the experience of many and imbued with metaphysical significance:

> [October 23, 1910.] (1) I lost the memory of everything, almost everything
> that has been, of all my writings, of everything that has brought me to the
> consciousness in which I now live. . . . How can one not rejoice at the loss of
> memory? Everything that I worked out in the past (if only by my internal
> labors, in writing) I live by all this now, I benefit from it, but the labors them-
> selves—I don't remember. It's amazing. And I think that this joyful change
> happens to all old men: life concentrates itself in the present. How wonder-
> ful! (58: 122)

The past disappeared: Tolstoy no longer remembered his history. In view
of his imminent death, the future was no longer there. It seemed that
time had come to a standstill: Tolstoy finally lived "a timeless life in the

[26] The *obmorok* (of which Tolstoy, obviously, knew little) was described in the diary of
Tolstoy's secretary N. N. Gusev (see 56: 482–83, n. 259).
[27] These episodes were recorded in the diary of a family friend, B. Goldenweizer: *Vblizi
Tolstogo* (Moscow: Khudozhestvennaia literatura, 1959), 1:207.
[28] This episode has a parallel in the life of Rousseau, recorded in his *Confessions*. In the
words of Starobinski, "Jean-Jacques experiences such awakenings as 'rebirths': he emerges
from nothingness and for an instant stands outside time" (Starobinski, *Jean-Jacques Rousseau*,
79).

present" (58: 122). But to make an account of the present was still far from easy: for one thing, he now frequently forgot what happened during the day. Occasionally, all he recorded was the fact that he did not remember: "*Feb. 22, 23, 24* [1910.] I poorly remember what happened in these two days" (58: 19).

In his last years, Tolstoy spent more and more time sleeping. More than once, on awakening, he would not regain but lose memory and consciousness of self: "I now more and more [begin] to forget. Just now I slept long and, having awakened, sensed a completely new emancipation from personality [*lichnost'*]: it is so wonderful! If only I could be emancipated altogether. Awakening from sleep, from dreaming, this is the model of such an emancipation" (January 31, 1908; 56: 98). In his quest for liberation from his *I*, Tolstoy apparently took sleep and awakening as an experience that was emblematic of life and death. In his late diary, again and again he drew an analogy between life and dreams. Reflections on his own experience went side by side with philosophical reflections, which frequently echoed thoughts formulated by his favorite philosophers. Thus, he found confirmation of his own intuition in Pascal's idea that the main difference between life and the dream was that life was a little more continuous; moreover, unlike a person's life experiences, his dreams were not shared by others (56: 91; January 13, 1908).[29]

As Tolstoy probably knew, the problem of how to distinguish between life and a dream (which went as far back as Descartes' *First Meditation*) was also addressed by his favorite philosopher, Schopenhauer: "We have dreams; may not the whole of life be a dream?" In search of a criterion, Schopenhauer turned to Kant, who, echoing Pascal, suggested that it was only the quality of continuity, that is, connectedness of representations, that distinguished life from a dream.[30] Schopenhauer presented life and dreams as two different strategies of reading the single book of life: "Life and dreams are leaves of one and the same book. The systematic reading is real life, but when the actual reading hour (the day) has come to an end, and we have the period of recreation, we often continue idly to thumb over the leaves, and turn to a page here and there without a method or connection. We sometimes turn a page we have already read, at others one still unknown to us, but always from the same book."[31] Judging by the representations of dreams in *War and Peace* and *Anna Karenina*, Tolstoy had long thought of dreams in similar terms.

[29] Pascal's *Pensées*, no. 386.
[30] See paragraph 31 of Kant's *Anthropology*.
[31] Arthur Schopenhauer, *The World as Will and Representation*, trans. E. F. J. Payne (New York: Dover Publications, 1969), 1: 16 and 18 (paragraph 5).

In his late diaries, Tolstoy's attention again turned to retroactive dreams, like the one he had described in "The History of Yesterday" sixty years earlier. Drawing a parallel between the experience of time in such a dream and in life as a whole, he now drew far-reaching metaphysical conclusions from his psychological observations:

> *March 25, 1908. Ia. P.* (1) The main likeness with respect to time is that in sleep, as in awakening, there is no time, but we imagine, we cannot not imagine, time. I remember a long, coherent dream, which ends with a shot, and I awake. The sound of the shot was the knock of a window slammed shut by the wind. I require time in remembering a dream. I need it, while awake, to place in order all my impressions from a dream. It's the same thing in remembrances of being awake: all my life is in the present, but in remembering it, or rather in being conscious of it, I cannot fail to arrange it in time. I—the child, the man, the old man—it's all one and the same, all present. I just cannot be conscious of it outside of time. (56: 114)

Tolstoy interpreted such dreams as experiential evidence that the passage of time was an illusion—a property of the world as representation. To extend Schopenhauer's metaphor, we misread the book of life, mistaking reading time for the time of the book's action. Concluding his reflections, Tolstoy actually expressed a hope that death would correct the corrupt text of life: "Just as, awakened by the knock of a window slamming shut, I know that dreaming was illusion, so too, upon my death, will I learn the same about all the earthly events which seem to me so real" (56: 115). Descriptions of dreams of this type, framed by reflections on the metaphysical significance of this experience, abound in Tolstoy's late diaries.[32] It was as if reexperiencing dreaming and awakening he was confirmed in the hope that in death one would instantly gain knowledge of life as it really was: in the terminal narrative, time would have not length but depth—a recess in which all the events, impressions, and thoughts of one's life occur simultaneously, defying the narrative logic of linearity and finitude.[33]

It was not long before Tolstoy noticed a fatal contradiction in his reasoning: there could be no such narrative, because thought itself, and its

---

[32] See, for example, diary entries for September 15 and 17, 1909 (57: 139–42).

[33] There is an interesting parallel. The German philosopher Carl Du Prel, in his 1885 *Die Philosophie der Mystik*, offered an interpretation of the dreams of the type reported by Maury which concurs with Tolstoy's. In such dreams, he noted, the effect precedes the cause and the beginning and end coincide. This "seeming duration" of time not only provides empirical evidence of Kant's idea of the purely subjective nature of time, but also opens access to a side of human consciousness in which the laws of causality and the "physiological measure of time" do not operate, giving way to the "transcendental measure of time" (Du Prel, 44–94). This made Du Prel recall the words of Luther: "God sees time not in its length, but in its breadth" (89).

forms, were a property of this world. On September 17, Tolstoy reminded himself of the ultimate limitation of speech and thought:

> I would like to say that life before birth was perhaps just the same, that the character that I carry into life is the fruit of previous awakenings, and that future life will be the same; I would like to say this, but I don't have the right, because I cannot think outside time. In true life there is no time, life merely presents itself to me in time. I can only say one thing—that this future life exists, and not only does death not destroy life, it only opens life still further. To speak of what *was* before life and what *will be* after life would be to use a mode of thought peculiar only to this life to explain other forms of life, still unknown to me. (57: 142)

For years, Tolstoy had been aware of this paradox: our knowledge is limited to what is representable; therefore, true life and the true self—life and self outside time, space, and language—are unknowable. The self is inaccessible not because of limitations inherent in the nature of thought and narrative, but because the true self—or rather the nonself of the true being—is precisely that which thought cannot grasp and language cannot formulate.

In his 1851 "History of Yesterday" the young Tolstoy, unaware of the essential limitations of human consciousness, had attempted to create a text in which the categories of time and space and the antithesis of the subject and object dissolved; in his late diaries, he seemed to have accepted the impossibility of such knowledge. In the epistemological skepticism of his later years Tolstoy was probably influenced by reading Kant and Schopenhauer.[34] The older (and better educated) Tolstoy was a wiser man: he did not solve the problems which had tormented him since his youth, but, learning from personal experience and the wisdom of others, came closer to accepting that they were insolvable. If there was any hope of finding such a solution in this life, it lay in religious experience—in something like the silent act of the Jesus prayer.

And yet, as long as he lived, Tolstoy did not stop trying. As in his youth, he recorded his experience in several parallel documents. In addition to

[34] See, for example, Schopenhauer's *Parerga und Paralipomena,* no. 5, "Thing Itself and Appearance," and no. 6, "The Indestructibility of Being," which could have served as a direct source of the September 17, 1909 entry. Tolstoy read Schopenhauer and then Kant in the summer of 1869 (see his letter to Fet of August 30, 1869, 61: 219). As he put it, in Schopenhauer, he found a confirmation of his own thoughts (61: 217). On Tolstoy, Schopenhauer, and Kant, see Eikhenbaum, "Tolstoi i Shopengauer (k voprosu o sozdanii "Anny Kareninoi")," *Literaturnyi sovremennik,* no. 11 (1935), and *Lev Tolstoi: semidesiatye gody,* passim; Sigrid McLaughlin, "Some Aspects of Tolstoy's Intellectual Development: Tolstoy and Schopenhauer," *California Slavic Studies,* no. 5 (1970); Gary R. Jahn, "Tolstoj and Kant," *New Perspectives on Nineteenth-Century Russian Prose,* ed. George J. Gutsche and Lauren G. Leighton (Columbus, Ohio: Slavica Publishing, 1982); Orwin, *Tolstoy's Art and Thought,* passim.

the regular diary (accessible to the members of his household), there were "secret" diaries,[35] notebooks (always carried in his pocket) in which he recorded thoughts, and almanacs of thoughts intended for publication. Arranged according to the calendar, these almanacs contained "thoughts" for every day of the year—Tolstoy's own thoughts (some of which had earlier appeared in the diary or notebooks) and aphorisms drawn from works of various authors, many of them heavily edited by Tolstoy. He conceived this idea in 1902, when, gravely ill and confined to bed, he "tore the pages off a wall calendar which hung above his bed and read the sayings of various thinkers printed on them."[36] When he had plucked all the leaves from this tree of life, Tolstoy decided to plant his own. After 1902, working on these almanacs was a central task of each day. The work went on ceaselessly: having barely completed the first such edition, *Thoughts of the Wise People for Every Day* (1903), he started an improved variant, *The Circle of Reading* (1906–7), then reworked it into yet another, *The New Circle of Reading*, or *For Every Day* (1909–10).[37] In these books, coauthored by Tolstoy and other wise men (from Socrates, Buddha, Confucius, Christ, and Mohammed to Augustine, Montaigne, Pascal, Rousseau, Kant, and Schopenhauer), "the consciousness of Lev T." was merged with "the consciousness of the whole world."[38] Issued in large-scale cheap editions, Tolstoy's almanacs were offered to readers as preprinted diaries of sorts: one could acquire a diary of Lev Tolstoy's spiritual life and live one's own in accordance with this paradigm. Tolstoy himself did that: he was both the "diaries' " author and their dutiful reader, perusing one or more of his almanacs daily. Such an almanac provided a "diary" that did not depend on "*e.b.zh.*"—each was guaranteed to make a complete circle. Moreover, they turned the world around Tolstoy into a friendly and predictable place, in which the lives of many people, along with his own, ran day by day in accordance with a prescriptive diary. One could live a life that had already been described.

After his final escape from home, at the monastic abode of his sister Maria (Masha), Tolstoy found and read a copy of his *Circle of Life*: he felt that the entry for the day (October 28) contained an answer to the question that tormented him at the time.[39] Thus, on one of the last days of his life, far from home, his almanac—this prewritten diary of spiritual life, shared with many—served him well. When Tolstoy died on November 7,

---

[35] For an analysis of this practice, see Morson, *Hidden in Plain View*, 31–32.

[36] From the commentaries to "Mysli mudrykh liudei na kazhdyi den'," 40: 479.

[37] "Mysli mudrykh liudei na kazhdyi den' " (1903), "Krug chteniia" (1906–1907), and "Novyi krug chteniia," or "Na kazhdyi den' " (1909–10), are published in volumes 40–45 of the Jubilee Edition.

[38] From Tolstoy's diary for April 21, 1908 (56: 123), where these phrases are used in another context.

[39] See his dairy entry for October 29, 1910 (58: 125).

1910, journalists reporting his death noted that the entry for that day in the *Circle of Life* was a perfect fit for Tolstoy's last day: "Life as a dream and death as an awakening." And in conclusion: "We can only guess what will be after death, the future is hidden from us. Not only is it hidden, but it does not exist, in as much as future implies time, but in dying we leave time."[40] It was as if through his almanac Tolstoy succeeded in bringing the narrative of life to its ultimate conclusion—asserting on the last day that the possibilities of representation stopped there.

From his early years, Tolstoy knew that his narrative utopia—to turn himself into a book—would remain unfulfilled. He left the gigantic text of his diaries—his own "critique of pure reason" and his own comment on the "world as representation"—as a monument to this failure, the inescapable failure of any writer (or reader) intent on the complete textualization of self. It was in death that Tolstoy hoped finally to experience a completely authentic being—a timeless, selfless existence in the present—that which language cannot formulate. For years, he was preparing himself, marking in his diary the process of shedding memories of the past, expectations, and even consciousness itself. Sometimes, he knew that to leave a record of the ultimate experience of this kind was as impossible as to transcribe one's dream as it occurred. Yet at other times, Tolstoy, who in his youth had attempted the latter, attempted to preempt the former. But in death he hoped finally to be able to take leave of his vocation as a writer: he would stop writing the book of his life (or reading a preprinted one) and, for a moment, see the light open on the unrepresentable. If only the author could share the experience of his heroine, Anna: "The candle, by the light of which she had been reading that book filled with anxieties, deceptions, grief, and evil, flared up with a brighter light than before, lit up for her all that had before been dark, flickered, began to grow dim, and went out for ever."[41]

[40] "Zamechatel'noe sovpadenie," *Rech'*, November 8, 1910. See also a penny-press organ, *Gazeta-kopeika* ("7–oe noiabria v 'Krugu chteniia,' " November 8, 1910). (For this information, I am indebted to William Nickell.)

[41] The Maude translation.

CHAPTER ELEVEN

Storied Selves: Constructing Characters in The Brothers Karamazov

WILLIAM MILLS TODD III

For a volume on "self and story" in Russian history, a study of Dostoevsky's last novel, *The Brothers Karamazov* (Brat'ia Karamazovy, 1881), which foregrounds its characters' uses and misuses of narrative as they attempt to understand the extreme possibilities of human behavior, offers many opportunities to reflect on both "self" and "story." In this essay I will outline a reading of the novel that focuses upon the central themes of this volume, illuminating them with modern theories of narrative which share Dostoevsky's own fascination with self and story. To the extent that *The Brothers Karamazov* constitutes not only a reflection on narrative in general but criticism of the kinds of story told by its culture, I will suggest how it can help make us aware of the ways late nineteenth-century Russians told stories. Here I will use modern theories of narrative to discuss the novel's own problematization of narrative, which is itself part of a long tradition in literature and in critical reflection.

Since Greek antiquity selves and stories have been inextricably intertwined in accounts of both "self" (or its rough equivalents) and "story." Our earliest theory of narrative, Aristotle's *Poetics*, may not entertain the notion of "self" in a recognizably modern sense, but it does have to deal with human agency in discussing actions, it does consider the social position of these agents, and it does endow them with character traits.[1] Subsequent theories, such as Propp's, at the very least entertain the first of these hypostases of character, the notion of agency. But most, whether

[1] For a discussion of Aristotle's treatment of character, see Seymour Chatman, *Story and Discourse: Narrative Structure in Fiction and Film* (Ithaca: Cornell University Press, 1978), 108–10.

266

normative or descriptive, will attempt to do more: dictate the types of characters most appropriate to a particular kind of narrative; posit what makes a character interesting or capable of generating narrative curiosity; study how characters can be constructed in narratives. Our most ornate and brilliant theory of narrative, Roland Barthes' *S / Z*, giving play to myriad critical discourses, jargons, and terms only to be found in a Greek dictionary, nevertheless makes problems of character and human agency central to the working of his five narrative codes.[2] Indeed, reversing the focus on action that has been the rule since Aristotle, Barthes argues that it is this movement of traits toward a proper name, not action, that is the property of narrative.[3] In plainer English, narrative becomes a process of endowing proper names with character. In any event, Barthes preserves and expands Aristotle's understandings of literary personages as agents, characters, and functions of context.

When we move from narrative in general to its principal modern literary manifestation, the novel, we see that theories of the novel are to an even greater degree fixated upon character, emphasizing to a greater degree, as is historically appropriate, issues of individuation and consciousness. Georg Lukács's famous inquiry defines novelistic plotting in terms of the movements and understandings of character: the "outward form" of the novel is the biography of a problematic individual, whose individuality is an end unto itself in a contingent world, while what Lukács calls the "inner form" of the novel is the problematic individual's journey toward self-recognition. "Outward" and "inner" in each case focus upon an individual.[4] Lukács's Russian contemporary, Mikhail Bakhtin, was drawn to and challenged such a conception of the novel, developing a number of different insights about narrative which explode the traditions of plot-oriented Aristotelian poetics. Speech, not action, becomes the center of Bakhtin's focus in his most developed essay, "Discourse in the Novel," and the "speaking person" becomes the novel's hero. But for all of Bakhtin's indifference to plotting in a traditional sense of the ordering of events, the testing or challenging of the hero in his theory of the novel do enter into a sort of master plot, the process of the speaking person's "coming to know his or her own language as it is perceived in someone else's language, coming to know one's own belief system in someone else's sys-

---

[2] The hermeneutic code, by which enigmas are posed and resolved, clearly deals with problems of human identity; the proairetic code, which governs actions, presupposes (as in Aristotle and Propp) human actors; the symbolic code organizes character as a function of rhetorical figures and tropes, such as antithesis; the cultural code views character as the product of regnant understandings, such as popular psychology; and the semic code attaches traits to a proper name. See Roland Barthes, *S / Z: An Essay*, trans. Richard Miller (New York: Hill and Wang, 1974).

[3] Barthes, *S / Z*, 191.

[4] Georg Lukács, *The Theory of the Novel* (Cambridge, Mass.: MIT Press, 1971), 77–80.

tem."[5] "Story," in short, has become inconceivable without not just actors or products of cultural contexts but also without "selves," individuated and coherent in varying degrees, depending on the theory in question.

But "self" is scarcely less conceivable without "story" in most modern treatments. Where it once may have been adequate to describe a character by measuring a person against an established norm or by attaching traits to a proper name—no small process of individuation, given that Webster's gives nearly 18,000 trait names[6]—a modern sense of self generally involves development over time. And the depiction of development over time inevitably calls forth narrative, our principal cognitive means, as Louis Mink has put it, for making comprehensive the many successive interrelationships that are composed by a career.[7] Cathy Popkin's paper for this volume shows how medical science of the late nineteenth century used narrative to constitute character according to disciplinary rules. We do not need to rehearse here the many different ways in which our various schools of psychoanalysis and developmental psychology construct, or deconstruct, individuated or integral selves, normative life histories, or case studies. The point is that all do this in story form.

Distinctions suggested by the novel itself aid our inquiry. These distinctions, in narratological terms, address three aspects of the poetics and pragmatics of narrative: the *plot*, the ordering of events and personages; the *narration*, the teller's presentation of events and personages; and the *reception*, the reader's or listener's processing of the story. The first aspect, plot, involves the openness of the story, the play that it allows for the subject's agency, potential, and own definition of self. It also involves the scope of the story: Is it a general account or a particular story? The whole story of the self, or just a part? The second aspect, narration, involves, primarily, distance and engagement: Is the story told with scientific objectivity, from a distance, or with varying kinds of personal involvement (egocentric / selfless) with the object of discourse? A related set of distinctions, ones involving the ideological involvement of the narrator, sets secular discourse against the insights of faith (scientific objectivity / loving empathy). The third aspect of the novel's stories of the self, reception, involves the participation of the listener, for many of these stories are told orally to personages, in their physical presence, making them the objects of dialogue, often heated or abusive.

[5] M. M. Bakhtin, *The Dialogic Imagination: Four Essays*, trans. Caryl Emerson and Michael Holquist (Austin: University of Texas Press, 1981), 365. Cf. Bakhtin's notion of "ideological becoming": the process of selectively assimilating the words of others, of liberating oneself from the authority of another's discourse, 341–48.

[6] Chatman, *Story and Discourse*, 125n38.

[7] Louis Mink, "Narrative Form as a Cognitive Instrument," in R. Canary and H. Kozicki, ed., *The Writing of History: Literary Form and Historical Understanding* (Madison: University of Wisconsin Press, 1977), 134.

The Brothers Karamazov, serialized over a two-year period in one of Russia's leading "thick journals" (1879–80), represents a field where Russia's various stories for constituting selves could, and did, confront each other. Or, more precisely, a field within a field, for the thick journals themselves, by bringing together fiction and literary reviews with articles on a variety of historical, scientific, and social-scientific topics, themselves forced confrontations between the discourses of Russia's incipient professions and academic disciplines. We may borrow the prosecutor's simile, "like the sun in a small drop of water," in turn borrowed from Derzhavin, to suggest this process of miniaturization, by which contemporary ways of characterizing the self come together first in the period's popular journals, then in Dostoevsky's last novel.[8] During the two years of serialization alone, *The Russian Herald* (Russkii vestnik) sandwiched the installments of *The Brothers Karamazov* among articles, many of them also serialized, on natural and physical science, military history, imperial history (the Polish and Eastern questions), religion, travel, the law (courts and prison reform), pedagogy, economics, music, art, and literature.[9] Contemporary readers of the novel would have these subjects before their eyes from this journal alone, to say nothing about what they would have encountered in rival thick journals, such as *The Herald of Europe* (Vestnik Evropy), *National Annals* (Otechestvennye zapiski), *Deed* (Delo), and *Russian Wealth* (Russkoe bogatstvo). The increasingly popular daily newspapers of the 1870s had come to carry the greater part of court and crime reporting, although Dostoevsky's one-man journal, *Diary of a Writer* (Dnevnik pisatelia), treated a number of trials at length as well as many of the social, cultural, and foreign-policy controversies of the time.[10] But Dostoevsky established a further journalistic context for his readers by setting his novel in the postreform late 1860s, when the journals—which then included *The Contemporary* (Sovremennik) and the Dostoevsky brothers' *Time* (Vremia) and *Epoch* (Epokha)—devoted more space to discussion of the judicial reforms as well as to deterministic theories of human development, such as we encounter in the novel in the writings and dialogue of the journalist Rakitin in *The Brothers Karamazov*.

The prosecutor accompanies his simile, however, with a specular metaphor: "in the picture of this fine little family it is as if certain general fundamental elements of our contemporary intellectual society may be

---

[8] F. M. Dostoevskii, *Polnoe sobranie sochinenii v tridtsati tomakh* (Leningrad: Nauka, 1972–90), 15: 125.

[9] For a more detailed account of this phenomenon, see William Mills Todd III, "*The Brothers Karamazov* and the Poetics of Serial Publication," *Dostoevsky Studies* 7 (1986): 87–97.

[10] For information on Dostoevsky and the court reporting of the time, see David Keily, "*The Brothers Karamazov* and the Fate of Russian Truth: Shifts in the Construction and Interpretation of Narrative After the Judicial Reform of 1864," Ph.D. diss., Harvard University, 1996; also T. C. Karlova, *Dostoevskii i russkii sud* (Kazan: Izdatel'stvo Kazanskogo Universiteta, 1975).

glimpsed—oh, not all the elements, and in microscopic view, 'like the sun in a small drop of water,' yet something has been reflected in it."[11] If one must have an optical metaphor, I would prefer "refracted," because it seems that when the novel deals with contemporary ways of storying the self, it does so by bending and ordering them from a particular angle, much as a prism would bend and order the intensities of a stream of light.

Through this prism of novelistic discourse the self becomes indeed storied, not only in the sense of the object and subject of stories, but also by being layered, as in the stories of a house. The personages of the novel become subject to many kinds of story, some literary, some scientific, some social-scientific. But we are never allowed to forget the angles of refraction, that stories are told by someone, to someone, and, instrumentally, for some purpose. This manifest refracting of stories of the self is evident from the opening pages of the novel, the passage "From the Author," which is generally ignored in the critical discourse. Here a sarcastic, maddeningly indefinite author figure presents Alesha, the youngest of the Karamazov brothers, from several different angles: as hero of the novel, as a character possibly not grand enough to play this role, as an indefinite figure, and as an eccentric, a special case, yet one which might represent "the heart of the whole" more than the other people of the era.[12] The author is fussy, hostile, on the edge of that aggressive buffoonery which character-narrators (Fedor, Maksimov, Ivan's devil, the defense attorney) will later adopt, on the edge of that clumsy, excited, at times ungrammatical, discourse that Valentina Vetlovskaia has accurately attributed to the novel's primary narrator.[13] This author figure's only solution to the problems he poses, including those of character, is his refusal to solve them. He makes a mockery of the notion that literature imitates reality by treating both text and reality in terms of senselessness and confusion (*bestoloch'*). Every aspect of the text, he promises, will be either ambiguous or muddled: its genre, both "biography" and novel"; the hero, an unheroic eccentric; and its structure—it begins with a preface the author calls superfluous yet nevertheless includes, and its significance will become clear only from the sequel, which the author does not, of course, include. The reader, assaulted by these equivocations, ambiguities, and muddles, finds him or herself projected, sarcastically, as one who will disagree with the "author," will have to guess at what the author is trying to say, and may even read through to the end, unlike the sixty or so unnamed "Russian critics" who took it upon themselves to review the novel before serialization was completed.[14] As a provocation to the reader, the narrator's own

---

[11] Dostoevskii, *Polnoe sobranie sochinenii*, 15: 125.

[12] Ibid., 14: 5.

[13] V. E. Vetlovskaia, *Poetika romana "Brat'ia Karamazovy"* (Leningrad: Nauka, 1977), 34–39.

[14] For a survey of these reviews, see William Mills Todd III, "Contexts of Criticism: Reviewing *The Brothers Karamazov* in 1879," *Stanford Slavic Studies* 4, no. 1 (1991): 293–310.

disjointed narrative becomes purposeful. The structure of the book will provide many patterns of repetition to guide the reader, as Robert Belknap has noted, and some of the book's characters, primarily Alesha and Zosima, will successfully "read" the other characters' stories with a measure of insight.[15] But these characters, whose insight is not infallible, will be the closest a reader comes to finding positive models of narrative reception in the text. The other characters, as narrators and listeners to narrative, provide only negative guidance: how *not* to process narrative and how *not* to understand character.

The author figure yields to the primary narrator as the novel opens, but "senselessness and confusion" echo from its opening pages through to the great trial scene in the novel's last book. Not the least of these enigmas concerns character, and the older two brothers, Dmitri and Ivan, represent its greatest mysteries and greatest breadth in the novel, with the principal female characters, Grushenka and Katerina Ivanovna, coming close behind. Dmitri poses the question most extravagantly, characterizing Ivan as a "tomb" and humanity a "riddle" and launching into his own refraction, in extravagantly aesthetic terms, of the spectrum of human capabilities:

> God sets us nothing but riddles. There the shores meet and all contradictions coexist. . . . It's terrible how many mysteries there are! Too many riddles weigh men down on earth. We must solve them as we can, and try to come out of the water with a dry skin. Beauty! I can't bear it that a man of lofty mind and heart begins with the ideal of the Madonna and ends with the ideal of Sodom. What's still more terrifying is that a man with the ideal of Sodom in his soul does not renounce the ideal of the Madonna, and his heart may be on fire with that ideal, genuinely on fire, just as in his days of youth and innocence. No, man is broad, too broad, indeed. I'd narrow him.[16]

The movement of the novel involves the reader in a quest to resolve these enigmas, as it does the characters. Multiple narrations construct incidents in different ways, indexing the characters with different traits. Dmitri himself will provide the richest examples, as he finds himself, even in the opening parts of the novel, the object of five different narrations of the thrashing of Captain Snegirev: by Fedor, who omits the specific nature of the captain's business; twice by Dmitri, who ignores the captain's lamentable family situation; once by Katerina Ivanovna, who adds the presence of the captain's son, and, finally, in excruciating detail by the captain himself, who adds Dmitri's viciously humiliating offer to fight a

[15] Robert L. Belknap, *The Structure of* The Brothers Karamazov (Evanston: Northwestern University Press, 1989). On the function of memory in the novel's poetics, see Diane Oenning Thompson, The Brothers Karamazov *and the Poetics of Memory* (Cambridge: Cambridge University Press, 1991).

[16] Dostoevskii, *Polnoe sobranie sochinenii*, 14: 104.

duel. Depending on the version, Dmitri comes off as noble officer, brute, or sadist—i.e., as the military equivalent of one who bears the ideal of Madonna or the ideal of Sodom. At the end of the novel, when he is tried for parricide, Dmitri will again be the object of multiple narrations, emerging with a similar range of "selves" from the narratives of lawyers, doctors, and witnesses.

Many of these stories collapse in utter futility; some—for the characters and perhaps for the reader—have the ring of truth. In a novel legendary for its ambiguities and confusion, how are these stories of the self ordered? Which emerge as plausible? By what criteria? Does the novel, adopting the grand ambitions of nineteenth-century science, posit laws by which the self may be known? Probabilities? Possibilities? Or does it, rejecting even the most modest of these conclusions, undermine all the stories by which the self might be known? Who pretends to story the self, by what authority, and how? Some of the answers involve recognizable scientific discourses, at times in the mouths of licensed representatives of Russia's incipient professions (such as lawyers or doctors), at times in the reports of educated laymen (such as the narrator or the journalist-seminarian Rakitin). It is not possible to account for every story told in *The Brothers Karamazov*, but we may essay some observations on these stories' attempts to deal with the characters of the novel.

Among the discourses the novel examines are those in which the observer tries to penetrate the secrets of the self and still, to borrow Dmitri's image, "come out of the water with a dry skin": medicine and "psychology." These attempts range from typification (as in the narrator's learned discussion of the abused women who become "shriekers") to specific diagnoses (the famous Moscow doctor's prescriptions for Iliusha, the court psychiatrists). Such stories told in the absence of the subject may have the ring of plausibility, as when the narrator explains the calming effect of the Eucharist on an hysterical peasant woman:

> The strange and instantaneous healing of the possessed and struggling woman as soon as she was led up to the holy sacrament, which had been explained to me as pretense and even trickery arranged by the "clericals," arose probably in the most natural manner. . . . With a nervous and psychically ill woman, a sort of convulsion of the whole organism inevitably took place at the moment of bowing before the sacrament, aroused by expectation of the inevitable miracle of healing and the fullest belief that it would come to pass; and it did come to pass, though only for a moment.[17]

The narrator's sympathy for the hard lot of rural women, expressed in the philanthropic terms of a socially and culturally superior observer, his es-

[17] Ibid., 14: 44.

chewal of an easy cynical explanation (a show staged by the clergy), and his rational, psychological account of irrational behavior make this explanation persuasive. At this relatively early point in the novel (Book Two, Chapter Three) we have nothing to contradict either its explanatory power or the narrator's credibility. Indeed, the early chapters feature a number of such commonsensical explanations, which the novel has not yet taught its readers to distrust. The narrator's presentation of Fedor Karamazov's first wife abounds in such explanations: "Adelaida Ivanovna's behavior was without doubt the echo of foreign influences, also the irritation from thought imprisoned. She perhaps wished to display female independence, to go against social conventions, against the despotism of her relatives and family."[18] The reader's subsequent acquaintance with the characters of the novel will reveal the superficiality and inadequacy of such seemingly plausible cultural, social, and psychological explanations.

Indeed, as the novel continues, commonsense psychological explanations become nuanced and undermined. Hysteria, for instance, becomes the property of all classes—and genders—of the novel's characters, and it is far from easily calmed by any treatment. Ultimately, the more rational—and the more scientific or professionalized—the story of sickness, the less adequate it becomes. The old German doctor, Herzenstube, is absolutely helpless as a physician, but his kindness touches Dmitri and is remembered by him. The district doctor, Varvinskii, is fooled by Smerdiakov, Markel's doctor mistakes religious enlightenment for brain fever, the confession of Zosima's mysterious visitor is taken for madness. The famous Moscow doctor's prescriptions for the impoverished Snegirev family create for them an absurd story that is cruelly impossible to live out: travel to Syracuse for Iliusha, to the Caucasus for Nina, to the Caucasus and to Paris for the mother. Medical science reaches the height of absurdity at the trial, where three doctors (Herzenstube, the Moscow specialist, and Varvinskii) debate the direction in which Dmitri, if sane, should have looked upon entering the court, to the left, to the right, or straight ahead.[19]

Ultimately the medical narratives, like the psychological ones, are subservient to the legal process, which brings not only the characters but also their stories together in the last, and longest, book of the novel. Here the reader sees that the plots and characters created by the novel's police investigators and attorneys likewise fail to come to grips with the breadth of the novel's personages. The story that the district attorney and his colleagues put together during the preliminary investigation (Book Nine) is based on their assumptions and on Grigorii's faulty evidence as well as on

[18] Ibid., 14: 8.
[19] Ibid., 15: 103–7.

what they can squeeze out of the exhausted, ecstatic Dmitri. It is remarkable for its deductive logic: they have decided that Dmitri is guilty, therefore they will assemble what they need to confirm that the murder is a rational, premeditated act. Dmitri counters their story of him with "his own story," as he calls it, that of an honorable officer who has had some difficulties, but who has not become a thief and who has been saved from murdering his father by his guardian angel. Dmitri's story lacks coherence, to say nothing of the weight of institutional authority, and it cannot counteract the police account of him as a rational killer. A third story of Dmitri's character is constructed during this investigation, however, this time by the narrator with help from the reader's ability to remember previous detail; this emerging story compares the former Dmitri to the one who develops during his ordeals. The new Dmitri still bears the traits of recklessness and impulsiveness but, as is seen in his dream of the baby, has compassion and concern for the suffering of others. His vision occurs toward the end of the interrogation, a process which has a profound moral impact upon him, stripping him of his superiority and his superficial sense of honor, the sense of honor that had, we may recall, led him to invite the helpless Snegirev to challenge him to a duel. As Dmitri is quite literally stripped, he loses his old attachments to life and turns, ever so slowly, toward new ones. It is, after all, hard to feel proud and superior in dirty socks and underwear.

The narratives constructed by the attorneys in the trial only compound the inadequacy of the preliminary investigation by adding the expert testimony of medical science and amateurish social science. Under Russia's recently instituted adversarial system, a trial had become a contest between storytellers, as Dostoevsky had pointed out in his journalistic pieces and demonstrates here, in Book Twelve of *The Brothers Karamazov*. To gain a conviction, the prosecution had to construct an airtight narrative in which some criminal event took place and its willing agent was the defendant. The defense was given a different storytelling task. To create the necessary grain of doubt, it had to break the prosecution's narrative down by showing that there was no criminal event or chain of events, or by showing that even if there was, the defendant was not the agent of these events.

In this trial both attorneys cut corners in their research and argumentation. The form of the story overwhelms its content; fiction-making talent comes to the fore. The narrator, lawyers, and witnesses use, in fact, a variety of literary terms to describe the trial and its arguments: "tragic," "comedy," "scenario," "spectacle," "fiction," "novel," "legend," "drama."[20] The

---

[20] The Russian word *roman* can be translated either as "novel" or as "romance." For an exploration of the storytelling manner of the two attorneys, see W. Wolfgang Holdheim, *Der Justizirrtum als literarische Problematik: vergleichende Analyse eines erzahlerischen Themas* (Berlin: De Gruyter, 1969). A large and growing body of contributions to the "law and literature"

prosecutor begins with the conclusion to the plot (that Dmitri with premeditation killed his father) and builds the story accordingly: this involves dismissing the intelligence, stability, and character of Dmitri's three witnesses (Alesha, Ivan, Grushenka). It involves constructing Dmitri's character to suit the plot and finalizing that character. For the prosecutor to tell us that there is a "real" Dmitri Karamazov ignores Dmitri's development and range of possibilities. Using this fictitious "real Dmitri," the prosecutor in turn shapes the events of the murder plot. This implicates Dmitri in a series of hypothetical actions which, as the reader by now knows, did not take place: Dmitri gradually spending the reserve of money, for instance. As if Dmitri could do such things in small installments! Or Dmitri consciously hiding the remaining 1500 rubles in Mokroe. As if Dmitri could have been concerned with anything but Grushenka at that moment. Ivan, whom the reader has seen undergoing the most profound transformation in the novel, is similarly grist for the prosecutor's mill. We see the prosecutor questioning why Ivan did not immediately come forth to report Smerdiakov's confession. The demands of legal narrative require that the prosecutor make Ivan a calculating, dishonorable slanderer of the dead, not a man wracked with guilt—and the prosecutor does precisely this. Finally, and pivotally, the prosecutor must, ventriloquized by Smerdiakov himself, construct a suitable biography and character for the only plausible alternative murderer, Smerdiakov. And in the prosecutor's "treatise on Smerdiakov" we see him doing just this. The result is a timid, sickly, "naturally honest" Smerdiakov who couldn't possibly have committed the crime that we know by this time he did commit. The prosecutor's loaded words in this treatise—"psychology," "fact," "natural"—conceal the extent to which psychology, fact, and nature are the prosecutor's narrative constructs, constructs that he has assembled in accordance with his needs and institutional requirements, constructs that he has borrowed wholesale from the murderer.

The defense attorney, Fetiukovich, adopts a different narrative strategy and tells a different story, using many of the same acts and actors. But, predictably, he provides different contexts and puts the acts and actors into different chains of events, drawing on different traits to characterize his personages. His institutional role requires him to see sudden acts and incoherence where the prosecution sees deliberate thought and action. Thus the "talented" Fetiukovich gives priority to acts and actors as potential plot material, not as products of his need for a particular outcome. He attacks the "whole logic of the prosecution." He dismantles the "combina-

---

movement in legal studies has begun to address problems of legal narrative, although rarely drawing on the full complexity of narrative theory. For an exception, with useful bibliography, see Keily, "*The Brothers Karamazov* and the Fate of Russian Truth."

tion of facts." And he reverses the psychology of all the characters, drawing on his famous maxim that "psychology is a two-edged weapon." To this end he employs his "talent" for humor, ridicule, and deconstructive logic. He takes each building block of the prosecutor's narrative—each character, each event—and gives it a different spin, a different place in a different story. Countering the dead certainty of the prosecutor's account and its determinism, which is based on notions of both the Karamazovs' heredity and their environment, the wily defense attorney constructs character and action in ways closer to the understandings of the loving Christian figures, Zosima and Alesha, namely, character as open construct and actions as sudden, spontaneous. Thus Fetiukovich makes Smerdiakov a much more clever, complex character than does the prosecutor, and this is, in fact, closer to the truth. Does this make Fetiukovich a spokesman for Dostoevsky? Or does it make him similar to Dostoevsky's greatest liar, General Ivolgin in *The Idiot*, who happened to tell the truth once, by accident? It is probably the latter. Fetiukovich's job is to sow doubt, not to tell the truth. His narrative, like the prosecutor's, is still a fiction, although a more modern, sophisticated one.

As these narratives, ostensibly created in the service of truth and justice, become increasingly a matter of personal competition between the attorneys, as, indeed, the medical experts' testimony had been a matter of personal pride and competition, we must turn to the second of the three aspects of narrative that the novel foregrounds, the teller's role in the story. The defense attorney's own term for the story with which he concludes his speech is "hypothesis"—i.e., an unproven fiction which might capture reality. This is a term that Kolia Krasotkin uses, as does Ivan Karamazov. It implies an intellectual detachment from life, from empathy. And here it becomes a masterpiece of equivocation on Fetiukovich's part. It is not enough for him to discredit the witnesses and to deconstruct the prosecution's story. He must become a romance writer himself. And so he reaches out to argue that there was no robbery and no murder. He must put his talent for rhetoric and casuistry to the ultimate test, to argue before a jury of patriarchal Russians that even if Dmitri murdered his father, it really did not count as parricide, because Fedor had not been a real father to him. One could only call it murder out of "prejudice." Fetiukovich concludes his speech with notions of salvation, penitence, regeneration, and resurrection, but the damage is done. He has been swept away by his talent, and both prosecutor and jury recoil from his flamboyant hypothesis by convicting Dmitri.

It is possible to argue that the defense attorney here is trying to mitigate Dmitri's guilt. Under the postreform judicial procedures, a simple majority of jurors could have called for clemency. But I would argue that Fetiukovich's argument is more a case of ego run amok, of the inspired lying one so often encounters in Dostoevsky's characters. The motives and interests behind his storytelling are clearly competitive and aesthetic. His wildly applauded performance is answered by Dmitri's simple but dignified final statement, in which he refuses to recognize himself in either lawyer's account.

This ineluctably self-interested aspect of the attorneys' stories is but a special case of most of the novel's stories; the teller's egocentricity becomes, paradoxically, most evident in those discourses that pretend to the greatest distance and objectivity. Not only are stories told in the professionalized discourses (medicine, psychology, law), then, limited by the rules of the profession, they are also limited by the vanity, competitiveness, and hostility of the speaker. This holds true for the journalists' discourse as well, that of both Ivan and Rakitin. The "little pictures" of Ivan's attack on God's world, culled from the newspapers, nevertheless are marshaled in an argument the basic aim of which is an attack on Alesha's faith and an attempt, momentarily successful, to seduce him to share in Ivan's unforgiving hostility. Rakitin's explanations in terms of heredity and environment, which so influence the prosecutor, emerge from the novel's refraction as the products of his greed, ambition, and resentment of Ivan. In each case any attempt to tell a truthful story is overshadowed by deeply personal attempts to exercise power or to gain vengeance. This, in turn, further compromises the professional discourses, which already appear inadequate for their rule-bound, limited view of the self.

Much of the dynamism of a Dostoevsky novel, and this one in particular, derives from the third aspect of stories of the self, their reception. Even the most silent listener to a story of the self, Christ before the Grand Inquisitor, makes a gesture of response, the kiss that may signify the forgiveness which undercuts the Grand Inquisitor's argument. The novel's nondivine characters typically respond more violently and vociferously to the storied selves which other characters create for them. From the beginning of the novel to the end, examples abound of these rebellious rejections of another's story—present, past, or future—about oneself. Fedor increases his buffoonery and lying after Zosima proposes to him that he try to stop. Grushenka turns savagely against Katerina Ivanovna because she refused to be the person Katerina Ivanovna wanted her to be; Grushenka refused to play the necessary part in Katerina Ivanovna's dream, as Dmitri astutely and gleefully notes: "She truly fell in love with Grushenka, that is, not with Grushenka, but with her own dream, her own delusion—because it was her own dream, her own delusion."[21] Captain Snegirev suddenly rejects and tramples a much-needed two-hundred-ruble gift from Katerina Ivanovna at the very moment when Alesha, his in-

---

[21] Dostoevskii, *Polnoe sobranie sochinenii,* 14: 143.

terlocutor, unthinkingly inserts himself into a story of the captain's future life, as Alesha subsequently comes to realize.[22] The captain tramples the money in trying to escape precisely that characterization of him which Alesha offers to Lise ("he is a cowardly man and weak in character"). Down to the last pages of the novel, when we see Dmitri railing against Claude Bernard, the famous French physician who was a darling of the journalists of the 1860s for his physiological explanations of human behavior, we see the novel's personages reject any sort of contextualization, any attribution of traits, or any assigned roles in another's narrative. They are quick to insist that these are not the whole story or the true story, and if the story seems too whole or true, they will do something to contradict it or otherwise show its inadequacy. The novel, then, develops a *negative* poetics for stories of the self, which its characters emphatically reject: excessive narratorial distance, egocentric narratorial involvement, rigid master plots, formal rules. Such plot schemes and ways of telling finalize character, they preclude agency and unexpected change on the part of the characters in the narratives, and they fail to allow for the possibility of unexpected change-producing events, such as Dmitri's vision of the baby.

Zosima's teachings, as they are constructed by Alesha in Book Six of the novel, offer an implicit *positive* poetics for the creation of stories that might be acceptable and effective: his teachings about the need for erasing the difference between servants and masters, his teaching about the interconnectedness of all, about the mutual responsibility of all for all, about mysterious seeds from other worlds all imply stories that would lack a hierarchy or distance among teller, subject, and listener; they suggest tellers as open to change and new understanding as the characters they are constructing; they remind us of Yuri Lotman's point that "events" are happenings that did not have to happen.[23]

Alesha's final speech once again adumbrates this positive poetics—indeed, ethics—of narration. It appeals to narrative, making Iliusha's life into an exemplary narrative which might be joined to the future narratives of his own and the boys' lives, and it appeals for narrative, the expression of the memory that will be a moral force not only for these young people, but for Alesha himself. Here Alesha does not, as narrator, separate himself from the events and characters of this concluding story, for to do so would manifest the negative poetics and pragmatics of narration which the novel has so rigorously exposed.

At the same time, however, the world of the novel shows its readers that even this ideal narrative communication, with its open endings and unfinalized characters, can be strenuously resisted by its characters, whose sus-

[22] Ibid., 14: 196.
[23] Iu. M. Lotman, *Struktura khudozhestvennogo teksta* (Providence: Brown University Press, 1971), 285.

picions and fears can lead them to see coercion and fixity. Zosima's life is filled with characters who have accepted stories—Markel, Zosima himself, Zosima's mysterious visitor—but it is not easy even for these parable-like figures to accept the "spiritual, psychological" process of transformation, supported by active love.[24] Of the Karamazov brothers, only Alesha seems to have accepted it by the novel's end. Ivan is suffering from brain fever; Dmitri realizes that his acceptance of grace is at best fragile.

Toward the very beginning of Dostoevsky's writing career, in 1847, his early supporter and critic, Belinsky, wrote: "With us the personality is just beginning to break out of its shell."[25] Dostoevsky's mature writings would show both how difficult it was to break out of that shell, and how inadequately the regnant discourses of his day described the process for personalities who would accept neither the traits, nor the contexts, nor the roles that these discourses assigned them. Stories and selves fit very poorly together in Dostoevsky's novels, which transform learned treatises into fiction, narrators into liars, and listeners into resentful rebels, especially when the stories concern themselves. The more authoritative, rule-governed, and professionalized the narrative, the more likely it is to fail its subject and object, generating in turn new stories. Whether addressing the memorably resilient selves of its characters or turning outward to reflect on history, thought, and culture, *The Brothers Karamazov* never lets its readers forget that stories are never detached, nor disinterested, nor predictably instrumental. Yet the simple fact that Dostoevsky included his critique of narrative within a narrative, a lengthy novel, testifies to the inescapability of storytelling in coming to grips with the elusive self. It also testifies to his hope that teller and reader might, at last, get the story right.

Attention to the terms and debates of narrative theory illuminates the complexities of Dostoevsky's storied selves. Multiple refractions await even the dimmest ray of narrative light. Turning outward from literature and literary theory to Russian history, politics, and culture, Dostoevsky's novel reminds its readers that the stories one tells are part of a process in which the role stories play is neither detached, nor disinterested, nor predictably instrumental.

[24] Dostoevskii, *Polnoe sobranie sochinenii*, 14: 175.

[25] V. G. Belinskii, *Polnoe sobranie sochinenii v deviati tomakh* (Moscow: Khudozhestvennaia literatura, 1976–82), 9: 682.

CHAPTER TWELVE

Self and Sensibility in Radishchev's Journey from St. Petersburg to Moscow: *Dialogism, Relativism, and the Moral Spectator*

ANDREW KAHN

Bad timing, more than revolutionary intent, earned Alexander Radischev's *Journey from St. Petersburg to Moscow* (1790) its reputation as a dangerous book.[1] Radishchev in fact had gained the approval of the censor before he went to press, but Catherine II reacted with violent dislike to what she saw as a seditious work. In 1858, when Alexander Herzen published the first subsequent edition, he conferred a political imprimatur that remained.[2] From the late 1920s onward, whether in a popular work like Ol'ga Forsh's multivolume fictional biography or in literary studies, Radishchev, lionized as a proto-Decembrist and therefore Bolshevik avatar, was read almost exclusively in Russia for narrow political purposes. Much attention, perhaps too much, has been spent on systematizing the political ideas that appear in the *Journey* as a supplement to Radishchev's own writings on natural law.[3] Among early scholars, V. P. Semennikov countered the political reading reinforced by Pavel Shchegolev's important edition of the text. He judiciously drew attention to Radishchev's expressions of anxiety at the outbreak of the French Revolution.[4] In the pe-

A prior version of this essay appeared in *Oxford Slavonic Papers* 30 (1997): 40–66.
[1] The definitive edition of the *Journey* is A. N. Radishchev, *Puteshestvie iz Peterburga v Moskvu*, ed. V. A. Zapadov (St. Petersburg: Literaturnye pamiatniki, 1992) with an authoritative discussion of the complicated history of its composition and revisions. Henceforth in the body of this essay the *Puteshestvie iz Peterburga v Moskvu* is referred to as the *Journey*. In the notes all references to the *Puteshestvie* are to this edition.
[2] *O povrezhdenii nravov v Rossii kniazia Shcherbatova i Puteshestvie A. Radishcheva* (London: Trübner, 1858).
[3] These are collected in *Literaturnyi Arkhiv. A. N. Radishchev: Materialy i issledovaniia* (Moscow: Nauka, 1936), 77–140.
[4] V. P. Semennikov, *Radishchev: Ocherki i issledovaniia* (Moscow: Gosudarstvennoe iz-

riod after the Russian Revolution it was not surprising that Semennikov's reservations went unnoticed. Yet even more recent scholars, although wary of anachronism and uniquely attuned to less partisan literary history, have been unable to stand outside this framework in evaluating Radishchev's writings despite the fact that further work on the manuscripts has revealed the extent to which Radishchev adjusted controversial passages even at a late stage.[5]

The immediate aim of this chapter is not to refute systematically these approaches, but rather, to show why Radishchev's text has meanings, both philosophical and political, that go far beyond them. Put at its most obvious, political readings that regard the *Journey* as an exposé of the ills of Catherinian Russia are inadequate because they cannot in the first instance motivate the range of stories that form the cycle. The fiction of sentimentalism loves victims, but in this work far from all the victims owe their plight to the government under which they find themselves, and far from all the stories indict the law for failing to eliminate social ills. Apart from the famous vignettes on serfdom ("Zaitsovo," "Peshki," "Mednoe") which are more specific to Russia, the narrative encompasses a story of a shipwreck ("Chudovo"); tales of excess and luxury ("Vyshnii volochok," "Peshki"); a monk's tale of earthly temptation; historical meditation ("Novgorod"); prostitution ("Baldai") and syphilis ("Iazhelbitsy"); the theatricality of court life and the artificiality of ranking ("Vydropusk"); censorship ("Torzhok"); charity ("Klin"); and versification and rhetoric ("Tver'," Chernaia griaz' "). What is most revolutionary about the *Journey* is its literary treatment of a range of philosophical and political questions. At the heart of the novel lies an attempt to problematize the representation of sensibility and the self.[6] Beyond the large repertory of topics that were common currency at the time, from the evils of slavery to the problem of excess and luxury,[7] what makes the *Journey* a classic text of the eigh-

---

datel'stvo, 1923), 3–43ff. The whole question of the immediate effect of the French Revolution on Russian literature and thought needs to be restudied. For an overview of the subject see Irina Reyfman, "La réception des révolutions Française et Américaine en Russie au XVIIIe siècle," in *Histoire de la littérature russe: Des origines aux lumières*, ed. E. Etkind, G. Nivat, I. Serman, V. Strada (Paris: Fayard, 1992), 670–81.

[5] For example, Iu. M. Lotman, "Otrazhenie etiki i taktiki revoliutsionnoi bor'by v russkoi literature kontsa XVIII veka," in *Izbrannye stat'i* (Tallinn: Alexandra, 1993), 2: 134–58; this article was originally published in 1965 and is reproduced in this collection without alteration.

[6] In *The Invention of the Self: The Hinge of Consciousness in the Eighteenth Century* (Carbondale, Illinois: Southern Illinois University Press, 1978) John O. Lyons argues that the distinct project of fiction is the depiction of various types of self that have been examined in the philosophy of the period. For an overview of English and French philosophical writing on the subject, see Jean A. Perkins, *The Concept of the Self in the French Enlightenment* (Geneva: Droz, 1969), especially 11–84.

[7] On luxury and its concomitant moral dangers as a topic in English and French literature, see John Sekora, *Luxury: The Concept in Western Thought, Eden to Smollett* (Baltimore: Johns

teenth-century Enlightenment and a uniquely complex work in Russian literature of the period is its demonstration that sensibility, the period's most influential theory of the self, must be tested against experience rather than acquired theoretically, and that, moreover, the most effective literary model for doing so is a dialogic one.

The monological and reductive reading to which Radishchev's *Journey* has been subjected does not only reflect the party-minded mentality of Soviet times. Literary analyses of the text have been stymied by a failure to see it as the free mixing of genres and discourse, and have been further bedeviled by inadequate responses to two related questions: what to make of its plotlessness, and what to make of its quixotic hero?[8] Two counterarguments can be put forward, one concerning its external status in the canon, the second concerning the literary properties of the work. First, what has in part led critics to neglect the artistic side of the text is its unexpectedness from a historical point of view and its disruption of standard views of the development of the novel within a national tradition. It is one thing when a self-conscious novel like *Tristram Shandy*, with its sophisticated deconstruction of key intellectual and literary fashion, appears at the end of a series of important fictions; its intertextuality can be accommodated with a standard account of the rise of the novel. In a tradition in which fiction has an uncertain status, and the novel has been a relatively minor genre,[9] it is harder to account for a work of the self-consciousness of the *Journey* and all the easier to be deflected by a political approach.

In the second place, the choice of form is integral to the meaning of the text: any ethical or philosophical message depends on its literary context and presentation, an apparently obvious point that is all too easily forgotten in criticism, and all too easy to forget in a text that courts nonfiction at times. It is important to bear in mind the different formal aims of specific kinds of texts. One recent historian of sensibility has observed that "the common concerns with models of social understanding of such differently organized texts as the philosophical and the novelistic may be

---

Hopkins University Press, 1977), 23–134. For a brilliant essay on pleasure, luxury, and excess and their place in eighteenth-century culture, see Jean Starobinski, *L'Invention de la liberté* (Geneva: Skira, 1964).

[8] In *Virtue and the Veil of Illusion: Generic Innovation and the Pedagogical Project in Eighteenth-Century Literature* (Stanford: Stanford University Press, 1991), Dorothea E. von Mücke examines a wide selection of paradigmatic literary texts that are formally innovative and also didactic. Radishchev's *Journey* would be at home in her selection.

[9] On the Russian novel in the eighteenth century, see V. Sipovskii, *Ocherki po istorii russkogo romana*, vol. 1 (St. Petersburg: Tip. St. Peterburgskaia Tovarishchestva pechat' i izd. Trud, 1909–10); P. Brang, *Studien zu Theorie und Praxis der Russischen Erzahlung 1770–1811* (Weisbaden: O. Harassowitz, 1960). On the development of the novel as a genre and the wide range of forms subsumed in the term from the 1750s, see John Ricchetti, "Introduction," in *The Cambridge Companion to the Eighteenth-Century Novel*, ed. John Ricchetti (Cambridge: Cambridge University Press, 1996), especially 1–6.

a temptation to synthesis, but should not be allowed to produce a history in which difference is forgotten."[10] As the author of treatises on philosophical and political subjects that could also be enveloped in fiction, Radishchev was sensitive to the different capacities of novelistic and expository forms.[11] He employed a wide range of subgenres and types of discourse, but their arrangement is as a syntagmatic set of encounters and moral challenges only tenuously linked by plot.[12] Most novels of sensibility have only the flimsiest of story lines, borrowing the episodic structure of the picaresque as a framework for the moral exhibitionism (but rarely development) of the hero. Plotlessness is therefore a generic property rather than an individual fault. A key to the sequence is less the interrelation of themes from chapter to chapter than the work's very shape. As one scholar has recently noted, what distinguishes the novel of sensibility in this period is that it is "the amalgamation of these differing discourses [where] sensibilities come together."[13] Like many a sentimental novel, the *Journey* exhibits a formal looseness and open structure, capable of "almost endless variation and innovation, committed to few rules about length, contents, or approach."[14] Yet in the *Journey* those qualities have been misread as signs of unpolished craftsmanship rather than taken as part of the unusually strenuous demands that the author makes on his readers (fictive, implied, and actual) who, implicitly, can only understand the ethical imperative of the text by being made to reflect on the act of reading.[15] To an extent unprecedented in Russian fiction of the period, though with a certain debt to key French texts like Montesquieu's *Lettres persanes* (1721) and the abbé Raynal's *Histoire des deux Indes* (1770), Radishchev exploits polyphony and blurs boundaries between fiction, autobiography, and expository writing. For the medium that Radishchev designed enacts his belief in the capacity of reason to make sense of experience from relative viewpoints and in the fragility of untested convictions.

Despite its acknowledged importance in the canon, the *Journey* has been seen as a problematic, and even unsatisfactory work, largely owing to

[10] John Mullan, *Sentiment and Sociability: The Language of Feeling in the Eighteenth Century* (Oxford: Oxford University Press, 1988), 14.

[11] This approach to the literary features of Radishchev's work is visible in Allen McConnell's *A Russian Philosophe: Alexander Radishchev, 1749–1802* (The Hague: Mouton, 1964). What remains the best introduction in English to Radishchev's thought is vitiated by his conclusion that "[Radishchev] has plainly no love for artistic effect, no supply of colorful detail. . . . His fellow travelers are almost never described realistically" (76).

[12] The structure has been well described in David Denby, *Sentimental Narrative and the Social Order in France, 1760–1820* (Cambridge: Cambridge University Press, 1994), especially 74.

[13] Markman Ellis, *The Politics of Sensibility: Race, Gender and Commerce in the Sentimental Novel* (Cambridge: Cambridge University Press, 1996), 8.

[14] Ibid.

[15] Most recently the criticism of the traveler's failure to develop has been restated in V. A. Gun'ia, *Khudozhestvennoe svoeobrazie "Puteshestviia iz Peterburga v Moskvu" A. N. Radishcheva* (Tbilisi: Metsniereba, 1990), 124.

the static nature of the traveler, whose characterization during the course of the twenty-one episodes fails to develop, both abetting and resulting from its plotlessness. The demand that is found in Radishchev criticism for a three-dimensional portrait of a realistic, psychologically nuanced narrator ignores the prevalent sentimental literary models of the 1790s where authors created first-person narrators with little regard for psychological plausibility. Put the man of sentiment within striking distance of a deserving victim and there followed virtuous displays of benevolence: weeping, blushing, and abundant pity described dutifully according to a predetermined plan. Because Radishchev's hero does not fall quite into this category of authorial *porte-parole*, critics have long insisted on (but not proven) a likeness with Yorick of *A Sentimental Journey* in the frustrated search for a clear template on which Radishchev patterned his own work.[16] Sterne's hero enjoyed overwhelming popularity across Europe, and his behavior was imitated in and out of texts. Nevertheless, as McConnell rightly realized, Radishchev's traveler does not approach Sterne's hero either in speech or narrative style or, finally, in behavior. Yet in answering the question why Radishchev's hero is neither faithful to the stereotype made popular by Thomas du Baculard Arnaud in his *Les epreuves du sentiment* (1772–80) or Henry Mackenzie's Hartley from *A Man of Feeling* (1771), the most fruitful approach is not necessarily in tracing the hero's genetic material back to potential models or a sentimental master plot.

The status of the narrator reflects Radishchev's sophisticated approach to the generic volatility of fiction and to the place of the first-person self within the world he creates. That world is one of constant exchange and dialogue, of story embedded within story, where the narrator functions as both author and spectator, for whom the main activity is conveying the stories of others and commenting on them. Insofar as his outbursts of feeling are limited and his ability to take initiative strongly curtailed, the narrator satisfies neither of the two modes of behavior typical of the fiction of sentimentalism; and insofar as the stories that he interpolates in the narrative comprise a catalogue of discourses and registers, he is far more attentive to other selves and other stories than the usual sentimental hero, whose greatest delight is not in watching others, but in watching himself emote. Where the hero of sentimental fiction at its peak is exemplary in his selflessness, endowed with exquisite sensibility and depths of moral sentiment (and at his worst a parody of gestures unmotivated by an ethical impulse), Radishchev's narrator seems to be at times almost with-

---

[16] The parallel was set out in G. P. Makogonenko, *Radishchev i ego vremia* (Moscow: Gosudarstvennoe khudozhestvennoe izdatel'stvo, 1956), 438–78, and has been perpetuated in recent criticism. See, for example, A. Lévine and I. Z. Serman in *Histoire de la littérature russe*, 464.

out a self.[17] The creation of a narrator whose sensibility is displaced and fragmented in the discourse of others, and whose moral sentiment constitutes a peripheral voice in a chorus of other tales, poses one of the most curious problems of the *Journey*.

Self and Other in Radishchev: Toward the *Journey*

The question of self has a broader context within Radischev's oeuvre and larger intellectual trends. Sensibility, formulated in the early part of the century in England by the Earl of Shaftesbury, revised by Francis Hutcheson and other followers of the moral-sense school, given philosophical exploration by David Hume and physiological definition by Robert Whytt in Scotland,[18] and systematized by Condillac in his *Traité des systèmes* (1749), was a scientific and philosophical attempt to describe the interaction between the self and the world.[19] It was a concept that informed numerous fields of knowledge, including aesthetics, religion, political economy, moral philosophy, and sociability in the form of conduct books.[20] Sensibility as an intellectual and cultural phenomenon is part of Europe's intellectual legacy to Russia, and its influence is felt most in literature. Animated by these inquiries on human sensibility, the second half of the eighteenth century in Russian culture, no less than its Continental models, can be fairly called an age of definitions of the self. Educated in Leipzig at the initiative of Catherine II, at one time a participant in the drafting of the *Great Instruction*, steeped in the philosophy of his time, Radishchev made the exploration of self rather than political theory his philosophical touchstone in a variety of writings.

Radishchev's longest and most complex literary work, the *Journey* is one of a series of texts treating sensibility and the self. Regardless of the genre in which he wrote, for Radishchev seeing the self seems always to begin in viewing the other. In the *Life of Fedor Vasil'evich Ushakov*, perhaps the outstanding intellectual biography of the period, Radishchev commemo-

---

[17] On the decline of the genuine man of sentiment into a cliché, see N. D. Kochetkova, "Problema lozhnoi chuvstvitel'nosti v literature russkogo sentimentalizma," *XVIII vek* 17 (1991): 61–73.

[18] Robert Whytt, *Observations on the Nature, Causes, and Cure of Those Disorders Which Have Been Commonly Call'd Nervous, Hypochondriac, or Hysteric* (Edinburgh: J. Balfour, 1765).

[19] For a brief description, see J. C. O'Neal, "The Sensationist Aesthetics of the French Enlightenment," *L'esprit créateur* 28, no. 4 (1988): 95–106.

[20] On sensibility and sentimentalism, see R. F. Brissenden, *Virtue in Distress: Studies in the Novel of Sentiment from Richardson to Sade* (London: Macmillan, 1974), and Janet Todd, *Sensibility: An Introduction* (London: Methuen, 1986); on the growth of sensibility and its wider ramifications, there is an interesting treatment in F. Baasner, *Der Begriff "sensibilitie" im 18. Jahrhundert. Aufstieg und Niedergang eines Ideals* (Heidelberg: C. Winter, 1988).

rated the life of his friend and schoolmate from their years together in Leipzig.[21] With a deliberateness indicated by the word *zhitie* in the title, Radishchev here uses biography to create a work of secular hagiography by seeing in Ushakov's actions the principles and deeds of an exemplary life. In an early section of this *vita* Radishchev devoted a description to Ushakov's reading of Roman authors and his study of ancient concepts of virtue. What interests Radishchev is the implication of parallel lives for his own readers. For what Bakhtin calls a ratio of simultaneity, Ushakov will be an exemplary figure to Radishchev's readers, as the Romans were to Ushakov.[22] But the work also allowed Radishchev to view his own formative years by recreating the perspective of a second self. Much like one type of novelistic hero who "must become another in relation to himself, must look at himself through the eyes of another,"[23] Radishchev used biography to view the development of his own moral and intellectual self. The work ends with a final apostrophe to his dead friend, calling attention to the ongoing relation between self and other "and you, if you now are able to harken to the voice of one who laments, incline, o beloved, to my soul, you will see yourself alive in it."[24]

The Diary of a Week (Dnevnik odnoi nedeli), one of Radishchev's most accessible and incisive works, is a literary experiment in transcribing consciousness.[25] Given its attempt to embody identity by recording a character's thought processes, there is no doubt that it transposes into literary form Radishchev's views on the identity and self, based at least on his reading of Hume's *An Enquiry Concerning Human Understanding* (1748) and owes something to Rousseau's *Confessions* for its theatrical sense and attempt to fix the *je* through discourse.[26] As in the *Life of Ushakov*, and in anticipation of the opening of the *Journey*, the stimulus for exploring sen-

[21] On this period in Radishchev's intellectual development see M. A. Arzurnanova, "O sviaziakh s Rossiei A. N. Radishcheva v leiptsigskii period," *XVIII vek* 3 (1958): 527–37.

[22] On the moral exemplum and idealized figure in Russian culture at this time, see Andrew Kahn, "Introduction" to M. N. Murav'ev, *Institutiones Rhetoricae: a Treatise of a Russian Sentimentalist*, ed. Andrew Kahn (Oxford: W. M. Meeuws, 1995), l–lii, with bibliography.

[23] Mikhail Bakhtin, "Author and Hero in Aesthetic Activity," in *Art and Answerability: Early Philosophical Essays by M. M. Bakhtin*, ed. Michael Holquist and Vadim Liapunov (Austin: University of Texas Press, 1990), 15.

[24] "Zhitie Fedora Vasil'evicha Ushakova," in *Polnoe sobranie sochinenii A. N. Radishcheva*, ed. A.K. Borozdin, I. I. Lapshin, and P. E. Shchegolev (St. Petersburg: Izdatel'stvo V.M. Sablina, 1907), 1: 45.

[25] The work has been difficult to date firmly, and conjectures have ranged from the 1770s to 1790. See G. Ia. Galagan, "Geroi i siuzhet 'Dnevnika odnoi nedeli' Radishcheva. Vopros o datirovke," *XVIII vek* 23 (1977): 67–72.

[26] Sound treatments of the Rousseau-Radishchev connection have emphasized questions of political philosophy rather than theories and fictions of the self. See Alan McConnell, "Rousseau and Radishchev," *Slavonic and East European Journal* 8 (1964): 253–83; Arnold Miller, "Rousseau and Russia: Some Uses of the *Contrat Social*," *Essays in Literature* 5 (1978): 119–27. There is very little on Radishchev in Thomas Paul Barran, "How the Russians Read Rousseau: 1762–1803," Ph.D. diss., Columbia University, 1984. The best treatment of the

sibility and defining the self is the relation to another. The diary records the thoughts of a first-person narrator who has been left on his own for a week. Here, as earlier, the departure of friends entails a loss of the other, resulting in the writer's sense of alienation: *skaz* technique is dramatically used to capture the narrator's crisis of identity. It is no accident that it is upon the return of his friends that the fragment breaks off. The narrator's compulsion to write and fix the self terminates with their advent. But even before the recovery of the other restores the narrator's poise and sense of identity, he makes clear the difficulty he has in conceiving and representing a self that is uncontrolled and unmediated, forever open and unfixed. Anxiety mounts and grips the narrator, who at first fears himself and finally recoils from solitary and microscopic introspection:

> O proud insect! Enter into yourself and understand that you are able to reason only because you feel, because your reason has its origin in your fingers and your nakedness. . . . But where shall I seek even a momentary slaking of my sorrow? Where? Reason announces: in yourself. No, no, for there I find ruin, there sorrow, there hell; let us go.[27]

On this occasion Radishchev homes in on a fictional first-person narrator for whom *écriture* represents the construction of a personal identity that enables the writer to behave as though he were the other and invent himself.[28] But it is part of Radishchev's purpose to show (*pace* Rousseau) that it is ultimately unsatisfactory, and even impossible, to invent the self without reference to another. It seems that it is precisely Rousseau's notion of the self that Radishchev backs away from. For Rousseau the self is defined in relation to its prior existence as figured in other texts; hence the construction of self in the *Reveries* incorporates and reenacts moments from the *Confessions,* which in turn derive from earlier autobiographical texts. Radishchev, on the other hand, is constantly trying to socialize the self as a dialogical construct given definition in relation to an other.[29] In *Diary of a Week* the attempt to create a monologic subject fails because in the end it is incompatible with Radishchev's conviction that to be human is to be engaged in active relation to another individually or collectively, and be-

---

reception of Rousseau's political works in Russia remains Iu. M. Lotman, "Russo i russkaia kul'tura XVIII–nachala XIX veka," in *Izbrannye stat'i,* 2: 40–100.

[27] Radishchev, "Zhitie," 7.

[28] On *écriture* and the self in Rousseau, see Huntington Williams, *Rousseau and Romantic Autobiography* (Oxford: Oxford University Press, 1983), especially the Introduction and chap. 4; and J. F. Maccannell, "The Postfictional Self / Authorial Consciousness in Three Texts by Rousseau," *Modern Language Notes* 89 (1974): 580–99.

[29] For this reason it seems to me that McConnell exaggerates Radishchev's artistic debt to Rousseau. If, as he maintains, Rousseau's influence on Radishchev is greater than any other writer's, I would argue it is only as a model against which Radishchev is defining himself.

cause attempts to view oneself from the outside fall into the trap of subjectivism.[30] Whether or not the *Diary of One Week* is better read as a fictional or an autobiographical monologue, there is also a case for construing it as evidence of Radishchev's evolving views on the literary self. The experiment in the monologic self, where hero is detached from author and other characters, ends in a rejection of texts that privilege only a single discourse and attempt to see the world through only one pair of eyes. It is significant, then, that the *Journey* makes clear from the outset that a dialogic structure and a dialogic approach to its entire spectrum of experiences and ideas are imperative.

The same process can be demonstrated with reference to the treatise *On Man, His Mortality and Immortality* (O cheloveke, o ego smertnosti i bezsmertii), where Radishchev is at his most effective in constructing a philosophical dialogue. In his writings on political theory and on the nature of man Radishchev showed his understanding of a basic tenet of the late eighteenth century, namely, that the age of reason arrives at philosophical and scientific truths through the evaluation of complementary and sometimes competing hypotheses and viewpoints. We have only to think of the *Encyclopédie* (1751–65) for one of the most visible and influential examples of the way in which various explanatory paradigms and types of scientific inquiry began to displace the authority of revelation and creed without coming to final conclusions: the only dogma was the faith in reason to establish the truth through trial and error.[31] In Radishchev's writings, relativism is a literary technique of defamiliarization used to challenge assumptions and cast philosophical certainty into doubt. This habit of mind first emerges in the quasi-literary treatise *On Man, His Mortality and Immortality,* and becomes an important feature of his novelistic writing in the *Journey.* The tendency to juxtapose points of view leads in *On Man* to positions that have sometimes been deemed contradictory

---

[30] The scientific language and image of the spectator link the quotation from the *Diary* to the following passage from *About Man:* "Arm your vision with telescopes striving for the furthest fixed stars; arm it with microscopes, magnifying millions of million times; what will you see? That you are unable to become separate from the existence that was given to you for even so much as a single trait. . . . And although you will see a part of the organ that gives you thought, but what glass will allow you to see your feeling?" (8).

[31] In the words of Robert Darnton, *L'aventure de l'Encyclopédie, 1775–1800* (Paris: Librairie académique Perrin, 1982), 31: "c'est cette rupture avec les idées établies sur la connaissance et l'autorité intellectuelle qui rend l'*Encyclopédie* aussi hérétique." Despite the paucity of evidence concerning Radishchev's reading, much material has been accumulated to show, first, his extensive and intensive debt to German and French thought, and second, even more important for our purposes, his eclecticism and comprehensive approach to a subject. On the paucity of sources for reconstructing his intellectual biography, see Makogonenko, *Radishchev i ego vremia,* chapters 1–2; Iu. M. Lotman, "Iz kommentariev k *Puteshestviiu iz Peterburga v Moskvu,*" *XVIII vek* 12 (1977): 29. V. P. Semennikov, "Literaturno-obshchestvennyi krug Radishcheva" in *Literaturnyi Arkhiv,* 213–89, remains a valuable profile.

when closer attention to the style of exposition might more convincingly resolve some of the antinomies. In the second section of this work Radishchev appears to be arguing that the soul is material, whereas in Part Three he seems to maintain that it is also immortal. Yet all of Part Two consists of a rather lopsided dialogue between Radishchev and an invented interlocutor who argues the materialist case forcefully. At the end of Part Two the treatise makes a sudden volte-face. A passionate denunciation of this position leads into the contrary proofs of the third part enunciated by the first speaker. There is no narrator to intervene and arbitrate, and the reader is left to weigh their respective positions without authoritative guidance.[32] In this respect the style of argumentation is imbued with the spirit of Kant's definition of Enlightenment as the "possibility man has of exiting from a minority that consists of himself alone. That minority is the incapacity to achieve understanding without the direction of another. Sapere aude! Have the courage to avail of understanding through your own effort."[33] This is a moral imperative for the reader as much as for the writer. The remainder of this essay examines a number of key episodes in the *Journey* that deploy literary devices and exploit linguistic ambiguity as a way of transforming reader response into a philosophical challenge by continually creating relative viewpoints on politics, literature, and the self.

The Seeing Self and Seeing the Self

Writings on the *Journey* often point to the second paragraph of the dedication as the moment when Radishchev flies the flag of his political program. In fact, the entire document well deserves to be read as part of the creation of the persona of the traveler. Eighteenth-century dedications, which were governed by strict conventions, can be studied fruitfully in writing the history of literary institutions, but their value is often sociological rather than aesthetic, since they speak almost exclusively to the patron rather than the reader. In its very opening, this dedication strikingly departs from that decorum: "Whatever reason and the heart might wish to achieve will be dedicated to you, my co-feeler! Although my opinions on many things differ from yours, still your heart beats in accordance with mine—and you are my friend."[34] Here, the language of friendship, socia-

---

[32] The full text of *O cheloveke, o ego smertnosti i bezsmertii* is in A. N. Radishchev, *Polnoe sobranie sochinenii*, 2: 3–141.

[33] See Immanuel Kant, "On the Question: What is Enlightenment?" in *What is Enlightenment*, ed. James Schmidt (Berkeley: University of California Press, 1996), 58–65. If Kant is a primary philosophical inspiration, a primary literary model here may be Montesquieu's *Lettres persanes* where adjacent letters argue opposite views. See, for example, Letters LXXVI and LXXVII, where the morality of suicide is disputed and upheld.

[34] Radishchev, *Puteshestvie*, 6.

bility,[35] and readership replaces that of patronage; expressions of difference displace the ritual obsequience; the language of feeling and suffering supplants the measured decorum and impersonal tone controlling the relation between writer and aristocrat. On the level of content the dedication signals a whole series of key terms and themes.

Equally important is the way in which the encounter with the addressee serves as an exmplary act of reading. In the *Journey* Radishchev will repeatedly draw attention to the physiological basis of sensibility by anatomizing his own reactions. In the opening of the second paragraph he tells the reader that his entire account begins as a reaction to his experience. Whereas Rousseau privileges hearing and the inner voice as the source of truth, in the *Journey* Radishchev makes sight the preferred cognitive sense.[36] Empirical knowledge of the world comes through observation, and knowledge of the self metaphorically derives specifically from looking both outward and inward. Sight is the operative sense in the dedication, and it is the spectacle of human unhappiness that makes him look inward: "I glanced around me—my soul is wounded by the sufferings of mankind. I directed my looks into my inner being—and espied that the sorrows of man come from man, and often only because he gazes incorrectly on the objects that surround him."[37]

As in *Diary of a Week*, it is the sensitivity to the physical world of nature and to the presence of the other that checks the move from outer perception to inner cognition.

> I awakened from my despair, to which sensibility and empathy had subjected me; I sensed in myself adequate strength to resist this mistake; and—ineffable happiness!—I felt that each person is able to be a collaborator in benefactions similar to oneself [compatible with oneself].—This thought aroused me to sketch out what I would read. But if, I said to myself, I find somebody who approves of my intention, who for the sake of a blessed goal will not find fault with the unsuccessful depiction of thought, who will suffer with me over the woes of one's brethren, who will support me in my action—will it not then be a marvelous fruit that comes from the labor I have undertaken? . . . Why, why

---

[35] For a history of the shifting meanings of the term "sociability" in French culture, see Daniel Gordon, *Citizens without Sovereignty: Equality and Sociability in French Thought, 1670–1789* (Princeton: Princeton Univeresity Press, 1994), chapter 2. The sociability that extends between Radishchev and Kutuzov creates one manifestation of sociability as an imaginary sphere in which virtue and autonomy can exist even in a society where political liberty is absent.

[36] Optical vocabulary predominates over auditory words in the *Journey*. See, *inter alia*, the entries for "videt'," "vid," "obrashchat' vzor," "zret'," "zrenie" in *A Lemmatized Concordance to A Journey from Petersburg to Moscow of A.N. Radishchev*, ed. Yasuo Urai (Sapporo: Hokkaido University, 1998).

[37] Radishchev, *Puteshestvie*, 6.

should I look into the distance for anybody? My friend! you live near my heart—and your name will illuminate this beginning.[38]

Under the cordial surface of sincerity and feeling, and when read in its intellectual and historical context, this passage can be seen to encode a polemic between two radically different approaches to the self as a philosophical and political entity, that is, between sensibility and freemasonry. The respective partisanship of the donor and dedicatee was not a secret to the small group of contemporaries and to Radishchev's immediate writers: Kutuzov's contributions the journal *Morning Light* (Utrennii svet) and his closeness to Novikov were clear signals of his masonic affiliation.[39] The source of ambiguity in the introduction is the deliberate application of a discourse common to both sensibility and freemasonry, including terms of philanthropy (*blagaia tsel'*, *blagodeistvie*), the notion of brotherhood with slightly militant overtones (*sobratie moe*),[40] the motif of sight and enlightenment (*ozarit sie nachalo*), and the theme of inwardness (*vnutrennost'*) and self-knowledge versus illusion (*zabluzhdenie*). The full implication of the dedication, and the gap that Radishchev opens between sensibility and freemasonry, becomes more apparent by way of juxtaposition with the opening passage of the *Redemptive Reflections* (Spasitel'nye razmyshleniia), one of a number of treatises published by Novikov in the 1780s, by which time Radishchev had begun writing the *Journey*. It is an example of the argument, the vocabulary, and the masonic commonplaces on which Radishchev draws as a way of alerting the reader to his book's ulterior polemic. The key term of comparison is *vnutrennost'*:[41]

God is sought in exterior things, bypassing one's inwardness, in which the closest God is. And because I turn from external things to inner ones, and

---

[38] Ibid.

[39] On this journal as the vehicle of the most radical masonic groups, see P. N. Berkov, *Istoriia russkoi zhurnalistiki XVIII veka* (Leningrad: Akademiia nauk, 1952), 314, 397–400; for a concise summary of Novikov's journalistic activity, see Iu. D. Levin, *Vospriiatie angliiskoi literatury v Rossii* (Leningrad: Nauka, 1990), 60–65.

[40] Fraternal language is part of the whole freemasonic cult and literary style. See, for instance, Lopukhin's publication *Bratskiie uveshchaniia k nekotorym vradiam svbdnm. kmnshchkm.* (Moscow, 1784). According to Margaret Jacob, *Living the Enlightenment: Free Masonry and Politics in Eighteenth-Century Europe* (Oxford: Oxford University Press, 1991), freemasonry as a form of association was based on egalitarian principles, above all the principle of merit. But she argues that this egalitarianism was part of an ethical rather than a democratic activism. It was accompanied by a desire to promote domestic virtue, religious feeling, and philanthropy rather than a desire to institute popular sovereignty, which, arguably, would have made the movement acceptable if not attractive to Radishchev.

[41] The entry in the *Slovar' russkogo iazyka XVIII-ogo veka*, vol. 2 (Leningrad: Nauka, 1987), gives five glosses. All but the third give citations referring to the natural sciences. Usage of *vnutrennost'* in the sense of the "inner, spiritual world of man" appears to be uncommon in literary texts as Radishchev is the main source given.

will ascend from inner ones to higher ones in order to learn where I have come from, or where I go, what I am, and what essence I possess, in this manner, having known oneself, one could come to the awareness of God. For the more I succeed in the knowledge of the self, the closer I come to the knowledge of God.[42]

For the freemason, self-knowledge means knowledge of God largely through a mystical apprehension of the divinity to which the senses contribute only secondarily. At the end of this passage sight refers to internal vision within the context of memory rather than an outlook onto the actual world. The masonic means of finding God is introspection, whereas for Radishchev man becomes godlike, what he calls the *bogochelovek*, only when turning outward in acts of benevolence and reason. Throughout the *Journey* Radishchev returns to the image of *vnutrennost'* to signify two things. First, it means the physiological capacity, akin to a moral intuition, that is either triggered by or registered as a reaction to the sight of suffering. Sentimental heroes have bad nerves because they are unusually predisposed to philanthropy, and, in the words of the Scottish physician Robert Whytt, "sympathy was no more than the communication of feeling between different bodily organs, manifested by functional disturbance of one organ when another was stimulated."[43] Hence, for example, at the end of "Liubani," the third station on the journey, where the narrator's meeting with a ploughman leads him to ponder the economic inequality of the peasant, his reaction is a marked display of a type of *vnutrennost'* at odds with the masonic meaning of the word: "Suddenly I felt a quick 'filth' flowing through my blood and, driving heat toward the top parts, forcing it to spread across the face. I became so ashamed in my innerness that I almost wept."[44] Here in the best tradition of sentimental fiction the body is the communicator of the ethical self.

There are also moments where *vnutrennost'*, extending the theme of the dedication, is used to relativize by parodying masonic discourse. In "Spasskaia polest'," one of the longest and most complex chapters, a physiological reaction serves as the bridge passage between the first section narrating a story of misfortune and the famous allegorical dream. Dreams

[42] *Spasitel'nye razmyshleniia o poznanii chelovecheskogo vnutrennogo i vneshnago sostoianiia, ili: o poznanii sebia samogo . . . s preizzriadnymi nravoucheniiami do vsekh voobshche, a osoblivo i bez iz''iatiia do kazhdogo imia Khristianskoe na sebe nosiashchogo kasaiushchimisia* (Moscow: Senatskaia tipografiia, 1784), 3.

[43] On physiological theories of sensibility, see Brissenden, *Virtue in Distress*, n. 30, 33–34; G. S. Rousseau, "Nerves, Spirits, and Fibres: Towards Defining the Origins of Sensibility," in *Studies in the Eighteenth Century: Papers presented at the Third David Nichol Smith Memorial Seminar*, ed. R. F. Brissenden and J. C. Eade (Canberra: Australia National University Press, 1976), 137–59.

[44] Radishchev, *Puteshestvie*, 11 ("Liubani").

in masonic literature are often a topos of divine revelation,[45] but when Radishchev's traveler looks inward, his dreams are of secular deities, his vision of a political program couched in a combination of symbols and discourse of natural jurisprudence that counterpose his vision to mystical revelation. While the arrangement of themes in the *Journey* does not fall into a strict pattern, Radischev tends to present major topics twice: the first time, a topic will be subordinated to another theme; in a later chapter the theme will be given more independent treatment.[46] *Vnutrennost'* as the path to divine recognition recurs a final time at the end of "Bronnitsy." The chapter deals with types of religious experience and stages a parodic revelation that can be read as a pendant to "Spasskaia polest'." Moved by the sight of a church erected on the ruins of a pagan temple, the traveler climbs a hill where he hears a sublime voice warning of the limits of human knowledge and the blindness of reason. The deity once again speaks in tones and terms drawn from the discourse of freemasonry before the revelation is puncuated by the obligatory thunderclap authenticating it:

> Why, o bold one! do you crave to know what only the single eternal thought can attain? Know that the unknowability of the future is commensurate with the fragility of your physical structure. Know, that happiness divined beforehand loses the sweetness of long expectation, that the charm of present joy, having exhausted its forces, is unable to effect in the soul the pleasant trembling that joy receives from anticipation. Know that doom known beforehand removes temporary tranquillity, poisons joys. . . . In returning to your home, returning to your family, calm the stirred thoughts; enter into your inner being; there you will find my divinity, there you will hear my message—And the crash of a strong thundering blow in the demesne of Perun resounded far and wide in the valleys.—I came to my senses.[47]

Yet at the end of the chapter another voice addresses the traveler, urging disbelief. Despite the powerful aesthetic experience of the revelation, the traveler admits that "reason prevents one from keeping both faith and the story; reason seeks convincing and sensuous conclusions." To the voice of revelation, therefore, the traveler opposes the discourse of literature, ending the chapter with an excerpt from Addison's *Cato*. This passage on the nature of historical cycles distills the traveler's earlier meditations on the varieties of monotheism throughout history and sets in relation to one

[45] Cf. P. Iu. L'vov', *Khram istiny, videnie Sezostrisa, Tsaria Egipteskogo* (Petropol: Akademiia nauk, 1790).

[46] For example, the theme of paternal and filial relations is first mooted and then expanded in the consecutive chapters of "Krest'tsy" and "Iazhelbitsy."

[47] Radishchev, *Puteshestvie*, 35–36 ("Bronnitsy").

another the claims of each religion to truth by placing them in a larger context. Second, rather than affirming either nature or God, it undermines revelation as an epistemologically privileged category by referring to it as a story, and by identifying man as the spectator to overriding cycles of history. While it would be possible to interpret the first part of the scene as Radishchev's criticism of superstition and bogus mysticism, it is clearly more than that. In both cases, the traveler leaves the reader to deliberate between two systems.

This implicit and explicit opposition of points of view through different types of discourse is not the narrator's only strategy for placing the burden of assessment on the reader. A favorite device of closure in the *Journey* is the ironical silence or gesture, the mere shrug that undermines certainty that the narrator must necessarily subscribe to every *bien-pensant* disquisition he relates. "Liubani" begins by depicting an encounter between the narrator and a serf, which prompts meditations on the inequity of all types of servitude. Jarred by the realization that in his own treatment of his coachman he may not be superior to the landowner, the traveler asks himself, what is the source of his authority over another person. The answer is the law. The fact that another intellectual system sanctions his position cannot stop the self-reproach of conscience. Yet, although the narrator weeps, reason subdues passion and prevents him from acting.[48] Similarly, at the end of "Vyshnii volochok," an ironic gesture sums up the traveler's response to a story on the evils of luxury and the economic exploitation of empire; the topic was one of the main themes of the abbé Raynal's *Histoire des deux Indes*, a work that Radishchev held in high esteem.[49] Clearly the traveler is gripped by the speaker's picture of the slave-based production of coffee.[50] He goes on to underscore the point by recounting a story that another friend has told him about agricultural exploitation in America. But as a resident of St. Petersburg he can hardly resist the temptation of coffee any more than he can not wear a wig: "the view of the prohibition accompanying this statement shook me to my inner being. My hand shook and my coffee spilled."[51] This typifies the constant alternation of perspectives in the *Journey*. It is also noteworthy that once again a moment of apprehension is construed in visual terms. The whole process of relativizing is a literary technique put to the service of philosophical advancement. Radishchev

[48] Radishchev, *Puteshestvie*, 12 ("Liubani").

[49] See Semennikov, *Radishchev*, 33–38; on the history of political economy in the Enlightenment, see Catherine Larrère, *L'Invention de l'économie au XVIIIe siècle* (Paris: Presses universitaires de France, 1992).

[50] On coffee as a luxury product and attitudes about its consumption, see Fernand Braudel, *Civilization and Capitalism* (London: Collins, 1988), 1: 256–62.

[51] Radishchev, *Puteshestvie*, 75 ("Vyshnii volochok").

does not believe in moral relativism, but for him, as for many thinkers of the Enlightenment, the definition of concepts like reason, truth, virtue, and freedom becomes in part a matter of personal judgment and reason based on the apprehension of another and sometimes contradictory point of view. No sooner are a position and judgment established than alternative possibilities are revealed.

The Dialogical Self as Moral Spectator

The narrator's compulsion to employ the technique of relativistic viewpoint, even while expressing sympathy, can be more closely correlated to Radishchev's intellectual context. Theories of sensibility posited different relations between the donor and the recipient depending on the place that the writer's theory of human nature accorded to benevolence. At the heart of such arguments were views on the relation between the passions and reason. The English "moral sense" school held that sympathy was activated by the observation of joy and grief in others. The mechanisms of sympathy are vicarious. In watching the outward signs of emotion we translate these signs into the emotions themselves. This process occurs because the expressions we observe in others are similar in all humanity and therefore familiar. Sympathy of a pleasurable or painful kind will be stronger in just proportion to the vividness of the impressions, and, according to Hume, can be experienced as readily in the theater or in reading as in life.[52]

There is a strong and instructive connection between Radishchev and the revision of sensibility produced by Adam Smith. His *Theory of Moral Sentiments* had formed the basis for a number of essays written by M. N. Murav'ev in the late 1750s, and was read in its own right.[53] There are two related components to this aspect of his thought which are relevant. First, in modifying Hume's claim of benevolence as a natural passion, Smith inserts a new stage between the acts of observation and sympathetic identification.[54] This new stage is one of willed uninvolvement in which the passions that are provoked by sympathy become subject to the regulation of an imaginary spectator who acts as an internal regulator and an observer to the subject in the act of observation, reinforcing the

---

[52] For a fuller discussion of these points, see the version of this article published in *Oxford Slavonic Papers.*

[53] See N. D. Kochetkova, *Literatura russkogo sentimentalizma* (St. Petersburg: Nauka, 1994), 122–34.

[54] On Hume's concept of benevolence, see *The Cambridge Companion to Hume,* ed. David Fate Norton (Cambridge: Cambridge University Press, 1993), 164–72.

distinction between the spectator and the agent as well as between the agent and the object.[55] In this model, sympathy becomes a secondary emotion that stems from the possibility of observing the "sympathetic passion of the observer." Sympathy articulates and controls the representation of the original passion to the self as a way of checking the overflow of sentiment and ensuring the sociability that can only be preserved through self-control.

The second part concerns the operation of this spectator and the figure of the mirror as an image for society.[56] In the 1759 edition of the *Theory*, from which Murav'ev translated excerpts, Smith wrote that "we must imagine ourselves not the actors, but the spectators of our own character and conduct."[57] Initially, the imaginary separation between the spectator (as a part of reason) and the agent creates the space for self-judgment. But this perspective on the self is further complicated by the presence of society as a mirror which is placed in the countenance and behavior of those we live with. Whereas Hume used the image of a chain of mirrors as a metaphor for the mutuality of sentiments that passes from one mind to another in human interactions, for Smith there is the single mirror that not only allows the one mind to become both subject and object, both agent and spectator, but also to be spectator on the self from the perspective of society.[58] Smith himself expressed this double function when he wrote in the 1761 edition (the basis for all reprintings henceforth) that this constitutes the process whereby "I divide myself, as it were, into two persons . . . the first is the spectator . . . the second is the agent."[59] When sympathy for another is provoked, this inner judge appears to change position, to step out of the self and treat it as another. It is this bifurcation of the self that facilitates examination of one's own conduct and the sympathy that allows one to place oneself in another's situation and to evaluate it in regard to one's self-interest: this capacity for judgment is meant to

[55] P. S. Ardal, *Passion and Value in Hume's Treatise* (Edinburgh: University of Edinburgh Press, 1966), 141; quoted in Mullan, *Sentiment and Sociability*, 45.

[56] On the moral spectator and Adam Smith, I have found the following works helpful: Mullan, *Sentiment and Sociability*, especially 43–56; Chris Jones, *Radical Sensibility: Literature and Ideas in the 1790s* (London: Routledge, 1993), 30–33; Istvan Hont and Michael Ignatieff, "Introduction" to *Wealth and Virtue: The Shaping of Political Economy in the Scottish Enlightenment*, ed. Istvan Hont and Michael Ignatieff (Cambridge: Cambridge University Press, 1983), especially 6–10; Nicholas Phillipson, "Adam Smith as Civic Moralist" in Hont and Ignatieff, *Wealth and Virtue*, 179–202.

[57] Adam Smith, *The Theory of Moral Sentiments*, ed. D. D. Raphael and A. L. Macfie (Oxford: Oxford University Press, 1976), 111.

[58] Mullan, *Sentiment and Sociability*, 48. It would be interesting to explore the possibility of reformulating Smith's use of the mirror in terms of the Lacanian *stade du miroir*. To what extent does the development of self-judgment in Smith's scheme parallel the site in the formation of the ego where the subject becomes alienated from himself? In this analogue society would be equivalent to the adult or the big Other that ratifies the subject's image.

[59] Adam Smith, *Theory of Moral Sentiments*, 113.

produce an impartiality that is both benevolent and at the same time immune to the passions.

The mirror as the instrument of self-improvement is a widespread topos in the moralizing literature of the eighteenth century.[60] In this type of didactic literature readers find not a reflection of themselves but their idealized image. Yet these didactic works hold up pictures rather than mirrors to the self; their discourse is univocal insofar as the reader or aspirant to self-improvement is not encouraged to view the self from the perspective of another. This static relation is precisely the opposite of dialogism where, as explained by Michael Holquist:

> All meaning is relative in the sense that it comes about only as a result of the relation between two bodies occupying *simultaneous but different* space, where bodies may be thought of as ranging from the immediacy of our physical bodies, to political bodies and to bodies of ideas in general (ideologies). . . . Bakhtin's observer is also, simultaneously, an *active participant* in the relation of simultaneity. Conceiving being dialogically means that reality is always experienced, not just perceived, and further that it is experienced from a particular position.[61]

The process Smith described, like Bakhtin's model, redoubles the dialogic self in making the spectator a mediator between society (here functioning as one other) and the self and the spectator (the second other).

This triangulation of the self is a notion that Radishchev invokes at one with Smith in his opening chapter. "Vyezd" is not only the traveler's send-off: it is a chapter in which all action is elided in narrative time. Attention is focused on the traveler's grief at departing and then moves on to his efforts to place himself in an imaginative space. Again, like the dedication, it is a passage filled with oblique instruction to the reader on how to approach the world Radishchev creates, and how to view Radishchev's own self as it is transposed in the figure of the traveler. The terms of this description are cast explicitly in the allegorical language of the moral journey, and they describe a loss of self caused by separation from the other

---

[60] For example, *Zertsalo vechnosti ili Razsuzhdeniia (1) O smerti. (2) O poslednem sude; (3) O adskom muchenii i (4) O radosti raiskoi: v koikh izobrazheny naibeditel'neishiia sredstva k udaleniiu sebia ot porokov i mirskikh suet* (St. Petersburg: Vil'kovskii and Galchenkov, 1787); or the less forbidding *Zertsalo zhenskoi drevnei uchenosti, ili Opisanie zhizni drevnikh filosofov. Soderzhashchee v sebe, ikh rod, proiskhozhdenie, postupki, deianiia i ucheniia* (Moscow: A. Reshetnikov, 1800). For an example of one of the most important examples of the sort of monological prescriptive approach to behavior that Radishchev is undermining, see *O dolzhnostiakh cheloveka i grazhdanina* (St. Petersburg, 1783). There is a translation and discussion in J. L. Black, *Citizens for the Fatherland: Education, Educators, and Pedagogical Ideals in Eighteenth-Century Russia* (New York: East European Quarterly, 1979), 209ff.

[61] Michael Holquist, *Dialogism: Bakhtin and his World* (London: Routledge, 1990), 20.

that is to be followed by a recovery that is enacted through the encounters of the *Journey*.

> Blessed is he who weeps while hoping for a consoler; blessed is he who lives in the future; blessed is he who lives in the process of dreaming. His essence deepens, pleasures multiply, and tranquility preempts the gloominess of sadness, arranging images of happiness in the mirrors of the imagination.—I lie in the carriage . . . . I see myself in an extensive valley that has lost from the heat of the sun all its pleasantness and the variegation of green; there is no source here of cooling, no arboreal shade for the moderation of the heat. Alone, abandoned, a wanderer amidst nature. I was shaken. "Miserable one," I cried, "where are you?"[62]

The sense of being outside the self described in this passage identifies a striking and highly unusual aspect of the traveler's characterization and calls attention to the notion of self as an important theme in the text. In sentimental fiction, and perhaps this is most true of fiction written from the 1780s onward, characters are always seeing virtue in distress and, depending on the degree of sympathy, exhibiting severe physical symptoms and then acting charitably. By contrast, although Radishchev's traveler is capable of munificence (he offers a handout once in "Klin"), he is much more the passive spectator, recounting and observing the plight of the subject. On occasion he becomes instructive and didactic in the manner of the earlier sentimental hero, but more frequently he then does not act, carefully maintaining his distance as a spectator of others' misfortunes, as recorder of his own reaction, and communicating to the reader the dilemma of relative points of view without endorsing action as virtue.

The role of the moral spectator is to gain a perspective on the self by assuming the viewpoint of another and to help the fictional reader and implied reader gain a perspective on others. There is no more artful example of this technique in the *Journey* than the story told in "Chudovo," where the layering of narrative frames asks us to read the tale as the interaction of contrasting sets of perspectives: the narrator (the traveler) on the secondary narrator (his friend the storyteller); a character in the story on the secondary narrator; and the reader's view of the tale as a real event, a political allegory, or a work of art.

At the post station at Chudovo, the narrator meets a friend he had left behind in St. Petersburg. After a festive few days in Peterhof and its environs the secondary narrator decided, for the sake of glimpsing nature ("blagost' prirody") and admiring the sunrise ("zrelishche voskhozhdeniia solntsa"), to hire a boat. The secondary narrator begins by telling

---

[62] Radishchev, *Puteshestvie*, 7 ("Vyezd").

how, as they sailed into a storm, he dispelled his anxiety by aestheticizing the experience, stepping outside the experiential frame of reference and into a canvas he paints along conventional lines:

> Poetic imagination had already relocated me in the wonderful pastures of Pathos and Amaphon. Suddenly the whistling of a wind rising in the distance dispelled my dream, and, oppressed, there appeared to my eyes thickening clouds, whose black heaviness, it seemed, directed them to our head and terrified with their descent. The mirrorlike surface of the waters began to show spots, and silence yielded its place to the incipient splashing of the waves. I welcomed this sight, observed the majestic traits of nature, and will say without vanity that what was beginning to terrify others made me happy. I exclaimed that it was like Vernet. Ah, how good![63]

In short compass this passage moves across two scenic frames as the narrator uses images to contain his expectations of nature and control his own emotions. The narrator begins by situating himself in a neoclassical landscape by tagging the picture with a reference to Greek places. As the narrator's perceptions change, the point of reference changes from this Claude-like picture to an invocation of Vernet, whose paintings of storms at sea, widely reproduced as prints, famously translated into pictorial terms the aesthetic of the sublime. The visual citation remains the key subtext in this narration. At the end of the first part the narrator speaks in terms closely reminiscent of Burke's classic treatise on the sublime, again suggesting that his retrospective account is a crafted literary performance, and that the act of recollection requires just as much distance as the act of controlling one's passions and distress during this sublime experience. He emphasizes the terror-*cum*-pleasure inspired by the force of the storm, by its majesty and power, creating a verbal chiaroscuro equivalent to the division of the heavens between clear and dark sky that is a standard feature in paintings. As the narrative gains in drama and is rendered in explicitly pictorial terms (*vzory, predstavlenie, zertsalovidnyi, cherty prirody*), Radishchev's narrator becomes the spectator of a narrator who is becoming a spectator of his own experience, creating a chain of viewers not unlike Hume's explanation of sympathy as the product of the minds of men arranged like a sequence of mirrors. This structuring of perspective stands in an interesting relation to the visual source. What the narrative owes to Vernet, and what gives the reader with a knowledge of the pictorial source an added pleasure and perspective, is its ability to contain within a single view a whole series of groups in which characters are clearly linked in their fates but also unaware of their interconnectedness;

[63] Radishchev, *Puteshestvie*, 12 ("Chudovo").

the paintings become an allegory of sociability under threat just as the re-counting of the tale functions to reestablish communcation.[64]

Although the perspective of the narrative as it unfolds is now told from the eye of the storm, the vivid detail and events appear to be patterned on Vernet as the narrator covers all the topoi of the canvas and actualizes the human drama of the painting. The focus shifts from the speaker onto the captain of the boat, who gradually disappears from view into the fore-ground as he heads in search of help. In the second frame, the speaker, re-creating the depth of the canvas, refocuses on the ship and describes the plight of the passengers as they await rescue. Again, in an attempt to create the perfect analogue of the painting the narrator relies on a pre-cise vocabulary to create perspective:

> Something black and moving spotted by us, it seemed, gradually grew larger; finally, as it approached, it presented to our eyes two small vessels heading straight for the spot where we were in our despair, a hundred times increasing our hope. As when the door suddenly opens in a dark temple com-pletely impermeable to light and a ray of light, flying straight into the gloom, dispels it, spreads through the shrine to its deepest recesses—thus, when we spotted the vessels, was the ray of hope for salvation that coursed through our souls.[65]

Radishchev's narrator signals pictorially the shift to a different story by moving the frame of reference out of the seascape inland and out of the picture. This visual cue marks the shift to another narrative, the account of the boat's captain which is embedded in the secondary narrator's story. This story of the rescue quickly turns into a series of encounters as the captain solicits help from the local customs agent where his pleas fall on deaf ears, and then the local garrison where he finds aid. Once the boat is beached, the captain returns to the customs house to remonstrate with the supervisor about his subordinate's inhumanity. He is rebuffed when the supervisor justifies the refusal on the grounds that it was not their duty

---

[64] For the possible literary sources of this episode, see A. Skaftymov, "O stile *Puteshestviia iz Peterburga v Mosvku*" in his *Stat'i o russkoi literature* (Saratov: Saratovskoe knizhnoe iz-datel'stvo, 1959), 77–103. The "tempête" as a subject became synonymous with Claude-Joseph Vernet (1714–1789). It is likely that Radishchev has no one particular painting in mind as the visual source. There is a suggestive parallel between Radishchev's verbal picture and Diderot's great celebration of Vernet in the Salon of 1767. See *Diderot on Art*, trans. John Goodman with an introduction by Thomas Crow (New Haven: Yale University Press, 1995), 2: 86ff. In his discussion of Vernet Diderot's narrator animates the landscape and tells his story from within it. Diderot's description here employs the categories of Burke's *Philosophical Inquiry*, but typically suppresses his source and diverts the reader onto less im-portant theorists. The *Salons* were circulated in Melchior Grimm's *Correspondance littéraire* of which Catherine II was one of the recipients. Whether Radishchev read Diderot's art criti-cism is unknown, but the parallels in narrative technique are suggestive.

[65] Radishchev, *Puteshestvie*, 14 ("Chudovo").

to aid them. Shocked by the callousness of this response, the narrator retires to St. Petersburg where his account of the adventure is greeted with sympathy but also, to his horror, acceptance of the custom agent's argument. Disgusted by this lack of humanity, the narrator decides to abandon the city altogether; it is at this point in his flight that Radishchev meets his old friend, who declares his misanthropy.[66]

The overall movement in the succession of episodes is from the aesthetic discourse of the sublime to the language of political allegory. This begins with the frame-narrative, where the narrator initially represents himself experiencing nature through the lens of culture, and then sees himself as man reduced to a state of nature. While the reference to Vernet is an important clue to the pictorial source of the story, it also functions metonymically as a cultural tag, locating the narrative self and story within their cultural frame of reference. The introduction of a second perspective that breaks the frame-narrative also introduces a second type of discourse. Verbal hints in the first part of the sequence had already prepared the reader for the political and social moral that the narrator draws from this experience. The first narrator speaks in terms of the "general good" (*obshchaia pol'za*), a direct calque on Rousseau's notion of the common good that binds primitive man together in society; the elemental ferocity of the storm. When the captain speaks about duty (*dolzhnost'*) the reader is forced into a revision of the first episode. What begins as an exercise in narrating the Burkean sublime is de-composed into the topos of an allegory of the ship of state.[67] Individual behavior during the shipwreck represents the opposition between moral conduct defined in terms of social contract (*dolzhnost'*) and passionate humanity (*iarost' chelovechestva*). And yet at the end, the secondary narrator, initially a spectator and then a moral agent, implicates himself in a contradiction, for his love of humanity causes him to abandon it. The primary narrator, however, stands as his interlocutor's foil insofar as he remains true to himself as the moral spectator by counseling reason without in the end attempting to restrain his friend. It can only be surmised that he would disapprove of the secondary narrator's Rousseauan retreat from society as another flight into an aesthetic system, for at no point does the traveler endorse any of the narrators or make an ethical pronouncement. In this he is consistent with Smith's view that to become the spectator is not to be possessed by the passion of others but to be the arbiter of all sentiments. The layering of stories and manipulation of perspectives make this episode function on multiple interpretive levels. Read as an autobiographical account, it explores the way in which a character can use one set

[66] Radishchev, *Puteshestvie*, 17 ("Chudovo").

[67] Edmund Burke's *A Philosophical Inquiry into the Origin of Our Ideas of the Sublime and Beautiful*, published first in 1757, would have been known in the French translation of 1765.

of artistic conventions to define the self, and what happens when experience outstrips the capacity of a style to contain it. Read as a species of cultural discourse, it is about the larger contexts in which such stories can implicate the self, expressed as a set of oppositions between city and country, society and state of nature, the individual and the community, the citizen and the human. Read as an emblematic episode set in this particular work, the chapter is about the dialectic between story and allegory that the implied reader must follow in order to experience the process of apprehending the multiple points of view that Radishchev places at the center of understanding the self.

The narrator of the *Journey* functions in the text as a moral spectator who sees the self in dialogical terms. As in this episode, it is the narrator who introduces the discourse of a whole range of further narrators, whose stories contain more drama and plotting, more emotion and detail, than his account of his own progress during the journey. What is novelistic about the *Journey* resides in the relationship of characters within the created world of the text. In acting and narrating their own tales, they achieve the freedom of the novelistic hero, if only for the ephemeral space of a single chapter. The narrator serves as a Janus-faced other both for the characters and for the fictional, implied, and actual readers.

What we have missed so far is a more significant link between the narrator and the author. While the use of the moral spectator as a narrator shows an instructive and ethical approach to literature, it also shows a wariness either to endow a hero with an independent personality and conscious life of his own or to gain distance from oneself by creating an autobiographical character. It might be thought that the *Journey* is in that respect the work of an intellectual rather than a natural writer of fiction. Yet even within the confines to which Radishchev has limited his authorial self, through a polyphony that causes the fragmentation and displacement of the narrator's own experience, it would be surprising and contradictory to find the author writing himself out of the text entirely. It might be thought that this view of the self and sensibility is authenticated (and our argument corroborated) when Radishchev applies his own model of self-understanding by figuring himself as a literary and rhetorical construct.

This is precisely what happens in two of the later episodes, "Tver' " and "Chernaia griaz'," each of which contains a famous literary centerpiece. Their significance depends on their being read together and taken within their larger context. Political readings of the *Journey* have relied on special pleading of unusual speciousness in accounting for their inclusion in the cycle despite the fact that, the excerpts from "Vol'nost' " notwithstanding, they hardly ooze Jacobin sentiment. "Tver' " begins with a discourse by a friend of the narrator's in which he compares and contrasts the different schools of Russian neoclassicism. While the speaker recognizes the contributions of Trediakovsky, Lomonosov, and Sumarokov, he singles out the poetics of the last of the trio for criticism on account of his preference for the iamb and the clear derivativeness of his style. The narrator hardly has a chance to defend Sumarokov, whose popularity peaked in the 1780s, before his friend pulls out a manuscript of the ode "Vol'nost'." Whether or not "Vol'nost' " is a radical incitement to revolution (as is often said), the argument that Radishchev attributes excerpts from his own poem to another narrator to mask his authorship is naive and unconvincing, particularly in light of the stinging historical survey of censorship given in "Torzhok." In "Vol'nost' " the poem is dismembered and made into a fragment from which only snatches of meaning are gleaned. The effect is dual. On one hand, it is a metatextual analogue to the narrative disruption of the authorial image that has occurred throughout. Just as quotation seems in this chapter to disrupt reading and interpretation rather than to facilitate it, the structure of the *Journey* as a sequence of dialogues and vignettes blocks the creation of the authorial persona or self. On the other hand and paradoxically, the act of criticizing the poem also represents the transformation of the self into another, giving Radishchev the distance on his own discourse in keeping with his narrator's performance vis-à-vis the discourse of his narrators.

In the last chapter, the famous tribute to Lomonosov removes narrative entirely from the realm of observation to that of reading, and from story to metastory. The traveler as author begins by creating a dialogical relationship with his predecessor, but soon moves to elevate Lomonosov to the place of a secular deity who created Russian literature. In terms again reminiscent of freemasonic language but now suffused with new meaning, Radishchev addresses the reader:

> But harken: before the beginning of time, when there was no basis to existence and all was lost in eternity and vastness, everything was possible for the source of forces, all the beauty of the universe existed in its thoughts, but there was no action, there was no beginning. And suddenly the almighty hand, having jarred the material world into space, gave it motion, The sun shone forth, the moon reflected light, and bodies surrounding the mass were formed. The first blow of creation was all-powerful; the miracle of the world, its entire beauty are only consequences. This is how I understand the action of reason on reason. In the field of Russian letters, Lomonosov is the first.[68]

---

[68] Radishchev, *Puteshestvie*, 123 ("Chernaia griaz' "). On associations of Lomonosov with the demiurge, see Irina Reyfman, *Vasilii Trediakovsky: The Fool of the "New" Russian Literature* (Stanford: Stanford University Press, 1990), chapter 1.

The paean to Lomonosov celebrates an exemplary literary figure by praising his contributions to versification, grammar, poetry, prose, and above all rhetoric as the art of civic discourse—all verbal forms that have been employed in Radishchev's text. This tribute reverberates with the language of Genesis because in his invention of a multitude of forms and discourses Lomonosov is seen as a godlike creator of heteroglossia. The tribute is a fitting one from a narrator whose performance is largely a matter of utterances, whose narrative is a complex tissue of genres and registers. Now self and other have been subsumed in the larger entity of a national literature. The creation of an absolute other who, godlike, embodies all the potential creativity of the language, whose lessons and rules have been absorbed by the inner voice, is for Radishchev the promise of a permanent dialogue and an unfixed self.[69]

In examining the *Journey* as a self-conscious fiction I have sought to revise an entrenched tradition of political readings that neglects the text's formal and ideological variety. For all its turgidity as a narrative, the *Journey* uses the resources of fiction in ways that complicate attempts to treat its political and moral themes as equivalent to the monological discourse of the conduct book, the law code, and even the political pamphlet. In the end it is worth wondering whether, by implication, the truly revolutionary act of this work is not the polyphony of discourses that Radishchev achieves. In Russian political culture, where the free exchange typical of civic discourse and philosophical debate was absent, and where the monarch could prescribe law and morality, a fiction that interrogated assumed values and countered the absolute with a relative point of view was bound to destabilize and to make a monarch uncertain of her certainties. The conventional interpretation of the *Journey* as an exposé of the evils of serfdom is unduly narrow; the true political power of this work derives from its literary and linguistic structures, which enact the relativism of the European Enlightenment.

[69] On Bakhtin's theory of the internalization of the other's discourse, see Caryl Emerson, "The Outer Word and Inner Speech: Bakhtin, Vygotsky, and the Internalization of Language," *Bakhtin: Essays and Dialogues on His Work*, ed. Gary Saul Morson (Chicago: University of Chicago Press, 1986), 31.

CHAPTER THIRTEEN

Enlightenment and Tradition: The Aestheticized Life of an Eighteenth-Century Provincial Merchant

DAVID L. RANSEL

Victor Terras observes rightly that "Russian literature views the merchant class almost always from the outside, if at all."[1] With regard to the eighteenth century, writers and historians alike could put the stress on "if at all" because of the dearth of source material. The recent discovery of the diary of Ivan Alekseevich Tolchenov, a merchant from the town of Dmitrov, permits somewhat greater definition than we have had of the personal world of a provincial trader of that era. The diary nevertheless has limitations for the study of personal narrative. The text is composed almost exclusively of brief references to church attendance, the names of visitors, and daily routines; Ivan rarely offers personal observations or comments on his own life, or even about events of great historical significance such as the Pugachev Rebellion, the French Revolution, and the overthrow of Emperor Paul, all of which occurred during the more than forty-five years covered by the diary (the work ends with Tolchenov's hasty departure from Moscow just ahead of its occupation by the Grande Armée under Napoleon in 1812). The diary follows the chronicle style typical of nearly all diaries and memoirs composed in Russia before 1760, even those penned by educated nobles.[2] Characteristic of the chronicle form are a division of material by years and reporting on purely external

Thanks are due to Laura Engelstein and Dale Peterson for their thoughtful comments on an earlier version of this chapter.

[1] *A History of Russian Literature* (New Haven: Yale University Press, 1991), 115.

[2] The chronicle form continued well past 1760 in many writings by nobles as well as commoners, indeed right into the middle of the nineteenth century in the case especially of non-noble writings. A. G. Tartakovskii, *Russkaia memuaristika XVIII–pervoi poloviny XIX v.* (Moscow: Nauka, 1991), chapter 1.

events. But in one respect, Tolchenov's diary departs from this form and exhibits a literary style associated with a more clearly articulated individuality. Starting about 1790, he begins to assemble his daily notes of comings and goings, meetings, and the like from earlier years into a clean copy to which he appends a summary that includes personal reflections on his successes and failures. In these sections, he adopts a different voice and becomes a self-conscious biographer of his former self.[3]

Diaries are a genre associated with the emergence of an articulated individual self-consciousness (individualism) in early modern Europe. Tolchenov's diary is one of only two merchant diaries from eighteenth-century Russia, and its largely first-person rendering supports the notion of individual consciousness, as does its evidence of the author's desire to stand out from the crowd, to give public display to his interests and tastes.[4] But the diary also constitutes a record of Tolchenov's connectedness, his bonds to family, church, and the other communities in which he fashions his personal identity.[5] Another seeming paradox distinguishes Tolchenov's self-presentation: while obviously fascinated with the rationalist and materialist devices of the new culture such as clocks, telescopes, and greenhouses, he deploys these devices not so much for business purposes as for symbolic and aesthetic effect. Likewise, his embrace of Enlightenment-era material and cultural elements fails to shake his commitment to traditional Orthodox Christianity and its Russian cultural expression, including a belief in miracle-working icons.

The story most easily told of Ivan Tolchenov's life is a familiar moral tale about pretensions and expenditures beyond one's means leading to economic collapse and public humiliation.[6] The diarist was the sole sur-

---

[3] The diary document, *Zhurnal ili zapiska zhizni i prikliuchenii Ivana Alekseevicha Tolchenova*, RO–BAN, shifr 34.8.15. kn. 1, is the product of a compilation by the author of notes (now lost) taken in the course of his daily life and work, which he began assembling in the 1790s in a clean draft ultimately consisting of three separate books. This compilation took place over the course of many years. A portion of the diary, mostly the first book, was published 1974 in a small rotoprint edition of 300 copies edited by N. I. Pavlenko, also called *Zhurnal ili zapiska zhizni i prikliuchenii Ivana Alekseevicha Tolchenova*, comp. A. I. Kopanev and B. Kh. Bodisko, Institute of History, Academy of Sciences of the USSR (Moscow, 1974). Citations in this paper are to the archival copy and will be rendered as *Zhurnal*, followed by the volume and page numbers.

[4] The other merchant diary from this era, the "chronicle" of Mikhail Tiul'pin, does not actually reveal his social position or commercial activities. V. Kolosov, *Letopis' o sobytiiakh v g. Tveri tverskogo kuptsa Mikhaila Tiul'pina 1762–1823 gg.* (Tver, 1902).

[5] Natalie Zemon Davis found in her studies of early modern France a process similar to this, in which the very embeddedness of a person in a web of social bonds and common experience may have been key to imparting a sense of one's distinctive history. "Boundaries and the Sense of Self in Sixteenth-Century France," in *Reconstructing Individualism: Autonomy, Individuality, and the Self in Western Thought*, ed. Thomas C. Heller et al. (Stanford: Stanford University Press, 1986), 53–63.

[6] I will merely summarize this story here, as I have told it in greater detail elsewere. See "An Eighteenth-Century Russian Merchant Family in Prosperity and Decline," *Imperial Russia: New Histories for the Empire*, ed. Jane Burbank and David L. Ransel (Bloomington: Indiana University Press, 1998).

viving son of an energetic and successful businessman from the town of
Dmitrov north of Moscow. His father, Aleksei Il'ich Tolchenov, had combined a considerable inherited capital with assets gained through marriage to become the richest merchant in Dmitrov.[7] He also enjoyed the
confidence of his peers, who elected him as their representative to
Catherine II's Legislative Commission of 1767–68. The family's principal
source of wealth was the grain trade. The diarist, Ivan Alekseevich, was
born in 1754 and by the age of fourteen was already actively working in
the family business, first under the supervision of a trusted agent of the
firm and then, at eighteen, on his own. Until the untimely death of his father in 1779 when Ivan was just twenty-five years old, he traveled much of
each year on a schedule that found him in winter on the lower Volga buy-
ing grain and in summer on the canals and lakes of the northwest accompanying the barge traffic to St. Petersburg. Some years he was on the road
for nearly two hundred days. Indeed, Ivan noted at the end of each year
the exact number of days that he had been traveling and did so in a way
that revealed his yearning for a settled home life; his formula was the
number of days he had been away from his wife (*v razluke c khoziaikoiu
nakhodilsia*).

Understandably, when his father died and Ivan inherited the entire
wealth of the family, he limited his travels to the surrounding area and
quickly settled into a more satisfying family life. His new role as head of
the family firm required him to be closer to the center of things. He was
no doubt expected to play an important part in the politics of his city,
where he was soon elected selectman (*burgomistr*) and then mayor (*gorod-
skoi golova*). But he also took this opportunity to indulge his tastes for the
good life, to build a magnificent town house, orangeries, fish ponds; he
entertained princes, clerics, and government dignitaries, financed charitable projects such as a bell tower and chapel for local churches, and engaged in gambling. These involvements and his official duties in munici-
pal government and local merchant estate organizations stole much of
the time he had previously devoted to business. More and more, his commercial affairs were left to agents, who without supervision either worked
poorly or siphoned off company profits into their own coffers. When Ivan
finally awoke to the disorder of his business affairs and mounting debts,
he faced two heavy drains on his remaining funds: expenditures for the
education and marriage of his first son and payment of a large sum held
in trust for his stepuncle, who had attained his majority. These shocks
brought the collapse of his financial position, and, after maneuvers that

---

[7] In 1774 he declared a capital of over 35,000 rubles. The next wealthiest merchant (not
counting the combined declaration of his brothers) was Stepan Loshkin, with a declared
capital of 10,000 rubles. Some additional information about the Tolchenov family can be
found in A. I. Aksenov, *Ocherki genealogii uezdnogo kupechestva XVIII v.* (Moscow, 1993),
74–85.

transferred some assets to his children and allowed them to remain for a time in the merchant estate (though at a lower guild position than their father), Ivan plunged from the elite first-guild merchant class to the *meshchanstvo*, a status so "contemptible," in his words, that he moved permanently to Moscow, where he managed a playing-card factory and other small enterprises until we lose sight of him in 1812.

We know this story because of Ivan's compulsion to tell it, first, through daily notes on his social contacts and comings and goings and, second, through his subsequent compilations of these notes and comments on them. It is not surprising to find the head of a large family firm in the habit of recording business transactions.[8] But Tolchenov's diary was different. Although he summarized his business dealings each year, his primary concern was to record daily social contacts, attention to religious duties, and work on his charitable and aesthetic projects. In other words, he was recording the development of a social personality, a cultivated individual who spent his time in the company of aristocrats, country squires, and high clergy, a person who surrounded himself with the material and symbolic elements of high status. The preferred "capital" of this merchant was his acquaintances, his aesthetic projects and indulgences, and these, no less than business transactions, required written expression if they were to be remembered and endure. This conceit of recording himself in the company of social superiors was consistent with the impulse that propelled his life along a course of expansion and collapse.[9] His desire to aestheticize his life through his cultural projects, display, love of theater, and reading likewise made his life more worthy of recording, and ultimately, as his fortunes collapsed, only a written record could preserve the aura of what was lost.

Geographic Orientation

The man was a traveler. Although Ivan ended his 200-days a year absences from home soon after the death of his father, he continued to travel—often two or three times a month—in a much contracted arena.

Ivan's travels mirrored the two prominent expressions of his identity: the new materialism and traditional piety. These secular and religious dimensions moved along two axes. The first followed a north-south line with Moscow at the southern point and his milling operations on tributaries of the Volga the northern arm. His hometown of Dmitrov stood about equidistant between the two. Moscow was his more frequent stop.

---

[8] Even if this runs counter to the intelligentsia stereotype of illiterate merchants who die with all their accounts in their heads.

[9] I want to thank Laura Engelstein for this insight and language.

The old capital was the hub of commercial and governmental affairs for the region. Ivan used its offices for transferring money for grain purchases and its markets for many necessities not available in his own small town. As an official of his city, he also had to report regularly to various government bureaus in Moscow and to the archbishop or metropolitan (the last two in regard to new religious structures and church repairs in Dmitrov). Here, too, were his in-laws, his stepmother's family and the large family of his wife, with whom in his early years he lodged on his trips to the capital. Later Ivan acquired his own apartment in the metropolis.

Equally important, Moscow was the source of expertise and supplies for Ivan's personal building projects, first and foremost, his elegant town house, designed by a Moscow architect and erected during the mid-1780s. Moscow also provided expertise for the home's adjoining fish ponds, gardens, and orangeries. Ivan had been touched by the "poetry of gardens," much as had the far more articulate Andrei Bolotov and many others of this era.[10] Orangeries and exotic trees were Ivan's special passion, and his trips to Moscow almost invariably included visits to the orangeries of prominent nobles and consultations with their gardeners. Finally, Moscow served Ivan as a place of edification and entertainment. He strolled in its gardens and visited palaces, he enjoyed its theaters, and he visited its many churches and monasteries, making a point of showing up for the sermons of his favorite prelates. In Moscow, he found a school for his son Peter, not the commercial school subsidized by Empress Catherine, but an expensive private *pansion*.

The northern end of this secular axis were three mills at which grain was ground into flour for delivery to market, either locally or in St. Petersburg. Ivan's father had spent much time at these mills, which were a key component of the family business. Ivan's own trips there, though frequent enough, were brief and often devoted less to work than to socializing with nobles who had estates in the vicinity, a lack of industry that he later cursed.[11]

A further extension of the north-south travel axis included Ivan's occasional journeys to St. Petersburg. Although, like many other Russians, Ivan experienced the northern capital as distant and different, he did not regard it as alien or a world apart, as some later Muscovites would. First, Ivan had emotional attachments to St. Petersburg. His mother had died there in 1768 while accompanying her husband to the second session of the Legislative Commission and was buried in the Alexander Nevsky Monastery. It was in Petersburg, too, that Ivan had received his only formal schooling (beyond basic reading and numbers, which he learned

[10] See D. S. Likhachev, *Poeziia sadov: k semantike sadovo-parkovykh stilei* (Leningrad: Nauka, 1982), especially chapter 5.
[11] *Zhurnal*, 1: 353. From notes made in 1796 in reference to his affairs in 1786.

from his father at home). For a few months in 1768, he studied geography under the tutelage of a monk and teacher at the St. Petersburg Seminary, a time when he also awakened to a love of reading, which he did independently on an increasing scale.[12] Ivan was impressed by the unusual splendor of St. Petersburg: the sumptuous palaces, the gardens, court life, and the theater of the city. In his early adult years, he enjoyed entrée to some court gardens and noble palaces through his acquaintance with gardeners or merchants who worked there. Later, as his circle of acquaintances among the nobility and high clergy expanded, he boasted greater access, several times being in attendance at mass in the court church in the presence of Empress Catherine and Grand Duke Paul.

If the north-south lines of Ivan's movement were primarily secular and material, the east-west axis was exclusively spiritual. To the east of Dmitrov stood the seat of his bishopric, Pereiaslavl'-Zalesskii, and the Trinity–St. Sergius Monastery. A couple of times each year the family traveled to one or both of these places, usually in connection with an important holy day when they could expect to hear mass and a sermon given by a prominent churchman.

The western extension of this religious axis lay in the small village of Vedernitsy, about twenty kilometers from Dmitrov. This village boasted an icon of the Savior that was thought to have curative powers. The icon, initially housed in a wooden church, attracted so many visitors and their monetary offerings that by 1780 the parishioners were able to replace the decaying wooden structure with a masonry building covered with highly plastic baroque designs.[13] Trips to Vedernitsy usually included a stop at the nearby Nikolo-Pesnoshkii monastery, which contained graves of noble families from the region. Among visitors to the shrine at Vedernitsy were some of Moscow province's most prominent families: those of Governor-General Lopukhin, Count F. A. Osterman, and Prince I. F. Golitsyn. Many other ordinary nobles, officials, and townspeople went there. Tolchenov's diary contains references to dozens of people who passed through Dmitrov on their way to Vedernitsy, often finding lodging at one or another of the large merchant homes of the city or merely stopping to have dinner with Tolchenov and his family. Pilgrims from Moscow, such as the governor-general or Tolchenov's own Muscovite in-laws, would visit Vedernitsy and the Nikolo-Pesnoshkii monastery as one point on a trian-

---

[12] *Zhurnal*, 1: 4–5.

[13] The icon was of the *rasslablennyi* type, Christ at the sheep basin curing the sick man. *Istoriko-statisticheskoe i arkheologicheskoe opisanie tserkvi vo imia spasa-istselitelia rasslablennogo v sele Vedernitsakh, Dmitrovskii uezd, Moskovskoi gubernii*, comp. I. Tokmakov (Moscow, 1895), 10–11. Description of the church in *Pamiatniki arkhitektury moskovskoi oblasti* (Moscow, 1975), 1: 75. See also V. Kholmogor and G. Kholmogor, *Istoricheskie materialy o tserkvakh i selakh XVI–XVIII vv.*, no. 11 (Moscow, 1911), 366–67.

gular excursion that went from Moscow to the Trinity–St. Sergius Monastery, then westward through Dmitrov to Vedernitsy before returning to the capital.

This shrine was also an important stop for Ivan Tolchenov and his family, in part no doubt because of the role the sacred icon was thought to have played in saving Ivan's own life in the spring of 1777 when he was stricken by a terrifying flu. The flu hit when he was transporting grain on the northern waterways and left him so weak he could not walk. He somehow got to an uncle's home in Torzhok and collapsed. Fearing death, he said confession and took communion. Soon he fell into "profound yearning and despair" and then into unconsciousness. His father rushed north to tend to his sole surviving child and obtained medical help, but medicines had no effect. They decided to bring him home, stopping at Vedernitsy, where among despairing relatives who had come from Dmitrov, they brought him the icon of the Savior and holy water. From that time onward, his condition began to improve.[14] In subsequent years, the family made regular excursions to Vedernitsy, sometimes on foot, an eight-hour walk from Dmitrov.

Temporal Orientation

Ivan Tolchenov's temporal orientation operated at several levels. The first was the rhythm of the seasons, the freezing and thawing of the river and land routes so critical to long-distance trade in agricultural commodities. Ivan continually tracked the weather and seasonal changes, noting their effects on the movement and pricing of products. At the close of each year's diary entries, he summarized the weather for that year, tracing the principal shifts in the patterns of heat and cold, precipitation and drought, as well as specific memorable events. Among the last were cases of lightning bolts that killed people or set homes afire, early or late frosts and heavy snowfalls, floods, and "terrifying northern lights"[15] (literary touches suggesting, too, that he was influenced by the sentimentalist writings of the age).[16] Weather changes were not only important markers of time but also matters of personal safety, especially for a person who traveled frequently by river and road. The unexpected early breakup of ice on rivers often made Ivan's crossings treacherous or impossible.

A second order of timekeeping was religious. The sequence of holy days, fasts, masses of remembrance, blessings of the waters, plus folk holidays such as *maslenitsa* (Mardi Gras) associated with religious observances,

[14] *Zhurnal,* 1: 78–79.
[15] *Zhurnal,* 1: 95.
[16] A point made by Tartakovskii, *Russkaia memuaristika,* 70.

marked the movement of time through each year. Ivan was steadfast in his religious practice, and a primary purpose of his diary may well have been to record his fidelity in attending to his religious duties, much like the English Puritans, who were the first diary keepers. Ivan noted each religious service he attended, whether it be mass, matins, vespers, or a vigil. He also recorded the name of the church or monastery at which he attended the service and, on special occasions, the priests or prelates who presided.

A third order of timekeeping was the daily rhythm of morning, afternoon, and evening. Ivan often tracked his days in this way. "In the morning, I was at the market. In the evening, I visited Uncle Ivan." "In the morning, I went to the Lugov mill; after dinner I rode over to see off Treasurer Stogov, who was leaving for Ruza."[17] Sometimes, however, he marked time in more precise ways that indicated the presence of a clock. He noted the hour some activity began or ended. On occasion, he moved to a level of accuracy that must have come from a watch carried on his person. The entries he produced in this way bore only a fictive precision, since no pocket watch in his day could actually render accurate time to the minute.[18]

This intrusion of a device of the age of rationalism with its precise divisions of the day into hours and minutes seems a sign more of Ivan's aspiration to a particular status than of his desire for precision in his business dealings and therefore a kind of modernism. In the diary as a whole, the precision of the clock is accorded most often not to business functions but to traditional observances such as important family events (births and deaths) and religious practices, especially pilgrimages. For example, his son Vladimir died "at the start of the 6th hour in the afternoon." His daughter Ekaterina was born at 5:20 PM and died a year later at 7:28 AM. Another daughter, Varvara, was born at 11:45 in the evening.[19] Easter services were noted with similar precision. "Easter mass began at 7:35" is a

---

[17] *Zhurnal,* 1: 183.

[18] David S. Landes, *Revolution in Time: Clocks and the Making of the Modern World* (Cambridge, Mass.: Harvard University Press, 1983), 133–34. A typical entry for Tolchenov's early years of business travel is one example:

> 1774. March 15th at 2:30 again left for Moscow with my wife, overnighting in Sukharevo. 16th at 7 in the morning we arrived safely. 25th heard mass at the Annunciation Cathedral. 27th at 3 in the afternoon left for the Shirin mill, overnighting in the village of Rastovtse. 28th had dinner in Gorodok and arrived at the mill in the evening. 30th in the morning started home. 31st at 9 in the morning arrived safely. April 8 at 8:08 in the morning left for the Tvertsa River and the village of Troitskoe for the loading into barges of the grain that had been stored there over the winter. (*Zhurnal,* 1: 27)

[19] *Zhurnal,* 1: 285, 2: 368, 1: 312.

typical entry for this important holiday.[20] The family's trips to the shrine at Vedernitsy were recorded with similar attention to the clock.[21]

In 1768, when Ivan was fourteen years old, his parents took him on a trip to Rostov and Yaroslavl to pray at the icon of the "Tolsk Blessed Virgin." Twenty years later, when his own eldest son Peter was fourteen years old, Ivan made the same trip, recording it with the kind of precision that to his way of thinking pilgrimages, and perhaps only pilgrimages, warranted.

> 28th. We left Ozeretskoe at 4:20 in the morning, arrived at Sergiev Posad at 7:38, and went to the monastery, where we visited the vestry and saw all the treasures kept there. Then we heard mass and prayed at the Holy Trinity Church. We had dinner at the home of my wife's cousin, the tax farmer Aleksei Petrov, and continued on our way at 1:45 in the afternoon.[22]

The entire trip, running for nearly two weeks, was recorded with this same to-the-minute accuracy. Ivan operated within the modern, rationalistic field of precision timekeeping, but he deployed this knowledge in the service of traditional family and religious obligation. If there was an element of efficiency or modernity in these efforts to sequester time, it was not the kind with which we are familiar. Perhaps it was a punctiliousness similar to that of English Puritans, who built a daily record of fidelity to religious duty. Yet it could as readily be understood as akin to the behavior of present-day parents who take a video camera or pair of binoculars along on a vacation trip in order to preserve or sharpen their observations (while displaying a status symbol), devices less often used at home, where other status markers are in evidence.

Traditional and Rational in Conflict

This impulse to order time minute-by-minute and yet to place this modern knowledge at the service of symbolic purposes was characteristic of Ivan's activities. This can be seen in his fish ponds, a technology that had been developing in his region since the seventeenth century. He and his workers would regularly catch fish in the rivers and hold them in a series of ponds, large ones at the Lugov mill south of town and smaller domestic ponds that provided immediate access to fresh fish for meals. Ivan was not putting his knowledge of ponds to work for business purposes, so far as I

[20] *Zhurnal*, 1: 298.
[21] *Zhurnal*, 1: 310.
[22] *Zhurnal*, 2: 51–52.

can determine, but using it to improve his diet and impress his guests with the quality of his table. The purpose was aesthetic, even if in the context of his aspiration to higher social position and style of living, this use of technology was hardly illogical or even "irrational" in an economic sense if it could have led to ennoblement (though one could well doubt the means).

Even more extravagantly, Ivan's orangeries bespoke his desire to sequester and control nature. But again, the goal was very specific. He was not putting technology at the service of commerce, as did one of his neighbors, an early textile manufacturer. Ivan sought to confine nature for purposes of display, to illustrate his mastery and refinement, and to provide exotic fruits for his dinner table.

The planned ordering of nature attracted, even fascinated Ivan when he could deploy this new way of seeing the world in a personal arena. He loved to show off his watches, ponds, plants, and greenhouses as marks of affluence and taste. But when notions of rational ordering were applied to society, they created problems for Ivan and ultimately played a role in checking his ambition to rise in the world. It is likely that Tolchenov hoped eventually to become ennobled. There had been enough cases of merchants being raised to nobility in the late seventeenth and eighteenth centuries that a man of Tolchenov's position might well have nursed such an ambition.[23] But whether his goal was nobility or merely an equalization of opportunity, respect, and display, the efforts of Empress Catherine to govern Russia as a society of estates (following the ideas of Montesquieu or, perhaps even more directly, the central European cameralist designers of Polizeiwissenschaft) were sharpening the lines between the estates and raising new obstacles to the merging of social status, including separate living spaces for different estates and enforcement of sumptuary laws.[24]

One such instance was the reorganization of the city of Dmitrov along a rational grid system, a process scheduled to take place during Ivan's terms as mayor in the 1780s and early 1790s. The reordering of city streets and squares emerged from the general survey of land begun near the start of Catherine II's reign but did not get moving until after the Moscow plague and the Pugachev insurrection in the early 1770s. In 1782 the Moscow military governor, Count Zakhar Chernyshev, sent a colonel to Dmitrov to

---

[23] For a list of such recipients of patents of nobility in the eighteenth century, see Arcadius Kahan, *The Plow, the Hammer, and the Knout: An Economic History of Eighteenth-Century Russia*, with the editorial assistance of Richard Hellie (Chicago: University of Chicago Press, 1985), 278. Also N. I. Pavlenko, "Odvorianivanie russkoi burzhuazii v XVIII v.," *Istoriia SSSR*, no. 2 (1961): 71–87.

[24] On the role of cameralist thought, see Marc Raeff, *The Well-Ordered Police State: Social and Institutional Change through Law in the Germanies and Russia, 1600–1800* (New Haven: Yale University Press, 1983).

survey the town and draw up a new plan for the city that designated certain blocks exclusively for nobles. However, nothing was done in Dmitrov until 1792, and then only after a new military governor flew into a rage over the delays, chased out Tolchenov's close associate and family friend, the police commissioner Anton Lezzano, and forced the destruction of fifty homes in a few weeks time. The city finally boasted a rational grid system, but its citizens and officials suffered much grief in the process.[25]

Just as the empress's urban plans began by defining precisely the borders of each city and then reorganizing the internal lines of communication within the newly established and socially defined boundaries, other reforms also applied principles of rationalization to the relationships of social estates. Catherine set these ideas out in a number of edicts, most prominently, in her Reform of the Provinces (1775), Police Ordinance (1782), and Charters to the Nobility and to the Towns (1785). These documents were responsive to some of the wishes merchants expressed at the Legislative Commission, affording the top ranks of merchants immunity from corporal punishment and the right to buy their way out of military conscription and labor obligations. But the new laws also drew precise lines between the estates in terms of sumptuary rules and government service and so checked the ambition of non-nobles to live above their station and rise into the nobility. To the extent that ennoblement of merchants and manufacturers was still possible, it became a three-generational process requiring remarkably enduring business success. Again, despite his delight in the symbolic use of the new mechanisms of the age of rationalism, the larger impulse to the tidy ordering of life proved to be more an enemy than a friend to Ivan Tolchenov.

Self-Identity Inscribed in Social Visiting

The diary's daily record of social and professional contacts provides the principal clue to Ivan Tolchenov's reflexive narrative of the self or the self-identity that a person creates and reorders in relation to the experiences of everyday life.[26] It is at this level of daily recording that his presentation of self is best captured. What activities and associations did Ivan most often pursue? What values did he seem to assign to particular projects or people? Fragmented and inexpressive though the record usually

[25] Of course, the reform had many purposes, including prominently fire protection and easy movement of police and military forces, not just social separation. The play between the lapidary daily entries about this change and Ivan's later more thorough retelling is fascinating but too lengthy to include here.

[26] I am borrowing the language of Anthony Giddens's *Modernity and Self-Identity: Self and Society in the Late Modern Age* (Stanford: Stanford University Press, 1991), which, though referring to a much more recent time, has been helpful in guiding me through the diary.

is, the picture has immediacy. Here Ivan occasionally surprises us with an exclamation about "terrifying" northern lights, an astonishing plant discovered in an orangery, or his disgust with doctors who cannot find a cure for him.

Another narrative, reflective rather than reflexive, can be read in the summaries of events attached to the end of each year's entries. These were composed when Ivan was transferring his original daily notes into a clean draft some years after the events they describe. Contemporary context, experience, and the action of memory allowed Ivan to reshape the daily record into a story that he constructed and reconfigured in annual increments. These reflective fragments contain elements of the classic moral tale of overreaching that I associated with the surface narrative. But, unlike a mythic tale, Ivan's story does not end in cathartic resolution. He commands sufficient psychic and social resources to sustain a coherent story of his life. He reflects on his aspirations and failures, offers his excuses and soldiers on.

First, the daily record, a self-monitoring begun at the age of sixteen that was no doubt bound up with the impulse to make his life worth recording, even if at first the record was inevitably prosaic. In the 1770s, before the death of his father, Ivan was on the road for long stretches as a junior executive in the family firm. He kept company mainly with business agents, river pilots, merchants, and local officials. At home, most of his socializing took place among members of his extended family. On occasion, the family associated with local nobles. The one person of real, if faded, prominence who was close to the family was Andrei Molchanov, a real state councilor.[27] Another acquaintance who gained in importance for Ivan over time was Prince Ivan Fedorovich Golitsyn, whose Danilovskoe estate lay on the outskirts of the city. A remarkable person to find in the provinces at the time, Golitsyn had been educated abroad and influenced by the manners of the French court. He served as adjutant to Peter III, remained loyal to him, and refused to take an oath to Catherine II.[28] Golitsyn therefore had to retire to his estate. The Tolchenovs did business with Golitsyn, and for major family events might even induce him to grace their home. Ivan was clearly impressed when in July 1774 he noted, "I went with my father for the first time to the village of Danilovskoe to Prince Ivan Fedorovich Golitsyn and dined there."[29] This was at the height of local panic over the threat from Pugachev's army when the Dmitrov elites were planning defense strategies. It was not a normal time. Golitsyn

[27] This office occupied the fourth position on the Table of Ranks.
[28] Though he relented twenty years later when he had to take the oath in order to serve as marshal of the local nobility, to which he was elected in 1782. *Dmitrovskii krai*, ed. I. N. Kurysheva and V. V. Gal'chenko (Dmitrov: Strelets, 1993), 76.
[29] *Zhurnal*, 1: 30.

did nevertheless join the Tolchenovs in their home the following month at a dinner for the new bishop.[30] A couple of years later, however, when Ivan on his own invited Golitsyn to a baptismal dinner, the prince refused. The same year, the family invited Archbishop Platon to visit when he was passing through town, but he too turned them down.[31] The aspirations were clear but not always fulfilled.

Ivan's almost yearly trips to St. Petersburg in the 1770s gave him opportunities to glimpse the life of the court and high society. In 1774, he went to Peterhof to visit a court purveyor and relative, Pavel Tolchenov, with whom he "dined and spent the day strolling in the gardens. From 7 o'clock and for the whole night I was at a masquerade in the palace and among the gardens and viewed a magnificent decoration of lights."[32] He left at "1:55," an event well worth recording to the minute!

Two years later, he again got a peek at court splendor when another relative sneaked him into the wedding of Grand Duke Paul and Maria Fedorovna. "In the morning, I went to the palace and found an opportunity through a cleric, my nephew Kheruvimov, to get into the court church by the altar, a good vantage point from which to view the marriage ceremony and prayer of thanks as well as the sermon given by His Holiness Platon."[33] A few days later, Kheruvimov got him into the court theater, where he watched a French comedy and ballet and then went to a masquerade until midnight.[34] In 1778, when again in St. Petersburg, he went with another friend, Semen Korob'in, to Tsarskoe Selo, where Korob'in knew a chamberlain (*gof-fur'er*) who showed them "all the splendid and remarkable things . . . the rooms of the palace, the chapel, gardens, grotto, hermitage, and other little houses and conversation nooks." But perhaps he was most struck by the orangery, where "we saw a flowering aloe tree that had prospered for 37 years through the talents of gardeners."[35] These experiences whetted Ivan's appetite for the finer things. But he was still very much on the outside looking in. He was not yet presenting himself as in some sense equal to those who could claim to be a part of high society.

During the 1770s, the other narrative level, the yearly summaries, did not diverge sharply from the daily story. The summaries commented on the family's business activities as well as on commercial relations more generally, the weather and its impacts, the deaths of friends, relatives, local officials and prominent national figures. Ivan also mentioned some

[30] *Zhurnal*, 1: 31.
[31] *Zhurnal*, 1: 60, 69.
[32] *Zhurnal*, 1: 29.
[33] *Zhurnal*, 1: 63.
[34] *Zhurnal*, 1: 64.
[35] *Zhurnal*, 1: 110.

political events, including the Pugachev rebellion, the introduction of a new system of taxation in 1775, a financial scandal in the local *voevoda*'s office.[36] But he fails to expand on these observations and scarcely mentions them at all in the daily entries.

If these larger events remain submerged in the daily record, the day-by-day entries register well Ivan's recasting of his life in his social contacts and activities, a process that can be seen most compellingly at fateful moments. In August 1779 Ivan's father died suddenly and left his only surviving child at twenty-five the wealthiest merchant in Dmitrov. Though stunned and initially busy organizing masses of remembrance and meals for the poor in honor of his father (while also dashing back and forth to his mills and Volga ports to put the year's trade in order), Ivan very soon began recording a life more to his taste than that of a peripatetic junior executive in the family firm. He spent much more time in Moscow, in part to dispatch agents for grain purchases and to pick up sheet iron to complete one of his father's charitable projects, the metal plating of the parish church cupola. But he also found time for the theater, the races, and orangeries. Indeed, within four months of his father's death, he had launched a project for his own orangeries in Dmitrov. "December 11, 1779. This morning I went to the orangery of Mr. Demidov, and his gardener gave me a plan for the building of my own greenhouse [*zelenaia*], afterward called an orangery."[37] Early the next year, he hired his own gardener, built his first orangery, over sixteen meters long, and purchased seventy trees for it, including orange, lemon, bayleaf, and peach. But this passion could not be contained in so small a space. By the end of the following year, 1781, Ivan had constructed a second orangery fifty meters long![38]

At the same time, Ivan expanded his social ties. His contacts with titled nobility were at first on a business basis; when he stopped to see them, he was not invited to their tables. But soon this changed. The breakthrough came in September 1780. "25th. In the morning I went to Peresviatovo to Prince Sergei Mikhailovich Golitsyn, who was there for the chase with his brother, Ober-Kamerger Prince Aleksandr Mikhailovich, and I was invited to the dinner table. Prince Ivan Fedorovich [Golitsyn] also came to dinner, and we were there until six o'clock. Then I went to visit [my] uncle Ivan Il'ich."[39] In the following years, Ivan became a regular visitor at the Danilovskoe estate of I. F. Golitsyn. On many Sundays during the year, he, alone or together with his wife, went to mass at the estate church and then

---

[36] *Zhurnal*, 1: 175.
[37] *Zhurnal*, 1: 147.
[38] *Zhurnal*, 1: 178, 206.
[39] *Zhurnal*, 1: 169.

stayed for dinner and the afternoon. By November 1781 he was at Danilovskoe with the prince riding to the hounds.

The best years had begun for Ivan. In February 1781 he was named to accompany his city's mayor to Moscow to pay respects to the new governor of Moscow province, and when the governor came to Dmitrov soon after, Ivan was flattered to be invited to dinner with him and asked to accompany him on an inspection of a famous porcelain factory in the vicinity. Despite his youth, he was now a family leader and was called in to advise on and arrange the marriage of his stepmother, a Moscow woman, to a Moscow merchant. By the end of the year, he was elected first selectman in Dmitrov (though not yet mayor, which occurred in 1786).

Much of Ivan's time was now devoted to attendance at the Magistrat, supervision of building projects of the city, such as refurbishing the Dmitrov Assumption Cathedral, or his own construction of a bell tower for his parish church. Further time and effort went to the heady task of hosting powerful visitors, for example, the military governor and former president of the War College, Count Zakhar Chernyshev, in August 1782.

> At dawn the *voevoda* and his officials and I with the city selectmen [*ratmany*] went to Danilovskoe to greet the count and were presented at 7 AM. We all immediately rode back to town and were received by the assembled merchants at 8 AM at the entry to Birch St. The count continued directly to the cathedral and from there to the chancellery and depot. As he exited it, he announced his intention to visit me and we proceeded on foot to my house while discussing commerce and other matters. Arriving at my house were Kamerger Prince Mikhail Vasil'evich Dolgorukii, Real State Councilor Petr Nikitich Kozhin, and General Adjutant Ivan Petrovich Turgenev. The count was kind enough to stay for a half-hour, having tea, and the others also vodka, and then got in a carriage and rode to the Magistrat.[40]

By this time, Ivan is throwing dinners for the town elite. Typical of several in 1782 was the notation for October 23, the time of balloting for town offices: "Dining at my house were Prince Ivan Fedorovich Golitsyn, [Naval Captain First Rank V. N.] Kurmanaleev, Prince Obolenskii, the district police commissioner [*gorodnichii*], and all the city judges and top merchants."[41] Visitors were, of course, treated to a tour of Ivan's gardens.

Until 1785 the reflective summary of each year's events follows the confident tone of the daily accounts, though usually emphasizing different matters. It is in the summaries that we learn the most about Ivan's building projects, including, most importantly, his masonry town house done

[40] *Zhurnal,* 1: 224.
[41] *Zhurnal,* 1: 228.

in the style of noble town houses of the day. But as early as this year of 1785, the narrative in the summary explodes with a comment on the disaster that looms ahead. Penned sometime in the early to mid-1790s, the summary notes that although Ivan earned an impressive 9,000 rubles in the grain trade during 1785, his expenses exceeded that amount, and receipts from Petersburg were slow due to problems with his agent there. And so, "I had to start borrowing up to 6,000 rubles with interest, which led eventually not just to the undoing of my commercial operations but to my complete impoverishment."[42]

From this point on, the two narratives diverge ever more sharply through the early 1790s. Looking back on his situation from the vantage point of 1796, Ivan can see where things had gone wrong. He had made very large profits in 1786, 13,000 rubles or "up to 34 kopecks on the ruble, which can be regarded as highly favorable trade." Yet his expenses continued to climb as well, including nearly 5,000 rubles on his new home, 3,000 on a bell tower for the parish church, and luxurious living, which reduced his overall capital by 1,500 rubles.

> In general, although in all three years in a row, i.e., 1784, 1785, and 1786, my commercial dealings were very favorable, I was unable to make any substantive increase in my capital. To be perfectly honest, I cannot attribute this to anything other than my poor management, for I did not give a thought to saving money and did not restrain myself from unnecessary expenditures, thinking that "of my abundance there could be no end," as the psalmist writes. Therefore I spent money, denying myself nothing that I desired. I paid little attention to my commercial affairs and everywhere handled them through agents and perhaps improperly. Not only was I lazy, but I also undertook the building of a house beyond my means and pursued other unnecessary projects and acquaintances merely for the enjoyment of them; and it should be said that I could not [find time] to go to St. Petersburg but instead allowed [my agent] Tiut'kin to make a mess of my affairs there, and I scarcely ever went to my mills [to check on] the grinding of grain, and when I did so I did not stay long, and the grinding took place with poor supervision and was not done as it should have been, the result being that a lot more flour was lost than was the case in the past. In a word, these prosperous years were wasted due to my inattention, and later I did not have such an opportunity.[43]

This later guilty recording of his failures reveals not only Tolchenov's slow awakening to his deteriorating financial position—caught up as he was in living the other, more glamorous story of his life—but it also tells us of some of the normative values of his class, to which he was not conforming.

[42] *Zhurnal*, 1: 319.
[43] Ivan penned this comment in 1796 when he was assembling his notes for the year 1786 and writing them up in a clean draft. *Zhurnal*, 1: 352–53.

Industry, modesty, personal attention to business matters, and suspicion of one's agents were evidently understood as the keys to success and essential to the proper conduct of one's affairs.[44] These values might be contrasted to the undisciplined behavior described by Lev Tolstoy in his moral self-accusations in Irina Paperno's chapter in this book.[45] While Tolstoy was making a moral and not a social commentary, one might also observe that because of a secure legal status, a wealthy hereditary noble could stay up late playing cards, rise after the noon hour, overeat, fail to conduct business on time, and yet not suffer loss of position. Tolchenov's self-indulgence and imitation of the idleness of his acquaintances in the nobility, without the security of rank and property they enjoyed, had fateful consequences.

Although losses and laments similar to those just noted characterize Ivan's summaries for the years through the early 1790s, his daily jottings register a much more buoyant story. At the end of 1785, he is elected mayor of Dmitrov and plays an increasingly important role in public affairs. When Empress Catherine returns from her trip to the southern provinces in 1787, Ivan and his family occupy a prominent place in Moscow for viewing the imperial entry and other festivities. This time he rents space for this purpose and does not have to rely on relatives to sneak him in. He also visits the Kremlin and attends balls for the elite.[46] In Dmitrov, he now regularly entertains visiting dignitaries in his home, including Bishop Feofilakt and Moscow Governor-General Lopukhin and his family (who were on a trip to Vedernitsy). No longer on the outside looking in in terms of his position at important events, Tolchenov's language also changes in his recording of his social associations; he places himself close to, if not altogether on the same level as, the nobility. In noting a party at a local estate, he writes that at "9 in the morning my wife and I went together with Iushkov and other local nobles to the squire Vakhromeev at the village of Alekseevo . . . where we arrived at 2 PM, had dinner, spent the evening, and stayed overnight."[47] Or, soon after, when Metropolitan Platon's new vicar, Bishop Serapion, arrived in town, Ivan writes that "I went to greet him at the monastery and was invited together with other city officials [*chinovniki*] to his dinner table."[48] At the time of

---

[44] An excellent example of faithfulness to these values can be seen in the life of Petr Mikhailovich Vishniakov, who lived during the reign of Nicholas I. *Svedeniia o kupecheskom rode Vishniakovykh, sobrannye N. Vishniakovym*, 3 parts (Moscow, 1903–1911).

[45] "Tolstoy's Diaries: The Inaccessible Self."

[46] *Zhurnal*, 2: 3–4.

[47] *Zhurnal*, 2: 54.

[48] *Zhurnal*, 2: 56. The mayor was not a *chinovnik* in the usual sense. Bishop Serapion functioned under the title of bishop of Dmitrov, although in fact he was appointed in May 1788 to assist Platon in conducting his administration of the Moscow metropolitanate and resided in Moscow. K. A. Papmehl, *Metropolitan Platon of Moscow (Petr Levshin, 1737–1812): The*

his reelection to a second three-year term as mayor later the same year, Ivan notes that "the entire local nobility and their families were at my house." And, again, a few days later: "In the morning, I was at the Magistrat. In the evening, all the local nobility and [my] relatives were at my house."[49] While Ivan increasingly associates and identifies with the local nobility, he never completely merges his identity with theirs and remains aware of the distinctions within and between the merchant estate and nobility. The number of nobles, especially those of pedigree, that he can claim for an event is clearly important to him. For example, in February 1788, he arranges the marriage of his stepuncle (a younger man and Ivan's ward) to a Moscow merchant woman and organizes the festivities. We hosted "a ball and supper of 37 place settings. Among the distinguished guests were Prince Ivan Fedorovich Golitsyn and his family, Ivan Andreevich Molchanov, squires Iushkov, Lavrov, Blagovo, and others."[50]

Again, we find him in 1791 on a visit to Petersburg in close proximity to the court. The daily entries note several occasions when he is at the court church while the empress and heir are in attendance. He makes the rounds of the top stores, purchases a telescope and tries it out from the top of a bell tower, and attends an art auction. Yet we know from the story running in the yearly summaries that he is close to bankruptcy, if not already there, and has begun to jettison his assets; for example, he relinquishes his lease of a mill belonging to Prince Sergei Mikhailovich Golitsyn. The daily record, though it registers the loss of the mill, continues to chronicle an impressive social life for a provincial merchant. In addition to almost daily socializing with a variety of friends from the local officialdom and squirearchy, his frequent dinners with Prince Ivan Golitsyn continue; in 1792 he adds regular visits for dinner or evenings to Countess Orlova, who lives on a nearby estate. His trips to Moscow in late 1791 include stops at the exclusive English Club, which he then joins in January of the next year![51] Even though the daily narrative starts to include more hints in the next years of assets being lost, the style of life remains the same. As late as January 1796, we find Ivan not only still at the English Club but also at the Noble Assembly in Moscow for the unveiling of a bust of Catherine II. A few days later, he is back in the halls of the Noble Assembly with his wife for a masquerade.[52]

Enlightened Prelate, Scholar, and Educator (Newtonville, Mass.: Oriental Research Partners, 1983), 53–56.

[49] *Zhurnal*, 2: 61, 62.

[50] *Zhurnal*, 2: 76.

[51] *Zhurnal*, 2: 179. "K istorii moskovskogo angliiskogo kluba," *Russkii arkhiv*, no. 5 (1889): 85–98, tells of the limited membership and exclusivity of the club after it restarted in 1802 (Emperor Paul closed it for a time), conditions that also obtained earlier. See also recent work by Aleksei Butorov, *Moskovskii Angliiskii klub, stranitsy istorii* (Moscow: Moskovskii Angliiskii klub, 1999).

[52] *Zhurnal*, 2: 301–2.

Looking back a few years later, Ivan assesses his state of mind in 1792. Despite success in trade, he writes, lack of capital for grain purchases kept his volume and hence his profits low, while

> domestic expenditures, interest payments, plus unfortunate (if not large) gambling losses and other outlays drew down my capital in that year by a substantial amount. My financial ruin was increasing such that I could scarcely muster the strength any longer to avert it. To conceal my unfavorable position and not completely lose credit, I did not alter my way of living and continued to hope for a fortunate turn of events.[53]

True, commercial success in Russia depended on personal credit (reliable financial institutions and legal framework did not yet exist), and credit worthiness might for a time be artificially maintained by an impressive self-presentation. But fateful moments not only require a person to act urgently in ways that could reshape their circumstances. They also have powerful implications for self-identity. Besides his need to manifest his credit worthiness, Ivan's statement seems to reveal his inability to surrender a style of life that had become integral to the self-identity that he had been creating and recording since boyhood. Instead, he chose to rely on the gambler's instinct in him: the next throw of the dice might bring a turn of fortune.

But his situation only worsened, and he sank into despondency, describing the position of his firm two years later as "similar to a ship that had lost its mast and was being tossed about in the sea at the whim of the winds."

> A kind of nonchalance took control of my reason, as I struggled against melancholy and despair. I was ashamed to reveal my dire situation not only to friends but even to my own family, and I spent much of my time with chimerical thoughts and gambling, which hastened my ruin, and by using my remaining assets on other diversions attempted to console myself and push away unpleasant thoughts.[54]

The end was in sight. The story in the yearly summaries reveals what has been happening, and from early 1796, it is difficult not to see it also in the daily jottings. Ivan sells his magnificent home, his exotic trees, even his serfs to wealthy merchants and nobles in the Dmitrov region and transfers capital thus acquired to his wife and children while dodging his creditors. Much of the middle of the year, he is hiding out at the last of his mills, and when he moves back to town, he pretends not to be at home or feigns illness to avoid paying his debts. The death of Empress Catherine in

---

[53] *Zhurnal,* 2: 202.
[54] *Zhurnal,* 2: 266.

November brings tears to his eyes but does not bring him out of the house to take the oath to the new emperor at the cathedral, as ordered. Instead, he takes the oath at home the following day in the presence of a cleric.[55] Even when in Moscow, Ivan has to live with his son Peter's father-in-law because his own apartment there is being watched by creditors. During this time, Ivan engages in a number of illegal maneuvers to save what he can for his family and to have enough to set up a new business in Moscow. In mid-March 1797, he and his family move to Moscow for good.

The daily entries record a striking juxtaposition of exhilaration and defeat. Ivan's move to Moscow coincides with the coronation of Emperor Paul, and he lovingly notes his sightings of the emperor and of the imperial family and entourage. He goes to the changing of the guard and decorations of light at palaces and on the streets, places his family opposite the Kazan Cathedral for an excellent view of the imperial entry, visits the Kremlin churches, and is present in the Synodal Palace for the preparation of the holy oil for blessing the new sovereign. He goes with his wife to view the coronation parade from the Assumption to the Archangel cathedrals.[56] Yet within days of having been captivated by the pomp of power, Ivan collided with another side of government. He was subpoenaed to appear before a bailiff and, on the request of one of his creditors, was sent to the police, arrested and held for two days before being ordered to appear before the Magistrat in Dmitrov.[57] There, he made arrangements to pay his debts over time and was allowed to return to Moscow.[58]

Although this particular humiliation was not repeated in the yearly summary, the two narratives begin again at this point to coincide more closely. The tension between the face Ivan was showing to the world and what he knew was his condition had necessarily in some measure resolved itself. His summary for 1797 describes this condition:

> In this year, I was compelled to leave my beloved fatherland, the city of Dmitrov, in which I was born and lived for more than forty-two years. I grew up there and partook fully in all earthly blessings, having inherited from my father a substantial capital. I myself engaged in trade there successfully and to good purpose for ten years and on the basis of my growing commerce built a lovely masonry home, orangeries, and had gardens and orchards, a fishery, and good servants. I deprived myself and my blameless family of all of this through my excessive luxury and inattention to business, added to which were some losses in Petersburg, such that from the honored rank of leading merchant of the city, I fell to a contemptible station, and from a beautiful

[55] *Zhurnal,* 2: 318–19.

[56] *Zhurnal,* 2: 338–40.

[57] *Zhurnal,* 2: 342.

[58] "Zhurnaly prisutstviia magistrata g. Dmitrova, 1797," TsGIAM, f. 37, o. 1, d. 809, ll. 271–75.

home I moved to the dark and noisy rooms of a Moscow apartment, where my sole occupation was the manufacture of playing cards, which in that year did not even yield a profit. In addition, I was constantly plagued with concerns about finding the means to keep my creditors at bay, and I increased God's wrath toward me by further illegal acts and deceptions.[59]

Despite this recognition of his fall from this-worldly (and that-worldly) grace, Ivan was not prepared emotionally to write himself out of the social circle to which his tastes and former life had accustomed him. Others, however, were willing to do so. Soon after his move to Moscow, he went to visit Countess Orlova, at whose estate he had been a regular for the past two years, but he "did not find her at home," a rare admission in the diary. After this we hear no more about Countess Orlova.[60]

Ivan's uncertain sense of his relationship to titled nobility is revealed in his comments about Prince I. F. Golitsyn. Golitsyn, who had suffered for his loyalty to Peter III, outlived Empress Catherine long enough to garner rewards from the heir. In reporting on the "special warmth the new emperor showed to surviving favorite officials of his father," Tolchenov noted that they "received extraordinary favors, including villages, money, gifts, and ranks. Among them was my benefactor and *in some sense even my friend* General-Major Prince Ivan Fedorovich Golitsyn."[61] Golitsyn died the following year, and when Tolchenov noted his death in the year-end summary for 1797, he did not repeat the reference to Golitsyn as a friend but retreated to the phrase "my true benefactor."[62] Possibly, Tolchenov's reduced circumstances by the time he composed the summary (sometime before December 1804) distanced him from the notion of friendships with princes: this despite the fact, evident from the daily entries, that Tolchenov was included in a group of noble friends of Golitsyn who made arrangements for the prince's solemn burial with full military honors at the Don Monastery—indeed the group met at Tolchenov's apartment for a review by him of the funeral procedures.[63]

One of the men present at this meeting, Afanasii Pavlovich Iushkov, was important in sustaining Ivan Tolchenov's sense of belonging in a social circle no longer consonant with his economic circumstances. Iushkov, who was approximately Ivan's age, proved to be extraordinarily loyal. When Ivan was recalling in his summary for 1797 the disasters of that year, he added a note about positive aspects of his life in Moscow that in small measure offset his losses:

[59] *Zhurnal*, 2: 358–59.
[60] *Zhurnal*, 2: 341.
[61] *Zhurnal*, 2: 330. My italics. The phrase in Russian is "moi blagodetel' i nekotorym obrazom dazhe priiatel'."
[62] *Zhurnal*, 2: 364.
[63] *Zhurnal*, 2: 356.

By way of salving my conscience for the dissipation [of my wealth] and humiliation of my family, our new life in Moscow served as some consolation. And, even more so, [it helped] to be occupied in abundance with new things to do and to be able to reestablish my acquaintance with squire Iushkov and, through him, also with other people.[64]

Indeed, in the last months of 1797, Ivan is almost daily with Afanasii Iushkov or his brother Nikolai Pavlovich. In September of that year, we find him briefly vacationing at the Iushkov country estate, running to the hounds and enjoying the diversions of the life of the landed nobility.[65] Little wonder that in noting Afanasii Iushkov's death in March 1804, Ivan could write in his later summary without qualification: "My friend and benefactor, Court Councilor Afanasii Pavlovich Iushkov, [died] and was buried in the Pesnoshskii Monastery."[66]

I say that Ivan only in some measure resolved the tension between his economic position and his aspirations to a life of leisure and elite tastes. As is evident in his friendship with Afanasii Iushkov, Ivan was able to make the most of his social opportunities and to turn them to his personal satisfaction. Gradually, however, as his former acquaintances from the nobility and high clergy either abandoned him or died, he settled into the life of a moderately prosperous Moscow townsman. Yet occasionally he had an opportunity to observe the difference between his education, interests, and tastes and those of impoverished members of the nobility. In 1805 Ivan and his wife took a trip to St. Petersburg. This time, instead of following the most direct route, they went to the north through Uglich and Ustiuzhna in order to make a pilgrimage to the famous monastery at Tikhvin. Along the way they encountered social situations sufficiently anomalous that Ivan remarked on them (a rare occurrence in the diary). For example, at the village of Novinki northwest of Ustiuzhna, he notes that

a large number of smallholding nobility live in the vicinity. Some of them not only do not have an education proper to their station but they even fail to perform service. Among them are three brothers by the name of Rozbitnyi who have 7 souls between them. They run the post station and themselves ride around on coachman's boxes wearing gray Russian kaftans and full peasant attire, and, to boot, all three are young.[67]

[64] *Zhurnal,* 2: 359.
[65] *Zhurnal,* 2: 351–52.
[66] *Zhurnal,* 3: 177, although the daily entry for March 11, 1804, reads simply: "In the morning, I went to say my farewells to [my] deceased benefactor Afanasii Pavlovich Iushkov." *Zhurnal,* 3: 158.
[67] *Zhurnal,* 3: 188.

A few days later, after an inspiring visit to Tikhvin, the couple stopped for dinner at the village of Savinka where "we dined at the place of a poor nobleman Obernibesov, who runs an inn and has a few acres of land, and it is by such means that he makes his living."[68] Whether observed with bafflement, compassion, or dismay (hard to tell from Tolchenov's flat description), these encounters underscored the importance of display and style in confirming and creating social status. The position of these nobles made quite a contrast not only with the life Ivan and his wife enjoyed in Dmitrov before his fall but even with the life they would participate in a few days later in Petersburg.

Their purposes in visiting the capital were to spend time with their two sons and grandson who were living there, settle a legal matter, and see the sights. While no longer in the regular company of titled nobility, they nevertheless enjoyed the kind of access accorded to educated people of means. A typical day read:

[My wife] Anna Alekseevna and I left after 10 AM from Tuchkov bridge in a canal boat and passing Krestovskii and Aptekarskii islands went to Kamennyi Island to the court church there for mass. The emperor and his august spouse were in attendance. Afterward, we were invited to lunch with [Commerce Councilor] Kusov [at his dacha]. We then went to the dacha of Count Stroganov and strolled in his gardens, returning by water to our apartment after 3 PM. In the evening, we went to the Bolshoi Theater.[69]

On another day, his son Peter, along with other local merchants, was invited to dinner at the Taurida Palace with the emperor and the entire imperial family. Ivan and his wife made the rounds of the most beautiful churches and palaces, attended parades and pageants (often sighting the emperor), went to the Senate, the Academy bookstore, the Kunst Kamera, and the theater.

Conclusion

Ivan's diary was found in three leather-bound volumes in which he transcribed his daily notes while appending to each year's entries a brief reflective summary. The title he gave his chronicle, "A Journal or Notes on the Life and Adventures of Ivan Tolchenov," leaves little doubt that he wished to associate it with the best-known work of Daniel Defoe or one of its many imitations circulating in Russia. But Defoe and his emulators

[68] *Zhurnal*, 3: 191.
[69] *Zhurnal*, 3: 196.

could scarcely have provided an exact model for Tolchenov's laconic diary. Whether the actual model was a church chronicle, a merchant's record book, a travel journal, or something else, Ivan was able to turn out a remarkable personal record of ups and downs and to sustain in his literary act a coherent story of his aspirations and failures.

Although Tolchenov engaged from the age of sixteen in a process of daily self-observation, only in the early 1790s did he become a self-conscious moralizing biographer of his earlier self; it was then that he began transcribing his daily notes into the large volumes and attaching yearly summaries. At this point, he already understood his worsening financial position and the unlikelihood of sustaining his ambitions (even while he retained a gambler's hope for a lucky turn of fortune). Interestingly, the worse he fared financially, the more readable his story became—full of unexpected turns, suspense, and emotional complexity. As he lost control of his life, his story related in his journal summaries gained in narrative coherence and literary power. These features, plus his choice of title and binding, suggest that the diary was his final act of self-fashioning, an attempt to preserve in literary form what had been lost in his life, his glory days among the wellborn and the powerful.

Why was this provincial merchant the first in Russia to leave such a record?[70] Did perhaps his position as the sole surviving child of a prominent family give him a feeling of providential distinction that allowed him to believe that his personal story was worth recording and preserving? He was the one child on whom the family placed its hopes for continued social prominence and business success. We know that at the time of his flu crisis in 1777, frightened relatives rushed across northern Russia to his aid. It is interesting, too, that the one insertion Ivan made into the daily records of the diary (as distinct from the year-end summaries) appeared at the entry on his father's death; there Ivan introduced a list of all nine children of his parents, with their birth and death dates, underlining his status as the only survivor.[71]

Ivan was special in another way, being separated from his local merchant counterparts (if not from some capital-city merchants) in his tastes, his aestheticized approach to life. His passion for gardens, exotic plants, pageantry and pomp, an elegant western-style home, and the theater represented more than a superficial westernization. His knowledge of gardening and arboriculture, for example, won the respect of his acquaintances among the nobility, who drew on his expertise in their purchases and the management of their own gardens and orangeries. His fascina-

---

[70] I omit here because of its remoteness and peculiarity the remarkable journal of the fifteenth-century merchant traveler Afanasii Nikitin, *Khozhdenie za tri moria*, 2d ed., 2 vols. (Moscow: Akademiia nauk, 1958).

[71] *Zhurnal,* 1: 13.

tion with the sequestration and artificial ordering of nature and time were of a piece with his aspiration to a westernized and aestheticized style of life.

Yet, like many other eighteenth-century Russians who shared his interests and tastes, Ivan remained securely rooted in Orthodox religious belief and practice. He was personally close to his local parish and monastic clergy (with whom he regularly exchanged visits), and he retained a firm belief in the power of miracle-working icons. It was the age of rationalism when people still believed that one could select from a varied palette of cultural choices, indulge the new without contaminating the old. Tolchenov was able to refashion himself from a junior executive in a provincial grain business into a man of comparative refinement, the owner of an elegant home and gardens, a merchant who nevertheless ran to the hounds at the estates of his noble friends and became a member of the Moscow English Club. Not even his financial collapse could completely erase his new self-identity, which a few residual contacts among the nobility allowed him to continue to indulge in small ways.

CHAPTER FOURTEEN

Personal Testimony and the Defense of Faith: Skoptsy Telling Tales

LAURA ENGELSTEIN

The merchant Ivan Tolchenov was not the only eighteenth-century Russian to acquire his social markings by design. For the Europeanized aristocracy, identity was always in quotation marks. They patterned themselves on a style that was highly ritualized and bore a foreign stamp. As Yuri Lotman writes, their "daily life acquired the characteristics of the theater." From this self-conscious perspective, the world beyond the ramp seemed authentic, inevitable, and unscripted. It was in opting for the attributes of a life marked by artifice (gardens that blossomed under glass, not in the open air), that Tolchenov associated himself with the upper crust. In some ways, it was the very act of choice that altered his social position. "The availability of *choice*," Lotman remarks, "sharply separated the nobleman's behavior from that of the peasant"—or other, tradition-bound commoner.[1] At least that is what a nobleman would have thought.

But were choices in fact unknown and self-reflection unthinkable for the inhabitants of the world that seemed, from one's own refined position, so natural when viewed from afar? The case of the so-called Skoptsy, or self-castrators, suggests, to the contrary, that ordinary folk were capable, too, of managing their identities through the adoption of customs and expressive forms that set them apart. In divesting themselves of reproductive organs, the Skoptsy rejected some of the basic processes of biological life. In violating the tenets of Orthodoxy, they retreated from the cultural common ground. They did not, however, abandon the physical

[1] Iurii M. Lotman, "The Poetics of Everyday Behavior in Eighteenth-Century Russian Culture," in *The Semiotics of Russian Cultural History*, ed. Alexander D. Nakhimovsky and Alice Stone Nakhimovsky (Ithaca, N.Y.: Cornell University Press, 1985), 70, 75.

space of the village or town, where they lived side-by-side with conventional neighbors. They relied instead on distinctive language and comportment to signal their allegiance to special beliefs and to ward off intrusion. Sensitive to the discursive environment, as it evolved over the course of 150 years, they managed to tell their stories in their own way while maximizing their chances of survival. Firmly attached to the original belief that their prophet was the reincarnation of Jesus Christ and that blood sacrifice guaranteed salvation, they were adept at changing with the times. The story of their encounter with the outside world, which brings them into the twentieth century, closes the circle where the volume begins, with the Soviet era.[2]

The existence of this heretical community among the peasants of Orel province was first uncovered by the authorities in 1772. The faithful distinguished themselves from Orthodox believers by their reading of Christ's injunction to sexual chastity ("eunuchs for the kingdom of heaven's sake," Matthew 19:12) as a call to sever the male genitals and remove women's sexual body parts—nipples, breasts, labia. The self-proclaimed born-again were not, however, eccentric individualists rejecting the collective world of village life for the outposts of personal conviction; they formed a collectivity in their own right, heeding the call in clusters of family and friends. Their leader was a charismatic vagabond, known as Kondratii Selivanov, probably a fugitive peasant, whose real name was never accurately determined and whose adventures were the stuff of myth. The story of his capture, punishment, and exile, rendered on the model of Christ's Passion and expressed in coded language opaque to the nonbeliever, constituted a foundational legend that further obscured his particular person in symbolic guise.

This narrative was a key element in establishing the Skoptsy as an interpretive community, with a story and vocabulary of its own. But the prophet and most of the early adherents were unlettered common folk. The fable was published only in 1845 by the Ministry of Internal Affairs, as evidence of the sect's doctrinal errors. It is possible, moreover, that the ministry's version was not a faithful transcription of some folkloric tale but the result of a folklorist's intervention. Publication was not intended to bolster the believers' sense of identity but to justify and facilitate persecution, with the goal of wiping them out. When the official edition was pirated, however, it became more widely available, including to those of the

[2] For a detailed study of the Skoptsy, see Laura Engelstein, *Castration and the Heavenly Kingdom: A Russian Folktale* (Ithaca, N.Y.: Cornell University Press, 1999). The author gratefully acknowledges funding for this chapter from Princeton University, the Woodrow Wilson International Center for Scholars, the National Humanities Center (with the support of the Lilly Endowment), the John Simon Guggenheim Memorial Foundation, and the Rockefeller Foundation Study and Conference Center in Bellagio, Italy. Thanks also to the staff at the Gosudarstvennyi muzei istorii religii in St. Petersburg.

brethren who had learned to read. Aware that the ministry's motives were unfriendly, the community nevertheless accepted the text as their own.[3]

The disclosure of ritual practices and beliefs always involved danger, because adherence to the faith was a criminal offense, and information leading to the identification of followers put them at risk. When discretion failed and congregations were arrested, the defendants were obliged to give an account of themselves in court. They often refused to comply or engaged in deliberate deception. The pledge of secrecy was not merely, however, a pragmatic measure. It was also an instrument of collective authority. Personal stories were not allowed; the faithful must follow a uniform script. The public lie was a ritual of communal belonging and submission to the rule. The pledge not to tell was a promise of loyalty. Telling was treason.

The relationship between revelation, self-definition, and self-defense did not, however, remain constant over the years. When the sect was first discovered in 1772, the believers ignored their oaths and readily described the circumstances of their conversion. Variations on a theme, their narratives conformed to a single type: encounter, inspiration, embrace. In later trials, by contrast, most defendants said as little as they could. Those who revealed the details of ritual castration and other secrets of the faith often cast themselves as the victims of proselytizing fanatics. Some wanted merely to avoid conviction. Others may have sincerely repented and wished to start new lives. Such was the intention of Gerasim Prudkovskii (1830?-1909), whose memoirs, published by a literary journal in the early 1880s, denounced the brethren as aggressive and corrupt. In betraying his fellows, Prudkovskii tried to establish his own innocence and take revenge for the harm he had endured. Writing was also an act of self-creation. Of peasant background, Prudkovskii had taught himself to read and write. By composing a story in his own words and seeing it appear in print, he was no longer a slave to formula or chanter of holy verse, but the author of a personal script, seeking the very attention that pious sectarians shunned.

Strategic and ritual silences, codes, refusals, and circumlocutions protected the community against internal deviation and external threat. By the end of the nineteenth century, however, the faithful began to use disclosure itself as a defensive tool. The writing or speaking self, as shaped in the narrative of revelation, might now serve the community as guardian or spokesman. The loyal self might undertake to preserve and transmit religious lore. Almost twenty-five years after Prudkovskii wrote his bitter exposé, Gavriil Men'shenin (1862–1930), another self-taught believer, also

---

[3] [Nikolai Nadezhdin], *Issledovanie o skopcheskoi eresi* (n.p.: Ministerstvo vnutrennikh del, 1845); reprinted in vol. 3 of V. I. Kel'siev, ed., *Sbornik pravitel'stvennykh svedenii o raskol'nikakh*, 4 vols. (London: Trübner and Co., 1860–62).

of peasant stock, published a collection of sacred texts and ritual verses proudly titled *Poetry and Prose of Siberian Skoptsy* (see *figure 23*).[4] Men'shenin acted as community spokesman in dealing with authorities and communicating with the outside world. He believed that self-representation was a source of strength. In pursuit of this tactic, he made contact with Vladimir Bonch-Bruevich (1873–1955), a Social Democrat who courted the good will of religious sectarians as a way of establishing a foothold in the countryside. The goal of political mobilization proved illusory, but Bonch-Bruevich gained the trust of various nonconforming groups who provided him with information for a series of documentary volumes. He was known, through these volumes and other writings and in his role as expert witness for the defense on behalf of indicted sectarians, as a reliable, though not uncritical, ally. A revolutionary by conviction and employment, Bonch-Bruevich was an archivist at heart and faithfully preserved the material he received in the holdings of the Museum of the History of Religion and Atheism in Leningrad, today the State Museum of the History of Religion in St. Petersburg.

This archive houses the record of how the Skoptsy (and other persecuted groups) wished to be remembered. The narrative and representational collage is a work of collaboration between the community and the man who began as a rebel and ended his career as a Soviet bureaucrat. His interaction with the few culturally ambitious self-made men of the people recalls the relationship between semieducated workers and their radical mentors that helped generate the Russian labor movement. In this case, however, Bonch-Bruevich was not trying to teach his correspondents a lesson. It was they who had a lesson to impart. Among the various self-styled Skoptsy intellectuals who responded to Bonch-Bruevich's call for documentation, one stands out as particularly inspired. After the 1905 revolution Nikifor Latyshev (1863–1939?) began recording his life story, as well as the saga of his family's travails (see *figure 24*). Sometime around 1912, he gave these manuscripts, which also contained reflections on Skoptsy belief, to Men'shenin, requesting they be sent to Bonch-Bruevich for safekeeping.[5] At the same time, Latyshev began a correspondence with the archivist, which lasted until 1939 and in which he recounted his and his family's experiences during the first two decades of Soviet rule.

---

[4] G. P. Men'shenin, ed., *Poeziia i proza sibirskikh skoptsov* (Tomsk: Levenson, 1904).

[5] Letter from N. P. Latyshev to V. D. Bonch-Bruevich (December 27, 1912), GMIR, f. 2, op. 5, d. 29, l. 3. Men'shenin took credit for giving Bonch-Bruevich these manuscripts: see A. I. Klibanov, *Iz mira religioznogo sektantstva: Vstrechi, besedy, nabliudeniia* (Moscow: Politicheskaia literatura, 1974), 24. On Men'shenin's relationship with Bonch-Bruevich in the Soviet period, see Claudio Sergio Ingerflom, "Communistes contre castrats (1929–1930): Les enjeux du conflit," in Nikolaï Volkov, *La secte russe des castrats*, trans. Zoé Andreyev, ed. Claudio Sergio Ingerflom (Paris: Les Belles lettres, 1995), xi–lxiii.

Figure 23. Gavriil Prokopievich Men'shenin (1862–1930). Photo A. Khaimovich, Tomsk, March 1907. GMIR, f. 2, op. 29, d. 108. (Copyright © GMIR.) As Men'shenin notes on the reverse of this portrait, he was forty-six when the picture was taken. In this same period, Men'shenin wrote of himself: "I have always fought against lies and many did not love me." Letter to V. D. Bonch-Bruevich (May 10, 1909). GMIR, f. 2, op. 5, d. 61, l. 2.

Figure 24. Nikifor Petrovich Latyshev (1863–1939?). GMIR, f. 2, op. 5, d. 261, l. 60. (Copyright © GMIR.) This studio portrait, which seems to be dated 1904, was included in a manuscript written in 1910. At the time of the sitting Latyshev was about forty years old and living with his family in Siberia. On his lap is a white cloth concealed behind an issue of the popular illustrated magazine *Niva* (The Grainfield). The objects represent the two components of Latyshev's identity: devoted to Skoptsy purity, he was also an intellectual of the people.

This essay will explore the three modes that characterize the Skoptsy use of telling and not telling as instruments of collective self-preservation and personal self-definition. In the first mode, believers asserted their identity with respect to the group by conforming to an established script that satisfied the pledge not to reveal secrets. To have chosen one's own words would have constituted a betrayal, a refusal to submit. That refusal was played out, when, operating in the second mode, disgruntled adherents spoke not *with* but *against* the group, signaling their departure. In exchanging the role of believer for that of victim, they also affirmed a new subservience: to Orthodox religion and the law. In other cases, rupture allowed the renegade to shape a separate identity—a new, highly articulated self that could not find expression in ritualized terms. The third mode of Skoptsy tale-telling involved speaking *for* the community. Self-educated, self-styled men of letters (correspondents, scribblers, or compilers) elected to represent the community by telling its story to the outside. Thus, Men'shenin assembled formulaic texts, and Latyshev recounted his life story, expounding the faith in his own voice. Their loyalty was no impediment to self-expression; indeed, faith provided a language and an occasion for addressing the world.

Who was listening in each case? To whom were the concealments and revelations addressed? The disciplined faithful no doubt believed that God himself heard their eloquent denials. Also listening were coreligionists and hostile outsiders—aggressive neighbors, judges, village priests. Among the denouncers, some aimed for legal clemency, others hoped to impress nonbelievers with their insider knowledge and, by the very act of speaking freely, establish residency in the outside world: they were not so much speaking *to* someone in particular as exercising speech. For those "setting the record straight," history seems to have been the target: some tribunal of truth-telling more abstract and enduring than any courtroom, but at the same time useful in courts of law as a counterweight to lies and falsehoods. This strategy involved translation into the outsider's idiom (the messengers were bilingual). It was a strategy that failed in Soviet times to save the Skoptsy from the obloquy they had suffered all along. Their remarkable adaptability to the shifting language regimes of the outside world did not save them in the end. But they were not alone in that failure.

Denying

The discursive discipline imposed by the sect affected ordinary adherents, many of whom could not read or write, but the mass arrests of entire congregations created a record in which their voices were inscribed. When charged with belonging to the sect, most followers denied the accusation. Take the case of twenty-four inhabitants of the city of Ufa. The group centered around three households. The merchant brother and sister, Andrian and Anisiia Ivanov, fifty-two and sixty-five years old, respectively, ran a shop employing various clerks, some of whom lived with them in the house they owned. They also owned land and maintained a household in a nearby village. Filipp Driamov, a peasant of sixty-three who dealt in trade, lived with his wife and children. Three Daletskii siblings, Nikifor, forty-seven, Irina, forty-five, and Dar'ia, thirty-seven, also peasants, shared another house with two younger relatives, Il'ia, twenty-one, and Ivan, eighteen, and some lodgers. During the winter of 1910, the police in Ufa learned of the community's existence from an anonymous source. When searched, the houses yielded ritual objects, sacramental clothing, sacred texts, books, photographs, and personal letters, suggesting the residents indulged in special ceremonies and shared some unorthodox faith. Of the eight women and sixteen men eventually charged with belonging to the sect, medical examination showed nine of the men lacked some or all of their genitals and one woman's nipples had been removed.

The accused were well aware of the terms under which they were being tried. To convict, the state would have to demonstrate not only that genitals and breasts had been severed but that an operation had been performed for this purpose in the context of and inspired by "fanatical religious belief." Absent the conjunction of belief (by definition "false," hence "fanatical") and the intentional destruction of body parts, the charge would not stand.

When interrogated, fourteen of the defendants denied all charges outright; nine offered partial denials; and one tried to have it both ways, alternately admitting and denying. People without physical marks found it easiest to dispute their involvement in the sect. Evdokiia Driamova, an illiterate peasant woman of forty-one, claimed to be a regular church-goer, though she admitted that neither she nor her parents ate meat. "I heard that our lodgers . . . were Skoptsy," she testified, "but I don't know what that is; it never interested me and doesn't interest me now. Are there Skoptsy in the city of Ufa? I don't know."[6] Nikolai Rabeev, a forty-seven-year-old unmarried semiliterate peasant who had worked for the Ivanovs for eighteen years and lived in their house, also professed complete ignorance: "I have no idea what the Skoptsy teach," he announced. "I have never been interested in the Skoptsy sect and have no interest in them to this day." He admitted not eating meat at the Ivanovs' but insisted he was sexually active. "I have sexual relations with women, for which purpose I visit brothels, but I cannot name even a single brothel I have visited. I re-

---

[6] Protokol doprosa: Evdokiia Filimonova Driamova (February 2, 1911), GMIR, f. 2, op. 5, d. 186.

call being in one brothel on Bogorodskaia Street, which has since burned down. In addition, I use streetwalkers."[7] Others also admitted to sharing Skoptsy dietary habits, but usually gave some mundane excuse: Ivan Daletskii objected to meat because it came from animals; Mariia Siutkina said she "used to eat meat but I don't any longer because a doctor told me it was bad for my health, but I don't know which doctor that was."[8]

Agaf'ia Sycheva and Grigorii Koloskov had to explain away more serious points: her nipples were gone and his testicles were missing. Both adopted a classic Skoptsy device: conceding the evidence but denying the cause. The forty-five-year-old peasant woman was illiterate and unmarried. "Twelve years ago," she reported, "I went to the field in a cart. Along the way my horse smashed into me and injured my breasts and I decided to cut them off. I myself took a knife and cut off my nipples, smearing the wound with the 'balsam' grass that grows in our field. I don't remember how long it took the wounds to heal."[9] Koloskov, an unmarried illiterate peasant of sixty-two, also denied belonging to the faith:

> In my defense I can say the following: twelve years ago I knocked my testicles against the pommel of my saddle, after which they became swollen. The testicles interfered with my movements and I decided to cut them off. With this in mind, I went to my apiary in the woods and severed them with an axe. I tied the testicles with a cord, placed them on a stump and hit the axe handle with the handle of another axe. Then I made a bandage out of canvas soaked in butter. I lay in the apiary for an entire day, then got up and walked around and left the apiary on foot a week later. When I was at the apiary no one else was there. I do not belong to the Skoptsy sect.[10]

Sometimes the denial was perfunctory but offered an occasion to talk about oneself. Thus, the peasant Dar'ia Daletskaia, an illiterate virgin of thirty-seven, insisted she was innocent while offering details of her personal and family life that contradicted this claim. Her family prayed like true Christians, she affirmed, adding that they "sang verses from the book *Poetry and Prose of Siberian Skoptsy*. I sang along with the rest. I don't know a single verse but sang in the choir. . . . To my testimony I would like to add that I married at age twenty and lived with my husband for a year and some months. I left him because he was incapable of sexual relations. My

[7] Protokol doprosa: Nikolai Petrovich Rabeev (February 2, 1911), GMIR, f. 2, op. 5, d. 204.

[8] Protokol doprosa: Ivan Grigor'ev Daletskii (February 1, 1911), GMIR, f. 2, op. 5, d. 181; Mariia Nikiforovna Siutkina (February 2, 1911), ibid., d. 203.

[9] Protokol doprosa: Agaf'ia Gavrilovna Sycheva (March 6, 1911), GMIR, f. 2, op. 5, d. 201.

[10] Protokol doprosa: Grigorii Andreev Koloskov (February 12, 1911), GMIR, f. 2, op. 5, d. 190. For earlier examples of this same device, see Evgenii [V.] Pelikan, *Sudebno-meditsinskie issledovaniia skopchestva i istoricheskie svedeniia o nem* (St. Petersburg: Golovin, 1872), 120; Appendix A, 11; Appendix B, 18–21, 25–27.

husband is called Fedor, but I do not know his patronymic, surname, occupation, or place of residence. I have lived with my brother Nikifor Daletskii for fifteen years, during which time I have not eaten meat. I have nothing else to say."[11]

It was probably the case that Dar'ia had indeed forgotten much about the husband, whom she had escaped in mint condition. But the volume of Skoptsy poetry and prose, assembled and published by one of their own, had become the community Bible. Her brother Nikifor, also among the accused, loudly proclaimed his affiliation: "I have heard the charges and admit being a member of the Skoptsy heresy, for which reason I am castrated. . . . It is my deep conviction that not being castrated I cannot be saved and this conviction I have kept to the present time." Castrated at age forty, only seven years before, his devotion was intense. The confession was not a betrayal. This literate, unmarried peasant, active in trade and the owner of land, remained true: he had no idea the Ivanovs were Skoptsy, he said, and had never attended a prayer meeting at their house.[12] But clearly, meatless dinners were not all he and Dar'ia shared.

Grigorii Koloskov's younger brother, Larion, also presented a curious contrast with his sibling. Where the castrated Grigorii denied belonging to the faith and blamed his condition on his horse, Larion, fifty-five years old, the Ivanovs' self-taught cashier, unmarried but with organs intact, said he had attended prayer meetings at his employers' and was proud to be one of their own: "I have heard the charges," he declared, "and plead guilty to belonging to the Skoptsy sect, although I am not myself castrated, because I consider myself capable of fighting carnal desires by fasting and prayer. . . . I have never had sexual relations with women and like all Skoptsy I reject marriage."[13]

Those not only castrated but also previously convicted could not but confess to something. They were careful, however, to keep the circle of implication small. The sixty-two-year-old peasant Stepan Kornoukhov, convicted in 1875 and pardoned after 1905, spoke eloquently on behalf of Skoptsy truth but insisted he had acted on his own: "No one induced me to undergo castration. I came to that conviction myself after reading the Gospels with special attention to Matthew 19:12. I castrated myself with no help from anyone else."[14] Arkhip Kulikov, a literate peasant bachelor of thirty-seven, also previously convicted and pardoned, echoed the same terms: "No one induced me to undergo castration," he affirmed, re-

[11] Protokol doprosa: Dar'ia Timofeevna Daletskaia (February 2, 1911), GMIR, f. 2, op. 5, d. 183.

[12] Protokol doprosa: Nikifor Timofeev Daletskii (January 30, 1911), GMIR, f. 2, op. 5, d. 182.

[13] Protokol doprosa: Larion Andreev Koloskov (January 30, 1911), GMIR, f. 2, op. 5, d. 191.

[14] Protokol doprosa: Stepan Ivanov Kornoukhov (February 1, 1911), GMIR, f. 2, op. 5, d. 194.

peating the familiar phrases. "I came to the conviction to be castrated on my own, after reading the Gospels. . . . I recognize the Skoptsy teachings as correct and will never renounce them." Arkhip's older brother, Grigorii, equally ardent and equally castrated, like Kornoukhov pretended to know nothing of the Ivanovs' beliefs.[15]

If taking responsibility upon oneself was one way of shielding the community, taking no responsibility at all was another. Iakov Labutin, earlier convicted then pardoned, a semiliterate peasant of forty-two, said his testicles had been severed when he was only ten, when he "understood nothing. I do not belong to the Skoptsy sect," he affirmed, "and do not observe its teachings. In my soul I am an Orthodox Christian and live by the teachings of Christ."[16] It is clear from correspondence confiscated by the police and from the record of his contacts with Bonch-Bruevich, that Labutin was an active member of the community.[17] He had simply lied. Only one man proved disloyal. When interrogated in February 1911 along with the others, Iakov Falaleev, who had been living at the Ivanovs' for two years, denied witnessing prayer services or discussing the sect, though he reported rumors that the couple's "beardless and whiskerless" visitors were in fact Skoptsy. By the time of a second interview a year later, Falaleev had changed his tune. Now he reported that the Ivanovs had tried to recruit him, that he had heard the sound of choral singing at their house, and that he had only affected an interest in the sect because he was living among them. Ivanov had told Falaleev to keep quiet, but he had disobeyed.[18] The rest had spoken only to affirm what they believed, while refusing to implicate others. In the end the betrayal was beside the point. All twenty-four of the accused were declared not guilty for lack of evidence in Ufa Circuit Court on November 27, 1912.[19]

Denouncing

The Ufa case shows that true believers sometimes confessed without renouncing the creed; others disavowed any connection with the com-

---

[15] Protokol doprosa: Arkhip Semenov Kulikov (February 1, 1912), GMIR, f. 2, op. 5, d. 195 ("oskopilsia" leaves ambiguous whether it was done to him or by himself); Grigorii Semenov Kulikov (February 1, 1911), ibid., d. 196.

[16] Protokol doprosa: Iakov Sergeev Labutin (February 2, 1911), GMIR, f. 2, op. 5, d. 197.

[17] Letter to Labutin from his son, in "Protokol osmotra naidennykh veshchei pri obyske u skoptsov" (n.d.), GMIR, f. 2, op. 5, d. 212, ll. 1–2. Also, Ia. S. Labutin to V. D. Bonch-Bruevich (May 2, 1912), ibid., d. 20; (August 16, 1912), ibid., d. 21; (October 21, 1912), ibid., d. 22; (October 22, 1912), ibid., d. 23.

[18] Protokol doprosa: Iakov Falaleev (February 2, 1911), GMIR, f. 2, op. 5, d. 228; Svidetel'skie pokazaniia po delu Daletskikh: Iakov Nikitich Falaleev (January 17, 1912), ibid., d. 215, ll. 4–5.

[19] Prigovor po delu skoptsov v g. Ufe: GMIR, f. 2, op. 5, d. 178, ll. 3–3ob.

munity but did not take the prosecution's side. Some confessions, however, were intentionally or functionally disloyal. Vasilii Kliukvin, an Ekaterinburg merchant raised in an Old Believer family, recounted his experiences among the Skoptsy in a personal diary, composed in 1826–27, which he turned over to church authorities, claiming to have posed as a recruit for the purpose of gathering information.[20] In 1826 officials recorded similar testimony offered by a state peasant named Ivan Andreianov, who claimed to have spent ten years with the Skoptsy.[21]

Kliukvin and Andreianov may perhaps have fooled the Skoptsy into trusting their good intentions or fooled the authorities into believing they had been pretending all along. Gerasim Prudkovskii, by contrast, did not enjoy the luxury of deciding whether or not to join the community he later tried to abandon. His memoirs begin with the story of his parents, who left the relative comfort of wealthy peasant life to devote themselves to salvation. Castrated as a boy at the age of ten, Prudkovskii eventually loses his faith and decides to unmask the sect's moral failings and describe its criminal practices with an insider's knowing eye. His account culminates with the dramatic report of his own castration, a narrative that indulges in shockingly graphic detail. In abandoning euphemism, Prudkovskii demonstrates that he is no longer a faceless sectarian vowed to sacred silence and ritualized evasion but a man of letters dedicated to telling secular tales. Yet the impact of the faith in which he was raised can still be felt. The account of his struggle to break away takes the form of a spiritual journey through suffering to the Light, structured much like the stories of conversion and redemption the faithful brethren told about themselves.[22] Prudkovskii's new self is not an entirely new departure.

---

[20] "Dnevnik ekaterinburgskogo kuptsa V. P. Kliukvina o svoem prebyvanii v sekte skoptsov": RGIA, f. 1005 [S. D. Nechaev-Mal'tsev (1792–1860), over-procurator of the Holy Synod], op. 1, ed. khr. 70 (1826–27), ll. 1–61. For the edited text, see: "Iz arkhiva S. D. Nechaeva: Donesenie V. P. Kliukvina o skoptsakh," pt. 1, *Bratskoe slovo* 2, no. 9 (1893): 717–35; pt. 2, ibid., no. 10 (1893): 770–87.

[21] Testimony in N. Varadinov, *Istoriia Ministerstva vnutrennikh del*, vol. 8: *Istoriia rasporiazhenii po raskolu* (St. Petersburg: II Otdelenie Sobstvennoi E. I. V. Kantseliarii, 1863), 247–66.

[22] [G. E. Prudkovskii], "Golos iz mogily zhivykh mertvetsov: Zapiski skoptsa," pts. 1–3, *Zhurnal romanov i povestei*, no. 1 (1881):1–70; no. 2 (1881):71–126; no. 1 (1882):127–78. The author's name appears only on the last part. The first page of *Zhurnal romanov i povestei*, no. 3 (1881), in the collection of the State Public Library in St. Petersburg, carries a penciled inscription in old orthography, presumably the hand of a librarian, that supplies the author's first name and patronymic and identifies him as a member of the Skoptsy sect, who died in 1909 in extreme poverty, his other manuscripts having been burned by fellow Skoptsy during the 1905 revolution. For more discussion, see Laura Engelstein, "Rebels of the Soul: Peasant Self-Fashioning in a Religious Key," *Russian History* 23, nos. 1–4 (1996): 197–213.

Defending

Prudkovskii's tone is hostile and aggrieved. He portrays his former associates in the darkest possible tones and revels in the act of betrayal. When Gavriil Men'shenin published the volume of Skoptsy texts in 1904, his purpose, by contrast, was to enhance, not diminish, the community's reputation. Where Prudkovskii revealed his insider knowledge to escape definition as "one of them," Men'shenin did the reverse, adopting the tone of knowing outsider, the scholarly expert, to qualify as representative of the group. The volume's introduction mimics the mode of many an introductory chapter in books written by true outsiders about the Skoptsy, tracing the origins of castration in ancient times, the attitudes of the early church, the early history of the sect. Men'shenin calls the prophet Selivanov a "fanatic." He analyzes the mixture of allegory and historical truth in the founding parable and draws his facts from the Ministry of Internal Affairs's violently hostile report on Skoptsy life and lore published in 1845.[23]

Though indignant at their misportrayal, the Skoptsy liked to read about themselves. When presented by a visitor with published commentary on their faith, Skoptsy exiles in the 1870s rejected some views and praised others.[24] Whether from vanity or in search of a fading past, Skoptsy city dwellers before World War I collected the classics of Skoptsy scholarship. As Nikifor Latyshev expressed it in 1913, referring to Bonch-Bruevich's promised study of the Skoptsy, which he never in fact published: "I'd like to take a look at [your] book on the Skoptsy, being one myself."[25] By far the most common volume on the sectarians' shelves, however, was Men'shenin's *Poetry and Prose of Siberian Skoptsy*, which became a handbook for true believers, a way to refresh and transmit community lore. Dar'ia Daletskaia in the 1913 Ufa trial claimed it served as the family prayer book, and it appears in the records of other cases as well.[26]

Even before the publication of this book in 1904, Men'shenin had felt a need to discuss the sect's beliefs and reach out to the world of letters. In 1898–99 he conducted a brief correspondence with Lev Tolstoy, in which he expounded Skoptsy teachings and argued with the great writer about true Christian belief. Tolstoy was the recipient of hundreds of such con-

---

[23] Men'shenin, ed., *Poeziia i proza*, 1–10 (introduction).

[24] N. M. Iadrintsev, *Russkaia obshchina v tiur'me i ssylke* (St. Petersburg: Morigerovskii, 1872), 256–57.

[25] Letter from N. P. Latyshev to V. D. Bonch-Bruevich (September 21, 1913), GMIR, f. 2, op. 5, d. 28, l. 7.

[26] For books on the sect in the possession of Skoptsy, see evidence, for example, from the 1910 Kharkov case: "Obvinitel'nyi akt po delu o sekte skoptsov" (Kharkov: Khudozhestvennyi trud, n.d.), RGIA, f. 821, op. 133, d. 233, ll. 160b.-17. For Dar'ia Daletskaia's statement, see GMIR, f. 2, op. 5, d. 183.

fessional letters and in this case actually replied. Men'shenin later claimed to have met with Tolstoy to discuss these matters in person.[27] He was certainly self-conscious about his role as community spokesman and intellectual-of-record. Sometime after 1905 Men'shenin established a similar but more enduring relationship with Vladimir Bonch-Bruevich, another intellectual occupied with fathoming the soul of peasant Russia.

Men'shenin had been castrated at the age of eight and taught himself to read and write at fourteen.[28] In his correspondence with Bonch-Bruevich, he presented himself as a source of authoritative knowledge. Gathering material for the historical record and working on memoirs and a diary, he repeatedly urged Bonch-Bruevich to complete his own scholarly efforts and publish the true story of the sect.[29] Once the Bolsheviks came to power, inaugurating the era of "freedom," as Men'shenin put it,[30] Bonch-Bruevich came to represent not only the principle of toleration but political authority itself. Men'shenin now appealed for help in gaining admission to official archives and asked Bonch-Bruevich to intercede on behalf of persecuted brethren and occasionally on his own behalf.[31] In 1924 Men'shenin wrote an open letter to the Central Committee of the Communist Party, addressed to Bonch-Bruevich at the Kremlin, in which he praised the regime's enlightened policy on religion.[32]

Though his tone began to darken in succeeding years, he did not lose faith in Bonch-Bruevich's good will. Knowing how to address his betters (having once called Tolstoy "Dear Count and Brother in Christ"),[33] Men'shenin now adopted the rhetoric of Soviet-style communication. While lauding the new regime and its admirable goals, he complained about the abuses and deficiencies of the local authorities.[34] In 1927 he assailed the antireligion campaigners for defaming Skoptsy teachings no

---

[27] Klibanov, *Iz mira*, 23.

[28] Letters from G. P. Men'shenin to L. N. Tolstoi (February 11, 1898), GMIR, f. 2, op. 5, d. 120, ll. 12–13 (castration); (March 31, 1898), ibid., ll. 18–19 (education).

[29] Letters from G. P. Men'shenin to V. D. Bonch-Bruevich (January 20, 1910), GMIR, f. 2, op. 5, d. 64, l. 1; (October 25, 1929), ibid., d. 85, ll. 5–140b. (answering questions); (August 21, 1916), ibid., d. 76, l. 2; (September 1, 1920), ibid., d. 78, l. 30b.

[30] Letter from G. P. Men'shenin to V. D. Bonch-Bruevich (December 28, 1917), GMIR, f. 2, op. 5, d. 77, l. 2.

[31] Letters from G. P. Men'shenin to V. D. Bonch-Bruevich: Interceding for others (May 25, 1920), OR-RGB, f. 369, k. 301, ed. khr. 27, ll. 22–24; (October 30, 1924), GMIR, f. 2, op. 5, d. 82, ll. 5–50b. Archives: e.g., (September 27, 1927), ibid., d. 85, l. 1; (January 28, 1928), ibid., d. 86, l. 1–20b. Apartment requisitioned as a radio station (September 24, 1920), ibid., d. 79, ll. 1–3.

[32] Letter from G. P. Men'shenin to Central Committee (July 15, 1924), GMIR, f. 2, op. 5, d. 121, ll. 3–30b.

[33] Letter from G. P. Men'shenin to L. N. Tolstoy (May 26, 1899), GMIR, f. 2, op. 5, d. 120, l. 20.

[34] See Sheila Fitzpatrick, *Everyday Stalinism: Ordinary Life in Extraordinary Times: Soviet Russia in the 1930s* (Oxford: Oxford University Press, 1999), 175–78.

less than Orthodox missionaries had once done.[35] In 1928 he condemned the arrests and mistreatment, which reminded him of tsarist rule.[36] In 1929 he appealed for help when his apartment was searched and his books and papers confiscated.[37] Bonch-Bruevich, not surprisingly, replied to Men'shenin's protests by defending Soviet justice. If the Skoptsy were being arrested, they must have broken some law. If their extreme beliefs could be understood—and should be viewed with compassion—as a reaction to the hardships of an earlier time, in today's perfect and enlightened world they had no place.[38]

Nikifor Latyshev was Men'shenin's exact contemporary, like him of peasant origin and similarly castrated at a young age. Latyshev's father had been one of the original members of a breakaway group that emerged in the 1870s, following a new prophet. Both Men'shenin and Latyshev had spent years in Siberia with other exiled Skoptsy. In 1910 Men'shenin contacted Latyshev, asking for information about his group. Latyshev at first hesitated, afraid that anxious brethren would object; wishing to avoid persecution, and also the shame of exposing an inner discord on issues of faith.[39] Latyshev eventually overcame these doubts and sent Men'shenin the notebooks expounding his community's perspective.[40] It was also through Men'shenin that Latyshev heard that Bonch-Bruevich was preparing a scholarly study of the sect. A newspaper account informed Latyshev of the acquittal of the Ufa Skoptsy, on whose behalf Bonch-Bruevich had testified as an expert witness. Latyshev thereupon wrote to offer the Bolshevik his services as a source of information about the "hidden secrets" of the Skoptsy faith. "I am not mentally ill," he added, anticipating an unbeliever's fears, "as people who talk about God and the truth are usually considered."[41]

In the twenty-five years of correspondence that followed, Latyshev had ample opportunity to define himself: in relation to the outside world, to his own community, to the new Soviet regime. Men'shenin was a compiler

[35] Letter from G. P. Men'shenin to V. D. Bonch-Bruevich (September 27, 1927), ll. 3–30b.
[36] Letter from G. P. Men'shenin to V. D. Bonch-Bruevich (November 6, 1928), GMIR, f. 2, op. 5, d. 86, ll. 5–60b.
[37] Letter from G. P. Men'shenin to V. D. Bonch-Bruevich (October 15, 1929), GMIR, f. 2, op. 5, d. 87, ll. 5–6.
[38] Letter from V. D. Bonch-Bruevich to G. P. Men'shenin (November 6, 1928), OR-RGB, f. 369, k. 173, ed. khr. 31, ll. 5–6.
[39] Letter from G. P. Men'shenin to N. P. Latyshev [1910], GMIR, f. 2, op. 5, d. 122, l. 1; from N. P. Latyshev to G. P. Men'shenin (November 18, 1910), ibid., d. 199, ll. 1–20b.
[40] N. P. Latyshev, "To, chto ia khotel by peredat' chitaiushchemu miru" (n.d. but after 1906), GMIR, f. 2, op. 5, d. 263, ll. 1–140b.; idem, "Nachalo moego povestvovaniia" (1910), ibid., d. 261, ll. 1–580b.
[41] Letter from N. P. Latyshev to V. D. Bonch-Bruevich (December 18, 1912), GMIR, f. 2, op. 5, d. 28, ll. 1–2.

of texts, a man with his name on the spine of a book, but Latyshev was above all a writer. In justifying his love of books and compulsion to write, Latyshev drew on models from different cultural spheres. On the one hand, he fancied himself a man of wisdom in a folkloric vein, following a sacred call: "I love to rummage around in books, searching for the merest shadow of holy truth."[42] On the other hand, he was a man of his time, alert to the existence of the secular public and the commercial press. This was the era of Charskaia's heroines and mass-market saints. "If I have written and continue to write it is exclusively . . . for the sincere love of God. And at the same time," he admitted, "also to inform my listeners, if there should be any." He showed "impatience to see my own thoughts, my own words in print." But "people are people and deaf to everything Divine and thus to my heartfelt declarations." He reproached Bonch-Bruevich, too, for doubting the value of these thoughts: "You look on all this (to you Mythical) from an entirely different angle. . . . I'm beginning to suspect that my . . . sincerely truthful words, will undoubtedly fail to achieve their goal. It is unlikely you will want to print them, because they contain nothing interesting or entertaining for the reading public." Envious of Rasputin, whose productions, he noted, had appeared in separate editions, Latyshev complained that the public had no taste for the truth, especially truth with "the slightest sectarian odor."[43]

Part of the drama he had to impart stemmed from his own position as victim of injustice and martyr to the truth. His writings were full of "twists and turns," he explained, showing courage on one side and fear on the other, because "each Word of God spoken aloud leads unavoidably to the constable's whip or fleabag jail, in the company of bandits or the unavoidable recidivist pickpockets." If Bonch-Bruevich would only take the cause of salvation more seriously to heart and publish Latyshev's ideas, then Latyshev would not "remain only the Voice of one crying in the people's wilderness."[44] But, he added defiantly, "I will keep writing, if not to you then to someone else. I love in general to preach God's Cause [*besedovat' za Bozhie Delo*]. I would be happy to find someone kind and tolerant to talk with, who would ask questions sincerely, without trying to trick me or mock me later." Bonch-Bruevich was, in fact, just this man. Latyshev feared he had offended his correspondent with the crude manner common to men inspired by faith, but he pleaded: "Don't ask more from a

---

[42] Letter from N. P. Latyshev to V. D. Bonch-Bruevich (October 1914), l. 4.

[43] Letter from N. P. Latyshev to V. D. Bonch-Bruevich (September 14, 1915), GMIR, f. 2, op. 5, d. 47, ll. 10b.–3.

[44] Letter from N. P. Latyshev to V. D. Bonch-Bruevich (September 14, 1915), ll. 4–5, 6. "The voice of one crying in the wilderness. Prepare ye the way of the Lord, make his paths straight" (Matthew 3:3). Latyshev adds the word "people's" to the scriptural phrase: "Glas vopiiushchego v pustyne [narodnoi]."

simple guy like me, please!"[45] An outcast, a man of the people: these were roles that Latyshev invoked as authorial personae. But he wanted his voice to carry across the cultural divide on which his identity depended. "Although I am a simple peasant [*muzhik*], I would like to be a gentleman [*dzhentel'men*]," he declared.[46]

How did Latyshev modify his self-image, or its projection, with the advent of Soviet rule, and how did he sustain the dialogue he needed? He hailed the triumph of Soviet power as the coming of "Might and Light" (a rough translation of the playful expression "*Sovet i Svet*") and claimed to have been constant in his "continuing simplicity" and devotion to shared spiritual goals. He was still Bonch-Bruevich's "humble little helper [*chelovechek sotrudnik*] in gathering the materials of enlightenment and the illumination of human darkness." But he had ceased being a "*muzhik*" and become a factory watchman. By 1920 he had gotten into trouble for corresponding with fellow Skoptsy, whom the police in Aleksandrovsk, Ekaterinburg province, briefly suspected of concocting "something political."[47]

In 1928, when Latyshev discovered that Bonch-Bruevich's 1922 study of sectarians cited his notebooks, his joy knew no bounds: "O! how happy and satisfied I am that my work, however minor, has been entered into History."[48] But the opportunity to tell the truth was no longer as promising as it had seemed with the onset of "Might and Light." By 1929 he was complaining to Bonch-Bruevich about arrests of the brethren in Leningrad and the heavy hand of antireligious censorship. Other Skoptsy were saying that if Bonch-Bruevich were to publish his research now, he would, "like earlier scribblers, have to cast a shadow here and there to lower the prestige of the faith in the readers' eyes." A mere ten years after the Revolution had raised the sectarians' hopes for tolerance and understanding, they were encountering the "same old persecution all over again."[49] This atmosphere only made them more reluctant to expose their beliefs. Although Latyshev assured them that "inquiry isn't inquest" (*issledovanie ne sledstvie*), they remained unconvinced. Still, the old folks—and

---

[45] Letter from N. P. Latyshev to V. D. Bonch-Bruevich (September 14, 1915), ll. 6, 7. "Beseda," meaning conversation, was the term used by Orthodox as well as sectarian folk to describe informal prayer meetings. In this context it can also mean preaching.

[46] Letter from N. P. Latyshev to V. D. Bonch-Bruevich (October 1914), GMIR, f. 2, op. 5, d. 32, ll. 3–4.

[47] Letter from N. P. Latyshev to V. D. Bonch-Bruevich (November 25, 1920), GMIR, f. 2, op. 5, d. 37, ll. 2, 30b. (quotations).

[48] Letter from N. P. Latyshev to V. D. Bonch-Bruevich (November 25, 1928), GMIR, f. 2, op. 5, d. 38, l. 3. The citations were originally published in "Tri skopcheskie rukopisi," *Sovremennik*, kn. 3 (1913); Latyshev would have found them in Vladimir Bonch-Bruevich, *Iz mira sektantov: Sbornik statei* (Moscow: Gosudarstvennoe izdatel'stvo, 1922).

[49] Letter from N. P. Latyshev to V. D. Bonch-Bruevich (October 9, 1929), including letter to Latyshev (March 1, 1929) from a fellow Skopets: GMIR, f. 2, op. 5, d. 39, ll. 3–30b.

himself in particular—were eagerly awaiting Bonch-Bruevich's promised tome.[50]

Meanwhile, in 1924 Latyshev and his household had suffered a brutal attack at the hands of local militiamen in Kursk Province, during which his brother Andrei had been murdered. Nikifor had since moved to the city of Osa in the province of Perm. There he and a spiritual sister kept a cow, but she had eventually tired of his presence and turned him out. In 1929, aged sixty-five, he was looking for a job. Could Bonch-Bruevich help him find something to do? "As for writing—I'm not a writer," he wrote coyly. "I have neither talent nor calling. I manage a bit, but in the long run I'm afraid of ruining my eyes. Something like a janitor, cleaning up, sweeping, keeping watch during the day, tidying the rooms, making tea." Did Bonch-Bruevich have "some kind of job in Moscow for an aged writer? I'm no great writer, but if my needs were met I might write something serious. And I would be able personally to explain many things to you for your book and research." Perhaps "dear Mikhail Ivanovich Kalinin" could help him get a pension for the five years he had served as a factory watchman in Aleksandrovsk, protecting state property. "Or," he suggested ingeniously, he might "count as a peasant-agriculturalist in Kursk province, according to the new law of 1928 or 1929. I'm a homeless, helpless old man of sixty-five, with the legal right to a pension of sixty-five rubles a year. These are the facts. Do what you can for a poor writer-peasant, or just because I'm an old man."[51]

Expert at survival, Latyshev knew which labels would get him ahead and which could do him in. In April 1932, he was interrogated by the OGPU and asked where he lived, what he did, and whether he was rich or poor. "I told the simple truth," he informed Bonch-Bruevich, "that I was never rich and have no tendency toward that class, being satisfied with my quiet, modest life. I am no threat to the Soviet regime and no criminal, I have never been involved in anything criminal, and despise those who misbehave." But they didn't believe him and seized his meager property—"a small little house, with two stories, it's true, but it brings in not a cent." By now he was calling himself a "worker-proletarian, a laboring Soviet citizen." Pleading for Bonch-Bruevich to intervene on his behalf, he claims to have told the interrogators: "What a pity that in Soviet Russia the innocent are treated so rudely. Only wreckers behave this way." For Bonch-Bruevich's benefit, he adds: "Of course one mustn't talk. One must exam-

---

[50] Letter from N. P. Latyshev to V. D. Bonch-Bruevich (March 25, 1929), GMIR, f. 2, op. 5, d. 40, l. 9–100b.

[51] Letter from N. P. Latyshev to V. D. Bonch-Bruevich (March 25, 1929), ll. 90b.–10. Until 1932 peasants viewed Kalinin, then a Politburo member, later president of the USSR, as a figure to whom one could appeal: see William B. Husband, "Soviet Atheism and Russian Orthodox Strategies of Resistance, 1917–1932," *Journal of Modern History* 70, no. 1 (1998): 89.

ine the situation carefully and not disgrace the Soviet regime. It has enough enemies already. . . . Though I am not a communist, I deplore the behavior of those who don't understand the behests of Lenin and other clever and noble communists."[52] A year later he was working as a carpenter in a factory, complaining about prices and the shortage of food, and calling himself "a real son of the proletariat."[53] Amazingly, the authorities declared Latyshev innocent. If he had trouble recovering his property, it was not for lack of trying. The income inspector, "a careerist, runs around like a bloodhound, asking everyone he meets: who's this Latyshev, was he formerly rich or poor. He tries to find the crimes I committed, but to his dismay there aren't any and never were. I don't dare ask the procurator how it will all turn out. . . . So I wait, pine away, despair, and grieve over the new life in Russia—on earth. If they're treating me like this, nothing much is new!"[54]

Latyshev ended his days in an old-age home in Dnepropetrovsk, in the company, as he put it, of "two or three ardent partisans, several nut cases, a few cripples, and some completely healthy lazybones."[55] In 1938, now seventy-five years old, he reflected on his continuing marginality. Because of his castration, Latyshev wrote, he appeared "in the eyes of all humanity, as a ruined creature, having lost the right to any form of PLEASURE or SATISFACTION, a person in short unworthy of attention."[56] "Wherever I have lived, worked, or held a post, supervisors and workmates have considered me a model worker, polite to everyone. But that wasn't enough for them to consider me their equal (by nature). I suppose it's because they are creators of life and in that respect I am dead, though this is not fair. Plenty of people capable of reproducing humankind have voluntarily refused this great honor. . . . From the perspective of nature it's just as harmful either way."[57]

When Latyshev's parents were sentenced to exile in 1875, he had been acquitted by virtue of his young age. Free to stay behind in European Russia and fend for himself, he felt out of place in ordinary life and eventually traveled to Siberia to join them. In the new era, the outside world remained a cruel place. The humility and self-abnegation involved in the sacrifice of progeny and pleasure earned him no credit in a regime that

[52] Letter from N. P. Latyshev, in Osa, to V. D. Bonch-Bruevich (April 25, 1932), GMIR, f. 2, op. 5, d. 42, ll. 14–16.

[53] Letter from N. P. Latyshev to V. D. Bonch-Bruevich (February 23, 1933), GMIR, f. 2, op. 5, d. 43, ll. 1–10b.

[54] Letter from N. P. Latyshev to V. D. Bonch-Bruevich (October 20, 1933), GMIR, f. 2, op. 5, d. 43, ll. 17–20.

[55] Letter from N. P. Latyshev to I. V. Stalin, sent to V. D. Bonch-Bruevich (December 22, 1938), GMIR, f. 2, op. 5, d. 49, l. 90b.

[56] Letter from N. P. Latyshev to I. V. Stalin (December 22, 1938), l. 4.

[57] Letter from N. P. Latyshev to I. V. Stalin (December 22, 1938), ll. 8–80b.

distrusted most forms of self-distinction, especially those with spiritual claims. Latyshev imagined what the people around him might be thinking: "Why aren't you like the rest of us? Perhaps you are more cunning, smarter than us. Perhaps in this way you want to be better than us. Therefore you're not as honorable as the rest of us. Perhaps that's it." The Skoptsy had always done well in practical affairs, adapting to worldly conditions, assuming cultural camouflage—orderly households, proper attire, economic achievement, even as they awaited the coming of the next world. Now, too, they conformed to local mores, but, once again, they felt unloved. "On this account," Latyshev wrote, "I wrack my brains wondering how I'm worse than others. Judging by my life, my proper life, I'm a great guy! My exemplary decent behavior admits me everywhere. What qualities are missing for me to be accepted as human. Better be a drunk, hooligan, roué, drifter, loafer, or malingerer—but not castrated! Nothing is more shameful among humankind. I've felt this on my own hide for 75 years."[58]

His thoughts were included in a letter addressed to Joseph Stalin, sent, not to Stalin himself, but to Bonch-Bruevich for inclusion in the archives. Like diary keepers of more exalted station, Latyshev imagined the record of his life surviving his disappearance. Not only despite, but because of his lowly status, he considered himself an exemplar of the human condition. "Knowing that among humanity I am nothing in comparison to others," he wrote Bonch-Bruevich, "I hesitated to send [the letter] to the addressee. I beg you to accept it for the State Museum, to preserve as a document. In 100 or 200 years it will speak of how the common folk understood the Greatness of the Great." In the cover letter, dated March 6, 1939, which was also his final communication, Latyshev took his leave. "My life is clearly on the wane," he wrote his correspondent, "my health is fragile, I feel my years. But when it comes to eternity I have no worries, there's no blot on my record!" With his usual disingenuous self-deprecation, he apologized for the torrent of thoughts he had inflicted on Bonch-Bruevich, but added: "You know I'm an odd duckie [*chudachka*]." "Vladimir Dmitrievich," he concluded, "don't take offense, forgive me the liberty I took, thanks to your noble relation to me, in sending you everything that happened in my life for the judgment of future people. I fully realize this isn't the end of the world! All manuscripts and letters a thousand years from now will be considered historical documents. In that far-off time they will seem wise and useful. Forgive me and farewell! Latyshev, N. P. March 6, 1939."[59] Eternity was gained, finally, not in holding one's peace but in making oneself heard.

---

[58] Letter from N. P. Latyshev to I. V. Stalin (December 22, 1938), ll. 8ob.–9.
[59] Letter from N. P. Latyshev to V. D. Bonch-Bruevich (March 6, 1939), GMIR, f. 2, op. 5, d. 50, ll. 50b.–8ob.

To be heard, someone had to listen. The Skoptsy, who distanced them-selves so dramatically from ordinary life and spent decades avoiding de-tection, defined themselves not only in contrast to the world but through interaction with it. Their story of origins begins at the moment when their cover is blown and they are first subject to interrogation. Court testimony then became a ritual of self-affirmation. A century later, a few emerged as intellectuals, devoted either to repudiating the faith or explaining it to a secular public. Silver Age writers liked to imagine the folk sectarians as ex-emplars of an archaic religious spirit and a repository of native tradition,[60] but the sectarians thought of themselves as timeless, and they changed with the times. Having made themselves pariahs, they nevertheless wished to get their message across, establishing their difference in a shared lan-guage. Men'shenin, Latyshev, and other Skoptsy scribes repeatedly asked Bonch-Bruevich to correct their grammatical errors. Urging him to pub-lish one of their sacred texts, Men'shenin suggested Bonch-Bruevich rewrite it "in a literary style."[61] The Skoptsy thus shaped an identity, both collective and individual, through the circulation of stories that translated from the religious to the profane, from the humble to the lofty. Occupying the very extremity of cultural life, they were also part of the whole.

[60] See Aleksandr Etkind, *Khlyst: Sekty, literatura i revoliutsiia* (Moscow: Novoe literaturnoe obozrenie, 1998).
[61] Letter from G. P. Men'shenin to V. D. Bonch-Bruevich (March 28, 1910), GMIR, f. 2, op. 5, d. 66, l. 1.

Notes on Contributors

EVGENII BERSHTEIN is assistant professor of Russian at Reed College. He received his M.A. in Russian from Tartu University, Estonia, where his research focused on eighteenth-century Russian poetry, and his Ph.D.from the University of California, Berkeley. His dissertation is entitled "Western Models of Sexuality in Russian Modernism." He has published several articles on eighteenth- and twentieth-century Russian literature and culture.

CARYL EMERSON is A. Watson Armour III University Professor of Slavic Languages and Literatures at Princeton University. She is a translator and critic of works of Mikhail Bakhtin, and has published widely on nineteenth-century Russian literature, on the history of literary criticism, and on Russian opera and vocal music. Her books include *The First Hundred Years of Mikhail Bakhtin* (1997) and a biography of Modest Musorgsky (1999).

LAURA ENGELSTEIN is professor of history at Princeton University. Her publications include *The Keys to Happiness: Sex and the Search for Modernity in Fin-de-Siècle Russia* (1992) and *Castration and the Heavenly Kingdom: A Russian Folktale* (1999).

JOCHEN HELLBECK is assistant professor of history at the University of Giessen, Germany. He is currently completing a monograph on diaries, subjectivities, and self-realization in the Stalin era, and his edition of *The Diaries of Stepan Podlubnyi* is forthcoming.

ANDREW KAHN is university lecturer in Russian at Oxford and fellow of St. Edmund Hall. His publications include *Pushkin's* Bronze Horseman (1998), an edition of M. N. Murav'ev's *Institutiones Rhetoricae: A Treatise of a Russian Sentimentalist* (1995), and articles on Tsvetaeva, Mandelstam, Pushkin, and eighteenth-century Russian literature.

SUSAN LARSEN is assistant professor of Russian literature at the University of California, San Diego. Her previous publications include articles on twentieth-century Russian drama and on contemporary Russian cinema. She is completing a book on girls' culture in late imperial Russia.

LOUISE MCREYNOLDS is professor of history at the University of Hawai'i. The author of *The News Under Russia's Old Regime: The Development of a Mass-Circulation Press* (1991), translator of E. A. Nagrodskaia's *The Wrath of Dionysus* (1997), and an editor of *Entertaining Tsarist Russia* (1998), she is currently coediting a volume on melodrama in Russia and writing a monograph entitled *Russia at Play: Leisure-time Activities in Late Imperial Russia.*

IRINA PAPERNO is professor of Slavic languages and literatures at the University of California, Berkeley. Her publications include *Chernyshevsky and the Age of Realism: A Study in the Semiotics of Behavior* (1988) and *Suicide as a Cultural Institution in Dostoevsky's Russia* (1997).

CATHY POPKIN is the Jesse and George Siegel Professor in the Humanities at Columbia University. Author of *The Pragmatics of Insignificance: Chekhov, Zoshchenko, Gogol* (1993), she is currently completing a book on epistemology and human form in the works of Anton Chekhov (*Bodies of Knowledge: Chekhov's Corpus*).

DAVID L. RANSEL is professor of history and director of the Russian and East European Institute at Indiana University. He is the author of *The Politics of Catherinian Russia: The Panin Party* (1975), *Mothers of Misery: Child Abandonment in Russia* (1988), and *Village Mothers: Three Generations of Change in Russia and Tartaria* (2000).

STEPHANIE SANDLER is professor of Russian and of women's and gender studies at Amherst College and visiting professor of Slavic languages and literatures at Harvard University. Her publications include *Distant Pleasures: Alexander Pushkin and the Writing of Exile* (1989) and an edited collection, *Rereading Russian Poetry* (1999). *Commemorating Pushkin: Russia's Myth of a National Poet* will appear in 2002.

WILLIAM MILLS TODD III is Curt Hugo Reisinger Professor of Slavic Languages and Literatures and professor of comparative literature at Harvard University. Author of *The Familiar Letter as a Literary Genre in the Age of Pushkin* (1976) and *Fiction and Society in the Age of Pushkin* (1986), he has edited several collections of articles, including *A Pushkin Collection* (in Russian, 1999). He is currently writing a book on the serialization of the Russian novel.

RICHARD WORTMAN is professor of history at Columbia University and the Harriman Institute. His most recent book is *Scenarios of Power: Myth and Ceremony in Russian History*, vol. 2: *From Alexander II to the Abdication of Nicholas II* (2000).

REGINALD E. ZELNIK is professor of history at the University of California, Berkeley. He is the author or editor of several books, including *Law and Disorder on the Narova River: The Kreenholm Strike of 1872* (1995); and *Workers and Intelligentsia in Late Imperial Russia: Realities, Representations, Reflections* (1999). He is currently preparing a history of the concept of the strike in Russia, Germany, and France, and, with Robert Cohen, a multiauthored history of the Berkeley Free Speech Movement.

ALEXANDER ZHOLKOVSKY is professor of Slavic languages and literatures at the University of Southern California. His many books include *NRZB. Rasskazy* (1991); *Text Counter Text* (1994, 1995); *Babel' / Babel*, with Mikhail Iampol'skii (1994); *Raboty po poetike vyrazitel'nosti*, with Yuri Shcheglov (1996); and *Mikhail Zoshchenko: Poetika nedoveriia* (1999).

Index